THE
STRUCTU
OF
INTERNATIONAL
SOCIETY

AN INTRODUCTION TO THE

STUDY OF INTERNATIONAL

RELATIONS

GEOFFREY STERN

PINTER

London and New York

Pinter
A Cassell imprint
Wellington House, 125 Strand, London WC2R 0BB
215 Park Avenue South, New York, NY 10003

First published in 1995
Paperback reprinted 1995

British Library Cataloguing in Publication Data
A CIP catalogue record for this book is available from The British Library

ISBN 1 85567 275 8 (HBK)
ISBN 1 85567 276 6 (PBK)

Library of Congress Cataloging-in-Publication Data

Stern, Geoffrey.
  The structure of international society: an introduction to the study of
international relations / by Geoffrey Stern.
      p.   cm.
  Includes bibliographical references and index.
  ISBN 1-85567-275-8 (hbk). – ISBN 1-85567-276-6 (pbk)
  1. International relations.   I. Title.
JX1395.S764   1995
327–dc20
                                                                    94-38367
                                                                    CIP

Typeset by Saxon Graphics Ltd, Derby
Printed and bound in Great Britain by
Biddles Ltd, Guildford and King's Lynn

CONTENTS

Preface vii

Part I Contending theories 1
1 Realism, rationalism and revolutionism 3
2 Behaviouralism versus traditionalism 17
3 Structuralism 31

Part II The evolution of international society 43
4 Pre-modern international societies 45
5 Modern international societies 60

Part III The state 75
6 Sovereignty: legal and political 77
7 Nationalism: the nation and the imagination 92
8 The making of foreign policy 106

Part IV Inter-state behaviour 121
9 Constraints and rules of international behaviour 123
10 Power balances and alignments 139
11 Diplomacy: old and new 153
12 Imperialism 167
13 War 180

Part V Non-state actors 195
14 International organisations: regional and global 197
15 Transnational movements and organisations 212

Part VI The international political economy 227
16 International economic order and disorder 229
17 Underdevelopment: causes and proposed cures 243

Part VII World society? 259
18 Planetary dangers and opportunities 261
19 Prescriptions and prospects for peace 274
20 Agenda for the twenty-first century 290

Selected bibliography 296

Index 301

To Tiffany, Jonty and 'Grandma' — with love

PREFACE

Having taught International Relations (IR) for more than 30 years and published a series of books and articles on subjects somewhat tangential to the central core, I decided it was high time to produce a text addressing IR's chief concerns. Since, however, the field is already overburdened with volumes assuming familiarity with the subject, but is somewhat deficient in readable and reliable introductions, I thought it best to offer a book for the beginner. Though students new to the subject may find the first five chapters rather daunting, I hope they persevere; once they have mastered the opening theoretical and historical sections, the rest will be much easier to grasp.

If *The Structure of International Society* represents in a sense nearly four decades of study and reflection, it is also a product of the distinctive grounding in the subject I received at the London School of Economics (LSE) first as a student, then as a colleague of such luminaries as Charles Manning, Martin Wight, Hedley Bull, Fred Northedge, Geoffrey Goodwin and Alan James (which, I suppose, places me in the 'English School' of International Relations). In addition, it owes something to the countless hours spent over coffees or Carlsbergs in discussion with students, many of whom taught me as much as I like to think I taught them. In its presentation and content I hope it bears the imprint of my moonlighting activities as a freelance broadcaster. For thanks to the BBC I have been able not only to keep abreast of a wide range of international developments but also to question at close quarters some of the people named in the text and whose thoughts and actions may well have affected the course of history. I would also like to hope that prolonged exposure to a medium which puts a premium on clarity of exposition may have had a positive effect on my writing, so that even if what follows is not profound, at least the reader may be spared the ordeal of having to plough through the kind of dense and opaque verbiage that sometimes passes for scholarship in the social sciences.

To all those colleagues, students and friends, past and present, who have enlightened and encouraged me and passed on their enthusiasm for the study, I should like to express my sincere gratitude. I should like in addition to thank my current colleagues Christopher Coker, Michael Donelan and Justin Rosenberg for their invaluable comments on the draft text and my secretary Judy Weedon whose labours on it were, as always, uncomplaining and undertaken with far more good humour than I deserved. I am also greatly indebted to Mark White for another of his highly imaginative cover designs, encapsulating in a single illustration the argument of a lengthy text. Needless to say the responsibility for errors of fact and of judgement are mine alone.

Finally, to my current students attending my lectures on the 'Structure of International Society' my apologies for retracing what may appear to be rather familiar ground. On the other hand the book does include material not in the lectures and, as ever, any constructive comments, critical or otherwise, and from whatever source, will be gratefully received.

Geoffrey Stern
London School of Economics
June 1994

PART I
CONTENDING THEORIES

CHAPTER 1

REALISM, RATIONALISM AND REVOLUTIONISM

The past few years have seen a dramatic change in the international land-scape, what with the collapse of Communist power in Eastern Europe and beyond, the reunification of Germany, the end of the cold war, the violent fragmentation of the Soviet Union and Yugoslavia and the return to tribal-ism in the form of 'ethnic cleansing', the end of white minority rule in South Africa, the cycles of war- and peace-making in the Middle East, the plethora of UN peacekeeping activities on a shoestring budget, the boom in Asian industry at a time of slump in much of North America and Europe and the appearance on the international agenda of such issues as famine in Africa, Third World debt, environmental degradation and resource depletion. For students and teachers of International Relations the obvious questions are: how significant are these changes, what new dilemmas do they pose for statesmen, diplomats, politicians, businessmen and ordinary citizens and what new posers do they present for the scholar? Readers who manage to get to the end of this volume should be somewhat the wiser, but as this is an introductory text to a subject that admits of many different approaches, it would be as well to clarify at the outset what *The Structure of International Society* as expounded below is not.

1.1 THE STRUCTURE OF INTERNATIONAL SOCIETY

Subject matter

Although references to recent and contemporary events abound, *The Structure of International Society* is not about current affairs as such. Nor is it focused on modern history, even though there are ample allusions to historical events and epochs. Nor is there a hint here of policy science. Even if the author's sometimes idiosyncratic views on, say, British policy, liberal democracy, North/South relations, the environment and the 'science' of Economics find their way into the text, the aim is not to pontifi-cate, propose or prescribe. If, therefore, it is neither current affairs, nor modern history nor policy science, what exactly is *The Structure of International Society*?

First and foremost, it represents an attempt to identify and define international society in terms of the literature, to examine the qualifications for membership, to analyse and explain its political and economic structure, to detail the various configurations—local and global—it can take, to outline the types and the patterns of interaction and the norms making for orderly and regular international intercourse and to assess its responsiveness to changing ideologies and technologies. In addition, the study focuses on some of the central dilemmas of statecraft, in particular the question of how, if at all, the need for order can be reconciled with the requirements for justice, in any sense of the term, and a concern for power, in its many forms, can be balanced with a concern for morality, also in its many different guises.

By way of exposition reference will be made to a wide range of historical as well as current events and to classical as well as contemporary theories concerning matters international. Although little or no attempt is made here to offer solutions to some of the world's perennial problems, its diagnostic approach should have practical relevance to those seeking, if not prescriptions, then palliatives—those, say, set on helping an ailing planet cope better with its problems, as a pair of glasses helps the myopic to cope with short-sightedness. If there is a philosophy underlying the text it is the reverse of Karl Marx's famous dictum: 'hitherto philosophers have attempted to understand the world. The point, however, is to change it.' Since examples abound of ignorant, insensitive but opinionated people of power who in the name of 'progress', 'morality', 'freedom', 'self-determination', 'the market', 'socialism', 'God' or whatever have merely compounded the problems they have sought to solve, the sub-text here is that action has to be preceded by understanding, and this volume is about fostering it.

Methodology

What approach will be taken? Unlike the historian, the student of international society tends to deal with the general rather than the unique—with, for example, wars rather than a particular war, revolutions rather than a particular revolution, sanctions rather than a particular boycott or embargo, the problems of peace-keeping rather than any specific example. Moreover, the methodology, in so far as there is one, tends to be analytical and comparative rather than chronological and sequential. For documentation we have to rely on what we can get—archival material at best, personal interviews, eye-witness reports and specialist articles in lieu of anything else.

More importantly, *The Structure of International Society* is designed to be an introductory course to the study of International Relations, but it may prove of interest even to the non-specialist in suggesting ways of organising one's thoughts about a complex world that often appears paradoxi-cal—with its tendencies simultaneously towards integration and disinte-gration, co-operation and conflict, internationalism and nationalism, order and anarchy, altruism and egoism, continuity and change, idealism and cynicism, reality and make-believe.

Shortcomings

Those of a scientific disposition hoping to derive from the study testable hypotheses which can be validated or falsified by experiment will find that in this respect it suffers from two separate but related handicaps. The first is that many, if not most, of its key concepts are essentially ambiguous. Such terms as 'the state', 'nation', 'international', 'sovereign', 'power', 'imperialism' and so forth can be conceptualised in different ways—mean-ing different things to different people, sometimes meaning different things to the same people, depending on the context. For example, in his much quoted book *Politics Among Nations*, the late American scholar Hans Morgenthau uses the term 'power' in almost a dozen different senses: as a means to an end, as an end in itself, as the capacity to produce intended effects, as the attainment of those effects, as a synonym for force, as a synonym for control, as a relationship, as something to be assessed in quantitative terms, as something to be assessed qualitatively, as being empowered to do something and so forth.

A second disadvantage stems from the fact that precisely because many of these same concepts tend to have no solid existence—ie no one has ever seen, felt, touched, smelt a sovereign state—we tend to personify them in our efforts to make them intelligible. We talk, for example, of the state as if it were a person. We refer to it as, say, getting angry, preparing for war, suing for peace, signing a peace treaty or joining an alliance. But, even if the state is as real to us as a table and a chair, to which there is, in the jargon, a concrete referent, it 'exists' on a totally different plane of reality. That is, it exists in our heads. Its existence is notional only. In the words of the late Professor C.A.W. Manning, the state exists in the realm of the 'in effect', not in the world of 'in fact'. Although in point of fact it does not exist, effectively it does, for it is a concept in terms of which people act.[1] Admittedly, in imputing personality to it, each statesman, diplomat, civil servant, journalist, citizen or whatever may entertain a slightly different idea of what the state is. But as will be immediately obvious to anyone following the turbulent events in Bosnia, Croatia, Serbia and the successor states of the Soviet Union, there are those for whom the state becomes a kind of god demanding service, deference and, if necessary, death. That is, having personified the state, people will sometimes go on virtually to deify it, being prepared to fight and die in its name.

In fact personification serves to reduce a complex reality to comparatively simple terms and is probably much more common than is realised. We speak, for example, of the university awarding degrees, the bank lending money, the trade union calling a strike, when the reality is of people playing roles as academics, bank managers and trade union officials. We may talk of the working class as being in revolutionary mood, when the reality is of individuals, many of them not themselves labourers, looking for radical change, while others who are labourers may be rather less enthusiastic about revolution. Those with musical inclinations may speak of the orchestra playing well or playing badly when the reality is, of course, of individuals banging, blowing and scraping to good or baleful effect. The way in which reality is conceived, imagined and understood is, thus, part of reality itself, and as students of 'Structure', we have to consider the situation as perceived at least as much as the situation 'out there'—by no means always an easy task. At the same time like the non-specialist, we are often obliged to use this kind of personified picture language ourselves, if only as a kind of verbal shorthand. The hope is, however, that we know what we are doing and why.

The need for 'linguistic analysis'

How then does the student cope with the conceptual difficulties the subject presents? The answer lies in what is called 'linguistic analysis', once, though no longer, *de rigeur* in Oxford and associated with people like A.J. Ayer whose *Language, Truth and Logic* is a classic in the field. Like the eccentric Cambridge don Ludwig Wittgenstein, he assumed that words do not have intrinsic meanings. They have uses, and our task with a word like, say, 'power' is to discover from the context how it is being used, whether it is to be seen as a relationship, a quality, a capacity or whatever. If the word is 'sovereignty', are we examining the legal, the political or the economic dimensions of the term? If the subject is 'imperialism', are we talking of the pursuit or acquisition of formal empire, the pursuit or acquisition of informal empire such as spheres of influence or economic client states, a structural relationship of dominance and dependency or a philosophy of expansionism, and if the latter, what kind of expansion, into and over what, by whom and so forth?

1.2 DEFINING 'INTERNATIONAL SOCIETY'

When 'the Structure of International Society' first appeared on the LSE syllabus, it reflected the then somewhat idiosyncratic understanding of its architect, Charles Manning, that the focus would be on the implications for the real world of the widely shared notion that there is in existence an international society, that its oldest and most durable members are states, but that it now comprised in addition a number of other politically significant legal persons. Among them were international organisations such as the UN, supranational bodies such as the Commission of the European Communities and transnational organisations such as IBM, Exxon and Rio Tinto Zinc, whose interests, as it were, knew no frontiers. Further, that there were in existence a host of political and economic entities—including rebellious colonies, secessionist groups and 'liberation movements'— anxious to become accredited full members of international society, and that this conceived of or postulated international society had become co-extensive with the globe itself, so that total isolation as practised by, say, Japan and China until the mid-19th century was no longer possible.

1.3 'SOCIETY', 'COMMUNITY' AND 'ANARCHY'

But why the use of the term 'society'? In 1949, when the 'Structure' course first appeared, the emotionally neutral, scientific-sounding expression 'international system' was not yet in vogue, while the terms 'international community' and 'international anarchy' both sounded inappropriate—the former due to its overtones of solidarity and cohesiveness, the latter because of its implication of disorder and chaos. People generally conceived of international relations as proceeding on the basis of a modicum of order and a shared interest in co-existence which is what, for Manning, the word 'society' conveyed. It was, of course, an unusual society both because it comprised states and other politically significant entities and because it was one without government, even though proceeding on the basis of rules and regulations commonly understood and in general self-administered and policed. For Manning the term 'society' had a further advantage, for it could be studied at several different levels of analysis: at a micro- or psychological level as individuals thinking and behaving; at a sociological level, in terms of group behaviour; and at a macro- or systemic level, when society itself is understood holistically, as a socio-political unit. As he says in *The Nature of International Society*: 'Meet my family (holism); meet the members of my family (collectivism); meet my brothers, Tom, Dick and Harry (individualism).'[2] For Manning, therefore, international society, like many other social institutions, could be investigated at the level of individuals entertaining ideas and notions; at the level of the state or other politically significant entities on behalf of which individuals operated, or at a holistic level when international society is conceptualised as a social whole with its own history and traditions.

If today the expression 'international society' is probably used less frequently than in Prof. Manning's day, that international relations are best conceived of as being to a degree orderly and predictable and that their perceived structure is worthy of investigation would hardly be controversial. It is in that spirit that the term is used as a basis for this text. It does mean, however, that in the study, the linguistic precision found in most of the physical and biological sciences is lacking. When, for example, a natural scientist proposes to test the boiling point of water, there is no problem about the meaning of 'test', 'boiling point' or 'water', whereas when the international relations scholar decides to investigate the international impact of 'revolution' or the effects of 'imperialism', we have semantic and conceptual problems *ab initio*; and, of course, whether or not one can actually test any hypothesis on either subject is debatable. But problems of semantics and of verifiability are not peculiar to the study of International Relations; they pervade the social sciences, even if some in the field—the economists in particular—are somewhat reticent about admitting it.

1.4 CLASSICAL THEORIES

There is a sense in which international relations of a kind has been a subject of study for more than two millennia. Round about 400 BC Thucydides wrote his *History of the Peloponnesian War* in order to enlighten those wanting to understand 'the events which happened in the past and which (human nature being what it is) will at some time or other and in much the same ways, be repeated in the future'.[3] Thucydides, in other words, had developed a theory of inter-state conflict, and in trying to account for war he suggested that a mixture of factors—geographical, demographic, economic, technological, political as well as psychological (he thought that human actions were motivated by greed, pride and fear)—would cause the power of one state to grow, thus inducing perceptions of threat in the other states. The result, in his opinion, would inevitably be war and the establishment of a new international system by the victor. In a sense Thucydides was the begetter of what became known as the Realist approach to international relations in his emphasis on power and power balances. About one hundred years later, the Indian statesman, Kautilya, in a treatise entitled *Arthashastra* might be said to have taken Realism a stage further in his unsentimental examination of the conduct of statesmen in their relations with one another. In it he essays, for example, the reasoning behind the time-honoured maxim: 'my enemy's enemy is my friend'. And sometime between Thucydides and Kautilya, the Chinese thinker Sun Tsu had addressed himself to one of Realism's central concerns, the question of strategy and tactics in warfare, and his guerrilla tactics were to prove invaluable to Mao Tse-tung in his path to power some two thousand years later.

In more recent times, towards the end of the middle ages, in 1513, a Florentine diplomat, Niccolo Machiavelli, produced a classic text, central to

Realism, *The Prince*, in which he muses on the nature of power and advises his aristocratic employer how to survive and prosper in a fragmenting and insecure world of political intrigue, assassination and diplomatic betrayal. But in the century which followed, several distinguished thinkers laid the framework for a more co-operative conception of international relations. The jurist, Hugo Grotius in *De Jure Belli ac Pacis*, written in 1625, spoke of a society of sovereign states and rooted it firmly in law. In many ways this was the first major text in what the late Martin Wight called the Rationalist tradition—which will be explored later in the chapter. The 17th century was, however, a period of turmoil—of religious wars which tore the European continent apart and of civil war in England; and the English philosopher, Thomas Hobbes, who had been one of the translators of Thucydides, took a far less optimistic approach than Grotius. In *Leviathan*, written in the 1650s, Hobbes speaks of a world where anarchy reigns in the absence of strong government—a notion having international as well as domestic implications. A hundred years later, the Scottish thinker, David Hume, issued a reminder that there was an alternative way of miti- gating international anarchy, and in a treatise *The Balance of Power* he both analyses and recommends the use of this age old diplomatic device. But by the end of the 18th century, the German philosopher Immanuel Kant was laying the groundwork for many an idealistic treatise on international rela- tions with his celebrated essay on the conditions for a cosmopolis or harmonious world society—*Perpetual Peace*, effectively a call to sweep away all those artificial barriers: dynasties, nations, states and so forth, which inhibit the creation of one world. Martin Wight dubs this the first major Revolutionist text.

Thus, by the end of the 18th century we have three different conceptual maps or paradigms, as Wight calls them, for analysing inter-state relations: Realism with an emphasis on power, Rationalism stressing co-operation and Revolutionism with an agenda for global transformation.[4] As indi- cated, the psychological universe—how people conceptualise the world— is for us at least as significant as the physical universe, since the way people imagine reality affects their behaviour and hence what happens in the real world. In this chapter are elaborated the three major traditions of thought about international relations developed in the years before anyone had taken up the sytematic study of those relations; and in the next chapter, how later generations of scholars amended and updated these classical paradigms in trying to understand contemporary interna- tional society. But first, a note of caution.

Any typology of this kind can only be a rough and ready method of categorising a bewildering variety of conceptions, and there is always the risk of misrepresentation, even of caricature. Clearly, within each of the categories identified there are bound to be significant differences of thought, and particular thinkers may straddle the fence between one tradition and another. Machiavelli, the apostle of 'power politics', was also something of a visionary, at least with regard to Italian unification. He was not himself, after all, a thoroughgoing Machiavellian, as anyone who has glanced at his writings other than *The Prince* can testify; while Marx, who also had views about the nature of international society, made it clear to an admirer that he was more revolutionary activist than dogmatic theorist and was, therefore, no Marxist.

The three major classical traditions of theorising about international relations have been variously described. Martin Wight typologises them as Realist, Rationalist and Revolutionist; his tutee and collaborator, Hedley Bull, as Hobbesian, Grotian and Kantian;[5] Keith Nelson and Spencer Olin dub them Conservative, Liberal and Radical;[6] Michael Banks designates them as Realist, Pluralist and Structuralist;[7] others, yet again, have depicted them as State-centrist, Internationalist and Universalist; State-centric, Multi-centric and Global-centric, and there are yet more designations! But what one derives from each body of theory is not just an analysis of the nature of international society but also a set of prescriptions about international conduct. And in the third of these traditions—the Revolutionist or Kantian school of thought—there is prediction as well as prescription.

Realism

The Realist or Hobbesian tradition, which may be said to include Thucydides, Kautilya, Machiavelli, possibly Burke and Hegel as well as Hobbes, is rooted in a pessimistic analysis of human nature. Humankind, in the Realist view, is deeply flawed—driven by self-interest, pride, ambition, anger and a host of other passions. Some Realists, indeed, see humankind as tainted with original sin. There is, thus, no question of human perfectability. On the other hand social order is possible, since the baser instincts can be kept in check by trained elites with the power to command and the authority to make their dictates effective. Order, in other words, depends on the acceptance of hierarchy and is to everyone's advantage, since the elites enjoy their responsibilities and the masses enjoy the benefits of an ordered and predictable existence and the feeling of belonging to a community long established. It follows from the Hobbesians' dim view of human nature that they are averse to individualism, equality, belief in progress and other such notions which threaten existing orders and hierarchies and disrupt what Burke called the partnership 'between those who are living, those who are dead, and those who are to be born'.[8] Basically it is a tradition which prefers inertia to innovation, stability to change and experience to experimentation and rejects assertions about 'human rights' on the grounds that they are abstract and unrelated to social context. It follows then that in a world of sovereign states, humanity's continued existence depends on the maintenance of those state structures. Further, that service to the sovereign state effectively means service to society and in this sense the state must be regarded as the highest focus of loyalty—all notions of law and morality deriving from it.

Thus what begins as a theory of human nature becomes a theory of the state—the state being regarded as a unitary actor which uses military and other power either as an end in itself (as a miser amasses wealth for its own sake) or as a means to an end—the end being the survival and enhancement of the state through which the life of the community is preserved.

From such bases, a number of propositions may be derived: first, that international relationships are characterised by neither community nor society. If we apply linguistic analysis, what 'community' seems to mean in this context is a collectivity whose members share a sense of solidarity, commonality and kinship; 'society' (implying something less cohesive) would appear to refer to an association organised for a specific common purpose, as in the case of a music or a dramatic society.[9] In the Hobbesian view, international relationships entail neither common sentiment nor common purpose. They are, therefore, anarchic and characterised by conflict and struggle as each state attempts to secure its objectives, often at the expense of others. Second, in such a condition of international anarchy, war is an ever-present contingency and peace, therefore, an interlude between wars. Third, international strife cannot be prevented by legal or moral rules, since rules arise only in the context of society, and no international society exists. Fourth, the presence of clearly recognised and accepted hierarchies, at both domestic and international levels, may serve to lessen the incidence of international conflict. This is because in a world of well-disciplined societies in which passions are kept in check, neither leaders nor lead are under pressure to force changes in the international status quo, and also because where there is an accepted international hierarchy in which the strongest powers want to maintain the status quo, peace can be preserved at least for a time. Fifth, since legal and moral rules are valid only in the context of domestic society, any legal or moral goals pursued internationally can only be those of the state itself. Anything going by the name of international law or morality must be a form of what Georg Schwarzenberger calls 'power politics in disguise'.[10]

What, then, is the Hobbesian prescription for national conduct in conditions of international anarchy? It is the pursuit of policies to preserve internal order and also to protect and promote those interests and values deemed important by the ruling elite. The only constraints on international activity recognised by the Hobbesians are those of superior force, prudence or expediency. Thus agreements may be entered into and kept if it is politic to do so but scrapped when no longer expedient.

Rationalism

Such a view of international relationships tended to gain currency at a time of international upheaval and rapid social change when values were in flux. Hobbes, for example, was responding to the turmoil associated with the religious wars in Europe and with England's civil war, Burke to the threat to the existing social and international order posed by the ideologues of the French Revolution. But, of course, theorists of a Grotian or Rationalist cast of mind—people like Locke, Montesquieu, Bentham and John Stuart Mill, as well as Grotius himself—would have been far more hospitable than Hobbes to many of the ideas of the French Revolution. After all, they shared with the Revolutionaries the notion of man as the possessor and beneficiary of natural rights, conferred on him by what was called natural law—possibly, but not necessarily, divine in origin. They also shared the notion that law had to be based on consent rather than command. As such the Grotians were in no way hostile to ideas of equality, individualism, progress and the like, since, as they saw it, any valid legal system depended on notions of equality before the law, law as guarantor of individual liberties, law as a body of binding rules which can develop as society changes. This latter consideration was fundamental, since Grotius was himself formulating a new theory to fit in with a new kind of world, as in the 17th century the institutions of medieval Western Christendom continued to disintegrate.

Where, then, did the Grotians stand in relation to the major preoccupations of the Hobbesians—man and the state? Needless to say their perspective was radically different. To the Grotians human beings were far more rational than the Hobbesians allowed and ready to recognise limitations on their immediate desires, for the long term good of themselves and of the society of which they were but a part. In short, there was a harmony of interests between self and society, wherever legal and other social institutions were perceived as representing a just and reasonable order of things. But this implied that those empowered to make laws—the state or other sovereign authority—must seek to serve society and that the lawgiver neglects that service at his peril, since people cannot indefinitely tolerate laws emanating from despotic or arbitrary power.

From such a view of man in relation to law, the Grotians derived their understanding of the nature of international society. They granted that in international as in domestic relationships there are conflicts. As against the Hobbesians, who regarded the international arena as one of unceasing strife, the Grotians held that—at least between Christian, that is, European nations—international disputes, like those occurring within civil society, could and should be mitigated, adjudicated or resolved through the application of generally recognised rules and procedures. But how could this be done in a world in which political power is dispersed and there is no accepted world sovereign or judiciary? The Grotians argued, as against the

Hobbesians, that society does not depend on government and that there obtained internationally a sufficient degree of order compatible with the notion of society. So what did they understand by society? Clearly they meant some kind of collectivity—not as homogeneous or as close knit as a community, perhaps—but whose members did have significant contacts and reciprocal interests and sustained orderly procedures and rules, explicit or implicit, as regards their inter-relations.

But the Grotians were not merely positing an international society. They believed they were describing one already in being or in the process of being formed. What was it that for the Grotians constituted evidence of international society? In the first place there was increasing acceptance among sovereign rulers of the body of binding rules understood as international law—recognition of sovereign status, sovereign equality, non-intervention, the right of national self-defence etc. Second, there was the development of the institutions of diplomacy, with resident ambassadors, as distinct from envoys *ad hoc*, and the evolution of diplomatic methods, procedures and rank. Third, there was the growth of trade on a regular and regulated basis. Fourth, there was the apparent existence of a residual sense of international moral as well as international legal obligation, presumably stemming from a common Christian ancestry. Fifth, there was the periodic existence of various Concerts of powers—usually great, satisfied and status quo powers—which together acted as self-appointed guarantors of international law and order. Sixth, there was the role of prudence in constraining the activities of states in their international dealings. And seventh, there was the manifest capacity of ordered international intercourse to survive hot and cold wars, ideological disputes and acts of international barbarism.

If all these were characteristic of international society, how did the Grotians explain the excesses of, say, the Spanish *conquistadores* in their dealings with the Aztecs or the colonisers of North America and Australia in their treatment of the indigenous populations? This is easily explained. For in the view of the Grotians, membership of international society was confined largely to those sharing a common Christian ancestry, ie the countries of Europe. In this sense, though the Europeans might have certain obligations to non-Europeans, these were not of the same order as their obligations to members of their own international 'club', and hence they were entitled to regard themselves as bearing the rights and obligations of tutelage until the non-Europeans were ready to join the family of civilised ie Christian nations. The Europeans, having drawn up the rules of membership in the first place, were to decide when that moment came, but we can each have our own theory as to whether those who set such appalling examples in far-off lands are morally entitled to set standards about anything.

Granted, then, that international society for the Grotians was confined largely to the European sphere, how did they account for war within and between European nations? Originally they were wedded to the medieval Christian idea of the 'Just war', involving: (1) a declaration of war by a properly constituted authority, like a king or a prince—ie they could justify neither random violence nor belligerent activity by unauthorised groups; (2) a just cause ie in response to a wrong inflicted; (3) a just means of prosecuting the war ie with as much economy as possible in terms of the lives lost and the damage inflicted (this ruled out such things as torture, the murder of innocent civilians, the wanton destruction of property and the use of weapons which were indiscriminate in the harm they inflicted); (4) the termination of war at the earliest possible time.

Subsequently the Grotians somewhat modified their position, admitting that the question of 'justice' in war might be more complicated, with each party to a conflict having in some sense a 'just' cause. At all events, as against the Hobbesians they came to see war as a breakdown rather than a continuation of policy.

What, then, is the Grotian prescription for national conduct in international society? Clearly, anything that makes for a good neighbour: mutual respect; the willingness to accommodate interests and minimise friction; the honouring of obligations—keeping pledges, pacts and commitments—and the principle of 'the lesser evil' as a guide to policy. Do that which entails the least sacrifice of value!

Revolutionism

If compromise, adjustment and accommodation were the essence of the Grotian approach, they were the very antithesis of the Kantian or Revolutionist position. For the Kantians, who included Rousseau as well as Robespierre, Marx, Lenin and a host of radical thinkers down to the Ayatollah Khomenei, entertained a vision of an ideal yet realisable society, holding that any accommodation with existing social, political and international orders, unless for strictly tactical purposes, represented in some sense a betrayal of principle. For accommodation implied some degree of acceptance, and since all existing structures were unjust, in that they deflected humankind from its true potential, any compromise was tantamount to an endorsement of that unjust order and hence a betrayal.

What then was humanity's true potential, and how was it to be attained? Each Revolutionist had his own view of that destiny. It was one thing for the Protestant at odds with a Catholic world; another for the bourgeois idealist struggling against feudal rule and privilege; another for the patriot or religious zealot whose country is under alien domination; yet another for the Marxist estranged from capitalist society.

For all their differences, they shared a number of attitudes: first, a common conception of the brotherhood (and sisterhood) of humanity, ie of a global community or cosmopolis in which the true interests of all are realised, and perpetual peace and justice are established; second, the notion that existing structures which condition perceptions and expectations impose artificial barriers between people and prevent humankind from achieving its destiny; third, and consequently, that such structures must be either destroyed by revolution or else eroded or transformed through constant pressure.

For all their faith in the ultimate perfectability of human arrangements, for all their rejection of existing institutions and hostility to compromise, the Kantians none the less had to have some kind of strategy for coping with an as yet unreformed and unregenerate world. What did they offer? Again, their prescriptions follow from the broad ideological screen through which they filtered all events. First, they made a clear distinction between those of the true faith who shared the same body of ideas and those not of their fraternity. Theirs was, so to speak, a polarised, dialectical view of the universe with the trustees of the potential community of humankind ranged on one side and those who would stand in its way on the other. Second, they believed themselves to be in a permanent state of hostilities—declared or undeclared, overt or covert, physical or psychological—against those who for whatever reason impeded progress to the inevitable goal. Third, they believed that the ends justified the means and that there was no room for compassion, sentiment or notions of moderation when there was so much at stake.

At its most extreme it could mean assimilate or exterminate, convert or destroy, and behind this way of thinking lay the tradition of the Crusade, of the jihad or Holy War. The irony was that a doctrine aimed at ultimate harmony and integration in practice tended to worsen existing divisions and to create a few more—and not just between the nations, but also within them, since the basic conflict which the Revolutionists diagnosed and promoted was one that cut across state boundaries. In the ideological divide between the harbingers of the new order and the supporters of the status quo, existing state structures were irrelevant. They were no more than projections of the interests of the elites, while the real struggle was transnational, horizontal, across the nations. The ties of loyalty and solidarity which bound the adherents of the true faith to one another took no account of state structures. In fact they wholly transcended them. Thus, if for the Hobbesians 'power' was the main consideration in an international context they deemed anarchic; and if for the Grotians 'order' was paramount in what they took to be an international society, for the Kantians, the pursuit of 'true justice' took priority in a polarised world destined to become a single global community.

1.5 ORIGINS OF THE SUBJECT

It is ironic that though men of letters had been been effectively musing on the nature of inter-state relations for some two thousand years, the term 'international' did not appear until 1780, when the philosopher Jeremy Bentham coined it in a text on inter-state law.[11] None the less, as a subject of systematic study, International Relations did not appear till the first decade of this century and even then not as an independent academic discipline. Until 1919, it was the province of the occasional lecturer in the occasional American university and mainly in the departments of History or Political Science. What had prompted its appearance was a characteristic American concern for solving problems. As the ancient Greeks had hit upon the study of Politics to deal with the problem of order in a civil society in a world of revolutionary change, so a few pioneering Americans early this century embarked on the study of what they called 'World Politics' to find an answer to the problem of war, which they feared to be on the horizon. In this they were quite right. They were unable, however, to find that elusive formula they sought, and, sadly, their successors have been scarcely more successful.

NOTES

1. Manning, C.A.W., *The Nature of International Society*, London, Bell, 1962, p.15.
2. Ibid. p.39.
3. Thucydides, *History of the Peloponnesian War*, trans. Rex Warner, Harmondsworth, Penguin, 1976, p.48.
4. See, for example, Porter, Brian, 'Patterns of Thought and Practice: Martin Wight's International Theory' in Donelan, M. (ed.), *The Reason of States*, London, Allen & Unwin, 1978, pp. 64–74.
5. See, for example, Bull, H., *The Anarchical Society*, London, Macmillan, 1977.
6. Nelson, K. and Olin, S., *Why War?*, Berkeley, University of California Press, 1980.
7. Banks, M., 'The Inter-paradigm Debate' in Light, M. and Groom, A.J.R. (ed.), *International Relations: A Handbook of Current Theory*, London, Pinter, 1985, pp. 7–26.
8. *Reflections on the Revolution in France*, [1790] New York, Dolphin Books, 1961.
9. In *Power Politics*, London, Stevens, 1964, p.12. Schwarzenberger, G. quotes the 19th-century sociologist Toennies as saying, 'the members of a society remain isolated in spite of their association, and those of a community are united despite their separate existence'.
10. This is the heading to Part II of his three-part volume, op.cit.
11. Wright, Q., *The Study of International Relations*, New York, Appleton-Century-Crofts, 1955, p.3.

CHAPTER 2

BEHAVIOURALISM VERSUS TRADITIONALISM

The previous chapter detailed some of the contending theories, paradigms or conceptual maps of international society developed long before anyone had taken up the systematic study of International Relations. This chapter examines some of the several paradigms that have gained currency especially in academic circles during a century which has seen the study come of age—transmuted from an isolated outpost in the odd American university to a fast expanding and 'respectable' subject taught throughout the world. Not that IR always has a department to itself. Even today it is often tucked away in a department of Politics or History. In some universities, moreover, it goes under the name of International Politics or World Politics, but the name often gives little clue as to subject matter. To discover what is in any course under any of these headings, it is always advisable to look at the syllabus and at past exam papers.

2.1 WHY STUDY INTERNATIONAL RELATIONS?

The rapid expansion of the study has been assisted in no small measure by the wide variety of purposes it appears to serve—academic, personal and political. Clearly, many of its teachers and students have a scholarly interest in acquiring understanding and knowledge for its own sake, and the idea of taking on a relatively new subject that appears to encompass as broad a prospectus as the great globe itself yet seems manageable, represents an exciting intellectual challenge. But IR is not just a formidable mental discipline. It also provides an avenue for both self-knowledge and personal advancement. In its focus not just on the world as it is but on the world as perceived, it can be a vehicle for greater self-awareness. At the same time, good and sometimes not so good graduates in the subject may well proceed to a diplomatic post, to some international organisation, to international business, to radio, TV journalism or the press, or, if they have nothing better to do, to teaching and research. Many also take to the subject, as they have always done, for political reasons. There are the 'super patriots' who hope that an understanding of the ways of the world may equip them better for service to the country. There are the ideologues endeavouring to further some particular right- or left-wing cause, and at the height of the cold war several American and Soviet universities were only too anxious to pander to their prejudices. Rather more common are those who hope through the study to find the intellectual tools to enable them to remedy what they see as some of the ills of international society—in particular, the persistence of war.

2.2 A DISTINCT ACADEMIC DISCIPLINE?

But does IR constitute a distinct academic discipline? Once again, linguistic analysis is called for. If by academic discipline is meant a field of study wholly distinct from any other, it was not, is not and probably never will be. It is difficult to see how one can develop a proper understanding of the many dimensions of International Relations without some knowledge of History, Geography, Political theory, Economics, International law and so forth, and in this sense IR may best be described as 'inter-disciplinary'. On the other hand if by 'academic discipline' one simply means disciplined study of a particular field, with or without the credentials of separateness or distinctiveness, then International Relations is, and always has been a discipline.

In fact, the first Chairs were established in Britain—at Aberystwyth in 1919, the LSE in 1923 and Oxford in 1930. On the other hand till comparatively recently those professing the subject were constantly on the defensive against the charge by historians, political scientists, international lawyers and economists that IR was not a proper academic discipline, and until the 1950s the study remained confined to a small group of specialist teachers, often themselves not graduates of the subject, at a few select universities and diplomatic academies in Britain, the United States and in Geneva. What is clear is that the development of this disciplined study, as reflected in the literature, has gone through several different phases, each to an extent the product of its time and place.

2.3 THREE POST-1919 PARADIGMS

The idealist/utopian

When the first two Chairs in the subject were established, much of the world was still traumatised by the effects of the world war, and the Wilsonian view that war was a product of elitist politics, secret diplomacy, imperialism, arms manufacture, insufficient attention to international law and organisation and inadequate understanding of world affairs seemed to be widely shared, especially within the victorious powers. The antidote, thus, seemed to lie in democratic control of politics, open diplomacy (President Wilson spoke of 'open covenants openly arrived at'), national self-determination (at least in Europe), disarmament, anti-war legislation, new international institutions to encourage co-operation, mutual aid and collective security, and, as a prerequisite, a better-educated public. It was with a view to their helping in the creation of that 'new world order' that Alfred Zimmern and Philip Noel-Baker were appointed to the new Chairs at Aberystwyth and the LSE respectively. However, neither stayed at his post for long—the cosmopolitan Zimmern soon falling foul of both the Welsh nationalists and the Welsh non-conformists for what is euphemistically called a 'moral indiscretion';[1] the equally passionate Noel-Baker deciding he would prefer the life of a disarmament salesman in Geneva to that of an academic in London.[2] None the less the idealism of their approach more or less permeated the teaching of the subject for some two decades. Until the late 1930s IR scholars toiled away with their tomes on international law, analysing treaties, examining legal sources and principles, commending the League of Nations, applauding such covenants as the Kellogg Briand Pact of 1928 outlawing war as an instrument of policy and devising schemes for new international institutions in what they took to be a shrinking world.

If the early exponents of the subject were a product of their time, so were their successors. For the heady idealism of the twenties was to be rudely shattered by the Wall Street Crash of 1929 and the Great Depression, the drive to protectionism and the rise of Fascism which followed in its wake. In 1931 the Japanese invaded and occupied Manchuria, in effect firing the opening salvo in what was to become the second world war. Later they made further incursions into China, setting the precedent for the Italians to seize Abyssinia in 1935 and Albania four years later, and the Germans to take control of Austria and the Sudetenland in 1938, the rest of Czechoslovakia and then Western Poland in 1939, triggering the second world war proper. Not to be outdone, the Soviet Union occupied eastern Poland and invaded Finland in 1939 and went on to seize Latvia, Lithuania and Estonia and to occupy Bessarabia and northern Bukovina which had been part of Romania. Though some International Relations scholars had begun to temper their idealism in the mid-1930s, many stuck to their principles, but by the late thirties it was becoming increasingly obvious, even to teachers of IR, that aspirations were no substitute for analysis and that the rule of law was no answer to people like Japan's General Tojo, Mussolini or Hitler. In academic circles, as outside it, there occurred what was to be called a 'paradigm shift': the earlier paradigm, with its Grotian prescriptions, now being regarded as inadequate in terms of both explanatory and prescriptive power. The publication in 1939 of E.H. Carr's seminal work *The Twenty Years' Crisis* marked the watershed.[3]

The Realist

Edward Hallett Carr was one of the most accomplished scholars ever to teach the subject. He had worked in the Foreign Office, was a leader writer for *the Times*, had already written the first of a score or more of distinguished books on contemporary history and held the Chair of International Politics in, of all places, Aberystwyth; in *The Twenty Years' Crisis* he launched a bitter attack on the previous generation of IR scholars, including the first holder of the Aberystwyth Chair, Alfred Zimmern. He dubbed them 'utopian' in their thinking, and in four major respects: first of all with regard to their objectives. Carr held that they were far more preoccupied with the 'ought' than with the 'is' and with the desirable rather than the feasible; second with regard to their perceptions. Carr saw them as culture-bound intellectuals who were often unaware of the collective self-interest behind their ideals. Those from the victorious powers were naturally interested in peace, disarmament and the status quo since their objectives had more or less been achieved. But why should those from the dissatisfied and aggrieved powers—'the have nots'—be expected to share the enthusiasms of the 'haves'? His third point concerned their dispositions. Carr saw them as far too judgmental in their approach to the problems of statecraft. They appeared to assume that those operating on behalf of the state had almost complete freedom of action, and they virtually ignored the role of necessity, contingency, determinism and chance in political affairs. His fourth criticism was of their understanding. Carr felt that in their preoccupation with co-operation as against conflict, with solidarity as against self-interest and with harmony as against discord, they showed little understanding of either history or human nature.

With Carr's study, the first of many major theoretical debates in the subject was launched, though the terminology 'Realists' versus 'Utopians' reflected the thinking of the former. Carr and his ilk claimed to be 'Realists', dismissing their opponents as 'Utopians', and though Carr himself does not altogether exclude ideals, ethics or morality from his analysis, he suggests that the ideals of his opponents are impracticable and hence 'utopian'.

So what was the new paradigm suggested by Carr, and later to be seized on by Georg Schwarzenberger at London University, Hans Morgenthau in Chicago, Henry Kissinger at Harvard, Raymond Aron in Paris and others? Basically, one on which students in Nazi Germany had already been hard at work for several years: namely, the importance of national interest, self-help, self-reliance and, if necessary, self-assertion. As Carr and the new breed of International Relations scholars saw it, what was needed in a world of power hungry dictators was a strategy for security and survival, and this in turn depended on an analysis of the uses and abuses of power in all its manifestations—as a resource, as a capacity, as a relationship and so on. Above all, each state needed to have, either on its own or in concert with others, sufficient military capacity to deter, or if deterrence failed, to defeat potential aggressors. And in an insecure world, foreign-policy considerations had to take precedence over domestic concerns. There was a role for ethics and ideals, but in international politics these had to be tempered by considerations of power; the desirable had to be sought within the framework of the possible. In short, IR had to exchange a largely Grotian for a mainly Hobbesian analysis, and in the select British and American academies that taught the subject, it did, remaining the dominant paradigm not just throughout the war period but also in the early years of the cold war. After all, by the late 1940s the Western powers saw themselves as having merely exchanged one set of enemies for another, and with Stalin now replacing Hitler as presenting the major threat to Western security and what were seen as Western values, there seemed no pressing reason for abandoning the broadly Hobbesian 'power political' approach, though the advent of nuclear weapons would eventually call for certain adjustments in the concept of 'power'.

On the other hand in rediscovering some of the Hobbesian postulates, the Realists of the forties and fifties did not necessarily go all the way with their mentor. True, they shared the state-centricity of the Hobbesian analysis. They regarded all other political, economic and social forces as contingent upon the state in interaction and saw national security and prosperity as scarce resources which constrained choices and led to intense competition between the powers, mitigated only by considerations of enlightened self-interest. But very few of the Western scholars would have identified themselves with the elitist and frankly anti-democratic character of Hobbes's original texts. Not all would have gone along with Hobbes's thoroughly pessimistic understanding of human nature. Nor did they necessarily take any delight in what they understood as the state-centric nature of the international system. For example, Martin Wight, who wrote one of the standard texts on *Power Politics*, was a pacifist. Perhaps, therefore, a distinction should be drawn between the analytical and the prescriptive components of Realism, when a scholar like Martin Wight can accept the diagnosis but be ambivalent about the implications.

The Stalinist/Marxist

While Western scholars were still wedded largely to state-centricity, a very different paradigm was being expounded in the Soviet academies and those Eastern European universities under Moscow's tutelage from the late forties. Its origin lay in a peculiarly Stalinist version of Marxism, a version owing at least as much to his country's recent history as to the notion of progress through conflict which lies at the heart of Marxist dialectics. As Stalin saw it, the Soviet Union, like Russia before it, had suffered much at the hands of foreign powers both to the west and east. After the Revolution of 1917 the country had been blockaded and subjected to the intervention of a dozen or more powers which gave aid and support to the anti-Bolshevik forces in the civil war and had the Red Army fighting at one time on 14 different fronts simultaneously. In the 20 or so years between the end of the intervention and the Nazi onslaught against the Soviet Union, there was Poland's invasion of the Ukraine, the *cordon sanitaire* of hostile Eastern European powers, Washington's diplomatic isolation of Moscow till the mid-1930s, the unremitting and unchecked rise of Fascism and Britain's appeasement of Hitler. Then in 1941 came Germany's second invasion of Russia in less than 30 years, in which the country lost one in nine of its population, followed by the West's lengthy delay in opening up a second front in Europe and its rejection of a role for Moscow in the management of Italy's affairs after Mussolini's defeat. There followed Washington's refusal to inform Moscow of the Manhattan project to develop the A-Bomb, the use of two such bombs against Japan and Washington's willingness to spirit away from Europe and use for militarily related purposes anti-Communist Nazis of considerable notoriety. The paradigm that emerged from Moscow, to be promulgated in what passed for seats of learning in all the countries under Soviet tutelage, put all of this in the appropriate ideological perspective.

Basically the Stalinist paradigm stressed the importance of class solidarity across frontiers and the comparative unimportance of national boundaries. The cold war, as indeed the hot war preceding it, was understood not in terms of competing alliance systems but in terms of competing ideologies based on class identification. War was a function of capitalist imperialism and a consequence of domestic class struggle. It would thus persist until the Communist millennium was achieved—a classless, stateless world of altruistic and versatile atheists. If it sounds familiar, it was, of course, a 20th-century variant of the Kantian revolutionary theme.

Although these three post-first world war paradigms—the idealist/utopian, the Realist and the Stalinist/Marxist—were by no means carbon copies of earlier models, nor indeed would their proponents have necessarily been familiar with the historical and philosophical genesis of any or all of them, some of the more recent controversies relating to the study can be readily understood in terms related to these earlier paradigms. What then of these contentions and controversies?

2.4 THE BEHAVIOURAL REVOLUTION

They were an almost inevitable product of the sudden influx of scholars into the field from other disciplines in the mid-1950s as people took stock of the frightening implications of the proliferation of nuclear weapons and as new kinds of international issues—North/South as well as East/West, environmental as well as economic—captured the imagination. In any case, the greater the number and variety of scholars in any particular discipline the greater the likelihood of disagreements among them. But with so many newcomers entering the field—some seduced from mathematics, others from the natural sciences, others, yet again, lured from the other social sciences and bringing with them, for good or ill, the very latest techniques of analysis—there were bound to be new methodologies, new concepts, new ways of defining the subject and its status among the other disciplines.

Equally there were almost bound to be exaggerated claims for some of those novel approaches and also resistance and hostility from scholars whose knowledge of and interest in history was generally much deeper and who felt that some of the 'new' techniques and methodologies were either not all that new or were irrelevant, pretentious, obscurantist or misconceived.

In a sense the first post-Realists offered not so much a new paradigm as more rigorous methods of enquiry. For Realism's basic assumptions could not, in their view, be substantiated. They were lacking in both proof and means of verification. In any case Realism was flawed conceptually since 'power' was far too vague to be a useful indicator of behaviour, international or domestic. As a prescriptive theory, too, it was deficient in that so many contradictory policies could be derived from it. Of what value was the approach when considerations of 'national interest' led Morgenthau to oppose US involvement in Vietnam and Kissinger to support it? As a description of international relationships it was likewise inadequate, since in its strong emphasis on the role of the state it underplayed the extent to which territoriality and sovereignty had been penetrated by international, transnational, subnational and supranational actors, movements and processes. Equally, in an age of nuclear 'overkill', 'spy-in-the-sky' satellites, common markets, debt crises, information explosions, population explosions, depleting ozone layers and Great powers being worsted by small powers, as at Suez, in Vietnam and Afghanistan, the Realist emphasis on national security and power balances seemed in need of drastic overhaul.

On the other hand the challenge of the early post-Realists was less to Realism's state-centricity than to its methodology. Even though a few Realists claimed their approach was 'science-based', most tended to rely on a mix of historical analysis, political theory and intuition and were concerned more with explanation than with prediction. In contrast the newcomers offered what they liked to call a 'behavioural, scientific approach' of the kind then fashionable in the social sciences. Basing themselves on the observable, the tangible and the measurable, they sought quantifiable data, testable hypotheses and verifiable knowledge of behaviour patterns and ranges of conduct. Above all they made a fetish of objectivity. Their 'science', so they claimed, was value-free. In addition, the self-styled 'scientists' offered a new kind of theorising based on models of the type used in psychology, anthropology, sociology and other such disciplines. These included game and bargaining theories, computer simulation techniques, systems analysis (from which was derived the notion of the complex of international relations as a system ie a web of interacting units with discernible or intelligible patterns and norms of interaction) and a host of other intellectual devices designed to give more rigour and precision to the study. On the other hand, the net effect of this dramatic influx was to stimulate yet another great debate in the subject, with the behavioural 'scientists' dubbing the Realists 'traditionalists' or 'conservatives' and chiding them for their failure to give precise answers to many of the questions they raised about the nature of power, national interest, security and the like; the Realists accusing the 'scientists' of a contempt for history, of dealing in measurable trivia and of obscurantism in many of their voluminous published works.[4]

2.5 REALISM RECONSTRUCTED

In point of fact, many of the 'traditionalists', as they were now called, were rather less conservative than they appeared and when the 'scientific' onslaught occurred, they were already in process of reviewing their ideas. The self-styled 'scientists' were pushing at an open door since even within the Realist fraternity, there was growing dissatisfaction with a conceptual framework from whose basic assumptions several contradictory conclusions could be drawn. For example, even if one granted the central importance of a national interest, precisely whose interest was involved and by what criteria could it be determined? What were the relations between ideology and interest? What did international stability mean and what form of the balance of power was most conducive to it—bi- or multi-polarity? Did the acquisition of arms contribute to national security or undermine it by encouraging opponents likewise to acquire arms? In the face of such questions the Realists had tended to speak with many voices. They could not agree on which policy options best served the needs of the state.

In any case a number of developments had seemed to require at least a review if not the replacement of the Realist perspective. These developments included: the spread of nuclear weapons, the constraints they implied and opportunities they afforded; the disintegration of formal empires and the proliferation of new and often unviable states; the penetration of state structures by transnational, supranational and subnational forces; the growing salience of the North/South divide; the mounting evidence of environmental degredation; the crisis in the international monetary system, the trend towards integration in Western Europe and so on.

In the light of such developments many Realists were beginning to jettison their more crude power political calculations according to which most outcomes are determined by relative strengths and starting to allot greater weight to economic factors, to the role of non-governmental organisations and subnational groups such as secessionist movements. Anyone picking up, say, *The Anarchical Society* by Hedley Bull or *The International Political System* by Fred Northedge will readily discover how far 'the traddies' had moved towards 'the trendies' since the heady days of Carr, Morgenthau and their minions.

If there had been a perceptible shift in subject matter and a slight shift in terminology—for example, many reconstructed Realists now preferred the word 'pressure' to the much more ambiguous and overused concept of 'power', there had been precious little movement in the way the so-called 'traditionalists' defined the subject. In answer to the question of why the primary focus should be on government-to-government relations when there were so many other significant interactions and relationships, Professor Northedge stated the archetypal modern Realist position. 'The political level of international relations is in itself an intellectual concern of heroic dimensions...If the entire social world of sovereign states is included, we run the risk of being defeated by the subject's sheer dimensions.'[5] Not so, said the 'scientists', for whom such a definition of the study was far too narrow and restrictive.

2.6 FOREIGN-POLICY ANALYSIS

The first and best-funded critiques of 'traditionalism' came, naturally enough, from the United States. Here, after all, was a country experiencing the ups and downs of superpowerdom and what has been called 'the pulling and hauling' process of decision-making, and many of its scholars had no time for what they saw as an oversimplified 'billiard ball' conception of international politics. In the late fifties and sixties, therefore, the 'scientists' lent themselves to pioneering studies of foreign-policy analysis, taking on board a host of theories derived from other social science disciplines.[6] As it happens, many continue to analyse foreign policy, though as a supposedly scientific and objective endeavour the study was somewhat discredited when some 'analysts', particularly in the US, used it as a rationalisation for justifying government policy and a tool to beat the Soviets. In any case, with its concentration on the policies of particular states, it tended to reinforce the state-centric view of international relations. On the other hand by revealing the extent to which decisions are less the product of rational choice and more the chance result of complex bargaining processes, involving informants, advisers, negotiators and envoys as well as official policy makers, it performed a valuable service.[7] Never again would the testimony of those statesmen and women who claim to have planned and masterminded virtually everything done in the name of their country be accepted without considerable reserve.

2.7 POST-BEHAVIOURAL PLURALISM

Hardly had the 'billiard ball' conception been disposed of when some of the self-styled 'scientists' decided that the new decision-making approach was itself inadequate to explain the complexities of what many were coming to call 'World Politics'. 'World Politics', they claimed, encompassed a far broader framework than inter-state relations, for it comprised several layers of analysis simultaneously: the human level, the state level, the international systemic level. At the same time analysis of the international system was to include study of the economic, technological, ecological, ideological and other environments within which international relations occurred, each of these environments lending itself to analysis as a separate system.

Where did this new perception of the world political process lead? It led to a mode of explanation which, like the 'traditionalist' model, deserves the name 'paradigm', if by paradigm is meant a kind of conceptual map, an overarching framework for structuring knowledge and analysing certain patterns of relationship. The new paradigm, espoused by scholars such as Robert Keohane, James Rosenau, John Burton and Michael Banks[8] was to be known by various names—Liberal, Pluralist, Internationalist, Transnationalist, Globalist. Its central assumption was that the contemporary international system differed fundamentally from previous systems, along several dimensions.

It held, first, that the traditional sovereign-states' system was a product of an era of comparatively low-level communication and interaction in which the idea of the self-contained, impenetrable sovereign state, acting rather like a billiard ball, may have had a basis in reality. Such an era was now past, and in an age of rapidly developing military, industrial and communications technology the notions of sovereign equality and independence were increasingly at odds with the practical realities. For now governments were incapable of exercising full control over the flow of information, ideas, funds, goods and peoples across frontiers and unable to protect their civilians against new and subtle forms of hostility, subversion or aggression from within or outside state frontiers or to defend them against nuclear or chemical attack. It also claimed that a sudden proliferation of regional and functionalist organisations, such as the European Coal and Steel Community or the wider European Community, and of non-governmental actors, such as the multi-national corporations (MNCs), many of which enjoyed financial resources exceeding the budget of all but a handful of states, were contributing to the state's obsolescence. Above all, it considered the various members of the international system to be interdependent to an unprecedented degree—interdependent in the sense of both sensitive and vulnerable to one another and in four clearly identifiable areas.

Economic interdependence

First, states were seen to be interdependent in the economic field—in international trade, investment and finance. There was now, the Pluralists argued, a complex international division of labour as a result of which such things as international business cycles, fluctuations in American or German interest rates, the decision of a Latin American country to default on its debts and speculative currency deals had 'knock on' spillover effects throughout the international system.

Political interdependence

Second, there was interdependence in the political arena, in the sense of multiple linkages between various governments and societies, of which Rosenau highlighted three. There were what he called 'reactive' linkages, as, for example, when the massacre of some 250 marines in Beirut affected the timing of Reagan's decision to invade/rescue Grenada only days later; or, perhaps, when domestic unrest encouraged General Galtieri to invade the Falklands. There were the 'emulative' linkages, where governments and social groups copied one another's policies or actions, as when there is a spate of incidents of air piracy, racist violence or of so-called 'ethnic cleansing'. And there were the 'penetrative' linkages, as when a political group in one country—say, UNITA of Angola, the Irish IRA or the South African ANC—tried to influence the policy of another.[9]

Military/strategic interdependence

Third, it identified interdependency in the military/strategic field. The vast increase in destructive potential created by modern technology and manifested in weapons of mass destruction had created a shared interest in avoiding a nuclear holocaust. For evidence the Pluralists could cite the reluctance of nuclear powers to resort to arms against one another (though, paradoxically, this might be an argument for possession of nuclear weapons rather than their renunciation). Moreover the escalating costs of weaponry had encouraged many powers to treat defence as a shared responsibility: some, indeed, hoping to place themselves under some kind of UN military guarantee.

Global awareness

Some Pluralists also pointed to a fourth, more controversial area of inter-dependence. Like the Kantian notion of *Perpetual Peace*, it was future orien-tated. They saw behavioural science as moving from 'islands of theory' in an ocean of ignorance towards a general theory of behaviour which would revolutionise our understanding of human relationships and facilitate both the prediction and the control of conflict at all levels. With this new understanding, they claimed, people's residual attachment to 'outmoded' notions of sovereignty, territoriality, ethnicity and the like would erode and we human beings would become conscious of the interests we share with every member of what they liked to call this 'shrinking planet', this 'spaceship earth', this 'global village'. At that stage, of course, there is no more war because no one has an interest in promoting it. By bringing ethics back in to the study, behaviouralists such as John Burton had moved beyond the objectivity they had formerly commended and might be said to have become 'post-behaviouralists'. Certainly the more extreme decided to abandon all talk of International Relations or even World Politics, since these were premissed on 'outmoded' inter-state concepts. Their preference now was (and is) for the term 'World Society', which suggests the multiple linkages or, to use one of Burton's favourite terms, the 'cobwebs' of relations comprising it.[10]

2.8 THE NEW AGENDA

But the Pluralists' assertion that the Realist paradigm was now obsolete had two further components in addition to the argument about the pene-tration of the state and the growth of interdependence. Rather like the idealists following the first world war, they contested the notion that force could still be an effective tool of foreign policy and that security still topped the list of government priorities. In the Pluralist view, military issues had declined in importance relative to other issues on the political agenda, and war was no longer a viable option for most decision makers.[11] Clearly these particular 'scientists' may not have noticed that there had been up to two hundred inter-state wars since 1945, and some three times that number if one considers civil or secessionist wars.[12]

What were the issues that in the post-behavioural perspective now topped the political agenda? They included such concerns as food distrib-ution, population growth, the debt crisis, the problems of pollution and the depletion of scarce resources—problems far too large to be solved by the traditional and hence 'obsolescent' state. To which the Realists would respond: if the state is outdated, why have the Slovenes, Croats, Bosnians, Latvians, Lithuanians, Estonians, Ukrainians, Kurds, Palestinians, Kashmiris, Eritreans, Quebeçois and other nationalists been so anxious to acquire sovereign statehood? But Realism's major counter-criticism was that the methodologies and measuring techniques of the natural sciences so favoured by the behaviouralists contained hazards of which they sometimes seemed blissfully unaware.

2.9 HAZARDS OF THE 'SCIENTIFIC' APPROACH

1. 'Complexifying' the obvious.
2. Employing misleading measurements: ie when inferences are drawn from statistical observations that are either unwarranted or else trivial in relation to the cost and effort of producing the figures.
3. Being conned by the computer into thinking that it can always improve on the data. The fact is: if you feed garbage into a computer, garbage is what you get out of it.
4. Gambling on gaming and being seduced by simulation. Computer simulation exercises, war games and the like are both fun and fine as teaching devices and from them one can learn much about the states of mind of those who have to make crucial decisions on the battlefield or at a time of economic or political crisis. But games and simulations are not real-life situations, and it is a mistake and sometimes a dangerous mistake, for example when intelligence agents and strategic analysts give advice to American presidents on the strength of such exercises, to confuse gaming with empirical reality.
5. Generalising from insufficient instances.
6. Claiming as of 'scientific' validity some conceptual scheme that is no more than a rationalisation of political prejudice. All too often pseudo-scientific verbiage serves as a cover for partisan views, complete with unwarranted assumption and preconceived conclusion. This last hazard is an ever-present danger in the social sciences and can apply as much to the Realist as to the Pluralist approach, even though Realists are not necessarily conservatives in politics nor Pluralists necessarily liberals. At any rate, it is as well to be on one's guard!

NOTES

1. See, for example, Appendix I to Porter, B. (ed.), *The Aberystwyth Papers: International Politics 1919–69*, London, Oxford University Press, 1972, p. 362.
2. Lloyd, L., 'Philip Noel-Baker and peace through law' in Long, D. and Wilson, P. (eds), *Thinkers of the Twenty Years' Crisis* Oxford, Oxford University Press, 1995.
3. Carr, E. H., *The Twenty Years' Crisis 1919–1939*, London, Macmillan, 1939.
4. For a representative sample, see Bull, H., 'International theory: the case for a classical approach' in *World Politics*, vol. 18, April 1966, pp. 361–77 and Kaplan,

M., 'The New great debate: traditionalism versus science in international politics' in *World Politics* vol. 19, October 1966, pp.1–20.

5. Northedge F.S., *The International Political System*, London, Faber, 1976, pp. 22–3.

6. Olson, W. and Groom, A.J.R., *International Relations: then and now*, London, Harper-Collins, 1991, pp. 165–70.

7. Braybrooke, D. and Lindblom, C., *The Strategy of Decision*, New York, Free Press, 1970 and Allison, G., *The Essence of Decision*, Boston, Little, Brown, 1971 were especially influential.

8. See, for example, Keohane, R. and Nye, J.S., *Power and Interdependence: World Politics in Transition*, Boston, Little, Brown, 1977; Rosenau, J.R. (ed.), *In Search of Global Patterns*, London, Collier-Macmillan, 1976; Burton, J., *World Society*, London, Cambridge University Press, 1972, and Banks, M. (ed.), *Conflict in World Society*, Brighton, Wheatsheaf, 1984.

9. Rosenau, J., *Linkage Politics*, New York, Free Press, 1969.

10. Burton, J., op. cit., pp. 35–45.

11. Keohane and Nye, op. cit., pp. 23–37.

12. See Kidron, M. and Smith, D., *The War Atlas*, London, Pan, 1983.

CHAPTER 3

STRUCTURALISM

This chapter focuses on a paradigm or conceptual map that entered the IR textbooks only comparatively recently. Known alternatively as 'Structuralism' or 'World Systems theory', it posits a world that is and has long been fundamentally one system but whose very nature determines significant divisions between its interacting units. Like other frameworks of analysis, Structuralism arose out of a profound dissatisfaction with the approaches to International Relations then on offer.

3.1 PARADIGMS AND METHODOLOGIES REVIEWED

First, there had been the paradigm stemming from the climate of ideas associated with President Woodrow Wilson at the end of the first world war behind which lay a complex of notions derided by E.H. Carr as 'utopian': that human nature was essentially good and capable of unselfish action, that there was a harmony of interests in international society and that there were clear and unambiguous moral standards on which to judge and base political action. Second, there was the 'Realism' counterposed to it, according to which conflict was to be regarded as the norm in a world of independent sovereign states lacking any political or legal superior and in which any sense of solidarity scarcely extended beyond state boundaries. Third was 'Behaviouralism', which brought new tools and methodologies in the pursuit of observable, testable and measurable data on inter- and transnational interactions and processes. The fourth paradigm was based loosely on the notion that societies were increasingly interacting in ways which were transnational rather than inter-state, making them sensitive and vulnerable both to one another as well as to the various political, economic, technological, ideological and other forces, processes and movements shaping their existence.

Each successive approach had been shaped by the changing climate of international events, but the 1960s, in which 'Structuralism' percolated the mainstream social science textbooks, had been a decade of exceptional social, cultural and, above all, political ferment. At that time the United States was in serious trouble—at home, with the seething unrest of the urban blacks; abroad, in Vietnam—and the revolt among potential conscripts on the American campuses had knock-on effects throughout the Western world. In 1968 at one university after another sit-ins, boycotts and anti-government demonstrations were staged—in France, Germany and, of course, in Britain, where the LSE, though by no means the most turbulent of the British universities at the time, was made to appear a hotbed of revolutionary activity, no doubt due in part to its proximity to Fleet Street (where the newspapers were then printed), Thames TV and BBC Bush House.

The Soviet Union, too, was under pressure. Czechoslovakia had repudiated the Soviet Socialist model and as Warsaw Pact troops suppressed the 'Prague Spring', Moscow's relations with independent-minded Communist states like China, Romania, Yugoslavia, Albania and the Communist Parties of Western Europe plummeted to new depths, as did the Soviet reputation further afield.[1] Meanwhile the entry on to the political stage of a large number of Third World states following decolonisation placed development issues high on the international agenda, and a new generation of scholars in North America, Britain and Europe decided to lend their 'science' once again to what they hoped would be the betterment of humankind, sparking off what was to become known as 'the post-Behavioural revolution'.

3.2 MORE ON 'POST-BEHAVIOURALISM'

In 1969 one of Behaviouralism's early enthusiasts sounded the alarm. Addressing the American Political Science Association, Professor David Easton claimed that too many behaviouralists had become obsessed with mere number crunching, that the hypotheses they tested were often trite and trivial and that they were neglecting many of the ethical issues which cried out for attention in a world of violence, oppression, poverty and hunger. And he concluded:

> It is more important to be relevant and meaningful for contemporary urgent social problems than to be sophisticated in the tools of investigation...To understand the limits of our knowledge we need to be aware of the value premises on which it stands and the alternatives for which this knowledge could be used...To know is to bear responsibility for acting and to act is to engage in reshaping society.[2]

Here was the clarion call for a post-Behavioural approach—an approach which, though based on careful observation and some quantification—went far beyond number crunching and the quest for value-free data. In effect it marked a return to ethics and ideals, but this time, so its proponents hoped, with analyses grounded in science.

Following Easton's plea, a super-abundance of theories appeared, loosely derived from the 'interdependence' paradigm. These went under a variety of names: integration theory, functionalism and neo-functionalism, regime theory, peace research, needs theory and world-order modelling—

all supposedly pointing the way towards the creation of better conditions for humankind.[3] For many of those involved in these post-Behavioural pursuits, the terms 'International Politics', 'International Relations' or even 'World Politics' suggested too strongly the state in interaction, and as if to stress the interdisciplinary nature of what they were engaged in, they tended to call their focus of study 'World Society'.

3.3 PLURALISM AND ITS CRITICS

The 'interdependence' paradigm was not without its critics. Some of the Realists, dubbed 'traditionalists' by the self-styled scientists, suggested that it was ahistorical and that the development of domestic trade and the growth of government responsibility for welfare and ideological orientation as well as security and prestige meant that interdependence was in decline, not on the increase. Nor was there any evidence that military power was losing its salience as arbiter in either international or domestic affairs. Others accepted that interdependence was growing but were by no means optimistic about its implications. 'Good fences make good neighbours' was their credo, and greater interdependence could only mean greater friction within and between political communities, increased transnational terrorism, more flights of capital, the growth of international drug cartels and transnational syndicates of organised crime.[4]

The criticisms came not just from hard-bitten traditionalists but from a very different quarter—from those who pointed out that the condition of interdependence applied to and only benefited a comparatively small group of developed, mainly Western capitalist countries who were increasingly trading with one another. The rest of the world had become far more dependent on those developed countries than the developed countries were on them, and in North/South relations, for example, there were serious and endemic imbalances or asymmetries in power and wealth. In short, the world economy, though a single economy, conferred unequal benefits and liabilities and, hence, a structure of dominance and dependency.[5] It is this approach that scholars refer to as 'Structuralism', in which the nature of the whole, as it were, determines the structural segments into which it is divided.

3.4 STRUCTURALIST THINKING

One can trace the rudiments of structuralist thinking back to Aristotle. But to understand its peculiar force today, one has to look at 18th- and 19th-century German philosophy—in particular the ethical imperatives of Kant, with his concern for justice, fairness and human solidarity, and the somewhat grandiloquent methodology of Hegel and Marx, with their claim to have divined the inexorable logic of history and, hence, the destiny of humankind. More significantly perhaps, one of their distinctive contributions to the analysis of society was what is called their 'holistic' approach. 'Holism' is probably best understood in terms of its opposite—'individualism'. An individualistic approach is one based on a study of individual psychology and which reduces all group behaviour to the level of individual interests, instigations and motivations. Holism, on the other hand, denies that social or for that matter international interaction can be reduced to mere individual psychology, for such a study could not explain such social situations as, say, the traffic jam or a sudden rise in inflation or unemployment, though it might provide some useful clues. The main presumption of holism is that recurrent patterns of interaction among groups of all kinds—political, economic, social, cultural, professional, sporting or whatever—taken together shape and guide behaviour, allotting 'roles' and establishing patterns of conduct independent of intention and motivation.

The holists claim that patterns of social conduct are constantly being reproduced, as happens when one crosses a field of corn and makes a path which others follow, as if it had been there for all time. Together with World Society enthusiasts and some Realists, Structuralists perceive as a system the network or web of interactions that some call international relations. As such they study its units, its rules of interaction—legal, moral, prudential or whatever—its forms of interaction ie how they interrelate economically, politically, socially etc; patterns of interaction in terms of configurations and structures; and the environment—technological, ideological, geographical and ecological—within which the interactions occur. Structuralists also believe that the overall characteristics and properties of the system determine the structural divisions within it.

3.5 TYPES OF STRUCTURALIST THINKING

Economic—Marxist, Marxist/Leninist and neo-Marxist

The Marxists among them hold that each existing system contains the seeds of its own destruction or transformation and its replacement by something better. From Karl Marx they derived the notion that for every superstructure of ideas, notions and concepts, there was an economic substructure or base. From that base, whether it be feudalism, capitalism, socialism or whatever, was determined the whole climate of political, legal, ethical, aesthetic and religious norms and traditions, and among the political superstructures was the concept of 'the state'. Like other such ideas, however, the state was a transitory phenomenon, destined to be transformed or to disappear altogether when the economic base altered dramatically, as in a revolution from world capitalism to world socialism. For the Marxists, then, the state was a mere projection of the class struggle, an artificial creation or construct of the ruling class which would last only so long as the social order it had created. In the meantime those acting on behalf of the state would continue to pursue foreign policies that were mere rationalisations of the interests of the ruling class.

Lenin took the standard Marxist argument a stage further. He formulated a theory to account specifically for imperialism. The unequal distribution of wealth within capitalist society had brought that system to the point of crisis. A few capitalists amassed great wealth, while the impoverished workers lacked sufficient purchasing power to sustain a domestic market with a large enough potential for profit making. The capitalists were thus compelled to reinvest any surplus capital in profitable ventures abroad, and at a time when the capitalist system becomes dominated by monopolies and cartels with overseas interests. But the search for profitable outlets, combined with the quest for overseas sources of raw materials, could only lead to fierce inter-state competition, to imperialism and eventually war—as in 1914. On the other hand the drive towards imperialism and war was not so much psychological as structural in origin. It was as independent of human will and conscious choice as any other form of socially conditioned behaviour. As the Marxist economist, Harry Magdoff, put it: 'Imperialism is not a matter of choice for a capitalist society, it is the way of life of such a society.'[6] It followed, that is, a kind of structuralist imperative, and the imperialist relationship was thus structurally conditioned. For Marxists, then, imperialism was not so much a policy consciously undertaken as a descriptive term connoting a structural relationship of dominance and dependency emanating from the system of world capitalism.

On the other hand, though traditional Marxists had seen capitalism as a progressive force—'an engine of growth', they called it—because of its key role in the downfall of feudalism and the creation of the political, social and technological conditions that would eventually produce a socialist order, more recent Marxist scholars have begun to have their doubts. Significantly, many of these neo-Marxist sceptics come from the lesser-developed countries (LDCs), and while earlier generations of Marxists had looked at the imperial relationship from the perspective of the advantaged, many of these neo-Marxists were peering from the other end of the telescope. The first influential body of neo-Marxists were, appropriately, from Latin America, where in the late 1950s there was a widespread perception that a century and a half of formal independence had generally failed to produce effective independence in either political or economic terms. Furthermore, although many of the countries of the region had indigenous wealth in the form of gold, silver, oil and other strategic raw materials as well as good agricultural land, most of their economies were

generally backward and their peoples poor. In their attempt at explanation, the Latin American neo-Marxists examined the assumptions of orthodox liberal economists as well as mainstream Marxists and found them
wanting.[7]

Both, liberals and Marxists, they argued, tended to equate development
with industrialisation and to see Western-style industrialisation as the
path to be followed by the LDCs. True, traditional Marxists advocated a
period of protectionism for infant industries together with import substitution, but in the view of the Latin American theorists—collectively known
as *dependendistas* (dependency theorists)—this was a mistaken policy:

(1) Because the internal market for consumer goods was too limited and
    the nature of the demand was determined by elites with a fondness for
    Western products;
(2) Because the process of import-substitution industrialisation tended to
    be based on capital-intensive enterprises which required little labour
    and, therefore, did little to stimulate demand; and
(3) Because such a strategy needed imported goods, materials and compo-
    nents which would reinforce dependence on multinational capital and
    foreign technology and only compound the crisis of debt experienced
    by so many Latin American countries.

In any case, for the dependency theorists, development did not necessarily mean Western-style industrialisation. There were a number of
successful Western economies—Denmark and New Zealand for example—
whose economic growth was based on agriculture; there were others, for
example Switzerland, whose development was based on service industries, insurance and banking; while yet others, like Sweden, could include
the generous state provision of welfare services as an indicator of development. Furthermore, even if Western-style industrialisation were desirable,
the Latin Americans held it to be unfeasible given their unenviable position in the international division of labour. Their reasoning went something like this.

Capitalism is the dominant mode of production, and its method of
exchange, ie for profit, is pervasive. There is, in other words, a world capitalist system which produces relations of unequal exchange between the
dominant 'centre' of developed capitalism and the dependent 'periphery'
of the lesser-developed areas. Incidentally for most of the *dependendistas*
the notions of 'centre' and 'periphery' here refer not to states but to socio-
economic structures, since relations between 'centre' and 'periphery' exist
within as well as between states. There are, for example, common interests
between the 'centre of the centre' and the 'centre of the periphery' ie the
elites of the LDCs.

Dependency theorists also claim that the hierarchical structures engendered by world capitalism ensure that the dependent economies remain

dependent and that underdevelopment, by which they mean subordinate status in the world economic system, is perpetuated in the periphery states, in several respects:

1. In that they weight terms of trade heavily in favour of the industrialised countries;
2. In that they facilitate alien penetration of development projects in the peripheral states through credit and other facilities which work, so the theorists claim, to the long term disadvantage of those states;
3. In that they accelerate international inequalities within the periphery states as the elites are 'bribed' or otherwise co-opted to serve outside interests;
4. In that they sap indigenous cultures of their appeal and vitality by subjecting them to a creeping tide of Westernisation—what is sometimes called 'cocacolonialism' and 'pepsicology';
5. In that they help reinforce ties of dependency through the discouragement of regional co-operation among the LDCs.

To those who pointed out that there had been industrial as well as other kinds of development in a number of states in the region, the *dependendistas* countered that it was what they called 'dependent development', dependent, that is, on trends in the world economy rather than being independently determined. Further, that many who begin the process of development, say, when cut off from the world economy, as in a world war, tend to find that growth stifled as they rejoin the world economic system. What follows is what Andre Gunder Frank calls 'the development of under-development'—in some ways a worse affliction than that of undevelopment, which was their condition before capitalist penetration occurred.

Economic—reformist and revolutionary

Whether or not these were serious arguments and not merely alibis for economic mismangement, such theories enjoyed and continue to enjoy considerable appeal in Latin America and throughout the LDCs and served as a basis for two types of demands. The first was a non-Marxist plea for reform of trade, aid and economic management expressed in the form of a New International Economic Order to meet the needs of the world's poor—a notion seized on with alacrity by Western statesmen such as the late West German Chancellor Willy Brandt and the former British Prime Minister Edward Heath, both emphasising the 'interdependent' nature of international relations. 'We must help them, otherwise we go down with them' was their platform.[8]

The second demand was much more Marxist in character and called for the adoption of more socialist strategies. For the traditional Marxist this meant preparing for world revolution; for the Marxist–Leninist (ie the card carrying Communist), it meant identifying with the policies of either Moscow, Peking, Tirana, Hanoi or Havana at a time when Communist rule was in full swing; for the neo-Marxist, despairing of there being Marxist-style revolutions in the forseeable future, it meant delinking the economies of the LDCs either selectively or comprehensively from the international division of labour and the world capitalist system, possibly with a view to forming some alignment with other 'peripheral' states who embark on a similar line of action.[9]

Theoretical weaknesses

While such theories have the merit of coherence and clarity and go some way to explaining both the economic backwardness and the enormous disparities of wealth in some of the LDCs, they have been criticised as resting on some dubious assumptions and leading to some questionable conclusions. First, the idea widely shared among dependency theorists that the world capitalist system has been in operation for some five hundred years requires some agile verbal juggling. True, they define capitalism, rather unusually for Marxists, not as a mode of production but as a mode of exchange, characterised by the search through trade for profits. It is still rather an eccentric notion, and not everyone would agree that the world capitalist system began in the early 16th century, when world economic exchange moved from the tribute system to the exchange of products conferring unequal benefits. Second, in their tendency to treat dependency and development as mutually exclusive, they would seem virtually to exclude the possibility of sustained economic development in the LDCs. Yet reference to the rise of Japan and the so-called NICs (Newly Industrialised Countries) of Asia such as Taiwan, South Korea, Singapore, Malaysia, Indonesia and some of the oil rich Sheikhdoms of the Middle East indicates what a questionable notion this is. And in the case of Communist China it could be argued that the country's development was hindered during precisely those years of the Great Leap Forward and the Cultural Revolution when it more or less decoupled itself from the world economy and that it is at its most impressive now, when it is firmly linked to the world system. Third, with their emphasis on structural economic factors, dependency theorists tend to underplay the extent to which indigenous socio-cultural factors—religions, customs, morals and mores—can affect development. Yet it can hardly be irrelevant to the economic development of Japan, for example, that traditionally its people had no sense of shame in adopting and adapting ideas from foreigners. After all, they got their culture from China and possibly in consequence never experienced the resistance of some of their neighbours to borrowing Western technology and managerial techniques.

Political—structural realism

Two structural theories with a political base have a particular claim to fame, the first by Kenneth Waltz—a structuralist in the Realist tradition. In his *A Theory of International Politics* he rejects the psychological basis of traditional Realism on the ground that its basic assumption regarding human nature is erroneous. For human beings are capable of altruism as well as egoism, unselfish conduct as well as self-interestedness. More importantly, he believes that theories regarding human nature are in any case largely irrelevant to an understanding of why states behave as they do. As a neo-Realist, he claims that international behaviour is the product not so much of human volition as of the precarious situation in which the state finds itself. For states are obliged to respond to the logic of international anarchy. In a world without government and with only a minimum of order, each sovereign entity faces a security dilemma which inhibits trust and limits co-operation. In Waltz's view 'the condition of insecurity— at the very least the uncertainty of each about the other's future intentions and actions—works against their co-operation'.[10]

Political—global systems

A second such influential theory is George Modelski's *Long Cycles in World Politics*.[11] Like the dependency theorists, he claims that a single world system has existed for the last five centuries or so but sees as the dominant factor not a single world economy but a global political system, comprising sovereign states and characterised by inter-state rivalry and conflict and creating cycles in the incidence of war. Like the dependency theorists, too, he divides the world into the dominant and the dependent, but in his theory the composition of the former changes as does the pattern of what he calls 'world leadership'. By world leadership he does not necessarily mean the exercise of 'hegemony'—a term suggesting a desire to dominate—because in his view not all world leaders seek power for the sake of it. Some such states try to act in the common interest and in that sense cannot be regarded as hegemonial in intent. So how may leading powers act in the common interest? Modelski suggests that they may perform five possible services:

1. Agenda formation, ie the clarification and definition of global problems and the assignment of priority tasks;
2. Mobilisation, ie building a coalition of support for law and order in the existing global system;
3. Decision-making about the political direction of the global system in the period ahead;
4. Administration of such decisions, together with the economic wherewithal necessary to promote them;

5. Technological and ideological innovation, and the dissemination of new ideas through education and the media.

In each system, when viewed in the long cycle, the balance shifts between the exercise of world leadership and the maintenance of hegemony, and Modelski identifies within the present world system five such periods: the first led by Portugal in the 16th century; the second by the Netherlands in the 17th century; the third by Britain in the 18th century; the fourth again by Britain in the 19th century and, of course, the fifth by the United States in this century. As Modelski puts it:

> Each [system] contains the same characteristic sequence of events: a global war; a world wide struggle of major proportions and consequences; an era of political and economic consolidation (world power), a mid course of political unsettlement...and a final sequence of rivalry and competitive disruption...setting the stage for another global conflict.[12]

It is a difficult, intriguing argument which, incidentally, throws an interesting light on the George Bush conception of a 'new world order' but involves a good deal of selection of evidence which in the view of its critics is the besetting sin of all such structural analyses.

Geopolitical

One final set of structural arguments stems not so much from political as from geopolitical assumptions. Here the world system is viewed in spatial or geo-centric terms, the perceived structure being the strategic imperatives posed by geography. Though geopolitics was somewhat discredited by its practical application in Nazi Germany, when it served as a strategic rationale for the policy of expansion into Central and Eastern Europe, it does have fairly respectable forebears and descendants. At a time when an American admiral, Alfred Mahan, was testifying to the political potentialities of sea power, the geopolitics of Sir Halford Mackinder, then Director of the London School of Economics, were land based and his understanding of what he called 'the geopolitical pivot of history' led him in 1904 to issue a prediction which was to preoccupy the Foreign Office mind for more than half a century. Basically he saw the future of world politics as being determined in one huge island land mass stretching from Ostend to Okhotsk, from Spitzbergen to Singapore and from Kamchatka to Cape Town. In other words, he held Europe, Asia and Africa to be one continent as there was no clear cut frontier between them, and because of its geopolitical importance he dubbed it 'The World Island'. His chief concern, however, was the centre of that World Island—roughly from the Rhineland through the Central and East European plain to the Urals and beyond. What Mackinder called the 'Heartland', since it was in the heart of Eurasia, held the key to the future. As he put it: 'Who rules East Europe commands the Heartland; who rules the Heartland commands the World Island; who rules the World Island commands the world.'[13]

It was this mode of thinking that appears in 1939 to have brought Britain into battle against Germany, a country which had neither attacked it nor threatened to do so. But Hitler had seized back the Rhineland, annexed Austria, incorporated the Sudetenland, taken control of the rest of Czechoslovakia and invaded Poland after making it clear in *Mein Kampf* that he intended to subjugate the Soviet Union, ie to take over the Heartland. By the same token, it seems to have been a similar consideration that led Britain as early as 1945 to seek an alliance against the Soviet Union after Moscow was perceived as having begun moves to take over the Heartland from the opposite direction.[14]

The major weakness in geopolitical theorising is the problem of determining criteria of significance. Mahan saw sea power as crucial, Mackinder a particular land mass. More recent geopoliticians have seen air power, the location of industrial capacity or of populations as critical. Interestingly enough, despite differences on other matters, most geopolitical experts testify to the strategic importance to exponents of guerrilla warfare of mountainous areas, and they counselled the UN and other interested parties to avoid a heavy ground commitment to Bosnia-Herzegovina where guerrillas successfully pinned down several German divisions during the second world war. One other weakness in geopolitical analysis is the extent to which technological innovations—the plane, the rocket, the A-Bomb, the H-Bomb, the chemical or bacteriological weapon—can make a nonsense of earlier geopolitical assumptions and priorities.

Having discovered the degree of division in the field of international relations, some readers by this time may have begun to wonder what is the point of studying 'The Structure of International Society' at all. Yet in almost any respectable study, there is contention, controversy and doubt.

3.6 THE ROLE OF CONTENTION IN INTERNATIONAL RELATIONS

Ever since Plato and Aristotle, if not before, philosophers have been at odds on the proper subject of philosophical enquiry and on how to approach it. Scientists, too, are often involved in heated controversy with one another. If one asks two scientists about the origins of the universe one is likely to get at least three different answers. And none of the social sciences is free from contentions and disputes. In Economics there are the Keynesians, the Chicago Free Trade merchants, the Marxists, the neo-Marxists and an array of others. In Psychology there are the residual devotees of Freud, of Jung, of Adler, of Melanie Klein, of Skinner, of a galaxy of other great names. In the arts, too, contention is king, whether the subject is English at 'Oxbridge' or music at the Guildhall. Indeed, it could be argued that controversy is the life blood of scholarship and that where the questioning of ideas, including one's own, stops, so in effect, does the academic enterprise. It is for this reason that the writer is always critical of those academics, on both sides of the Atlantic, who seem to prefer cyphers to scholars and want their tutees merely to regurgitate what they hear in the lectures.

What is required of an academic environment is that it should serve as a kind of intellectual hothouse within which the student mind can grow. It should be taken as a sign of intellectual vigour not of weakness where academics engage in spirited debate with one another about the appropriate structure, content and methodology regarding a field of study. On the other hand if scholars are going to criticise a particular mode of thought they need to ensure, first, that they do not misunderstand it; second, that they do not misrepresent it and; third, that they at least give it due respect, since in the end it may prove to be no less valid than their critique of it.

NOTES

1. Stern, G., *The Rise and Decline of International Communism*, Aldershot, Elgar, 1990, pp. 205–9.
2. Easton, D., 'The new revolution in political science' in *The American Political Science Review*, December 1969, pp. 1051–2.
3. Such theories are detailed in Olson, W. and Groom, A.J.R., *International Relations: Then and Now*, London, Harper-Collins, 1991, pp. 171–6 and 190–217.
4. See, for example, Morse, E., *Modernization and the Transformation of International Relations*, New York, The Free Press, 1976, p. 14.
5. For a characteristic exposition see, for example, Wallerstein, I., 'The rise and future demise of the world capitalist system' in *Comparative Studies in Society and History*, vol. 16, no. 4, 1974, pp. 387–415.
6. Magdoff, H., *The Age of Imperialism*, London, Monthly Review Press, 1969, p. 26.
7. Their deliberations are encapsulated in Harris, N., *The End of the Third World*, London, Penguin, 1986, pp. 11–29.
8. The argument is summarised in the Brandt Commission's Report: *North-South: A Programme for Survival*, London, Pan, 1981.
9. The arguments are essayed in Cardoso, F. and Faletto, E., *Dependency and Development in Latin America*, Berkeley, University of California Press, 1979.
10. Waltz, K., *A Theory of International Politics*, Reading, Mass., Addison-Wesley, 1979, p. 105.
11. Modelski, G., *Long Cycles in World Politics*, London, Macmillan, 1987.
12. Modelski, G., 'Long Cycles and the Strategy of U.S. International Economic Policy' in Avery, W.P. and Rabkin, D.P. (eds), *America in a Changing World Economy*, New York, Longman, 1980, p. 100.
13. Mackinder, H., *Democratic Ideals and Reality*, New York, Henry Holt, 1919, p. 150.
14. See Bell, C., *Negotiation from Strength*, London, Chatto and Windus, 1962.

PART II
THE EVOLUTION OF INTERNATIONAL SOCIETY

CHAPTER 4

PRE-MODERN INTERNATIONAL SOCIETIES

4.1 THE VALUE OF HISTORY

In this chapter we move from theory to history, trying to trace the evolution of international society. But why bother to make an excursion into history at all? In the first place, because any political or international occurrence is located in time, and to fully comprehend it we must be able to place it in context, in the sequence of events. What were the earlier situations out of which, say, the current (1994) bloodletting in Rwanda grew; what are the elements of continuity linking it to what had gone before; what the elements of change marking it out as different? Second, though history cannot prove our theories or ideas, it can give us the evidence we require either to make out a case or to cast doubt on one.

4.2 CONTENDING INTERPRETATIONS

On the other hand history is another of those studies that admit of contradictory interpretations since both the facts and their exact significance may give rise to controversy. On the problems of factual evidence one has only to consider such questions as: did a revolution or a *coup d'état* propel Lenin to power in Russia 1917? Did six million Jews die in the Holocaust? Who started the cold war? Who really murdered President Kennedy and was there only one assassin? And even where the facts are not generally in dispute, there is always the thorny question of interpretation. In 1992 some celebrated the five hundredth anniversary of Columbus's discovery of the Americas. Yet many marked the anniversary not in celebration but in sorrow for the cruelty and exploitation they alleged he brought to the New World. As to the French Revolution, we know the facts by and large, but what do we make of them? Asked once to give his opinion on the outcome of that Revolution, the late Chinese Premier, Chou En-lai, is reported to have said that since it had occurred less than two hundred years ago, it was far too early for a verdict.

One such thorny historical question: 'When did modern international society originate?' seems uncomplicated enough until one begins to consider the conceptual conundrums that this apparently simple query conceals. For what in this context is meant by 'international society' and also by the term 'modern'? Once again a bit of linguistic analysis is called for. Suffice it to say: like many other political expressions, the term 'international society' was coined long after the appearance of the political phenomena it purports to designate, and if one is to give definition to the notion of 'modern international society', an examination of earlier networks of relationships would seem to be required. In that way the peculiar and distinctive features of more recent international relationships can be thrown into sharp relief. Where, then, do we begin our analysis?

We could go back to the dawn of history—to primitive man who formed the earliest social units with primitive woman, to their families and extended families, to the clans and tribes emanating from the various forms of intercourse in which they engaged. We could start with the more complex social arrangements that evolved subsequently, when nomadic hunters and gatherers stopped their wanderings to become cultivators of a fixed territory and to rely on one another for the tasks that needed to be performed for the benefit of the whole. But *our* starting point is not the organisation of the community or society as such but of relations between them, and by 'relations' one means not just random haphazard interaction but something more protracted and continuous.

4.3 WHAT IS AN INTERNATIONAL SOCIETY?

The major requirements for the student of international society are the existence of: (1) separate and autonomous political units such as empires, city states, principalities, feudal fiefdoms, sovereign states or nations; (2) significant interactions, co-operative and conflicting, between them which to an extent condition their behaviour; and (3) the existence of a dominant culture that shapes the norms, codes of behaviour and institutions that exist between the political units.[1] At the same time, each such web of interaction should be capable of analysis in respect of at least five separate but related dimensions: (1) types of political community comprising those units; (2) forms of interaction, from co-operation through compliance to conflict; (3) overall structure of power in terms of dominant and dependent relations; (4) rules of conduct, explicit or implicit, between the units; and (5) the environment—geographical, political, economic, technological etc—in which the web of interaction operates and where significant changes could affect the society's structure and functioning.[2] As regards the use of the term 'international', in examining the evolution of international society we have to use the expression loosely since in its modern usage it connotes a network of relations in which a central role is played by the sovereign state, while within the compass explored here are networks of relations that long predate it. Further, we are concerned with international societies that were, in effect, regional, ie confined in area, rather than global, as international society is today.

Given the three criteria identified here, ie the existence of separate and autonomous units and of significant interactions between them within a dominant culture, it is possible to identify at least seven such major societies prior to anything resembling the kind of international society with which we have become familiar. What is so striking about them is the diversity of their modes of organisation. At the one extreme there is the network of relations with a manifestly dominant state or group of states that tries to unify the known world under a single command and set of political ideas. At the other is the loose association of kindred independent communities each with a degree of self government and interacting in terms of diplomacy, trade, war and the migration of peoples.

4.4 PRE-MODERN INTERNATIONAL SOCIETIES

Ancient empires of the Near and Middle East

If we take as our first set of examples of pre-modern international society the ancient empires of the Near and Middle East—Sumerian, Egyptian, Babylonian, Assyrian and the Persian from roughly 4000 to about 400 BC— we find the city states of these regions too small and too weak to resist for long the forces of amalgamation and integration. Moreover, as they became dependent on water supplies for irrigation, usually a very costly undertaking, they created the conditions for the concentration of power into the hands of an individual—an individual who financed and supervised the irrigation projects, governed as god-king and became the sole source of legislative, executive, and judicial authority. Control was maintained and consolidated by a variety of methods. For example, the Assyrian monarchs imposed a common religion and transplanted their conquered peoples from one part of the empire to another. The ancient Egyptians planted garrisons among their subject peoples. Though the conquered peoples were usually left with a semblance of self-government, they were often compelled to pay tribute and contribute manpower for the service of the god-king. The rulers of these massive ancient empires had no conception of either legal equality or the right to independence. They regarded all not yet under their rule as potential vassals or enemies, though very occasionally, when expedient, they would conclude temporary treaties, as did the kings of Assyria with the rulers of the Chaldean and Babylonian peoples.[3]

The Chinese system

The pattern was similar in the case of the second of our pre-modern international societies ie the Chinese empire. There was, however, a crucial difference, for it continued its existence, though with often lengthy bouts of internecine war, leading to changes of dynasty, from the 18th century BC right down to this century—in fact, to 1911. On the other hand the pattern in China was established in virtual isolation and in virtual ignorance of the structure of relations of the empires of the Near and Middle East. As in the case, for example, of the Egyptians, the traditional attitude of the Chinese rulers towards neighbouring peoples and states was one of superiority, though unlike the Egyptians the notion was based not on wealth, power or race but on culture and bred of centuries of continuous settlement and civilisation. China was the *Chung Kuo*, the Central Land, or the *Chung Hua*, the Central Splendour, an island of elegance located in the middle of the world and surrounded by political barbarians or tributaries—barbarians if they had not yet imbibed Chinese culture, tributaries if they had. Moreover, while the educated Egyptians or Persians knew that they had to deal with other peoples at least as advanced and as sophisticated as themselves, until recently the educated Chinese entertained no such notion.

China was a vast, populous and for a time technologically innovative civilisation surrounded by peoples far less advanced with which Peking had no need to deal unless forced to by invasion. As for the peoples farther afield, they usually came to China as pirates or adventurers—again, merely reinforcing the Chinese view of the inferiority of the non-Chinese. Significantly the Chinese emperors, believing themselves to have 'the Mandate of Heaven', claimed exclusive sovereignty not only over China proper and what became known as Outer China—Manchuria, Mongolia, Sinkiang and Tibet—but, in theory at least, over the rest of the world as well. They talked not of acquiring but of recovering territory. Though aware of the independent existence of peoples like the Tatars, Huns, Indians and Japanese, the Chinese were quite unable to accept them as equals, and when Buddhism penetrated China in the sixth century BC, like subsequent creeds, including Communism, it had to be 'sinicised' ie made Chinese. Meanwhile, throughout this lengthy period, the emperors continued to enjoy ceremonial deference throughout the empire, including the payment of tribute, even in periods when the structure of the system had changed from feudal hierarchy to the virtual anarchy of conflicting rival states. Until comparatively recently, therefore, Peking (Beijing) could have no conception of a world of sovereign states based on the notion of equality before the law.[4]

The Indian system

As in Imperial China, so in the kingdoms of ancient India there was no conception of a world society of legally equal states. Nor was there any notion of equality among India's diverse states, even though the Aryans, who had migrated from Persia to establish their domain over much of the sub-continent in about 1000 BC, had imposed a common language, Sanskrit, a religion and a set of customs which blended into earlier ways of life to form a common Hindu civilisation. Rather like classical Greece, to be discussed below, or medieval Germany, the region was for the most part divided into a large number of independent and often warring units despite the existence of a common culture. Uniquely, the local rulers seemed to consider it legitimate and even praiseworthy to acquire territories at the expense of their neighbours, but they also accepted that they should not disturb the laws, customs and economic life of a subject country. No doubt this had something to do with the Hindu tradition of respect for the natural order of things, but it also meant that the time-honoured caste system which divided and stratified the various Indian states survived virtually intact.

However, fresh incursions from the Persians in the sixth century BC and from the Greeks in the fourth century BC, together with the introduction of Buddhism in the sixth century BC began to shake up the value system in the sub-continent. From this ferment of ideas emerged two men who were to shape the political destiny of the region for some two hundred years and to leave an imprint on international politics to this day. The first was Chandragupta Maurya who in 300 BC was able to fashion in Northern India an empire based on a mixture of Indian and Persian values; the second was his prime minister and mentor, Kautilya, who had produced a manual, *Arthashastra, Book of the State,* on constructing a Persian type of empire in the area, which foreshadowed Machiavelli's treatise on Italian unification, *The Prince.* His basic strategy: to aim at dominion but always permitting substantial local autonomy in an attempt to win over the subject peoples to the imperial system. The Mauryan empire effected in 300 BC lasted until the death of Chandragupta's grandson, Ashoka, in 231 BC, when the submerged desire for independence was reasserted and India reverted to the traditional pattern of the warring states described and deplored in the *Arthashastra.*[5]

Anyone reviewing the *Arthashastra* today would be struck by its remarkable prescience and modernity, for much of it might have been written about Europe in the years since 1914. For instance, in a chapter entitled 'The decay, stabilisation and progress of states' Kautilya identifies several kinds of policies all of them utterly familiar in 20th-century terms: 'peace', by which he means 'concord supported by pacts'; 'war', implying 'armed aggression'; 'neutrality' meaning 'nonchalance'; 'armed intervention', which means what it says; and what he calls 'biformal policy', by which he

means 'making war with one and suing for peace with another'.[6] Another
striking feature about Kautilya's treatise is its brutal realism. The world he
describes as characteristic of the Indian sub-continent before the Mauryan
empire was not dissimilar from the world Martin Wight portrayed in his
Power Politics, the first edition of which was written at the end of the
second world war. Basically they both depict a merciless jungle, lacking
effective law, order or scruple and in which security is understood in
terms of the overthrow of other states, automatically deemed hostile.

The Greek city states' system

It is only when we come to the fourth international society—that of the
Greek city states of the fifth century BC—that the pattern of the ancient
world seems to be broken. For, though the Greeks tended to exhibit
towards the outside world the same kind of disdain or hostility as their
predecessors (they called non-Greeks 'barbarians' because their speech
was unintelligible and sounded like 'bar bar bar'), within their own
world—that of the Hellenes, a people with affinities of language, religion,
descent and culture—they had a code of honour towards one another and
practiced a system of politics not all that different from our own. For
example, they held that Greeks should never enslave other Greeks, that in
wartime olive groves should never be burned or otherwise destroyed and
that after battle armies should leave the people in peace to bury their
dead—something which some of today's civil warriors in Bosnia, Angola,
Rwanda or Afghanistan have yet to learn. It was a code which was of
mutual benefit and made it easier for today's enemies to become tomor-
row's allies.

What, then, of the polities—the word comes from 'polis', the Greek for
a state and from which we derive the word 'politics'— which regarded
themselves as bound by such codes? There were 1,500 or so fiercely independent city states throughout mainland and insular Greece as well as in
what was called Greater Greece ie Greek settlements in Sicily and southern Italy, many of them little more than fortified villages and most
governed by corporations of citizens rather than by kings. However, about
a dozen became important states (in modern parlance great powers)
including Athens, Sparta, Thebes and Corinth on the mainland, Rhodes
and Lesbos among the islands and Syracuse in Sicily; and they maintained
an intricate web of relations with one another, including the apparatus of
diplomacy. Though their envoys were messengers rather than negotiators,
they generally enjoyed what would we would now call diplomatic immunity and in the name of their governors would offer trade agreements,
mediation or arbitration in disputes and alliances; they would also issue
threats and challenges and sue for peace in time of hostilities. All that,
however, was before the war which shattered the world of the Hellenes in

much the way the first world war had shattered Europe. The Hellenic 1914 came in 431 BC. Thucydides, an Athenian general who wrote a masterly treatise on it, called it the Peloponnesian war. It was a titanic struggle between the two superpowers of the time—Athens and Sparta—and was to last, with brief moments of respite, for nearly three decades, during which standards of inter-state conduct began to decline.

None the less the pattern of inter- and intra-Greek politics during this period continued to bear striking resemblances to more recent times. First the Peloponnesian war was itself an outcome of the previous cold war between the main ideological rivals of the day: Athens, wealthy, democratic and expansionist; and Sparta, militarised, authoritarian and interested in preserving the international status quo. Furthermore in their competitive co-existence prior to war they had acquired a host of client states and satellites. Athens was at the head of the Delian League of mainly island states, Sparta presided over the Peloponnesian League of states opposed to Athenian domination. Just how and why the war came about is instructive. As in our own day, the members of the international society of the Hellenes were as much divided within as between, the main internal stratification being based on class which is perhaps why Greek society so fascinated Karl Marx. Such divisions frequently lead to revolutionary upheavals, and, as in more recent times, in a roughly bipolar world there is always a tendency for outside powers to intervene, at the very least to preserve stability at home and, more particularly, to try to create a more favourable political balance internationally. Such revolutionary struggles for power which involved the use of internal or external force to alter the way a city state was governed was known as *stasis*. Given the bipolar tension in the Hellenic world of the fifth century BC there was always the danger that, as in 1914 or 1939, a sudden increase or decrease in power by one side might spark off a conflagration involving the two major protagonists and their allies and satraps, and that is precisely what happened in 431 BC.

It began with a revolt against Corinth, Sparta's major ally. When Corcyra (modern Corfu), a Corinthian colony, staged an anti-colonial rebellion, it secured the assistance of Athens, always eager to side with an enemy's enemy. Naturally Corinth called on Sparta to help contain the rebellion, and soon the rival alliance systems were battling it out in a conflict as 'total' as the technological resources of the age allowed, the theatre of operations gradually widening to include most of the Hellenic world. It had become a struggle between a power bent on reshaping that world and those determined to resist, and for some time the Athenians and their allies, who had command of the seas, had the upper hand. But after Persian gold and military equipment was thrown into the fray, Sparta was able to meet Athens on equal terms at sea and eventually emerge victorious. The Peloponnesian war had demonstrated what was to become

an all too familiar motif in international relations: a power aiming at hegemony is likely sooner or later to face a hostile combination which will
eventually defeat it. It is on the basis of that recurrent pattern that the
theory of the balance of power rests.

On the other hand, the failure by Athens to unify the Hellenic world in
the fifth century BC was by no means the last such attempt. For after 404
BC, when the Peloponnesian war ended, the much vaunted independence
of the Greek city states was frequently under threat, either from within or
outside the Hellenic world. The Persians, whose assistance had been so
invaluable to Sparta, were to throw their very considerable weight behind
the Athenians when Sparta, contrary to tradition, sought its own hegemony in the region, but then the Persians switched back again in support
of Sparta when Athenian power seemed to be growing dangerously strong
again in the Aegean. Anyone who knows anything about Britain's traditional policy of acting as power balancer, 'holding the ring' between
competing states, will at once find Persia's political strategy at this time
strangely familiar.

It was, however, an unstable situation, and in the fourth century BC
when Persia was in retreat, two rulers were eventually to destroy the
Greek multi-state system and to establish their hegemony over all Greece.
Both came from the part-Greek, part-Persian kingdom to the north—a
country which was to become a serious bone of contention in the 1990s
between Greece and its neighbours—Macedonia. Philip II, King of
Macedonia from 359 to 336 BC, was well aware of the political and military
weaknesses of both the Hellenic city states and the Persian empire and
used a combination of diplomacy and force to establish control of the
former. As such he preserved the form but little else of the polis. However,
an assassin prevented him from completing his self-imposed mission to
add the Persian empire to his domain, and it was left to his son, Alexander
the Great, to lead a conquering coalition of Macedonians and Greeks to
fulfil his father's grandiose dream, in 330 BC proclaiming himself the legal
successor of the Kings of Persia.

Alexander's military achievement transformed the eastern Mediterranean
lands from a complex of relatively small competing sovereignties into an
empire stretching from Macedonia to the borders of India. Though it was
short lived, for Alexander died of fever in 323 BC, aged only 33, and his
domains were subdivided into three large Hellenistic kingdoms, the old
Greek multi-state system was gone. Henceforth the city states were effectively subservient to one or other of the large kingdoms into which
Alexander's world state was now divided—the Seleucid Empire in Asia
Minor, Macedonia and Egypt. Between these vast kingdoms a new kind of
balance of power system was to be played out until the first century BC. It
was a system resembling that of 18th-century Europe in which, rather like
a kaleidoscope, the few great powers of the period combined and recom-

bined in various permutations without the emergence of any major political alliance system or dominant power. And yet in the two centuries between Alexander's death and the establishment of the Roman domain in the eastern Mediterranean, Hellenism flourished, economically, scientifically, philosophically and culturally.[7] It was in many respects a golden age, its achievements in no way dimmed by those of its illustrious successor whose inter-relations form the fifth international society to be discussed.

The Roman system

With the Roman system we come to the climax of the lengthy, gradual but perceptible return of the Near Eastern and Mediterranean worlds from multiple and independent sovereignties towards the imperial end of the international spectrum. Yet Rome had begun as just another city state on the western fringe of Hellenism. How had this central Italian state, much given to *stasis* especially in its early years, been able to rise to become the greatest power in all Italy between the eighth and third centuries BC and then to become the world's largest and most durable empire? How had it been able to to bring under one order peoples and lands from Scotland to north Africa, from Spain to Iraq and beyond? How was it that Roman law, administration, architecture, transportation, communications, poetry, philosophy and Roman-inflected Christianity became, as it were, the property of the world?

In the first place, Rome had a geographical advantage. Situated midway up the western coast of Italy, with its long-settled communities, good harbours and hilly vantage points, it was strategically well placed. Second, it was well situated politically. Its early years of *stasis* had encouraged it to seek a formula for stability and order, and it had found the answer in the creation of a strong, centralised, popular administration in which the masses were drawn in to the patrician-dominated government, were allowed the vote and a tribune of their own which acted as a watchdog on administration. Its success at home led the Romans to export a modified version to their colonies, to whose people they generally extended the privilege of Roman citizenship and the advantages of Roman law and order, and on the whole these served to defuse hostility to colonial rule. Third, it had a superior political strategy. Despite its own periodic disposition to *stasis*, its various political rivals were prone to even greater instability, and the Romans were able to exploit the divisions both within and between them to establish dominion. The process was piecemeal, the political dominoes, so to speak, falling one by one, with the Romans securing first the city states of central Italy, then the Etruscan communities to the north, then the Greek city states to the south. Before long, they had refined and perfected a technique of political control which later generations of imperialists, including the British and the Russians, were to use to advantage—*divide et impera*, divide and rule!

But none of this would have worked had it not been for a fourth, and perhaps decisive ingredient, its military superiority. The Roman talent for organisation and engineering was to give its army the edge over its rivals in almost any conflict. For in weaponry, mobility, training, dedication, command and control it was more than a match for any opponent, and by the time of Rome's epic struggle against Carthage towards the end of the third century BC, it was able to draw on the manpower of the whole of Italy, now under its control. It was a resource which in the end not even the Carthaginians with their north African reserves could match, and with the defeat of Carthage in 202 BC, Rome was able to add north Africa to its growing list of provinces. It was a crucial step to what we would now call 'superpower' status. By the end of the second century BC Rome had taken in turn the territories in Greece, Asia Minor and Egypt once ruled by Alexander the Great, and there was no power strong enough to halt it. Even before the formal establishment of the Roman empire by Augustus Caesar in 27 BC, it was a formidable empire in all but name. Each province was under the control and jurisdiction of a governor, often a distinguished Roman general, appointed by the Senate in Rome.

From 27 BC when the Roman empire formally came into existence, central control was tightened still further. The emperor as the permanent and indisputable commander-in-chief was at the apex of the system of control, the provincial governors now being known as *legati Augusti*, the emperor's lieutenants, but to give the inhabitants of the provinces a stake in the system, some were allowed to hold positions of power in Rome, even, on occasion, becoming emperors themselves. The recent French practice of according representation in the National Assembly to their overseas colonies bears a distinct resemblance to Roman procedure but with one critical difference. No one has ever suggested that the French president is divine (even if they have sometimes behaved as if they thought so themselves), whereas the Roman imperial system rested on the divine authority of the emperor. In addition, all law for the empire was made in Rome and administered by Roman judges, even if it incorporated certain features of provincial law existing prior to the Roman conquest. On the other hand it did bestow the blessings of comparative peace and relative prosperity upon the Mediterranean world and beyond for upwards of four centuries.[8]

Some have seen the empire as a possible model for a future world government. But as Robert Purnell suggests in his book *The Society of States*, this would seem to be open to three major objections. First, it was based on conquest; second, it was obliged to devote considerable resources, both human and material, to the needs of internal and external security, and, third, increasingly its rulers were the creatures of contending warlords at the head of embattled legions. Though the period from AD 96 to 180 was the high noon of the *Pax Romana*, its complex of inter-related structures were subject to increasing strains, not least because of the mounting burden of defence, and as regional priorities reasserted themselves, the centre could not hold.

In the century and a half following the death in AD 337 of the Emperor Constantine, the empire split into a Latin western and a Greek eastern imperium, the former still based on Rome, the latter based on Constantinople. In the meantime Christianity had become the official religion of the empire, and when the western empire came to a formal end in 476, to be partitioned into kingdoms dominated by Germanic tribes, the only institution to survive that stood for the former unity was the Church. However, before long that, too, was fragmented. In the eastern so-called Graeco–Byzantine empire, which survived the western empire for a further thousand years, possibly because of its adept use of military pressure, diplomatic intrigue and political intelligence, Christianity began to take on an oriental hue, and proclaimed itself as authentic and Orthodox a faith as Catholicism. Other rifts and divisions within the Church were to follow, and there was to be a further major schism not long after when Western Christendom acquired a temporal in addition to a spiritual head, the Holy Roman Emperor, a position established, ironically with papal blessing, in 800 AD.

For some two hundred years—from 1076 to 1268—Pope and Emperor waged a war for supremacy which enfeebled both and destroyed the political and religious fabric of medieval European society. In the meantime, in having to devise new strategies to deal with the rising tide of Islam, which was spreading over the southern and easternmost parts of the empire from the seventh century onwards, Byzantium's ethics and political vocabulary came increasingly to resemble those of the *Arthashastra*. It turned friendship of its enemy's enemies into a fine art and attempted to win converts and supporters by encouraging the translation into the vernacular of the Orthodox litany and scriptures and the establishment of national churches such as the Serbian, Bulgarian, Romanian and Russian within the Orthodox tradition.[9] What of the international system—our sixth—which having seized its capital, Constantinople, was to destroy the Byzantine Empire in 1453—Islam?

The Islamic system

The Islamic era can be said to have begun in 622. That was when Muhammad, a reasonably successful Arab trader, and the followers of his message of community based on submission—Islam—to one unique all-powerful, all-merciful, all-compassionate God—Allah—were forced by idol-worshippers in his native Mecca to flee to Medina some 300 miles to the north. It quickly became a military as well as a religious and political movement, and its advance, compared with earlier expansionist movements, was remarkably swift. By the time of Muhammad's death in 632, the new religion already controlled the whole of the Arabian peninsula, and within a further two decades had spread to the fertile crescent, from Syria to the Gulf, to Egypt, to the heartlands of the old Persian empire as far as the Afghan marshlands and into Tunisia, along the southern Mediterranean. Within a few more years its writ ran from Tripoli to the gates of India and from the Nile as far as Armenia. And in a second wave of conquests and conversions in the eighth and ninth centuries it had reached down into the land of the Berbers of North Africa, into Morocco, had swept through Spain to the borders of France, and had penetrated further into Asia as far as the Indus valley and into Sind, now part of Pakistan. Although Mecca, possessed of a black stone with reportedly magical properties, had been a place of pilgrimage for Arab idol worshippers, it was hardly known outside the peninsula. How, then, did this somewhat obscure trading centre come to spawn the world's fastest-growing religion and become a place of pilgrimage for hundreds of millions of people?

Certainly the high morale, dedication, commitment together with the ruthlessness of its leaders served to inspire those troubled with uncertainty and looking for a God-centred creed which, unlike Judaism, which is not a proselytising religion, appeared to be available to all. More importantly, because of its geographical origins, it had a special resonance to those speaking a Semitic language, as in much of the Near East, irritated by the intrusions of Byzantine or Persian imperial politics. In addition, its universal message of brotherhood and equality under God had an especial appeal to the poor, the weak and the dispossessed—in fact wherever people felt oppressed by some divisive heirarchical or caste system. Moreover its conception of a single community, *umma*, of the faithful had an obvious attraction wherever tribal and inter-tribal squabbles, blood feuds, vendettas and the like made life intolerable for those not wishing to get involved.

On the other hand had the existing empires not already been in a process of decay, it is doubtful if the spread of Islam would have been quite so rapid. None the less, having emerged from the desert and being unfamiliar with the ideas and skills of the civilisations they overran, the Islamic conquerors were quick to learn from those now within their domain. From their Syrian capital Damascus, and their subsequent capital, Baghdad, they encouraged translations of and commentaries on Greek, Persian and Indian philosophy, mathematics, science and literature, passing them on to Europe where they were to become a vital force in the Renaissance. It is at this time, for example, that the cumbersome Roman approach to number with its X's, V's, I's, M's and C's was abandoned in favour of the simpler Arabic numerals, and algebra (*Al Gebr*) arrived. So, too, did a number of Arab ideas on medicine, chemistry and astronomy.

At the same time, and contrary to the picture often portrayed in the West, where we tend to hear only one side of the story of the Crusades, the Muslims, though prepared to use the sword to make converts, came to learn the value of tolerance, and rather like the Persian Empire of old evolved a formula for dealing with people of other faiths. Though they regarded other belief systems as inferior, Christians and Jews were allowed to maintain their religious traditions and most of their laws, provided they lived in autonomous communities and paid extra taxes. It was this tolerance, for example, that enabled the three monotheistic religions to co-exist reasonably satisfactorily in medieval Spain until the Church began its forcible conversions, the Inquisition and the Crusades.

The Muslim conquerors divided the world into two. There was the *dar al Islam*, an area of peace and harmony wherein lived the faithful and which in time would encompass the planet, and the *dar al harb*, an area of war, where conflict with non-Muslims was always a possibility. With the authorities in the *dar al harb* there could be accords, provided these were both expedient and temporary, but Islam drew a distinction between different kinds of infidel negotiating partners. It tended to be much more tolerant of Jews and, till the Crusades, of Christians because they were people of the Book than towards those it regarded as idolatrous heathens, which is in part why relations between Hindus and Muslims have often been so turbulent. But there was trouble, too, within the *dar al Islam*: the death of Muhammad had left a problem of succession that had led to a serious rift stemming from rival claims to the caliphate, the political centre of the movement. This was the origin of the great schism between the Sunni and the Shiah, and it widened still further when the vast wealth acquired in the course of Islam's expansion was distributed in a way which would cement loyalties rather than in accord with the equalitarian precepts of the faith.

Such rivalries led to bitter conflicts between the protagonists, generating a further series of rifts and divisions, opening up a wide chasm between the theory and practice of the *dar al Islam*, which the Muslim community has never properly succeeded in bridging. All this made for instability—an instability compounded by a weakness at the heart of Islam, the fact that in its bedouin origins it was hostile to political power structures and even to settled government and yet was unable to do without them.[10] Further, as the great 14th-century Islamic scholar, Ibn Khaldun, pointed out: the social solidarity of the tribe tended to be undermined in the ease and luxury of city life, and there is no doubt that the rulers of Islam tended to neglect high moral principle in the Courts of Damascus, Baghdad and, later, when the destiny of Islam was in the hands of the Ottoman Turks, Istanbul.[11]

The schisms as well as the contradictions between Islamic theory and practice were to create in the empire a kind of paradoxical or dialectical process. Though Islam embodied probably the most total and unified way of life, secular and religious, ever devised, it was fragmented politically almost from the start and never in practice attained the cohesion or status of, say, the Roman or Chinese empires, even if it achieved something more regulated and ordered than the city-state system of the Greeks. No doubt its many strengths contributed to its rising fortunes until the 19th century; its weaknesses, however, account in large measure for its more recent setbacks, partly at the hands of Western colonialism, partly self-engendered.

The medieval European system

Reference has already been made to the final pre-modern international society, medieval Europe. Serving as an important link with later systems, it will be covered in greater detail in the following chapter. Although the system inherited some of the religious and political ideas of the past—after all, the papacy still claimed to be the centre of religious orthodoxy, with the local ruler, in theory, a viceroy of the pope—theory and reality were increasingly at odds. Moreover, the rivalry between Byzantium and Rome and within the Catholic sphere between Pope and Holy Roman Emperor, paving the way for further rifts and divisions, served to establish conditions essential to the emergence of a modern international system—ie the secularisation of politics and the creation of sovereign political units with their own *raison d'être* and, more importantly, perhaps, their own *raison d'état*. At the same time, in medieval Italy new diplomatic practices were beginning to come into play that were to leave their imprint on the international societies of the future, in effect shaping first European then global diplomacy.

NOTES

1. See, Bull, H., *The Anarchical Society*, London, Macmillan, 1977, pp. 13–16.
2. This framework of analysis is adapted from Holsti, K.J., *International Politics*, Englewood Cliffs, New Jersey, Prentice Hall, 1967, pp. 27–9. The following text owes much to Bozeman, A.B., *Politics and Culture in International History*, Princeton, Princeton University Press, 1960; Wight, M., *Systems of States*, Leicester University Press, 1977, and Watson, A., *The Evolution of International Society*, London, Routledge, 1992.
3. For detailed analyses of such ancient societies, see, for example, Garnsey, P. and Whittaker, C.R. (eds), *Imperialism in the Ancient World*, Cambridge, Cambridge University Press, 1976; Kramer, S.N., *History Begins at Sumer*, New York, Doubleday, 1959 and Oppenheim, A.L., *Ancient Mesopotamia*, Chicago, University of Chicago Press, 1977.

4. For detailed analyses of the Chinese system, see, for example, Hirth, F., *The Ancient History of China*, New York, Columbia University Press, 1923; Rubin, V.A., *Individual and State in Ancient China*, New York, Columbia University Press, 1976 and Fitzgerald, C.P., *The Chinese View of their Place in the World*, London, Oxford University Press, 1964.
5. See, for example, Majumdar, R., Raychandhuri, H. and Datta, K. (eds), *An Advanced History of India*, London, Macmillan, 1964. Also Thapar, R., *The Penguin History of India*, Volume I, Harmondsworth, Penguin, 1966.
6. *Arthashastra*, trans. Shamasastry, A., Mysore, Wesleyan Mission Press, 1929.
7. See, for example, Boardman, J., *The Greeks Overseas*, London, Thames and Hudson, 1980; Burn, R., *Persia and the Greeks*, London, Arnold, 1972 and also Meiggs, R., *The Athenian Empire*, Oxford, Oxford University Press, 1972.
8. Badian, E., *Roman Imperialism*, Oxford, Blackwell, 1968; Luttwak, E., *The Grand Strategy of the Roman Empire*, Baltimore, Johns Hopkins University Press, 1976; and also Millar, F., *The Emperor in the Roman World*, London, Duckworth, 1977.
9. Obolensky, D., *The Byzantine Commonwealth*, New York, Praeger, 1971; Ostrogorsky, G., *History of the Byzantine State*, Princeton, Princeton University Press, 1969 and also Urbanski, A.B., *Byzantium and the Danube Frontier*, New York, 1968.
10. See, for example, Gibb, H.A.R., *Mohammedanism*, London, 1950 and Arnold, T., *The Caliphate*, London, Routledge, 1965.
11. See, Schmidt, N., *Ibn Khaldun: Historian, Sociologist and Philosopher*, New York, Columbia University Press, 1930.

CHAPTER 5

MODERN INTERNATIONAL SOCIETIES

5.1 THE MEDIEVAL EUROPEAN SYSTEM

The medieval system may be said to have begun when the European body politic experienced something akin to a collective nervous breakdown with the demise, after a long illness, of the Roman empire in AD 476. As recent experience has shown, it is by no means unusual for the disintegration of a political personality such as an empire or a state to be followed by a period of turbulence. We saw it earlier this century with the decomposition of the Ottoman and Austro-Hungarian empires, which engendered a series of wars including, of course, the first world war, and produced a number of unstable regimes in the years after hostilities. It happened in many parts of Asia and Africa as the so-called *Pax Britannica* entered its final phase, and, of course, it is to be seen now following the demise of the 'Pax Sovietica' and the disintegration of what was Yugoslavia. As the discipline of centralised administration is eroded, long-standing tensions and grievances are apt to surface, resulting in a patchwork quilt of warring religions, ideologies, ethnic groups and nationalities in contention for a share in the succession. Meanwhile living conditions tend to worsen, aggravated by the collapse of an integrated economy and communications infrastructure. Moreover, the struggle of new and inexperienced leaders to inaugurate a new order in face of conservative sentiment and the opposition of unreformed and unregenerate officials of the old order merely compounds the problem of establishing stable successor goverments.

In the case of medieval Europe the period of nervous collapse probably lasted until the early 11th century as the successors to the now divided empire further fragmented in both their religious and their secular domains, while regular communication and trade almost ceased altogether in the wake of repeated conflicts within and between the nascent political communities. In fact the various bodies politic that inherited the decaying corpse of the former Roman empire became increasingly isolated at the cost of their economic health.[1]

Here the medical analogy is helpful, since, as the psychiatrist William Sargent reminds us in his book *Battle for the Mind*, which explores various techniques of conversion and brainwashing, it is at periods of nervous collapse that patients tend to be at their most suggestible.[2] He argues that

the patient who has reached the depths of despair often becomes unusually receptive to new ideas: to the therapist who counsels a fresh
approach, to the priest or pastor who offers religious salvation, to the
politician who proffers an earthly paradise, to the playmate who tenders
gratification, to the performer who provides fresh distractions. Before that
stage is reached, however, there are generally moments of lucid rationality
when the patient appears to behave like the integrated personality he or
she once was.

In the case of medieval Europe during the so-called Dark Ages there
were two major attempts to return to the imperial womb. From
Constantinople in the East, the Emperor Justinian in the sixth century
recaptured for the empire parts of Italy, Spain and Africa, at the same time
reviving the Roman notion that secular and spiritual power were to be
regarded as one. However, hopes of reviving imperial fortunes in the eastern Mediterranean were soon to be dashed by the advance of Islam. The
second bid at restoration came from the west and was the joint endeavour
of Charlemagne, the king of the Franks, and the Pope. On Christmas day
800 in the now dilapidated city of Rome, the pope crowned Charlemagne
Holy Roman Emperor, hoping that henceforth western religious and secular authorities could work together to recreate the unity that had been lost.
After all, Charlemagne's existing realm was already bigger than anything
seen in the West since the Roman empire, but the rivalries of his descendants reduced the Empire to a fiction and before long Pope and Emperor
were at war, the former supported by the Italian city states, the latter by
German troops.

Apart from these abortive efforts, papacy, Church, missionaries and
monks made other attempts to keep alive the idea of Christian empire—an
endeavour which found a kind of confused, even corrupt expression in
the Crusades against Islam. But it was a forlorn hope: although conversions, forced and voluntary, ensured that nominally Europe represented
in some sense one Christian civilisation, it was about as Christian as post-
1945 Eastern Europe was communist. The reality, that is, was often far
removed from the body of doctrine on which it was based, and the divergence between theory and practice merely encouraged religious dissidence and hence greater fragmentation within the so-called 'body of
Christ'.

What of the political reality? In fact by the 11th century, Europe had
been divided into a series of decentralised feudal entities centred around
castles and towns, within which service and deference were accorded by
serfs and vassals in exchange for protection and maintenance from the
chieftain, lord or warlord. Yet the wars, conquests and migrations that had
destroyed the old order and helped to reshape the political map of Europe
had also produced that receptiveness to new ideas that we associate with
the process of recuperation and recovery following a nervous collapse. As

the small feudal units began to be amalgamated into larger units for greater security, the notion of the nature of political obligation began to change. There was to be a significant shift, too, in the notion of religious obligation, as local merchants wrestled with abbots, Christian kings with bishops and, of course, Emperor with Pope. A still greater catalyst for change was the rivalry between western and eastern Christendom, leading, in 1204, to a western Christian Crusade against Christian Byzantium. Here a crusading army robbed, burned, pillaged and raped its way through Constantinople, thereby widening the growing rift between the two wings of Christianity which has never even to this day been truly healed. One has only to think of the recent tensions between the Catholic and Orthodox churches in, say, the Ukraine, and the savagery that characterised the bloody struggle between the Croats, supported by the Vatican and co-religionists from Italy, Germany, Austria and Hungary and the Serbs with the assistance of their sanctions-busting Orthodox friends in Greece, Russia and Romania.[3]

The prospects of a revolution in loyalties towards the end of the Middle Ages were to be given added impetus by the start of the Renaissance in the late 15th century. For this marked the culmination of a period in which ideas and inventions were diffused which were significantly to alter both social structures and material conditions. Not that these notions were all by any means novel, for both the monastic orders within Europe and the Islamic invaders from outside were disseminating long-neglected learned Greek and Roman texts, while the Muslims were also conveying to Europe some of the ingenious discoveries of the Orient, and in particular China, a civilisation which had tended to invent but not to utilise. The cumulative effect was profound: in agriculture—more land under cultivation, the wheeled plough, the nailed horseshoe enabling the horse gradually to replace the ox, the growing use of water and wind power and the introduction of olives, apricots, rice, sugar, oranges, lemons and other new crops; in industry—the introduction of gunpowder for quarrying, of jib cranes for lifting, of the blast furnace and of geared wheels, ratchets and pulleys for machinery; in construction—great Gothic cathedrals, battlemented castles and tile and brick to supplement stone. Later, the invention of the printing press served to shape both language and literature and in turn political organisation. At the same time, the appearance of the mariner's compass and improvements in the techniques of shipbuilding and seamanship ensured that the cross-fertilisation of ideas would be on an ever-widening canvass. Fifteenth century Europe was on the verge of the great voyages of discovery that were to lead to the colonisation of whole continents and a vast increase in international trade.[4]

The revolution in loyalties was to result in the gradual transfer of allegiance from religious to secular authorities and from local to something akin to national governments. One of the key factors in giving coherence to this process was the spread throughout Europe of the mystique of monarchy which in the course of time gave, as it were, a kind of legitimacy to what had generally begun as successful brigandage. Thus the political units to which post-medieval Europeans were expected to pay at least deference, if not more, were states, and because they were under the control of royal or at least princely households these self-same states were themselves to be accorded sovereign status. Just what that implied will be discussed in the next chapter. What is of interest is that many took as their model the experience of the wealthy Italian city states of Venice, Milan, Florence and Naples which in the late 15th century had pioneered an approach to politics and diplomacy that meant a final break with the aspirations of Christendom.

5.2 THE ITALIAN CITY-STATE SYSTEM

In contrast to the bewildering hierarchies of authority elsewhere in Europe, by the late 15th century the Italian city states had developed efficient, if not always stable, polities under rulers whose ambitions were unashamedly secular. They made no claim to religious principle and entertained no moral inhibitions or scruples on the acquisition of power. For them policy was to do with the pursuit of material advantage, and the justification lay in what was to become known as *raisons d'état*, reasons of state. It was not, however, a licence for unrestrained savagery, as had often characterised conflicts between peoples claiming to have God on their side, as in the Crusades or in the religious wars that were to come. For as A.J.P. Taylor recalls in *Rumours of War*, the tally of casualties in so-called 'just' wars involving conflicts of principle is usually far in excess of that in so-called 'necessary' wars ie arising out of conflicts of interest.[5] In fact precisely because they were unconstrained by dogma or by considerations of moral rectitude, the rulers of the Italian city states saw nothing wrong in making compromises, doing deals with the enemy or in acting with the utmost caution and prudence, when expedient. Since by the time of the Renaissance each such state had more or less accepted the existence of the others, they developed novel techniques for managing their inter-relations. To those Italian city states we owe our diplomatic system with its attendant embassies and privileges.[6]

Admittedly, the Assyrians, Egyptians, Greeks, Romans and others had also employed envoys and ambassadors, but these were for particular missions, to be withdrawn when the mission had been accomplished. What the Italians had invented was the permanent embassy and the career diplomat, complete with privileges and immunities. Moreover they charged their professional diplomats with many, if not most of the functions we associate with them today—communication, representation, negotiation, ingratiation (ie winning friends and influencing people) and, above all, extracting information, not least after a bottle or two or a romp in the hay with some well-placed wench.

On the other hand where diplomacy failed, the Italian rulers had, as Machiavelli, secretary to the republican regime in Florence, points out in *The Prince*, a whole arsenal of alternative pressures and inducements, including bribes, threats, subversion, assassination and, ultimately, war. On the other hand such wars were generally fought not between individual citizens, as so often in the past, but between mercenaries in receipt of *soldi*—the word means money or pay and is the origin of our word soldier—led by professional officers under contract to conduct a given campaign, which is why they were generally of short duration. Furthermore, the aim was never the destruction of the opponent since this might encourage the other states to form a hostile coalition. The objective, as befits those whose main concern was banking, was to establish a favourable balance but not at the cost of the stability of the states' system. Again the Italians had taken an *ad hoc* arrangement used by the Persians and the Greeks, among others, and turned it into a permanent institution—to be known as the 'balance of power'.

Unfortunately it was the broadening of this concept to include an outside power, France, who had responded to a plea from Milan to intervene in the peninsula to deter a threatened offensive from a neighbour that was to lead to the end of the cosy, if cynical, relationship between the Italian states. For nearly four centuries following the French intrusion into the peninsula in 1494, they were to become mere objects of the rivalries between the new dynastic states of France, Spain and Austria. On the other hand neither the Italian example nor the writings of Machiavelli, which had so deftly characterised Italian politics, had gone unnoticed in the rest of Europe. After all, in their secular dispositions and dispersal of power, the Italian states had effectively broken with the past and in this way were to form a vital link between the medieval and the modern conceptions of an international society. Some scholars see the roots of modern international society in 15th-century Italy.[7] Others, however, trace its origins to the time when the concepts of sovereign equality and territorial integrity entered the European political vocabulary, neither of which would have been readily understood in Renaissance Italy.

What the rest of Europe derived from the Italian experience was a clear alternative to the complex and diffuse layers of authority, spiritual and temporal, local, provincial and central, territorial and extra-territorial that characterised European politics. The Italian city states were administered by rulers with the power to command, and their example had appeal wherever religious doubt, pride in secular languages and literature and nascent capitalist activity contributed to the rejection of the Pope's intrusive authority. Since, moreover, those rulers that began to identify with the Protestant Reformation, which occurred at about the same time as the Renaissance, were increasingly disposed to determine the religious affiliations of their subjects, they were in effect simultaneously adding to both their power and their legitimacy. On the other hand, in the best balance of power tradition, Reformation bred Counter-Reformation, and before the ideal of a Commonwealth of Christian societies had finally given way to a conglomeration of independent secular states, Europe experienced a prolonged and exceptionally bloody struggle culminating in the Thirty Years war of religion that virtually tore the continent apart.

In France, Spain, Portugal, Italy and Poland the Protestant reformers were eventually crushed. In England, Scotland and Scandinavia they emerged victorious. In Ireland, a small minority of Scottish and English Protestants imposed their rule but not their faith on a Catholic people, giving rise to resentments that have lasted to this day. The Netherlands and Germany were partitioned after decades of internecine strife, which eventually brought prosperity to the former and utter devastation to the latter, combined with a feeling that despite their cultural kinship, the Germans were unlikely ever to achieve any satisfactory political unity (a feeling never entirely dissipated and much in vogue today with the rising tensions between the western and eastern wings of the country).

5.3 THE WESTPHALIAN SYSTEM

The Thirty Years war ended in 1648 with the Treaties of Westphalia, which for the first time outside of Italy elevated *raison d'état* to the level of principle and helped crystallise a framework for the existence of tolerable relations between states with conflicting interests. For scholars such as F. S. Northedge and Hedley Bull, Westphalia marks the formal beginning of modern international society, or at least of the European states' system. Others see it as ratifying a system already in existence and marking its coming of age.[8] Ironically, Westphalia did not bring an end to war. Hostilities between France and Spain were to continue for a further decade or so and in a century which saw only seven complete calendar years free of bloodshed between European states.[9] Indeed, the feeling that Westphalia had changed very little caused Thomas Hobbes to publish his famous *Leviathan* three years after the settlement. To him international relations were characterised by anarchy, and peace was a mere interlude between wars. Yet by the end of the century it was evident that Westphalia had, indeed, marked some kind of watershed, given definition to the political shape of Europe and provided for a modicum of order in inter-state relations.[10] In what way?

Sovereign statehood

First and foremost, Westphalia formally broke with many of the medieval constraints on government and with the universal laws which were supposed to regulate the conduct of rulers in medieval Christendom. Henceforth neither Pope nor Emperor could order kings and princes to undertake action without their specific consent. In other words, Westphalia gave official currency to the principle of sovereign statehood. So long as a state was recognised as sovereign it would be legally free of outside interference and accorded equality before the law and the sole right to enter into treaties. By implication this meant that a state not so recognised was not entitled to membership of the European 'club'. Like a colony or protectorate today, a state whose ruler lacked supreme authority over the lands he claimed or whose country was not constitutionally or juridically self-contained, such as a duchy within France or one of the various states around the Baltic, had no legal standing in European international society. But how could this legitimation of the sovereign principle provide the basis for international order?

In the first place, if a sovereign state was one which could not permit other political entities to make or apply their rules on its territory without its express consent, it had the corresponding obligation not to intervene in the internal affairs of other states or compromise their territorial integrity. Admittedly the principle of non-intervention may well have meant turning a blind eye to the most appalling misdemeanours within a state, but Westphalia put a premium on orderly relations, and considerations of justice for individual citizens and groups were not a major concern. Second, no matter what the divergencies in size, location, population or military capability between the sovereign members of international society, all were to be regarded as equal as regards legal rights and duties, including the right of self-defence. Third, all sovereign states were duty bound to honour their treaties and other obligations under international law. But this immediately raises the question: how could a state be sovereign and yet subject to law?

International law

To this conundrum there were to be at least three alternative answers. Those looking back to medieval times and even before held that the relationship between states was governed by mandatory rules of conduct incumbent on all individuals and social institutions according to what they called 'natural law'. Most such theorists argued that natural law was divine in origin and discoverable through the exercise of what they called 'right reason' (a question-begging phrase, if ever there was one). Others, the so-called 'positivists', were to argue that states were subject to law because their rulers had indicated their consent to international legal principles by seeking sovereign status for their respective countries. The accord of sovereign status, that is, only made sense within a legal framework. Recognition was, after all, a legal act from which obligations as well as rights flowed, and among the obligations was respect for legal principle. International law had not been imposed from above. It was a body of rules established between sovereigns for their mutual benefit. But were the rules binding on them? To Professor C.A.W. Manning they were, their 'bindingness' being not a demonstrable proposition but an ascription. In speaking of law we generally imputed to it a binding quality. To speak of a non-binding law would be as anomolous as to speak of a four-sided triangle or a non-circular circle ie it would be to use the term in a highly eccentric fashion.[11] If law is binding by definition, the operative question is whether it functions effectively in an international context, an inquiry to be pursued in a subsequent chapter. One other school of thought, associated with one of the earliest systematic exponents of international law, the Dutch lawyer Hugo Grotius, held that sovereign states were subject to law on both natural law and positivist principles. They were obliged to obey because they were mandated to and also because they had consented to, though it is interesting to note that to write his seminal work *De Juri Belli ac Pacis* (the Law of War and Peace) in 1625, Grotius had to escape his native Holland in a trunk to avoid the horrors of the Thirty Years war, which had engulfed his country.

Given that international law had to function between sovereign authorities, its implementation clearly had to be different from the application of law in a domestic context. (Which is why some who ought to know better ask: is international law really law? It all depends on what one means by 'law'. If it refers to a body of rules with the status of law and deemed to be binding, then international law is law.) Unlike domestic law, however, any such agreement between sovereigns has to be self-policing. Is that so unusual? Anyone mystified as to how a system of law can operate in the absence of government might reflect on how a rule-governed enterprise such as a game of bridge, billiards or table tennis is sustained. For though not necessarily free of controversy, such contests do not usually appear to require a referee, umpire or the intervention of the police. Like a game of bridge, the international legal 'game' tends to proceed more or less satisfactorily, since the regulations are generally regarded as of mutual benefit. Naturally, if one partner constantly breaks the rules, it soon finds the others refusing to play. Applied to international relations, the habitual law breaker tends to be treated as a pariah, the other 'players' severing diplomatic ties.

Diplomacy

Diplomacy was a second post-Westphalian instrument for containing international disorder. Following Italian practice, European diplomacy shifted from a fitful to a permanent activity and tended to continue even at times of hostilities. Indeed, one could well argue that in time of war the negotiating and intelligence functions of the diplomat were needed more than ever, and on a reciprocal basis he received the full protection of the law as both his person and his embassy were legally inviolable. What was novel in post-Westphalian Europe is that diplomacy began to be organised as a profession. The diplomatic resources of states started to be arranged between separate ministries; diplomatic dispatches began to be regarded as state property and not the personal property of the envoy, and in the course of time the profession started to develop its own social manners and rules of procedure, styled largely on French diplomatic etiquette. By the end of the 17th century the profession appeared to have a corporate identity, much in evidence at the various congresses called to settle outstanding issues at the end of a war.

Balance of power

A third mechanism for managing the affairs of what was being called 'the European system', post-Westphalia, was the 'balance of power'. Though there has always been controversy about its precise meaning, it clearly had to do with strategies—military, political or economic—for ensuring that the existing power of the state in relation to other states was preserved and, if possible, enhanced. As will have been clear from the previous chapter, variants of balance of power politics were to be found in pre-modern international societies—among the Indians, the Greeks and the Romans even prior to the establishment of empire. However, in its post-Westphalian sense it became a conscious policy to secure political advantage at the least possible cost to self or society. Indeed, in the 18th century it was generally spoken of as if in some sense an indispensable adjunct to international law, and at the Treaty of Utrecht, which ended the war of Spanish Succession in 1713, express reference was made to the balance as a principle of foreign policy. Like the solar system revealed by Newton, states were understood to exercise attraction and pressure in proportion to their mass and the distance they kept from one another. If one power in the system grew stronger or weaker, the others would have to adjust, and the objective was to prevent the domination of the system by any one power or group of powers. Though the balance in this sense did not necessarily mean the absence of war, it did mean that war was generally a last resort and fought by limited means for essentially limited ends. Thus the cost of combat in both human and material terms in the years between 1648 and the end of the 18th century was as nothing compared to the religious wars preceding Westphalia or the national wars following the French Revolution. In the so called 'Age of Enlightenment' warfare had become a demonstration of power rather than an orgy of destruction.

In addition to international law, diplomacy and the balance of power, there was to be a further foundation to the framework of order established in the wake of Westphalia. For all their insistence on sovereign independence, the rulers of 18th-century Europe and those working in government service were linked to one another by a common culture. They generally spoke French, continued to identify themselves as upholders of Christian values and accepted the principles of royal legitimacy and dynastic succession. If proof were needed of the degree to which the 18th-century state system still possessed a common culture, it is to be found in the numbers of Germans serving in the Russian court, of Italians in the French court, of Englishmen, Irishmen and Germans in Spanish diplomatic and military service and the fact that in 1688 a Dutchman, William III, and in 1714 a Hanoverian, George I, became king of England.

On the other hand for all the factors making for order there were, as there usually are, countervailing forces which would undermine the system and eventually bring about its disintegration. For the dynasties of the time often treated populations, their own included, like bits of real estate and would transfer territory and peoples from one area to another regardless of tradition or the wishes of inhabitants. The fragmented domains of Germany and Italy were constantly being reallocated from one dynasty to another as if pieces on a chessboard, a process eventually leading at the end of the 18th century to the partitioning of Poland, when certain powers deemed it preferable to divide much of it between Prussia and the Habsburgs rather than allow the whole state to fall under Russian control. The idea that sovereigns were in charge and that the will of their subjects did not matter much bred increasing resentment, especially among those peasants and townspeople under despotic, corrupt or alien rulers. The time bomb ticking away under the post-Westphalian order that would eventually destroy the Europe of the dynasts was, of course, nationalism—a movement which in its initial phase set out to shift the locus of sovereignty from ruler to people.[12]

5.4 THE NATIONALIST REVOLT

In North America Europe had had in the third quarter of the 18th century an indication of what was to come. For since the 15th century, Europeans had settled in the Americas, transplanting their culture to much larger areas than those in which it had developed. At the same time the rulers of Europe tended to regard such settlers and the lands they colonised in the Americas and elsewhere as mere sources of revenue and continued to do so long after the settlers had spread inland out of reach of any effective control from the mother country. By the mid-1770s the British-Americans began to question their subservience to Britain. Heavily taxed but denied any say in the spending of national revenue, their trade, including their tea exports, sacrificed to the interests of the British Crown, they demanded 'no taxation without representation' and threw cargoes of tea imported from the London-based East India Company into Boston harbour. When the British government attempted to arrest two of the protesters near Boston in 1775, the first shots were fired in what was to become America's War of Independence, and in 1783 at the Peace of Paris, the Thirteen Colonies, from Maine to Georgia, were to become a union of sovereign states.

The significance of what had been agreed at Paris in 1783 had not been lost on the taxpayers of the French capital, comprising most adults save those of the nobility and clergy who were protected by a system of exemptions. Soon anger began to mount, especially among those of the country's middle class familiar with the ideas of philosophers, such as Rousseau, who had begun to challenge the whole edifice of privilege and patronage on which the 18th century idea of 'legitimacy' rested. To them a state might be lawfully sovereign, but it could not be truly 'legitimate' if it oppressed the mass of the population, politically, socially or economically. As Rousseau had claimed in the first chapter of *Social Contract*, written in 1762: 'Man is born free, yet everywhere he is in chains.'

In 1789 a shortage of bread combined with the financial embarrassment of a spendthrift monarch who had squandered much of the taxpayers money triggered off an attempt led by the Parisian middle class to break the chains that were hampering freedom of association and enterprise and a career open to the talents. In the name of 'liberty, equality and fraternity' they expounded a doctrine with profound implications for the European international system. For they were intent on replacing tradition by consent and dynastic by popular sovereignty, but in proclaiming their new doctrine, they introduced a fanaticism into international relations that Europe had not seen for a century and a half and that was entirely alien to the international order post-Westphalia. For their ideas knew no frontiers. They wanted to spread them throughout Europe and beyond, and any power that opposed them stood in danger of having to face France's new citizen army. Incidentally it was at this time that a new word entered the political vocabulary—'ideology'—to describe the new political creeds displacing the old religious dogmas. For Cambridge historian, F.H. Hinsley, it is when France tried and finally failed to force the states of Europe into a common mould that the modern European states' system was completed.[13] It is with the Europe of the nations rather than the Europe of the states that for Harry Hinsley modern international society originated—yet another idiosyncratic conception as to its genesis.

The violence of the French Revolution was rather less than legend suggests. In fact, fewer Frenchmen died in the worst months of the Terror than in the few weeks following the suppression of the Paris commune in

1871, and, for that matter, fewer people fled abroad to escape the turmoil than had emigrated from the American colonies during the American Revolution.[14] None the less its psychological impact throughout the world was profound. Executing a monarch in the name of the nation and expressly breaking with Christianity conveyed to the world the possibility of massive social change and identified politics as a mechanism for challenging vested rights and interests. In the broadest sense political debate was now about a single issue—stability or change, conservatism or liberalism, immobility or innovation—and the French in 1789 invented two terms to characterise the protagonists. In the National Assembly those opposing further change sat on the right of the president, those for reform sat on his left, and the terms 'right' and 'left' entered the political lexicon as indicators of political orientation. Like all such expressions these were over-simplifications. By this test the former British Prime Minister Margaret Thatcher is a woman of left-wing inclinations: the former Soviet President Mikhail Gorbachev had become a man of the right. None the less the terms have their value.

Far more problematic, however, was the inconsistency of the claims of the revolutionaries regarding fundamental rights, one of which was the right of the people to sovereignty. For what if the people, or at least their spokesmen, wanted, for example, to persecute minorities, to silence the press, to hang so-called 'wrongdoers' and so forth, which, as it happens, they frequently did? Which right was to take precedence? As we know, in the name of the people of France in 1789, of Russia in 1917, of Germany in 1933, of China in 1949 and elsewhere, the most terrible deeds have been done, to say nothing of the deeds perpetrated by, say, the Americans in the name of 'freeing' the people of other countries such as Vietnam, Nicaragua or Panama. In any case were 'liberty' and 'equality' compatible? After all, if an equalitarian society was what was required, then surely those who did better would have to be held back in some way, which would be an infringement of liberty; if the emphasis was on individual freedom, then some would do better than others, and an inequalitarian society would result.

Leaving such issues aside we can say that if the theory underlying the French Revolution represented a standing reproach to the principles of the post-Westphalian international order, its militant policies at home and abroad soon alienated those intended to be its strongest supporters. For a series of coups and counter-coups in Paris, the promiscuous use of the guillotine and the behaviour of republican troops in looting the lands they were supposed to be liberating turned potential allies into real foes. And when the French armies were finally beaten back and the Emperor of 11 years' standing, Napoleon, suffered defeat by British, Belgian and Prussian forces at Waterloo in 1815, a kind of order was restored. Yet it was to differ somewhat from Westphalia in that it was to be managed by the great powers of the day. The informal directorate of powers instituted at the time of the Vienna settlement was to go under the name of the Concert of Europe. In the event, however, the Concert was to be less than harmonious since its five principals—Britain, France, Russia, Prussia and Austria—were to diverge markedly in attitudes and interests.[15]

5.5 THE CONCERT SYSTEM

True, many of the most important changes in the post-1815 system were imposed by the Concert powers, which held periodic summit conferences to discuss and if possible settle matters of common concern. Through multilateral action—a novel concept—the Turks were forced to grant Greek independence, the Dutch to yield Belgium (like Switzerland and Luxembourg to be neutralised), while the autonomy of Egypt, Serbia, Romania and Bulgaria and the partition of Africa were all decided by the Concert. On the other hand no such international 'management' could work at times when the principals were engaged in hostilities against one another, as in the Crimean War in the 1850s or the conflict between Prussia and Austria a decade later. In any case nationalist sentiment, which was on the rise in Europe throughout the 19th century, could not always be channelled in the direction desired by the Concert Powers, two of which—Austria and Russia—held substantial European possessions.

According to Evan Luard,[16] at least three-quarters of the wars between 1815 and 1914 stemmed from attempts by European nationalists to secure an independence which their imperial overlords were determined to resist. There was, in any case, growing resentment among the smaller powers at the way in which their sovereign rights tended to be disregarded by the greater. Sometimes, tensions within Europe would be relieved by expansion outside it, but in the end, a combination of declining Austrian, Russian and Ottoman power and rising German power was sufficient in 1914 to bring down the whole diplomatic edifice erected a century before. At the same time, the revolutions in the art of warfare— with the invention of the tank, the torpedo, heavy artillery and aircraft— ensured that the casualties inflicted during the first world war were for a conflict of four years' duration the worst on record.

5.6 THE VERSAILLES SYSTEM

Yet another international system may be said to have been inaugurated at the Peace Conference at Versailles following the first world war—one built on the ruins of European empires, and in accordance, at least in theory, with the principle of national self-determination. This fact led Evan Luard to identify 1918 as the year when contemporary international society came into effect.[17] But the new states that came into being after Versailles were hardly exemplars of the nationalist principle. Yugoslavia and Czechoslovakia, as has become only too obvious, incorporated an ill-assortment of peoples, as did the newly revived Poland, which was less than 60 per cent Polish. Meanwhile, the resentments building up in Germany, Italy, Japan and other countries believing themselves to have been deprived by the 'peace-makers' of their rights to full self-determination contained the seeds of another world war less than 20 years after the end of the first.

5.7 WORLD POLITICS

It is interesting that so many scholars, particularly American scholars, perhaps familiarising themselves with international politics for the first time, choose to call the era since 1945 the 'modern' period—a period they characterise as one of cold war between two sets of hostile nuclear powers. But now that the cold war is over, do these self-same scholars believe we are entering into yet another kind of international society—perhaps 'post-modern' in character? There is an alternative way of depicting the post-1945 era ie as the period when international society became truly global in the wake of decolonisation, with the expansion of the ideas on which the European state system was based, the proliferation of new states and the development of new technologies with implications for the future of the planet.

In sum, when precisely modern international society evolved and whether it has completed its course depends on how one chooses to define both 'modern' and 'international society'. What is clear, however, is that the two concepts are bound up with a third—'sovereignty'—to which we turn in the following chapter.

NOTES

1. See, for example, Talbot Rice, D. (ed.), *The Dark Ages*, London, 1965.
2. Sargent, W., *Battle for the Mind*, London, Heinemann, 1957.
3. On relations between medieval Rome and Byzantium, see, for example, Roberts, J.M., *The Triumph of the West*, London, BBC, 1985, pp. 149–74 and Obolensky, D., *The Byzantine Commonwealth*, New York, Praeger, 1971.
4. See, for example, Roberts, J.M., op. cit., pp. 175–202.
5. Taylor, A.J.P., *Rumours of War*, London, Hamish Hamilton, 1952, p. 44.
6. See, Mattingley G., *Renaissance Diplomacy*, London, Cape, 1955.
7. Wight, M., *Systems of States*, Leicester, Leicester University Press, 1977, pp. 110–13.

8. Ibid., pp. 129–52.
9. See, Mowat, R., *The European States System*, London, Oxford University Press, 1923, pp. 14–32.
10. See, for example, Keens-Soper, M., 'The Practice of a States System' in Donelan, M. (ed.), *The Reason of States*, London, Allen & Unwin, 1978, pp. 25–44.
11. Manning, C.A.W., *The Nature of International Society*, London, Bell, 1962, pp. 103–6 and 160–1.
12. Hobsbawm, E., *Nations and Nationalism since 1780*, Cambridge, Cambridge University Press, 1990, pp. 18–24.
13. *Power and the Pursuit of Peace*, Cambridge, Cambridge University Press, 1967.
14. Roberts, J.R., op. cit., p. 284.
15. For a range of conflicting views about the origins and effects of the Concert see, Holbraad, C., *The Concert of Europe*, London, Longmans, 1970.
16. *Conflict and Peace in the Modern International System*, London, University of London Press, 1970, pp. 10–11.
17. Ibid., p. 11.

PART III
THE STATE

CHAPTER 6

SOVEREIGNTY: LEGAL AND POLITICAL

What do Afghanistan and Albania, Cambodia and Costa Rica, Lebanon and Lesotho, Vanuatu and the Vatican have that Kashmir and Kurdistan, California and Catalonia, Cabinda and Katanga, Queensland and Quebec do not? The answer is sovereign status. Each of the former is recognised in international law as a sovereign state, even though most of the latter, which are not so recognised, are far larger and more cohesive. This chapter seeks to explain how and why such an anomolous situation can arise and to unravel the mysteries of sovereignty in legal theory and political and economic practice.

6.1 STATE SOVEREIGNTY: PREREQUISITES

The first and most obvious question is: how and when did sovereignty as a legal concept come into being in the first place? The very notion of legal sovereignty, which connotes authority and dominion, would have been inconceivable without the disintegration of the medieval framework of ideas and institutions. For the medieval conception was essentially hierarchical and based on the idea that despite the collapse of the temporal power of Rome and the division of its religious domain into rival realms, a unified Christendom would again be restored one day. Even by the 14th century when the great Italian poet, Dante, in his *De Monarchia* expressed his yearning for the days of order and cohesion under the empire, it was clear that Christian universalism had disintegrated beyond repair. Indeed, many of the feudal lords who had proliferated in the wake of Christendom's decline and had arrogated to themselves the title of duke, prince or king had acquired control of vast territories which were soon to become recognisable as the future sovereign states of Europe. In what became known as France, England, Spain and Austria, kings created dynasties and son followed father to the throne, and the mystique of modern monarchy was born. As the new rulers consolidated their domains, so they also greatly enhanced their authority against the claims of Pope, Emperor and local barons. In *The Prince*, written by the 15th-century Florentine, Niccolo Machiavelli, ambitious monarchs had a practical manual on how to rid themselves of medieval constraints. But

Machiavelli left it to others to erect a scaffolding of theory to justify that independence, and it fell to the Frenchman Jean Bodin to furnish the requisite doctrine. In his *De Republica* of 1576 and subsequent works, he elaborated a series of precepts on which the modern doctrine of state sovereignty rests.[1]

6.2 SOVEREIGNTY AS A POLITICAL CONCEPT

Bodin's starting point was that the medieval confusion of unco-ordinated independent authorities with residual ties to a distant Pope or Emperor was a recipe for chaos and bloodshed; what was required in each state was a single and ultimate temporal source with 'the power to give law to all the citizens'. For Bodin, then, such a ruler would represent the *summa potestas*, the supreme or sovereign power, and in an attempt to justify the centralisation of royal authority since the time of Louis XI in the 15th century he argued that such power emanated directly from God. The sovereign was God's appointed representative for the earthly affairs of his country, and though he might be subject to divine law, natural law or the laws of the realm, including those he had himself promulgated, he could not be otherwise called to account. Indeed, since he ruled by 'divine right' any challenge to his power was effectively a challenge to God.

Though it might be thought that such an idea would be popular only among rulers, in fact it also had considerable appeal among the ruled. In a continent torn apart by religious strife, the concept of centralised orderly rule attracted the rising commercial classes with a vested interest in counteracting the chaos and uncertainty of the time. It also struck a chord wherever a nascent sense of political identity was beginning to emerge— the kind of sentiment that was to culminate more than two centuries later in the phenomenon of nationalism. On the other hand in defining sovereignty as 'absolute and perpetual power within a state' and locating that power in the institution of monarchy, Bodin was propounding a theory that would later be challenged by liberal thinkers such as John Locke, by populist theorists such as Rousseau and by legal authorities such as John Austin or A. V. Dicey who rooted sovereignty in parliament and in judicial institutions.

Bodin's theory of sovereignty had been essentially political in character. It justified a particular kind of rule, if only as a recipe for effective government, and identified what had already become a political reality in many countries, including his own, namely, the monarch's assertion of his authority against all comers. Although essentially concerned with political organisation, it had legal implications—and not just in respect of relations between rulers and ruled but also regarding the state in relation to other states. For if a sovereign was a ruler acknowledging no political superior, was this not also true of the state over which he presided? Bodin's theory, in other words, seemed to suggest that any state with what lawyers called 'internal sovereignty', and, hence, under the effective control of an identifiable supreme authority, must have external sovereignty as well ie sovereign status in the world at large. Yet as indicated earlier, clearly some states under exclusive sovereign control do not have sovereign status in the world at large. For example, though Tibet claimed sovereign status after the collapse of the Chinese empire early this century, its credentials were never accepted in the wider international community. Nor were those of Ian Smith's Rhodesia or of Rauf Denktash's Republic of Northern Cyprus. Conversely, some states in which all authority appears to have broken down such as Afghanistan, Somalia and Bosnia continue to be regarded as sovereign. How come?

6.3 SOVEREIGNTY AS A LEGAL CONCEPT

By way of an answer we must examine how sovereign status is acquired in international society.[2] Since the origin of the international legal system in the 17th century and though never clearly articulated till the Montevideo Convention of 1933, there have been legal criteria for the attainment of sovereign statehood. These include the existence of a defined territory, a population inhabiting it more or less permanently, an effective government which receives allegiance if not deference and is capable of entering into relations with other states and willing to abide by its legal obligations. There is in practice, however, a further hurdle a state has to overcome before being accepted into the 'club' of sovereign states. It has to have sovereign status conferred on or imputed to it by the governments of other sovereign states. On the other hand governments are free agents and are not duty bound to confer legal recognition even on a state that fulfils all the necessary legal criteria. For though legal consequences flow from the grant and attainment of sovereign status, recognition is itself a political act and it is up to each and every government to determine whether or not it wishes to accord sovereign status to another administration or state.

It is for this reason that some apparently independent states go unrecognised, while countries such as Israel and the Democratic Peoples' Republic of Korea (North Korea) can be recognised as sovereign by some governments and not others. This does not mean that such states are semi-sovereign, for in the eyes of international law, sovereignty is like virginity: you either have it or you don't. Israel and North Korea are wholly sovereign to those recognising them as such. To those not so recognising them they can at best only have a *de facto* not a *de jure* status, which inhibits what they are legally permitted to do in international society. Just why such micro-states as Nauru, Vanuatu or Liechtenstein; shambolic states such as Afghanistan, Bosnia or Somalia; or states under virtual foreign occupation such as Panama or Lebanon or some of the Eastern European countries in Stalin's time have continued to enjoy recognition is a political question which need not concern us at this stage. On the other hand the tragic fate of states such as Bosnia and Croatia indicates the folly of disregarding the criteria for recognition drawn up by the international lawyers long ago. For the decision of the EC countries to accord sovereign status to those two states whose governments were known to lack effective control over crucial regions of the territories over which they claimed sovereignty only added to the existing divisions in both countries, giving the Serbs a pretext for intervention.

But legal doctrine and political and economic reality may be two different things, and the possibility of a divergence, even a conflict, between theory and practice may apply as much to the internal as to the external dimensions of sovereignty. For example, since in Britain there is no body like a Supreme Court with the power to review or question the constitutionality of what the sovereign does, in theory the Queen in Parliament can make or unmake any law. In practice, however, the Queen in Parliament has only limited capacity to instigate laws against powerful associations or groups. Already vested interests have made a nonsense of the Sunday trading laws, the attempt to secure payment of the 'poll tax' and the Queen's own desire to curb press speculation about the sexual preferences of her family and the marital and extra-marital relations of her siblings. And, of course, the vagaries of international finance, to say nothing of the exactions of the European Union, render the exercise of sovereign power all the more problematic. At the other end of the globe, in Communist China, often described in the West as 'totalitarian', implying a state under total government control, not even the ultra-radicalism of The Cultural Revolution was able to stamp out the corruption and nepotism, racism, drug abuse, gambling, prostitution, female infanticide and so forth declared illegal at the beginning of the Party's rule in 1949. Even where the authorities are able to exercise control, the exact source of their power may well be different from the constitutional position. For example, although according to the Soviet constitution supreme legal authority rested with the Supreme Soviet, it was, until Gorbachev, largely a rubber-stamp parliament and the real decision-making power rested with the score or so people in the Soviet Communist Party's Politburo and Secretariat, whose exact legal standing was somewhat unclear. Thus both the locus of internal sovereignty and its degree of effective authority may be rather different in practice from the official theory.

6.4 LEGAL IMPLICATIONS OF STATE SOVEREIGNTY

When we come to the external dimensions of legal sovereignty ie the state in respect of other states, the relationship between theory and practice can be even more remote. But since it sets the state apart from other social organisations, what does the status of external sovereignty imply? Here sovereignty does not connote 'supremacy' as in the domestic setting, for a sovereign state is not above the law. In attaining sovereign status a state has equality in terms of the law which means that it is entitled to a number of rights, powers and privileges:[3]

1. First and foremost, the exclusive power to control its own domestic affairs, to make ultimate decisions concerning the lives of its citizens and take actions regarding any matter within its territorial confines to the exclusion of other sovereign states;
2. Freedom from outside intervention, unless sanctioned by some legally constituted body, like the UN, in response to a gross breach of international law;
3. The right of self defence and, if necessary, of retaliation against an unprovoked attack;
4. The right to make and amend treaties;
5. The right to participate as a full member in the work of international organisations;
6. The right to participate in the creation or amendment of international legal practice;
7. The rights to its diplomats abroad of all the customary legal privileges and immunities;
8. The right to the sole jurisdiction of crimes committed within its territory;
9. The right to sue in the international courts;
10. The power to admit and expel aliens, and so forth.

Legal equality and inequality

Even on a formal, legal basis, even before we examine the discrepancies between theory and practice, there are *de facto* inequalities.[4] Built into the structure of the UN, for example, is the glaring inequality of the special prerogatives of the members of the Security Council and of the veto powers of its Permanent Members. At the other end of the political scale are the micro-states such as San Marino and Liechtenstein, whose foreign and defence policies are determined by others, despite their sovereign status. On the other hand such infringements of the principle of sovereign equality may be regarded as more apparent than real, since in their sovereign capacity the relevant states may be said to have expressly agreed to these inequalities in the first place. The veto of the five Permanent Members of the Security Council was accepted by all the powers at the UN's inaugural meeting in San Fransisco in 1945, though admittedly somewhat under duress since the Soviet Union and the United States had indicated that without the veto they were unlikely to join the world body. As for the micro-states, they could only afford to participate as full members of the international 'club' if other states agreed to be responsible for their defence and foreign affairs, so that again they may be said to have opted for second-class status.

There are also a number of other seeming legal inequalities which can be made to appear compatible with the notion of sovereign equality. Many of the apparent anomalies concern the question of jurisdictional independence. Though freedom from the juridical authority of outside bodies would appear to be a fundamental attribute of sovereign status, many a state seems to lack full control of its legislative, executive or judicial functions. With regard to the question of law-making capacity, in some countries the decisions of bodies such as the UN are automatically considered to be part of the law of the land, while the decisions of the European Council of Ministers are regarded as mandatory for the members of the EU. In addition, Community officials have the right of access to member countries to investigate any matter of common concern, regardless of whether or not their presence is desired in the country in question. The judgments, moreover, of the European Court of Human Rights have often overruled decisions of member parliaments, banning long-established practices (some might say perversions) such as the predisposition of the Courts of the Isle of Man to sanction a peculiar kind of beating for male offenders, known as birching, or of teachers in the rest of the United Kingdom to administer corporal punishment.

An even more seemingly fundamental infringement of sovereign status would appear to occur when one state is accorded the right of armed intervention in another—as was Britain as one of the guarantors of the independence of Cyprus in 1960. Ironically it was Britain's failure to intervene legally in response to the Greek inspired crypto-Fascist coup on the island in 1974 that led to the illegal, if understandable, intervention by Turkey, whose troops continue their occupation of the north of the island to this day. But if the presence of Turkish troops in Cyprus lacks legal sanction, there are plenty of instances where the appearance of foreign troops can be viewed as fully in accord with the law. For example, following the onset of the cold war in the late 1940s several states made over part of their territory for use by Soviet or American troops, in effect giving Moscow and Washington the right to exercise jurisdiction, since their bases were often granted certain immunities from the authority of the local courts. Perhaps the most glaring example is the continued use by the United States of the Guantanamo base on Cuba, a hangover from the days when the island was used as an American playground, casino and brothel. Meanwhile, the despatch of UN forces, whether to Korea, Kashmir, Egypt, the Congo, Cyprus, Cambodia, Croatia, Bosnia or wherever also entails certain immunities. Finally, there are instances, though declining in number, when the judicial authorities of one country are empowered to make decisions affecting the constitutional structure of another. For example, the House of Lords sitting in a juridical capacity retains the right to commute death sentences in as well as sanction changes in the constitutions of more than a dozen former colonial countries, now members of the Commonwealth. Though it has tended to act as a rubber stamp for what the legislators of those countries want, in recent years both Canada and Australia have had to take steps to, as it were, repatriate their constitution at times of political and legal turbulence.

Sovereign inequality?

In most though not all of the cases just outlined, the apparent inequalities can be explained as consistent with sovereign equality in that in their sovereign capacity, and for whatever reason, the powers whose rights have apparently been infringed have specifically agreed to such intrusions and to accept limitations on their exercise of sovereignty. Nor is there anything unusual in this since even the greatest power will agree to constrain its freedom of action if it believes its interests will be served thereby. After all, that is what happens whenever a state participates in a multilateral alliance. In this sense, there is no derogation of sovereignty. What, then, in law is this 'sovereignty' which is not necessarily infringed, eroded, violated or compromised by the kinds of examples just quoted? It seems that the irreducible minimum is what Professor Alan James calls 'constitutional self containment': in other words, when a country is not part of another's domain.[5] For example, even if, as is often said, California has the world's eighth-largest economy, it cannot sign treaties, exchange ambassadors or join international organisations because it is a part of the constitutional structure of the United States. By contrast Vanuatu and Nauru can do these things because they are constitutionally self-contained.

And here is a possible answer to those claiming that membership of the European Union means a loss of sovereignty. For no state is forced to join the organisation. However, if one joins that particular 'club' one agrees, as one does in becoming a member of any club, to abide by the rules. If one objects to the rules one can leave, though the political and economic costs of relinquishing membership of the European 'club' would probably be rather greater than that of leaving the Athanaeum or the MCC.

So far we have explored the sorts of inequalities that could be construed as being compatible with legal equality. But there are many inequalities that cannot be so regarded, and since some states are better placed than others to exercise and utilise their sovereign status, it is necessary to consider 'sovereignty' in a more broadly political context. Here the issue is no longer one of form as of substance: in particular, how far the sovereign authorities within the state are free to articulate and implement what they consider to be that state's interests. For though in law there cannot be degrees of sovereignty, politically, economically or culturally some states can be more sovereign than others, in the sense that they can exercise greater independence of initiative. Ever since the break up of Christendom, structural inequalities in the inter-state system have produced a kind of international political hierarchy.

6.5 CONSTRAINTS ON THE EXERCISE OF SOVEREIGNTY

In point of fact the various powers that make up the society of sovereign states are so disparate that their capacity to exercise their sovereignty can be affected by many different factors. As such they can be classified and ranked in diverse ways,[6] each giving some insight into the structural factors constraining state behaviour; the first is the relatively changeless factor of geography.

Geography

Though one should always be wary of anything resembling geographical determinism, there is no doubt that a country's place on the world map can condition and often seriously constrain what it is able to do internationally. At the one extreme there are the land-based, land-locked continental powers such as Austria, Zaire and Mongolia; at the other end of the spectrum are the maritime or oceanic states like Britain, Japan or New Zealand; and in addition there are countries like France, Germany and the United States which have both continental and maritime outlooks.

Evidence suggests that being a small offshore island off a politically restless continent has markedly affected the history, national attitudes and policy options of a Britain or a Japan. On the one hand there has been the perceived security need of strategies to prevent the domination of their respective continents by any state that could menace its security. In Britain, repeated 'Kraut'- and 'Frog'-bashing by the tabloids serve as a reminder that France and Germany have traditionally been seen as posing the major threats. In Japan, reluctance to relinquish the so-called 'northern islands' is a legacy of historic rivalries with Russia and China. On the other hand, their understanding of geography impelled both countries into overseas adventures and the acquisition of empire, formal or informal, and prompted reliance on the navy to protect trading and supply routes. This explains perhaps why Tokyo reacted so violently to Washington's threatened oil embargo in the late 1930s and London to Nasser's nationalisation of the Suez Canal Company in 1956. Meanwhile their respective insular positions have bred in both countries a kind of insular mentality, which expresses itself in national self-absorption and a resistance to continental labels, such as 'European' and 'Asian'.

Have the policies of the landlocked or continental powers been very different? Not necessarily, and yet it seems that a country occupying a land mass lacking any clear geographical boundaries with its neighbours—as, for example, Germany or Poland—will have its own distinct order of priorities and preoccupations. Germany was a reluctant overseas colonist, its main avenues of exploration and exploitation were over land, and since Poland stood in the way, the relations between the two countries were often fiercely antagonistic. At the end of the 18th century Prussia was largely responsible for Poland's disappearance from the map for a century and a quarter, and, together with Russia, Berlin secured in 1939 yet another carve-up of its Eastern neighbour. Not even their shared experience of Communist rule could eradicate the traditional ill-will between the East Germans and the Poles, and now that Communism has collapsed in both countries we see neo-Nazi violence in eastern Germany directed, among other targets, against Polish refugees.

Among other geographical variations is the spectrum between states in the vicinity of the traditional epicentres of conflict in the international system and those in much more remote areas. States inhabiting regions contiguous to the great trade routes, the strategic waterways or the sources of raw materials where the ambitions of the powerful tend to cut across one another suffer from a double disadvantage. They risk getting caught in the crossfire between antagonists and being drawn into a war not of their own choosing. Alternatively, they are in constant danger of becoming the client state of one or other antagonist in a high-risk tension area. This seems to be the fate, for example, of many a state in the Balkans, the traditional powder keg of Europe, and in the Middle East; whereas in areas remote from the main highways of world politics, in Iceland, perhaps, New Zealand or Portugal, no such dangers arise.

The social matrix

A second method of classification, with also a basis in geography, relates to what might be called the 'social matrix'. Clearly states characterised by a considerable degree of ethnic and cultural homogeneity such as the Scandinavian countries, Hungary and, again, Portugal may be spared some of the secessionist problems of heterogeneous states lacking any clear sense of identity or national solidarity. Unfortunately many of the Third World countries, being accidents of colonial rule rather than the products of indigenous social growth, are so prone to separatist revolts that their capacity to pursue coherent and effective policy is often severely impaired. There are also states where a combination of geography and history have left a legacy of political schizophrenia where they are torn, as it were, between competing cultures which can only complicate the process of policy-making. For example, the recently revived dispute in Russia between the Slavophiles and the Westernisers as well as the current contention in Turkey between the Islamicists and the secularisers reflect the geopolitical dilemmas of states with mixed European and Asiatic roots. In both countries, the instability that results from their political ambiva-lence has 'knock-on' effects not only in respect of their neighbours but with regard to their minorities such as the Chechen and Ingush peoples and, of course, the Kurds, who are frequently used as scapegoats when things go wrong for the government.

Political values and orientations

A related method of classifying states is in terms of political culture, value systems and behaviour patterns. For these may serve to shape not only a state's policies but also the process by which they are arrived at—demo-cratic, oligarchic, autocratic or whatever—and, in addition, the country's diplomatic style: combative or conciliatory, inflexible or flexible, assured or uncertain. From the time of the Peloponnesian war, ideological factors, and in particular the professed beliefs of ruling elites, have tended to heighten existing inter-state conflicts. They may also give rise to neutralist sentiments where certain powers refuse to take a stand between ideologi-cal antagonists. Often, however, as indicated in the previous chapter, ideo-logical disagreements compress into a simple antagonism—between those broadly in favour of the prevailing international status quo and the 'revi-sionists' desiring radical change. In between there may be those satisfied in respect of the system overall but dissatisfied with the state of affairs in a particular region, as was the United States with the balance in Eastern Europe during the cold war. Alternatively, a state might be content with the status quo in a particular region, as was the Soviet Union in respect of Eastern Europe, but dissatisfied with the general balance of advantage in world politics. Again, a state may appear 'revisionist' in relation to some countries, status quo in relation to others. It may also give different impressions to friend and foe. While, for example, the Soviet Union appeared to many in the West as a radically dissatisfied power which would stop at nothing to secure change in favour of Communism, the governments of Communist China, Albania and North Korea came to see Moscow as a broadly conservative force (as indeed did those in the West who felt that Washington was constantly overstating the Soviet 'threat').

Perhaps one should add, as a caveat, that while there are competing claims, interests and idea systems in the world, few governments can ever be wholly satisfied with the international order they face. On the other hand any power spearheading the struggle to preserve as much of the old order as possible tends to gather to itself a friendly constellation of the like minded as does the major proponent of change. But there remains the thorny question as to how far contending value systems cause and how far they reflect and rationalise conflicts of interest.

Position in the world economy

A further disparity among the states concerns their position in the world economy. Until comparatively recently the existence of economic inequality was more or less taken for granted. The division between rich and poor was regarded as a fact of life. However, with decolonisation and the plethora of new states—many industrially backward, suffering from rural overpopulation and the effects of low literacy, technical skills and per capita production—came the demand for an economic status commensurate with the sovereignty newly acquired. Thus the question of reforming the world economy was thrust on the international agenda. In the meetings, say, of the Non-aligned Movement, the UN Conference on Trade and Development (UNCTAD) and the Group of 77 (now expanded to over 130 countries), the demand was for a New International Economic Order. What was sought was: (1) a transfer of resources from richer to poorer states by means of development assistance; (2) easy access to Western markets and a preferential position in trade; and (3) a greater voice in the decision-making machinery of the International Monetary Fund (IMF), World Bank and other such institutions.

If the LDCs were hoping for a meaningful dialogue with the developed countries they were to be sadly disappointed. For while some influential Western voices like Brandt and Heath spoke of an interdependent world in which the fate of rich and poor were bound up together, others were far less sympathetic to the plight of the poorer countries. Some saw the so-called 'North/South divide' as a straightforward conflict of interests between free-market and Socialist economies. Others were not opposed to Western assistance as such but were strongly against the provision of government-to-government grants or subsidised loans. As the late Professor Peter Bauer wryly observed: such support amounted to 'poor people in rich countries [subsidising] rich people in poor countries';[7] and when the Group of 77, representing the more 'needy' states, tried to discuss matters with the 'rich man's club' known as G7, what followed was often a dialogue of the deaf.

True, at a time when dollars earned from the sale of oil ('petrodollars') were flooding into Western banks there was not just a willingness but an eagerness to lend to almost any potential customer. But when many an LDC found the burden of interest repayments far too onerous, the

Western finance institutions were often less than sympathetic, with the result that today many an LDC finds itself, like many a British mortgage holder, facing interest payments far larger than the capital originally borrowed. On the question of access to Western markets and a greater voice in the IMF, the Western powers have yielded little, and though they encourage the LDCs to raise export production, if only to pay off their debts, they often refuse—GATT notwithstanding—to take the goods the LDCs wish to sell.

In fact, many recent developments have conspired to widen the North/South gap. Naturally the wealthier countries have more capital to invest in new technologies which effectively reduces their need for the raw materials of the LDCs. The mass production, for example, of synthetic fibres lowers Western demand for the raw cotton or wool produced in the Third World, leading to a fall in their price on the world market. In addition, the technological inferiority of many an LDC, if combined with destabilising political and ethnic divisions and the baleful effects of often corrupt and inefficient government, produces spectacular falls in living standards, in countries such as Somalia, Angola and Mozambique taking a heavy daily tally of lives. Though various aid agencies try to fill the breach, their help is nowhere near sufficient to provide first aid, let alone aid for development.

In face of the failure of the West to meet many of the demands of the LDCs, some radical economists and political scientists have suggested radical solutions such as world revolution, self-sufficiency, self-help among the LDCs and selective delinking from the world economy. In practice, however, both liberal/conservative and radical panaceas have often proved woefully defective. Socialism has not been a conspicuous success in the Third World, nor the free market in the post-Communist states of Eastern Europe. On the other hand the experience of the NICs like Singapore, South Korea, Taiwan, Indonesia, Malaysia as well as the oil-rich states of the Middle East indicates that change is possible and that the old North/South division can be bridged if pragmatism replaces dogmatism.

There is, however, a paradox about the distribution of economic wealth. Ironically, many so-called 'poor' countries are far more richly endowed with resources than many of the so-called 'rich' countries. In terms of raw materials, Japan, Taiwan and Singapore are far less well supplied than China; Germany has far less mineral wealth than Russia, and it is hard to see what Switzerland produces in abundance other than magnificent scenery and chocolate bars. Yet these largely under-resourced countries are among the world's top economies. What seems to be crucial, therefore, is less what a state has in terms of resources as what it does with those it has. Certainly the most successful appear to have education and enterprise in abundance. Perhaps the LDCs would be better advised to invest in these rather than, as so often, in prestige projects and arms.

Military capacity

In many ways the diversity which most graphically underlines the divergence between sovereignty in principle and in practice lies in the ranking
of the powers in some kind of pecking order from small to medium, to
great to superpower status.[8] Such classifications of the standing of particular countries represent a kind of international consensus as to the range of
interests of particular powers—whether local, regional, intercontinental or
global—their ability to defend those interests, their influence among the
nations and the extent to which their concerns need to be taken into
account by others. Such estimates tend to be based in part on some of the
classifications already alluded to—geography, social mix, ideology and
economic strength—but also on a calculation of potential military capacity
in the light of past military achievements. The ascription, for example, of
'great power' status suggests a state that cannot be ignored in diplomatic
discussion because it has world-wide interests and influence and a more
than even chance of attaining objectives. In this sense 'greatness' bears no
relation to size, since some of the powers meriting that ascription—
Holland and Britain, for example—have been comparatively small in area.
Clearly, however, with the imputation of 'greatness' goes the responsibility for maintaining what is called 'world order' (another of those tricky
concepts, to be discussed in a later chapter). In the 19th century it was left
to the Concert of Europe: in the 20th century to those with permanent
seats in the Councils of the League and the UN.

6.6 THE GRADING OF THE POWERS

As international politics are a dynamic process, ascriptions of rank tend to
change with changing circumstances. Since the standing of at least three of
the permanent members of the Security Council—Britain, France and
Russia—has been much reduced in recent years, there is a real question as
to whether they should be allowed to maintain their veto powers at the
expense, say, of countries like Japan and Germany, whose interests and
influence are probably no less than theirs. Conceivably we may now be
moving into a world in which the chief criterion in determining a country's esteem is not so much its military as its economic potential, and in
this sense there could be many a new great power on the horizon, with a
corresponding reduction in rank for some of the old; though doubtless
they will strive to cling on to the privileges as well as the responsibilities of
imputed greatness.

Given that recent military, technological and economic developments
are often said to have eroded the base of sovereignty, it is as well to
conclude with a discussion of why sovereign status remains such a live
issue.

6.7 THE CONTINUING RELEVANCE OF SOVEREIGNTY

In the first place, while it is obvious that nowadays the state is neither invulnerable nor impermeable, it is questionable as to whether it ever was. Yet the principle of sovereignty was able to withstand centuries of penetration from international, transnational, subnational and supranational forces, and there seems no reason why it should not continue to endure, even if the doctrine of non-intervention is not as hallowed as it once was.

Second, recent developments in technology have, if anything, enhanced the ability of the medium and small powers to exercise sovereignty.[9] The very strength of the Soviet Union and the United States tended to make them musclebound to a degree, and in the end Moscow proved unable to prevail over its recalcitrant neighbours to its east, west and south, while the United States failed to humble Vietnam, Cambodia, Laos, Iran, Iraq, Lebanon, Libya and Cuba.

Third, while secessionism poses a very real threat to the political contours of many existing states, it represents no threat to the state system as such. Secessionists do not want to destroy international society. They want to join it.

Fourth, the fact that the present number of sovereign states is nearly four times that of 1945 and rising suggests that the sovereignty principle is as much prized today as it ever was. Kashmiris and Kurds, Palestinians and Punjabi Sikhs, Abhazians and Basques all want to be allowed to give political expression to their sense of separateness. If they want *de jure* rather than *de facto* sovereignty, who are we to tell them that it is illusory and that they simply cannot run their own show?

Fifth, if many who lack sovereign status wish to have it, it is also increasingly clear that those, say, in Western Europe, afraid that they might lose sovereignty to the bureaucrats in Brussels, wish to reassert it. That, surely, is the real message of the recent rows over Maastricht, the Exchange Rate Mechanism (ERM) and the voting procedures to follow the enlargement of the Union.

NOTES

1. Bodin, J., *Six Books of the Commonwealth* (trans. Tooley, M.J.), Blackwell, Oxford, undated.
2. On the establishment of sovereign statehood see Brierly, J.L., *The Law of Nations*, New York, 1949, pp. 122–35.
3. Goodwin, G.L., 'The erosion of external sovereignty' in *Government and Opposition*, vol. 9, no. 1, Winter 1974.
4. See Duchacek, I., *Nations and Men: An Introduction to International Politics*, New York, Holt, Rinehart and Winston, 1971, pp. 146–8.
5. James, A., *Sovereign Statehood*, London, Allen and Unwin, 1986.

6. For a thoroughgoing taxonomy see Northedge, F.S., *The International Political System*, London, Faber, 1976, pp. 154–76.

7. Bauer, P., 'The case against aid' in *Millennium*, vol. 2, no. 2, 1973, p. 13.

8. Purnell, R., *The Society of States*, London, Weidenfeld & Nicolson, 1973, pp. 66–107 and Wight, M., *Power Politics*, London, Penguin, 1979, pp. 61–7 and 295–301.

9. A point noted by Herz, J. who, in an article, 'The territorial state revisited', *Polity* 1, 1968, pp. 11–34 revised the main thrust of his argument on 'The rise and demise of the territorial state' in *World Politics*, 9, 1957, pp. 473–93.

CHAPTER 7

NATIONALISM: THE NATION AND THE IMAGINATION

In *The Invention of Tradition*, a book he part-edited, the Marxist historian Eric Hobsbawm points out that many of the things we assume to have existed since time immemorial are of comparatively recent origin and the product of conscious design. For example, the 'traditional' British Christmas, complete with carols, Christmas trees, yule logs and Santa Claus was largely a 19th-century creation in which two people played a key role—Prince Albert with his memories of Christmas in Germany and Charles Dickens with his tale, *A Christmas Carol*. Likewise, what we know today as the Scottish kilt, widely regarded as of ancient lineage, was invented in the 1730s by an English Quaker from Lancashire, while the tartan whose colour and pattern are supposed to be an indicator of clan was designed as part of a pageant devised by Sir Walter Scott in the early 19th century. And if these 'inventions' did nothing else, at least they offered a life line to the Scottish home woollen industry.

As to the ceremonials associated with the British royals, these, according to the same source, are also comparatively recent inventions. Until the mid-Victorian period, people were on the whole indifferent or hostile to royalty because of the sexual exploits, extravagance and political interference of the often foreign-born monarchs, and any regal ceremonials would in any case have aroused little interest. In fact not until the 1870s, by which time the electoral franchise had been extended and Queen Victoria had given up any pretension to a political role, was she required to engage in public ceremonials and parade periodically in a splendid state coach. Meanwhile, the clergy, now dressed in copes and coloured stoles, were on hand in an increasingly media-conscious age to give a spectacular religious aura to whatever ritual the politicians devised for her. Soon there were invented or reinvented such 'traditions' as the ceremonial state opening of parliament—parliament itself being a largely 19th-century reconstruction in Gothic style—the anointing of the monarch in coronations, the lying in state at royal funerals, the 'traditional' Christmas message and other such 'showbiz' spectaculars for the benefit of a public now being encouraged to admire or even love the royals.

7.1 THE 'NATION' AND THE IMAGINATION

According to the same source, like the 'traditional' Christmas, the 'traditional' royal ceremonials, the 'traditional' tartan and kilt, nationalism and the nation to which it refers are also of comparatively recent origin, even if they relate to forms of identification that are much older. Often, Hobsbawm contends: 'even historical continuity [has] to be invented, e.g., by [the creation of] an ancient past...either by semi-fiction'—a reference here to characters such as Boadicea—'or by forgery', and he mentions the 'manufacture' in the 17th century of supposedly early texts designed to show that the Scottish highlanders were an indigenous people and not the descendants of fairly recent invaders from Ireland. He goes on to detail the fabrication in the 18th century of symbols such as the national anthem or the national flag and of images—'Marianne' and 'Germania', pugnacious 'John Bull' and the lean Yankee, 'Uncle Sam'— 'designed to foster national sentiment'. And he continues, 'the very appearance of movements describing themselves as "traditionalist"... indicates a break with the past...Where the old ways are alive, traditions need be neither revived nor invented.' Later he talks of 'innovators...generating their own invented traditions', including, significantly, the rewriting of history. 'The history which [becomes] part of a fund of knowledge or the ideology of nation, state or movement is not what has actually been preserved in popular memory, but what has been selected, written, pictured, popularised and institutionalised by those whose function it is to do so.'[1] As an historian Hobsbawm should know!

To anyone such as the present author who has actually witnessed the invention of an historical tradition, as when in the days before the current turmoil in what was Yugoslavia he saw builders in the historic city of Dubrovnik constructing totally new 'medieval' ramparts, all this has the ring of truth.

7.2 THE EVOLUTION OF THE NATIONAL IDEA

The idea of the nation as essentially a construct built on myth is the theme of another volume also written by a Marxist, Benedict Anderson, and with another revealing title, *Imagined Communities*. In seeking to place nationalism in historical perspective he argues that five major factors encouraged its rise: first, the decline of the universal Church and the growth of separate and largely autonomous national or state churches; the invention of the printing press which, harnessed to capitalism, facilitated the transmission of novel ideas; the slow but perceptible displacement of Latin in official communications by indigenous vernacular languages; the gradual weakening of dynasticism and monarchy in the 18th century; and changing conceptions of time in which a concept such as the nation could, rather like the *New Testament*, be made to appear simultaneously as both radically new and yet encompassing the best or even the fulfilment of some earlier tradition.

The most original part of Anderson's thesis relates to the geographical genesis of nationalism. Most scholars have tended to accept that nationalism, whether or not an invention, originated either in Europe or among Europeans. Not so, says Anderson, who traces the concept to the Creole communities of Central and Latin America in the wake of the tightening of Spanish control, together with the spread of Enlightenment ideas in the latter half of the 18th century. However, neither is sufficient in itself to explain the political contours of Latin-American nationalism for, according to Anderson, 'the very vastness of the Spanish American empire, the enormous variety of its soils and climates and, above all, the immense difficulties of communications in a pre-industrial age' combined to ensure that any sense of nationhood was based on 'the original...American administrative units marking the spatial limits of particular military conquests'. How such administrative units came to be conceived of as fatherlands, says Anderson, was the work largely of disaffected Creole functionaries, indispensible to the stability of the empire and yet economically subjected and exploited, 'even though in terms of language, religion, ancestry or manners' they were 'largely indistinguishable from the Spain-born Spaniard', who tended to fare better.[2]

Yet, it might be objected, it is all very well to dismiss nationalism as an invention and to locate its origins somewhere between the Gulf of Mexico and Tierra del Fuego, but what of the claims of the Egyptians and Ethiopians, Chinese or Celts, Greeks or Jews who believe they are in some sense special and that they can trace their national ancestry back thousands of years? Are they not entitled to assert an unbroken sense of nationhood thousands of years old? Well, yes and no.

7.3 PRE-NATIONAL SOCIAL GROUPS

First, no one, not even Eric Hobsbawm or Benedict Anderson, suggests that the national idea emerges in a vacuum. Before there were nations there were social groups such as extended families, clans and tribes as well as societies with some sense of a common ethnic, cultural or religious identity; there were also socio-political entities such as city states, provinces and principalities, which produced local loyalties as well as select groups of state functionaries who identified with associations larger than themselves or their immediate family.

Moreover, some of the sentiments we associate with modern nationalism were not unknown in an earlier age. In, for example, Shakespeare's evocation of England in *Henry V*, such emotions are given powerful expression:

> This fortress built by nature for herself against infection and the hand of war; this happy breed of men, this little world, this precious stone set in the silver sea, which serves it in the office of a wall, or as a moat defensive to a house, against the envy of less happier lands; this blessed plot, this earth, this realm, this England.

In another work, *Nations and Nationalism since 1780*, Hobsbawm dubs such sentiments 'proto-nationalist', suggesting a kind of inchoate, inarticulate, ill-formed, primitive nationalism.[3] And if to the early 18th-century writer Dr Samuel Johnson, 'patriotism', that is, civic loyalty, love of country and of service to the state, was 'the last refuge of a scoundrel', he was presumably alluding dismissively to a sentiment reasonably widespread at the time. And, indeed, the word 'patria', like many of the other terms from which the vocabulary of nationalism is derived, has a long history. References to the 'patria' or fatherland can be found as early as Roman times. The Romans also used the word '*natio*', by which they meant people lacking political community or direction, a term which they applied to, among others, the Jews. In medieval Spanish the word was used as a synonym for 'foreigner'—as when they talked of 'nations' of foreign merchants—and it was more broadly used of a community of scholars, as in the German, Czech and Polish 'nations' of Prague University when it was founded in the 14th century. And though as early as the 16th century the term '*Volk*' began to be used in German of a group of people of common descent (thereby anticipating some of the modern associations of the term 'nation'), by the 18th century the term seems to have been used to indicate the entire population of a province or state regardless of origins.

On the other hand even if terms such as '*natio*', '*patria*' and '*volk*' had a history, it is clear that their early connotations were rather different from their modern implications, though both ancient and modern usages testify to the fact that humans need to feel a part of some sort of community or imagined community which appears to enshrine their hopes and to serve their interests. But though the sense of solidarity and the feeling of fellowship remains through time, the national idea, superimposed on earlier concerns for commonality, represents something new.

7.4 THE NOVELTY OF 'NATIONALISM'

What was novel and distinct was that its defenders from the late 18th century onwards had sought to identify the nation in terms of a specific location and composition and to give to it a specifically political and secular dimension hitherto lacking.[4] Though there might have been disagreement on the precise origins and political contours of the nation, most nationalists assumed that nations could be identified objectively, that they had interests, discoverable by those entitled to act as interpreter and that those interests were to be given appropriate political expression. Though this doctrine of national self-determination generally implied sovereign statehood, Puerto Rico's emphatic rejection of independence in 1993 and the Welsh nationalist bid for little more than cultural autonomy suggests a more varied nationalist agenda. Even so, there remained the problem of the precise definition of the nation, of determining which of the many human collectivities should be labelled in this way and of distinguishing it from other kinds of socio-political organisations.

7.5 CRITICAL DISTINCTIONS

Perhaps the first distinction to make, since the two are often interfused, is between state and nation. Though the term 'state' can be used in a number of different senses, in discussions relating to international relations and world politics it generally refers to an administrative unit based on territoriality. If, moreover, the unit in question acquires legal status we call it a 'sovereign state'. But the nation is not an administrative unit, nor does it ever have sovereign status. It comprises a group of politically aware people, but rarely does any state encompass all the people and only the people who wish to identify with it—and in this sense seldom do nation and state coincide. It is a pity, therefore, that in American English the term 'nation state' tends to be used as a synonym for sovereign state, that Jeremy Bentham invented the term 'international relations' when by and large he was referring to inter-state relations and that we refer today to the League of Nations and the United Nations, thereby confounding still further an already confusing set of concepts. Apart from anything else, the idea of the state was in existence long before the modern notion of the nation, and in this sense the sentiment of patriotism—of love of country and of loyalty to the state, conceived of as a fatherland—was around well before the rise of modern nationalism.

Another important distinction is between tribe and nation. A tribe comprises a group of people with certain characteristics in common, physical as well as cultural. Its basis, therefore, is ethnic. Ethnicity, cultural and physical kinship and tradition, is what differentiates one tribe from another. The nation, too, refers to a group of people but is an infinitely more elastic concept than that of the tribe; and attempts to give it precise definition are usually doomed to failure, not least because its defenders have tended to be more interested in propaganda than in description.

7.6 THE NATION: 'OBJECTIVE' CRITERIA

Language

In the 19th century, many writers, especially in central, eastern and south-eastern Europe (people like the German Fichte, the Czech Palacký and the Russian Danilevsky), claimed that 'language' was 'the badge of nation-hood', that which distinguished 'us' from 'them', the lofty civilisations from the barbarians who made incomprehensible noises.[5] After all, the fact that our first impressions in life are formulated and expressed in the language we hear in our infancy tends to establish in our minds an intimate association between our speech and the wider society from which we take our word-stock. We talk, in fact, of a 'native tongue', even though in the era before mass education, only the literate elites could have had access to anything resembling a national language. For the rest there were just local dialects transmitted orally from one generation to another. In this sense national languages were the opposite of what nationalist propagandists supposed them to be. They were not the primordial formulation of national culture but the constructs of those who wanted to devise a standard idiom out of a multiplicity of spoken dialects and for the purpose employed a host of grammarians, orthographers who created a written language and lexicographers who compiled dictionaries. Yet as if oblivious to this point, 19th-century Polish, Czech, Hungarian, Croat, Norwegian and other nationalists began to encourage the development and study of what they called 'indigenous' literature, while other nationalists devoted themselves to the study of languages that had seemed in terminal decay such as Irish, Welsh and Hebrew. If language was the decisive factor, what of the Swiss with their several languages? What of the English- or Spanish-speaking peoples, so divided in their national loyalties or of those linguistic Poles and Slovenes who preferred to think of themselves, for whatever reasons, as Germans or Austrians respectively?

Religion

Others sought to root the nation in religion which might have seemed plausible to the Poles, the Irish or even the Jews but would hardly have applied to the British or Germans with their several religious denominations. Nor is there much evidence that a common religious heritage, say, as between Iran, Iraq and Syria or between Pakistan and Bangladesh makes for a common feeling of solidarity.

Ethnicity

Others again claimed to see the key in ethnic identity. But with the depopulation and resettlement of large areas of the world in face of the ravages of man and of nature, common descent is difficult to establish. People tend to be multifarious in their origins. In any case, though ethnicity as a basis for the nation might have a certain appeal to the Armenians, the Greeks or even the Basques, it would hardly strike a chord with the polyglot Americans or, indeed, the Somalis, whose perceived common descent engenders no corresponding sense of national solidarity. Conversely one often finds among the most ardent champions of a particular nation people who have little or no historical claim to it. Napoleon, for example, was not French but Corsican, Hitler was not German but Austrian and probably part-Jewish, Stalin was not Russian but Georgian, while the Cossacks who fought so valiantly for Russia throughout the ages were polyglots. If none of the objective tests is entirely satisfactory, perhaps the key may be found in subjective factors—in collective consciousness and the sense not of nationality (which normally refers to citizenship) but of nationhood, a far more nebulous concept.

7.7 THE NATION: THE SUBJECTIVE APPROACH

Here philosophers, historians and psychologists can come to our aid. According to the 19th-century British philosopher J.S. Mill, the nation comprised people 'united among themselves by common sympathies, which do not exist between them and any others—which make them...desire to be under the same government and desire that it should be government by themselves or a portion of themselves exclusively'.[6] A nation, according to another 19th-century thinker, the French historian Ernest Renan, 'supposes a past, but it is contained in the present in a tangible fact: the common feeling, the clearly expressed desire to continue life in common. A nation...exists by virtue of a daily plebiscite.'[7] In other words a nation is a self-contained group of people who put loyalty to the group as a whole above competing loyalties. And an American psychologist, W.S. Pillsbury, writing after the first world war summed up the nation as offering for each member 'something more than an abstraction. He identifies himself with it as a part of himself, he suffers pain when it is diminished, he rejoices with it as it thrives. It becomes almost as much a centre of his emotion as is himself.'[8] By this test, then, the nation would appear to be the repository of the same kinds of partisan sentiments as are generally reserved for *our* team, *our* tribe or *our* faith at a time of challenge.

Anomalies

Even if the nation is best discussed in subjective rather than objective terms, here, too, there may be anomalies, especially when membership of a particular nation is claimed on behalf of people who may not wish to be so considered: for example, when children of Jamaican immigrants to Britain who see themselves as British are regarded by their parents or by their black friends or by white racists as Jamaicans; or, again, when children of Irish, Polish, Pakistani, Chinese or Jewish parents are similarly classified by others as belonging to a national category from which they may wish to escape. On the other hand, these are anomalies, and if we take the national idea to rest on a collective sentiment the obvious question is how does this national self-consciousness arise? To this question several objective answers are possible since historically the notion of the nation has arisen in different parts of the world in response to different sorts of stimuli.

Prerequisites

If, as was argued earlier, the state, in the sense of an administrative unit based on territoriality, preceded the nation ie people conceiving of themselves collectively as constituting a nation among nations and wishing to give political expression to their shared sense of solidarity, the earliest indications of national self-consciousness in a modern sense must have occurred within the established sovereign states of Western Europe. On the other hand, such sentiments could not have been properly developed until a kind of cultural fusion had occurred. After all, each such state comprised an often lethal cocktail of peoples. In medieval England there were Saxons and those whose language was French, Cornish or Welsh; the English language emerging eventually from a synthesis largely of Saxon and French. In France there were the Bretons, Normans, Provençaux, Burgundians, Flemings, Germans, Basques and Catalans in addition to the French, themselves largely an amalgam of Gauls and Romans. In Scotland the blend was of Celt, Saxon and Norwegian, while in Spain the mix comprised people of Roman, Visigothic, Arab and Basque origin as well as peoples of even remoter antiquity; the Spanish language emanating from Castile. Even after the consolidation of the various monarchies of these countries, there would have been for some time little in the way of a national consciousness given that people's physical horizons were largely confined to a few miles from their place of birth and their intellectual horizons governed by the teachings of the Church or Mosque and circumscribed by their inability to read or write.

However, once developments in commerce and communications had made travel, both internal and foreign, easier, at least for the nascent middle class, and the kinds of provincial loyalties displayed in, say, the Wars of the Roses were displaced by a broader sense of obligation to central authority, the potential was there, if not for proto-nationalism, then at least for patriotic sentiment, especially in time of war. After all, as suggested earlier, people do like to support their team and by the end of the 18th century many writers and composers, priests and prelates, traders and merchants had become accomplices, wittingly or unwittingly, in an attempt by court officials and government administrators to convince fellow citizens that the state and its citizens constituted just such a team. It was a process assisted in the 18th century by the circulation of materials designed to emphasise, even exaggerate, the differences between 'them' and 'us'. There were quasi-historical fantasies dwelling on 'our' virtues in contrast to 'their' failings; there was a growing litany of national saints, heroes and martyrs for our emulation, of sinners, villains and reprobates for our condemnation, in addition to the anthems, emblems, flags, monuments, shrines and other symbols designed to arouse feelings of national solidarity. By the time of the French Revolutionary wars there were Frenchmen, rather than Burgundians and Normans, Englishmen rather than men of Kent or Sussex, Spaniards rather than Castilians; and objective conditions began to favour if not national self-consciousness as such, then at least nationalist movements, many led by intellectuals—the quintessential inventers of tradition—whose function was to generate national self-awareness.

The role of the adversary

On the other hand the existence of a suitable adversary which could be portrayed as the national enemy probably contributed most to the rapid spread of nationalist sentiment. Indeed, nationalism, rather like Communism with which it has a number of common characteristics, is often in part a creation of its enemies. That is, it has tended to arise in a context of perceived deprivation seemingly occasioned by power-holders utterly impervious and unresponsive to pleas for changes in the structure of political or economic power. In this sense nationalist movements come to serve as repositories of discontent and instruments for securing what their adherents conceive as justice. As often as not their demands or claims are based on a highly selective understanding of history, but it is partly because so many nationalist movements define themselves primarily in terms of what they are against that the phenomenon of nationalism has come to be associated with so many apparently incompatible political platforms: from extreme left to extreme right, from popular sovereignty to 'ethnic cleansing' and 'the final solution', from the ballot to the bullet, from a platform for political integration to a programme for political fragmentation.[9]

If Anderson is right, then modern nationalism in its negative guise first surfaced in Latin America as the Creole functionaries sought to right what they considered a double wrong: subordination to a foreign country, Spain, and further subordination to Spanish- and American-born Hispanics. Here, therefore, nationalism is identified not just with anti-imperialism but with anti-colonialism and anti-racism as well ie with resistance to domination by so-called 'thoroughbred' settlers from the mother country and their descendants. However, there would seem to be a problem in equating such anti-imperialist, anti-colonialist and anti-racist sentiments with nationalism. For once the source of the discontent is removed, as when, for example, Spain finally relinquished its American colonies and the expatriates lost some of their privileges, how much of a sense of solidarity remains? What, in other words, of the nation? True, the two-week so-called 'football war' between Honduras and El Salvador in 1969 following a disputed result in a match between the national teams suggests that some Latin Americans literally support their country as people support a team. But the experience of much of Latin America, together with much of Africa, Asia and Eastern Europe is that either the sense of national self-consciousness is altogether lacking or that narrow parochial or tribal loyalties still prove far stronger than loyalty to the whole state and its citizens, with often catastrophic results for internal order.

The next manifestation of nationalism in its negative guise is well documented: the revolt of the 13 American Colonies against the unrepresentative and exploitative power of the British Crown. Here the mainspring is also anti-imperialism, even though some of the complainants would have been expatriates from the country they now accused of oppressing them. However, the institution of slavery and the experience of bloody civil war in the 1860s indicates that once again the success of an anti-imperialist strategy failed to consolidate any feeling of nationhood. The American federalist motto 'E pluribis unum' seemed for a long time more an aspiration than a reality. On the other hand, despite vast disparities and distances between one part of the United States and another and periodic eruptions of racial violence, it would be difficult to deny the development, albeit recently, of a sense of American nationhood. Here education, the media, the manipulation of symbols and rituals have all played their part. Once again the existence of perceived adversaries had been of invaluable assistance in speeding the process. First there were the 'heartless' Spanish and British imperialists, then the 'Godless' Nazis followed by the 'Godless' Communists...and now what? Could some prominent Americans be desperately searching for an enemy to try to piece together a Union that is in danger of falling apart at the seams? If so, could they have found the answer in either Islamic fundamentalism or Japanese protectionism?

Following the American revolution, the next major manifestation of what is called nationalism was in France. Here, however, the adversary was not foreign but domestic. Armed with the ideas of the Enlightenment and with Rousseau's call to break the 'chains' inhibiting man's freedom, the revolutionaries declared war on feudalism, patronage and privilege in the name of the French 'nation', by which they appeared to mean just about anyone entitled to French citizenship. Basically their nationalism was an assertion that government should be by consent and that the locus of sovereignty should be transferred from monarch to people. There were, however, two problems with French revolutionary nationalism. One was that the revolutionaries sought equality and fraternity as well as liberty, and the two are not always easy to reconcile. If you want an egalitarian society then you have to curb the liberties of those who do better than others, as is supposed to happen in a Socialist country; if the emphasis is on freedom, an inegalitarian society is likely to be the result. The second problem was that France was far too large to be run like the Swiss cantons Rousseau so admired, in whose governance theoretically every adult male had a voice. In general, therefore, Rousseau's 'general will' required interpretation, and as so often happens the interpreters tended to be self-appointed and at odds with one another. Hence during the revolutionary period the country lurched from one kind of rule to another, ending up with the Napoleonic dictatorship. Once again the attempt to effect an apparently liberal doctrine had had unexpected and untoward results.

Moreover, the greater the dissension between France's new rulers, the greater their tendency to want to internationalise the struggle against the old order. Thanks to that peculiar institution of revolutionary nationalism, the *levée en masse* (conscription), France had a formidable array of armed might at its disposal to force, as it were, the rest of Europe to be free. For a time it succeeded. By 1812, at the height of the Napoleonic dominion, the only entirely independent states left in Europe were Britain, Russia and the Ottoman empire—all on the margins of the continent and largely immune to the revolutionary appeal.

On the other hand the revolutionary message the French forces took with them was to prove only too attractive. For the peoples now under French hegemony were being treated as subordinates, not equals, and sought liberation from their somewhat oppressive 'liberators'. Once again nationalism had emerged in the guise of anti-imperialism, but this time it also evoked more positive feelings as well, and these were to remain following the final defeat of Napoleon in 1815. In Western Europe the national idea continued to mean what it had meant for the architects of the French Revolution—individual liberties and constitutional guarantees against arbitrary power. By and large that is what they got, and the peoples of Western Europe now felt themselves to be citizens rather than subjects and came to see their states as an expression of their nationhood. However, in Central and Eastern Europe it was a different story.

Here, within the vast empires of the Ottomans, Russians and Austrians as well as the politically fragmented regions of Italian and German civilisation, the priority among nationalists was not so much the civic virtues of liberal democracy as the eradication of all impediments to cultural and linguistic self-expression. That Greeks should have to speak in Turkish in official communications, that Poles should have to speak in Russian or

German and Czechs in German or Hungarian was increasingly unaccept-able, though no more intolerable than that Italian- and German-speaking peoples should be parcelled out among a number of different states; and so the nationalist emphasis shifted from a political/territorial to a cultural/linguistic concept. In its Central and Eastern European guise, nationalists came to reverse the traditional state/nation process. Here nationalist movements sought a redrawing of the political map along linguistic and cultural lines, and between the 1820s and the 1920s they more or less succeeded. But at a price.

7.8 IMPACT ON WORLD POLITICS

In the first place, national liberation did not necessarily bring with it indi-vidual liberty, and many within the new nations probably had less personal, political and economic freedom after independence than before. In this sense there are some interesting parallels with the more recent post-imperial experience of countries like Iraq, Malawi, Burma and, of course, Bosnia.

Second, far from exhibiting satisfaction with their countries' newly acquired independent status, some of their leaders were constantly seek-ing to expand their terrain at the expense of their neighbours, while depriving their national minorities of the kinds of rights they had claimed for themselves. It is this kind of behaviour that discredited nationalism in the eyes of many liberals who had originally endorsed it, and in turn it generated a plethora of destabilising claims from the so-called 'suppressed' and 'submerged' nationalities against the so-called 'historic' nations: with Slovenes and Croats disputing the historic claims of nation-alist Italy; Slovenes, Croats, Serbs and Romanians repudiating the whole idea of a Greater Hungary; the Czechs questioning German predominance in Bohemia; the Ukrainians, Byelorussians and Lithuanians challenging the political contours of the newly restored Poland in 1920. The national principle may have united 19th-century Italy and Germany but has contin-ued to cause the disintegration of far more states and has repeatedly injected fresh uncertainties into the workings of international society.

Third, since the end of the 19th century, nationalism has been hijacked by ideologues, left and right, religious and secular to suit their various purposes, again having capitalised on popular discontents and resent-ments. As E.H. Carr put it in his book *Nationalism and After*, 'the socialisa-tion of the nation has as its natural corollary the nationalisation of socialism'.[10] In the newly Socialist states capitalism, Western imperialism and religion were the proclaimed enemies. However, in a country like Nazi Germany, where nationalism tended to become the ideology of the right, the enemy was the Socialist, as well as the Jew, the pacifist, the gipsy or the socially inadequate who could be portrayed as having sapped the country of its vitality. And of course in much of post-war Asia and Africa nationalism served both left- and right-wing ideologues, first in the cause of freedom from imperial rule and then against a host of domestic or foreign targets which could be blamed for all or most of the new country's problems. Where, as in its most recent manifestation, it becomes identified with some kind of religious fundamentalism, as in Iran, India, Israel, Bosnia or even Northern Ireland, it tends to be especially intransigeant and prone to violence.

7.9 NATIONALISM: RISE AND FALL

Thus nationalism is a sufficiently plastic notion to have been equated with all manner of contradictory phenomena—with popular sovereignty and liberal democracy, with anti-imperialism, anti-colonialism and anti-racism, with Socialism/Communism, with Conservatism, with Fascism, Nazism and religious fundamentalism. It is also the word we use of governments which behave internationally in an especially aggressive way and of a group of people seeking to secede from such states. In addition we use it of political movements which try to whip up national sentiment and also of governments attempting to create a unified state out of a host of tribal, ethnic and linguistic groupings in a country whose political contours are an accident of colonial rule. How they do it today in countries such as Nigeria, Bangladesh and Croatia is the way they have always done it—by the creation of myths, the use of symbols and rituals and by the invention of traditions.

But what accounts for the sudden rise of a nationalist movement? In the cases of, say, the Palestinians or Bangladeshis it can be attributed to a sudden shared predicament or misfortune. The Six-Day war which saw the Israelis in occupation of the West Bank and Gaza from 1967 helped to solidify among people that had formerly considered themselves to be Arabs or Bedouin a sense of Palestinian self-consciousness. A series of disastrous floods in East Pakistan in 1970, combined with the failure of the government in West Pakistan to disburse to the East the massive aid which had flowed in, led to a sudden rise in Bangladeshi national self-consciousness and a desire to be rid of the now thoroughly alien government in Islamabad. By the same token, when the conditions that gave rise to nationalist sentiment disappear, that heightened sense of national identity can disappear with it and more parochial feelings surface which in time can give rise to secessionist impulses.

Finally, to return to the question posed earlier, cannot many modern nations claim their ancestry from peoples of ancient times? Possibly, but given the degree of inter-marriage, miscegenation and of illegitimacy throughout the ages, it is doubtful whether any such claim can be very meaningful, and this is precisely where the element of myth and make-believe tends to come in. Could it really be that Mussolini, that obese narcissistic little man with the loud voice who created Fascism in Italy, was a true descendant of those Romans that conquered and civilised whole continents? Was the dark little man with a black moustache and an ill-fitting raincoat who invented National Socialism really a product of Aryan culture and race? And can the Aryans be considered a race at all? And do some of those agnostics presiding over Israel's fortunes today have much in common with the 12 desert tribes of biblical times wandering in search of a theocracy? More importantly, perhaps, could any so-called 'ancestor' have thought in terms of the secular territorial state, a standard national language, representative government and some of the other notions many contemporary nationalists appear to cherish? In all these and more there would appear to have been a decisive break with tradition.

NOTES

1. Hobsbawm, E., 'Introduction: Inventing Traditions' in Hobsbawm, E. and Ranger, T. (eds), *The Invention of Tradition*, Cambridge, Cambridge University Press, 1983, pp. 1–14.
2. Anderson, B., *Imagined Communities*, London, Verso, 1991, pp. 47–58.
3. Hobsbawm, E., *Nations and Nationalism since 1780*, Cambridge, Cambridge University Press, 1990, p. 75.
4. Gellner, E., *Nations and Nationalism*, Oxford, Blackwell, 1992, pp. 1–7 and 49–62.
5. Hobsbawm, E., op. cit. pp. 51–63 and 93–100.
6. Mill, J.S., *Utilitarianism, Liberty and Representative Government*, London, Dent, 1910, pp. 365–6.
7. Quoted in Zimmern, A., *Modern Political Doctrines*, New York, Oxford University Press, 1939, pp. 202–5.
8. Pillsbury, W.D., *Psychology of Nations*, London, Macmillan, 1919, p. 59.
9. Hobsbawm, E., op. cit., especially pp. 163–72.
10. Carr, E.H., *Nationalism and After*, London, Macmillan, 1945, p. 19.

CHAPTER 8

THE MAKING OF FOREIGN POLICY

It has become fashionable among the more 'trendy' teachers of International Relations to claim that domestic and foreign policy are so closely interlinked that there is little point in trying to differentiate between them. And yet almost anyone familiar with the layout of a newspaper or of a radio or television bulletin will know the distinction between a foreign and a domestic news story, and if a particular item merits a political response, the Foreign Office will be called upon to frame one towards the former and the Home Office towards the latter. And certainly, when in 1992 the American electorate chose Clinton in preference to Bush, many made it clear that they were backing a man who had promised to put domestic policy first, as against an opponent whom they saw as having neglected the domestic arena in a quest for foreign approval. If lay persons can tell the difference between domestic and foreign policy, why not some of those with a claim to expertise on these matters? Part of the problem, as so often in this subject, is linguistic. Clearly foreign policy is one of those maddeningly ambiguous concepts whose very existence seems designed only to plague the student of International Relations. But is it also as outdated a notion as it is ambiguous?

8.1 A DISTINCT FOREIGN-POLICY ARENA?

Pluralists like James Rosenau and John Burton contend that in an age of interdependence, of global environmental concerns and of multiple unofficial and informal economic and political ties across frontiers, all policy has internal as well as external dimensions.[1] They would point out, for example, that the decision of the Bundesbank to maintain comparatively high interest rates has profound international ramifications, though presented as a domestic policy; that a policy to phase out British coal gives a boost to the coal industry in Germany, Poland, South Africa, Australia, Colombia and elsewhere; that 'ethnic cleansing' has serious repercussions abroad in terms of mass migration and problems of resettlement, the mounting demands for humanitarian intervention in a country like Bosnia and the growing sense among the wider international Muslim community that the West had religious rather than strategic reasons for failing to halt the onslaught against Bosnia's Muslims. Furthermore, they would maintain that the distinction between domestic and foreign policy has long been an artificial one. For did not high American tariffs in the 1920s, imposed for largely domestic reasons, make a world depression inevitable and, incidentally, contribute thereby to the development of Fascism? Did not the removal of American price controls in 1946 worsen the 'dollar gap' and create such severe imbalances in the world economy as to require in turn a massive assistance programme to Washington's friends in the West? The Pluralists would also contend, by extension, that a policy pursued in the arena beyond a state's jurisdiction can have an effect—beneficial or adverse—within it, affecting, say, its domestic currency reserves, balance of trade or payments, interest rates, welfare provisions, even perhaps its domestic stability or the popularity or perceived legitimacy of its government. At the same time they could argue that today European Union directives on such subjects as seat belts, food hygiene, Sunday trading, corporal punishment, the transportation of animals, employment opportunities and the conservation of fish stocks defy the conventional categorisation of external and domestic realms.

Clearly, those 'traditionalists' who continue to separate domestic and foreign policy into mutually exclusive packages have a case to answer. On the other hand it is a claim which perhaps the Pluralists take too far, since rather like knowledge, which is a unity but tends to be compartmentalised into various specialisms and focuses of interest, so policy, which might similarly be regarded as one, is best charted and understood if compartmentalised. Even if the distinction between domestic and foreign policy is today less clear-cut than it once was, the latter remains an activity of government both directed at and implemented largely in an environment external to the state in question. As such it is generally formulated in greater secrecy and by fewer hands than domestic policy.[2] Moreover, the various specialised departments associated with it generally try to ensure that what the government regards as vital information—information which might, say, be of use to a potential enemy—is denied to the general public. For example how much do we know, even now, about 'Irangate', let alone 'Iraqgate', which is of much more recent vintage? In this sense the inquisitive politician, journalist, business executive or academic anxious to know more than has already been divulged about the details of foreign policy is at a disadvantage.

However, the foreign-policy decision-makers may themselves be at a disadvantage in having to act under the pressure of events, often at great speed but with insufficient information for a properly judicious deliberation. Though they may sometimes benefit from the fact that the general public tends to be less interested in foreign than in domestic policy, perceived success in foreign policy and a good name abroad will not necessarily save a politician in trouble at home (as Mrs Thatcher and her friends Presidents Gorbachev and Bush found to their cost).

8.2 FOREIGN POLICY: DIVERSE MEANINGS

But what kind of activity is foreign policy-making? Does it resemble the creation and implementation of a Grand Design, as in architecture? Is it better understood in nautical terms, as the navigation of a course towards some given destination? Does it concern itself with diagnosis and prescription, as in medicine? Or is it more akin to some mechanical contrivance whereby a given stimulus produces an automatic response? In fact as a process foreign policy-making encompasses planning, analysis, steering, reacting to international circumstance...and more besides. But foreign policy is more than a process and has half a dozen or more different dimensions.

In the first place, it can refer to the goals, purposes or objectives sought by political authorities in the arena beyond a country's national jurisdiction. Such goals can be: of different degrees of precision, ranging from the abstract such as prestige to the concrete, the possession of a piece of territory belonging to another power; positive, by way of seeking to attain something, or negative, designed to deprive someone of something; long term, relating to some distant aspiration, or short term, connected to more immediate concerns; conservative, concerned with maintainance of the status quo or revisionist, seeking to enhance a country's overall position in the international system.

Second, foreign policy can mean the norms and principles from which such goals are derived, ranging from the fundamental precepts of self-preservation and enhancement to the more altruistic tenets of respect for international law, rendering humanitarian assistance where needed, peaceful coexistence between ideological rivals, and so on. Such principles may also be of a more explicit nature, for example, Imperial Preference (the economic orthodoxy of the old British Empire), Manifest Destiny (the political orthodoxy of 19th- and early 20th-century America), Lebensraum ('living space'—the basis of Nazi expansionism), Islamic Fundamentalism, Zionism, Marxism–Leninism. Alternatively, the operative norm may take the form of a strategic or geopolitical theory like the Monroe doctrine, whereby Washington insisted on the Europeans keeping out of Latin American affairs in return for an American commitment not to intervene in Europe; 'containment', whereby the United States sought to counteract Soviet influence; or the 'domino theory' by which Washington was persuaded that once North Vietnam succumbed to Communism, the rest of South East Asia and beyond would fall to 'the Red Menace' like dominos.

Third, foreign policy can refer to the inventory of methods, measures, stratagems, tactics and devices by which political authorities seek to obtain their goals in the international arena. These can range from the most coercive such as the threat, display or use of force or of subversion to the most genteel, a plea for support, an appeal to sentiment based on ideological or religious affinity, kith and kin and so forth.

Fourth, foreign policy can refer to a range of decisions or courses of actions, innovative, adaptive and reactive in pursuit of a goal or goals or with reference to a particular area. Britain's policy, say, in respect of France or towards the Balkans would come into this category. Fifth, it can refer to a particular decision or action undertaken in pursuit of a particular objective: for example the American decision to involve the UN in removing Saddam Hussein's forces from Kuwait. Sixth, it can refer to an accumulation of piecemeal and pragmatic day-to-day reactions to situations, events and pressures emanating from the international arena. Nor does this list exhaust the possible meanings of the term 'foreign policy'.

But does a country always need to have a foreign policy? Before the mid-19th century neither China nor Japan had one. Until the Western powers forced their attentions on them, they were able to remain isolated and detached from the affairs of the world. And in 1917 when Trotsky became Foreign Commissar (Minister) of Soviet Russia immediately after the Bolshevik Revolution, he also assumed his country would not need a foreign policy. Expecting the withering away of the state in the wake of a global revolution he declared: 'I'll just make a few revolutionary pronouncements to the world and then shut up shop.'[3] However, within days he had to admit he had been mistaken and that his country did after all need a foreign policy. Why? Because the international system was now global and for a state participation in it was unavoidable. Given its territorial associations, a state could never escape its near neighbours. But with more recent developments in science and technology, a state can hardly evade its more distant neighbours either. As Abraham Lincoln once indicated: though man and wife might go their separate ways and divorce, states are unable to part in the same way. Even after hostilities they are obliged to find some basis for interaction,[4] and this calls for precisely the kinds of undertakings that go under the name of foreign policy.

8.3 FOREIGN-POLICY FORMULATION

Given that policy-makers have only limited control over the international environment and limited resources with which to pursue objectives, how do they set about the task of framing an appropriate policy? Clearly this depends in part on who they are, and this is to a degree determined by the nature of the political system. Whether the country in question is a parliamentary or presidential democracy, under an ideologically grounded party dictatorship or ruled by monarch, sheikh, military officer or civilian despot can affect the way foreign policy is formulated. On the other hand a country's political structure can only be a rough indicator of decision-making responsibilities.

In the first place formal positions and designations are not always reliable guides to the degree of effective power exercised by those in high office. When it comes to foreign policy-making foreign ministers are frequently less influential and well informed than some of their cabinet colleagues. When, for example, Andrei Gromyko first became Soviet foreign minister in the late 1950s, party leader Khrushchev said of him, 'he does exactly what we [meaning the Politburo] tell him, and if he doesn't we get a new foreign minister.' To Henry Kissinger, later US Secretary of State, Khrushchev summed up Gromyko's position even more graphically. 'If we told him to take his pants down and sit on a block of ice, he'd do it,'[5] meaning, of course, he would have to do it. Later Gromyko was to take much greater responsibility for foreign policy, but it is clear that at first he had virtually no input into decision-making. Indeed, presidents, prime ministers, kings and emperors may also have rather less say than is commonly assumed. For example till the final surrender to the Americans, the foreign political preferences of the late Japanese Emperor Hirohito seem to have counted for comparatively little, despite his semi-divine status, whereas the views of the rather less-divine Margaret Thatcher (who, it is said, liking a compliant cabinet generally got one) would usually prevail. In other words, personalities matter—in foreign policy-making as in other kinds of political activity.[6]

But who determines policy is not just a matter of political systems and personalities. It is also a product of pressures and institutions. As the issues become more complex, foreign policy is seen to require, in virtually every political system, a host of government organisations and agencies to gather relevant information, find the necessary expertise to interpret and evaluate the evidence and to tender advice to the decision-makers. In the process some of those working behind the scenes may have a direct effect either on the political agenda or on the policies which emerge.

8.4 THE NATIONAL INTEREST

Whether or not foreign policy is the product of many or comparatively few hands, its formulation generally centres around yet another ambiguous concept—that of 'the national interest'—a term fraught with all manner of conceptual booby traps but none the less suggesting a set of stable, relatively unchanging foreign-policy goals which can be identified and recognised by enlightened statesmen and rational observers.[7] On the other hand its very vagueness appears to suit both governments and their critics. Governments use the expression to give legitimacy to their external objectives and to suggest that those opposing them are somehow unpatriotic and disloyal. When oppositions use the term it is to imply an objective standard to which the government is oblivious or from which it has deviated or fallen short. Given, however, its often polemical use—as a justification or a critique of policy—can so elastic a concept have any settled meaning at all?

At the very least it must have two separate if related connotations, stemming from the ambiguity of the word 'national'. It could be a reference to the state as such or to the people of a state. In either case, it is what is perceived as the relevant interests which count, and, of course, in their perceptions, the policy-makers might be informed, influenced, misinformed or prejudiced by all manner of considerations. Marxists, believing that all perceptions are class-based, claim that what is presented as the national interest is in fact in the interest of the ruling class, though some might regard the concept of a ruling-class interest as no less threadbare and insubstantial than that of a national interest. Undoubtedly, many governments, in an attempt to cling to office in times of trouble, equate the administration's interest with that of the state. Indeed, it has become standard practice for governments to claim that the country would suffer greatly were there to be a transfer of political power to the opposition. This is not to say, however, that 'the national interest' is merely a rhetorical device to serve the interests of the ruling elite. For the operative decision-makers may genuinely believe that their conception of it advances in some sense 'the general good'. But in determining its content, they may allow personal vanity, regional bias, religious fanaticism, ideological zeal or gender-based considerations—in particular the idea that a woman prime minister or president can be as tough if not tougher than a man—to enter into the calculations.

8.5 SHAPING FOREIGN POLICY

The historical dimension

On the other hand, foreign policy-making does not arise in a vacuum. Though its formulation may have to bow to ever-changing military, political or economic realities—the end of a cold war, the onset of international recession, an apparent and sudden deterioration in the ozone layer, a series of natural disasters, perhaps—the interaction between pressures internal and external to the state have a certain perennial quality which tends to give to foreign policy a degree of continuity, regardless of who is in power. In other words, the persistence through time of the general features of the international system combined with the geographical situations of the various states and their space relations vis-à-vis one another give to the process of defining national interest an historical dimension. Notions of wherein that interest lies tend to be passed from one generation to another, reflecting the fact that people inhabiting a particular land mass and whose neighbours—near and far—are relatively unchanging inherit a framework of perceptions and expectations about the world, are apt over time to dream the same dreams, indulge in the same prejudices and experience the same fears.[8] For example because their country had twice been wiped off the map as a result of a Russo–German accord, the Poles tend to have an understandable fear of any renewed accord between their eastern and western neighbours and an interest in an element of friction between them. The Armenians, having for centuries been in religious and political conflict with their Turkic neighbours and having been massacred by the Turks in 1915, retain both an historic fear and suspicion of Turks and Azeris; and the bloodshed over Nagorno-Karabakh, the Armenian enclave in Azerbaijan, has to be seen in that context. As for the current hostility between the Vietnamese and Cambodians, it is in many ways the latest round in an age-old struggle, temporarily halted by French colonialism, between the Cambodian Khmer empire and their Vietnamese neighbours.

Influential individuals, lobbies and interest groups

At the same time particular formulations of national interest can be shaped or reshaped by influential individuals within the administration such as strategically placed civil servants, by people outside of government—for example wives (Hillary Clinton is only the latest of a series of politically influential spouses), personal private secretaries, lovers (often the same thing as personal private secretaries)—by pressure groups and lobbies and, of course, by the media, which governments sometimes ignore at their peril. It is doubtful, for example, whether successive French governments would have been so wedded to the Common Agricultural Tariff had not the French farmers been such an influential lobby, with powerful backing from the press. Similarly, successive American governments have bowed to pressures from Zionist, cotton and oil lobbyists in pursuit of Middle Eastern policy. All three lobbies were influential in Washington's decision to refuse funding for Nasser's Aswan Dam electrification and irrigation project in 1956. Whether or not decision makers have a personal, regional, religious, gender- or class-based stake in the outcome, sooner or later in attempting to give definition to the concept of the national interest, they have to sort out the greater from the less salient objectives. Generally speaking governments dub 'vital' those interests for which in the final analysis they are prepared to use methods of coercion. They term 'secondary' those interests deemed to be of lesser importance and from which *in extremis* they would be prepared to retreat.

8.6 PRIORITIES

Security: military and economic

Though the ranking of interests alters over time, in accordance with changing conditions and perceptions, those seen as preserving the sovereignty and territorial integrity of a community still tend to take priority in many, if not most states. Till recently this was understood as a function largely of military strength. Today, however, bearing in mind that security can be jeopardised by forces within as well as between the states, many understand the maintenance of physical integrity in political, economic and diplomatic terms. For example, awesome military strength alone proved insufficient to preserve the Soviet state, while countries with but a fraction of the armed might of the former Communist power—Switzerland, for example, or Singapore—survive and prosper, in large part because of the judicious economic and other policies pursued by their governments. Also high on the list of most interpretations of national interest is the notion of independence, or rather of as much freedom from outside interference as is possible in an interdependent world. As the countries of Western Europe have amply demonstrated in the recent past, independence and interdependence are matters of degree. As any self-possessed, critically self-aware child who grows up in a rather restrictive household could testify, independence and interdependence need not be mutually exclusive.

Prestige

A further perceived interest relates to the esteem in which a country is held ie to its prestige. At one time the main preoccupations in this regard were with power, authority and status. A state like Britain, France or Germany, for example, would glory in its military reputation. Nowadays, however, in an age of mass communications and mass literacy, the question of credibility seems to be especially important. If a country A makes a commitment to country B and then reneges on it, as the Clinton administration seems to have done more than once, the general credibility of its commitments is thrown in doubt and the country's reputation suffers accordingly. But what happens when a country makes a commitment which turns out to be excessively costly, manifestly unsuccessful and perhaps unwise?

While at Harvard in the mid-1960s, the author discussed the question of Washington's commitment to South Vietnam with Henry Kissinger, then a Professor of International Politics. Originally strongly opposed to the commitment to Saigon on the grounds that it was tactically unwise to make a stand against Communism in such unpromising terrain, he was then of the opinion that Washington was now effectively stuck with that commitment, no matter how questionable its origins. As he put it: 'To give in now would be to suggest that American commitments aren't worth anything.' A further problem was that: 'we'd be seen as yielding to pressure from campus militants and left-wing ideologues and our prestige would suffer accordingly.' To the suggestion that Vietnam was a war the United States could not win, Kissinger said, 'if you can tell me how we can get out of it with honour, I'd be delighted to pass your recommendation on to the White House'; to the contention that Washington was unlikely to get out of Vietnam with honour, that the later the withdrawal the greater the dishonour, he had no answer. In fact, by continuing the conflict, losing it and then having to abandon its Vietnamese allies, the United States did indeed suffer a shattering blow to its prestige and its credibility.

The effect on a government of loss of prestige, or, as they call it in the Orient 'loss of face', can be seen in two earlier examples: first, the French humiliation of 1940, when Paris pulled out of the second world war and adopted a pro-Hitler policy. The sense of shame this produced, especially in the French army which had surrendered in 1940, is said to have been largely responsible for its tougher, evidently far more brutal tactics in Indochina and Algeria in the 1950s and 1960s,[9] though in the end these proved no more successful, and France was further discredited. Another example is the abortive American landing in Cuba's Bay of Pigs in 1961. The mishandling and failure of this enterprise is said to have so wounded Kennedy's pride that in the following year during the 'eyeball-to-eyeball' confrontation with the Soviet navy following Moscow's emplacement of missiles in Cuba less than a hundred miles from the US mainland, he was prepared to go to the brink of nuclear war to produce a Soviet climbdown.[10] But, as is clear, prestige, credibility, esteem and self-esteem matter, and in this way what may start as an unwise commitment can be raised to the status of a vital interest.

Preserving a stake in the international system

Somewhat less abstract than prestige is the concern of decision-makers for the preservation of a country's stake in the international system ie the rights, privileges, assets and amenities it enjoys beyond its frontiers. These would include, first, its strategic interests: the security of its allies and alliances, its overseas possessions, bases, staging posts etc from armed attack; the security of communications with its overseas markets and sources of supply and the maintenance of a perceived global or regional balance in its favour. Second, there are its political interests, in particular the maintenance of a type of international order consistent with a state's political ideals and structures. Third are its economic interests, and in particular the maintenance and enhancement of the country's share in

world trade and investment. They would also include its ideological interests—its way of life or style of politics, so that its aspirations and values are
projected on to the international system and protected against the
encroachment of alternative and hostile ideologies.

8.7 A RATIONAL ENDEAVOUR?

In practice, however, the ordering and interpretation of those interests are
normally matters for argument. Whether guns are to take precedence over
butter, conflict over co-operation, confrontation over appeasement, and
whether security is to be sought by strengthening one's allies, buying off
opponents or going it alone has to be thrashed out by those in the decision-making process. It used to be assumed that a serious evaluation of
such things as intentions and relative capabilities, existing and potential,
trends in the world economy and developments in military and industrial
technology were a prerequisite to such discussions, and that in devising,
amending or pursuing foreign-policy options the individuals concerned
would consider possible alternatives, selecting those most likely to
advance particular goals at the least possible cost. Often this does happen,
but by no means always.

Sometimes there is no time for considered reflection. An unforeseen
crisis—the Japanese bombing of Pearl Harbor, the North Korean incursion
into the South, the Argentinian landing in the Falklands or Iraq's invasion
of Kuwait—can occur overnight requiring an immediate reaction, often in
ignorance of the full facts and under the kinds of stressful pressures which
can distort judgment. At other times rational decision-making may be
impaired by the effects of previous mistaken policies which produce a
chain of circumstances from which, as Kissinger had suggested in the case
of the commitment to South Vietnam, a state may find it difficult to extri-
cate itself. A third impediment to rational policy can result from the
attempt to implement contradictory and incompatible goals. This can stem
from a failure of proper co-ordination. More often than not it is the product of loose thinking. How often do we hear that it is a government's
policy to seek 'peace' and 'security', as if these were always compatible
goals? But are they? When Britain's Prime Minister Chamberlain returned
from a meeting with Hitler in September 1938 claiming that he had
secured 'peace in our time', had he not in fact jeopardised the security of a
continent by allowing the Führer to take over that part of Czechoslovakia
which contained one of Europe's most important arsenals, one of its best
equipped air forces and 35 military divisions—all of which were to
contribute greatly to the Nazi war machine? By the same token, of course,
going to war may be a way of safeguarding security, in the sense of securing a long-term balance.

But irrationalities may occur not only in the implementation but also in the formulation of policy, as a number of writers point out. For example Graham Allison in his *Essence of Decision* dealing with the Cuban missile crisis points to two forms of policy-making in which the outcome is more the result of chance than of serious deliberation. In charting policy by what he terms 'organisational process', and here he would seem to have the United States very much in mind, decisions are the product not of choice but of a bargaining process involving 'pulling and hauling' between the representatives of different government departments, each functioning according to standard operating procedures. It is a process which produces a policy to which no one strongly objects, even if, equally, no one is especially happy with it. Allison also speaks of decision-making according to 'bureaucratic politics' where policy is, again, the product not so much of careful selection but of a power struggle among key individuals in the bureaucratic elite whose several objectives, personal, political as well as professional, may well be incompatible with one another. Here, too, policy emerges at the end of various complex bargaining strategies in the process of which individual preferences and prejudices—including that of the leader and the foreign minister—may be entirely submerged.

In another study, simply entitled *Understanding Foreign Policy*, Michael Clarke, one of the editors, suggests that the process of decision-making may sometimes be even less rational than that depicted by Allison. He submits that in a world in which the foreign-affairs arena is broadening to encompass a host of political, economic, military, diplomatic, legal, scientific, technical, cultural and even sporting activities, decisions of consequence traceable to particular personalities probably account for but a small proportion of foreign-policy outcomes. Nowadays in a rapidly changing international environment, foreign policy-making tends to involve so many different hands—informants, advisers, envoys, negotiators as well as official decision-makers—that it is sometimes difficult for even the participants to discover who precisely is responsible for what.

Moreover, says Clarke, what appears to be a 'decision' may in fact lack that element of conscious choice and selectivity that the term normally conveys. It may be the resultant of habit, inertia or of mindless routines and standard practices, as when a given aid programme is maintained regardless of significant changes in economic circumstance and bilateral relations. It may be the product of a fragmented process in which officials exercising their discretion according to their field of competence make a series of minor decisions the cumulative effect of which is to produce a momentum in favour of a particular course of action but which no one in particular has willed. For example the unplanned and unwelcome chill in East–West relations in the wake of President Nixon's fall in 1974 appears to have been the product of a combination of actions, none particularly significant in itself. Clarke goes on to reiterate Allison's point about decisions that are the product not of any careful consideration of alternatives but of a bargaining process among key individuals that produces an outcome which, in the jargon phrase, 'satisfices', is just about acceptable to all, even if it gives total satisfaction to none.[11] Alternatively it can stem from a refusal to recognise that any choice exists. How often do we hear the phrase 'there is no alternative'?

Even where particular foreign-policy outcomes can be readily attributable to particular individuals it cannot be assumed, suggests Clarke, that either rationality or 'the national interest' will necessarily have prevailed. All too frequently rational decision-making is impaired by erroneous intelligence and further marred by misperception, prejudice, lack of understanding or empathy, wishful thinking and the kind of intellectual short-sightedness that goes under the name of 'tunnel vision'. What psychologists term 'cognitive dissonance', in which any information conflicting with cherished beliefs, values or desires is rejected and the facts distorted to fit in with pre-existing notions, can add a further impediment to rational policy. Here one thinks, for example, of Stalin's dogged conviction after his quarrel with Tito in 1948 that Yugoslavia must return to the Soviet fold because he believed it was quite impossible for a state to be under Communist rule, yet anti-Soviet—a view incidentally shared by many in Washington who, as a result, failed for so long to understand the depth of the Sino–Soviet antagonism after 1960. They thought it was a 'disinformation ploy' to lull the West into a false sense of security. An example of 'cognitive dissonance' perhaps? Nor should one overlook the impact on policy of domestic electoral considerations. The desire to be seen as 'doing something' so as to enhance personal or party fortunes or to appease a particular interest group may be the mainspring for a foreign-policy pronouncement, overseas trip or adventure. It would not be difficult to recall the names of leaders whose penchant for overseas summits appears to grow in proportion to their domestic unpopularity.

8.8 THE ROLE OF LEADERS

Even though leaders often exaggerate their own role in getting things done and take the credit for popular and successful policies instigated by others, in point of fact their room for manoeuvre tends to be rather more limited in external than in domestic policy. Often they are circumscribed by a host of geopolitical, technological, military, economic and psychosocial factors, to say nothing of the legal, political and what are perceived to be moral obligations by which, as will be discussed in the following chapter, states are generally deemed to be bound. As the late Professor F.S. Northedge put it: 'Effective freedom in foreign affairs...is the capacity to choose between relatively few options.'[12] In consequence, leaders are apt, perhaps after an initial attempt at setting the foreign-policy agenda, to become pragmatic operators rather than grand strategists. If they have a foreign political role, it is frequently confined to adjusting commitments to capabilities and aspirations to practicalities. Here short-term expedients to buy time, to sow confusion among enemies and reassure friends or simply to avoid having to make a decision at all may have to be substituted for principle. These are essentially behind-the-scenes exercises and often masked by an official rhetoric designed to suggest purposeful activity, progress and continuity.

On the other hand that there are still leaders able to devise and implement plans for creating new nations, uniting ethnic or religious kinsfolk across frontiers, spreading a particular gospel or establishing novel international institutions cannot be denied. After all, the roll call of great statesmen did not end with Bismarck, Ataturk, Masaryk, Woodrow Wilson and Lenin. In a world, moreover, in which the forces of international integration are constantly vying with the factors of national disintegration, opportunities for high-profile political activity are not lacking, even if they are not necessarily seized. And in crisis situations when there are heightened threat perceptions and serious time constraints, leaders are often well placed to 'make history'. Sadly, it is often at such times that they are at their least rational and are either paralysed or, alternatively, driven into misplaced hyperactivity by either a dearth or a surfeit of relevant information.

Notwithstanding the continuing ability of leaders to 'grab the headlines' in foreign affairs, there does seem to have been a perceptible shift away from the kind of high-profile leadership much in evidence from the mid-19th to the mid-20th century. If so, perhaps this is due not just to the complexities of modern statecraft but also to the fact that a post-colonial, post-Communist era leaves comparatively little scope for political messiahs and charismatic rulers. Moreover, as time seems to have dented the reputations of many recent political 'giants'—and from Kennedy to Gorbachev and from Gandhi to Mao, of whom so much was expected, the idols crumble under scrutiny—there is not perhaps the same incentive as before for political heroics.

What are we to conclude? Was the 19th-century literary historian Thomas Carlyle right to see 'great men' as the motive force behind history or was the late Harold Macmillan nearer the mark when he claimed that the most difficult things an administration has to face are 'events'? Did Chamberlain mould or reflect British opinion in appeasing Hitler? Was Churchill's role in Britain's war effort critical or did he merely, as he claimed with unaccustomed modesty, give the 'roar' to 'the British lion'? Did Gorbachev 'kill' European Communism and with it the cold war, or was he the instrument of an historical process already underway? Such thorny issues will doubtless long continue to be the subject of debate, though Professor John Garnett in *Common Sense and the Theory of International Relations* has taken some of the heat out of the discussion with his claim that 'policy makers are never as free as their critics think they are'[13]—something Bill Clinton had to take to heart early in his administration.

NOTES

1. See, for example, Burton, J., *World Society*, London, Cambridge University Press, 1972, and Rosenau, J. (ed.), *The Scientific Study of Foreign Policy*, New York, Free Press, 1971. Also Mansbach, R. and Vasquez, J., *In Search of Theory*, New York, Columbia University Press, 1981.
2. Franck, T. and Weisband, E. (eds), *Secrecy and Foreign Policy*, New York, Oxford University Press, 1974.
3. Quoted in Carr, E.H., *The Bolshevik Revolution, Vol III*, Harmondsworth, Penguin, 1966, p. 28.
4. See Dent, J.M., *Abraham Lincoln: Speeches and Letters*, London, Everyman, 1936, p. 172.
5. Quoted in Kissinger, H., *The White House Years*, Boston, 1979, p. 788.
6. See, for example, Stern, G., *Leaders and Leadership*, London, LSE/BBC World Service, 1993, pp. 185–91.
7. For a useful, if critical review of the literature on the concept, see Rosenau, J. (ed.), op. cit., pp. 239–49.
8. Northedge, F.S., 'The nature of Foreign Policy' in Northedge, F.S. (ed.), *The Foreign Policies of the Powers*, London, Faber, 1974, pp. 13–14.
9. Thornton, A.P., *Imperialism in the Twentieth Century*, London, Macmillan, 1980, pp. 290–93.
10. See, for example, Allison, G., *Essence of Decision*, Boston, Little, Brown, 1971.
11. The phrase was coined by Herbert Simon. See his *Administrative Behaviour*, New York, Macmillan, 1959.
12. Northedge, F.S. (ed.), op. cit., p. 16.
13. Garnett, J., *Commonsense and the Theory of International Relations*, London, Macmillan, 1984, p. 61.

PART IV
INTER-STATE BEHAVIOUR

CHAPTER 9

CONSTRAINTS AND RULES OF INTERNATIONAL BEHAVIOUR

There was a time was when some of the leading authorities in International Relations such as Carr, Schwarzenberger, Morgenthau and Wight could draw only the most pessimistic conclusions from their study. They had examined the writings of an earlier generation of scholars and statesmen like Zimmern, Noel-Baker and Woodrow Wilson and found them wanting in both explanatory and prescriptive power. In short, these were 'utopian'. They had also studied far earlier texts by people like Thucydides, Machiavelli and Hobbes and found them if not comforting then at least familiar. And, of course, they were writing at a time when the world appeared to be lurching from one deadly imbroglio to another: in the 1930s a trade war, followed by the second world war within a generation; thereafter, cold war in Europe, colonial and civil wars in Asia and Africa. Not surprisingly, the specialised literature tended to deal with crises, hostilities and conflagrations. At least two of the major texts in the subject were entitled *Power Politics*,[1] and the term was widely used to depict both the ends and the means of international activity and to distinguish the international arena from other theatres of politics. But was 'power politics' an appropriate designation, and does it epitomise the distinction between international and domestic politics? That depends on what the phrase is intended to imply.

9.1 'POWER POLITICS': THE HALLMARK OF INTERNATIONAL RELATIONS?

The various connotations of 'power'

The problem with 'power' is that it has so many different connotations that no single and agreed meaning to suit all contexts or occasions is possible.[2] For 'power' can suggest the sum total of a country's capabilities—military, economic, technological, diplomatic and political. It can refer to the various means by which a government can attempt to secure a particular objective. It can also imply one set of means in particular—the coercive—when 'power' becomes a synonym for 'force', 'might', 'muscle', 'strength' or, alternatively, for the type of behaviour we associate with such activity—'assertive', 'aggressive', 'forceful' and 'vigorous'. But 'power' can be a reference not simply to means but also to ends: such objectives as ascendancy, control, dominance, hegemony, imperium, mastery, sovereignty, supremacy. In addition, it might indicate a structural relationship, as it were, legitimised by society. Here the emphasis is on such notions as 'authority', 'competence', 'empowerment', 'prerogative', 'warrant' and so forth.

The various connotations of 'politics'

But if power can take on a variety of different guises, so can 'politics', though mercifully the range of possible meanings is not quite as great.[3] One helpful way of delimiting the general area of interpretation is to consider the antithesis of the word 'political'. Since 'apolitical' suggests 'apathy', 'disinterestedness', 'non-involvement', 'unconcern', 'not taking sides', the word 'political' must have to do with commitment, interest, involvement, concern, partisanship and in a context concerning government, rule, regulation or authority, since it is derived from the Greek word for the governance of the city state. Broadly speaking, a political arena is a social framework within which (1) there is contention and disagreement about either the structure of authority or about purposes, procedures or priorities; (2) such contentions, though necessarily partisan and often passionate, occur below the threshold of serious, organised and protracted violence, and are adjudicated according to recognised procedures such as a vote, a consensus, an administrative act or a decree; and (3) the possible outcomes of such procedures are the victory of one side, a compromise between protagonists, the eradication through obsolescence of the issues in contention or an agreement to continue the disagreement until victory, compromise or the displacement from the political agenda of the issues in contention.

9.2 A POLITICAL ARENA

In its most narrow interpretation, politics is an activity or a process under formal government as in a cabinet meeting, a parliament, a local council or at election time. In its broader connotations politics—non-violent contention within an ordered framework—can occur in any social situation. One can talk, therefore, of the politics of the classroom, of the student's union, of the mother's meeting or of the family as, for example, when a divorcing couple bid against one another for the sympathy and support of the children. By the same token we can talk of international as well as national politics ie between governments in a global environment with a framework of order but lacking any formal central structure.

From the various connotations alluded to, it is clear that the notion of 'politics' and of 'power' are closely inter-related, and in this sense it would be somewhat illogical to suggest that international politics are unique in being 'power politics' since the contest for attention, authority, influence or decision-making power is of the very essence of politics in any social framework.

9.3 'POWER POLITICS' AS APPLIED TO INTERNATIONAL RELATIONS

What, then, did people such as Carr, Schwarzenberger, Wight and Morgenthau intend to suggest in alleging that international politics were uniquely power political? Frankly, it is not always clear, but if their implication was that the international arena is one in which the politics of not being overpowered are a major consideration, in which the dealings of the great or superpowers form the backdrop against which international relations occur, in which the expectation of inter- or intra-state violence is pervasive and a relatively low moral tone prevails, they had reasonable grounds; but it is doubtful if the expression 'power politics' accurately conveys the situation. If, however, they meant by 'power politics' that the parties to the political process have an inordinate 'lust for power', that all inter-state relations are governed by ratios of physical strength and determined by threat, display or use of military power and that international relations are best described, in Hobbes's words as 'a war of all against all', they were, to my mind, overstating the case. Certainly there may have been times when international relations have approximated to that portrayal, but such times are exceptional, and the idea that force is always the arbiter of international outcomes is mistaken.

9.4 DOMESTIC CONSTRAINTS ON THE USE OF FORCE

Moral

The fact is that if there were such ready resort to violence in the international arena, then sustained international relations would surely be virtually impossible, and the state system that was, as it were, validated at Westphalia in 1648 would hardly have lasted 35, let alone nearly 350 years. For the maintenance of relations between human groups always requires an element of constraint, and the continued existence of so many weak and vulnerable states indicates that controls and regulations have never been entirely absent from the international relations of the past three centuries and a half. In the early days of the Westphalian system there was still an ethos of common obligation, buttressed by international law, diplomatic procedure and a host of tacit understandings stemming in part from the common Christian heritage of the elites determining policy. Though such a sense of obligation was bound to dissipate as international society expanded to include revolutionary states which expressly repudiated Christianity and countries lacking a Christian background, the governments in an enlarged international society shared a number of concerns which found expression in rules and institutions for sustaining a modicum of international order.[4]

Psycho-social

Though there have been primitive tribes who delight in combat, and, in less primitive societies, Social Darwinists who believe that organised military activity is good for the soul, creating the kinds of comradely feelings that bind a people together, such people are today mercifully as rare in administration as outside it. Moreover, far from spoiling for a fight, governments often try to shy away from a fray for as long as possible. Indeed, it was because others did not want to become involved that empire builders such as Alexander the Great, Attila the Hun, Genghis Khan and Napoleon were able to make such massive conquests, dealing with their victims one by one. And through his adroit use of intimidation between January 1933, when he came to power, and 1 Sept 1939, Hitler had been able to annexe one country after another without firing a shot. Thus, even though international society is riddled with competing and conflicting interests, there is no war of all against all—necessarily.

Political

What are the constraints on international violence? Talk of constraint suggests an activity, thought process or passion in need of restraint, but are humans all that bloodthirsty? Even were we to subscribe to the most pessimistic theories of Hobbes, Morgenthau or even Freud, it still would not follow that we are all basically homicidal maniacs looking for the opportunity to kill. For aggressive individuals are not necessarily violent individuals, and even violent individuals who inflict suffering do not necessarily have the urge to kill. It is significant that during military training people have to be taught to kill by sticking bayonets through sandbags, as if to counteract all those years of conditioning by which we learn to live in society, co-operate and develop a moral sense. Moreover, when organised groups engage in organised conflict, it is usually because they have important interests or a cause to serve, not because they want to let off steam.

Even where there are conflicts of interest or of principle between states, there is no automatic recourse to coercive measures. Whether or not a government contemplates their use in support of policy has always depended on at least five factors: first the salience of the matter at issue. If the issue in contention is perceived as of comparatively minor importance, and the possible benefits outweighed by the potential costs of a military riposte, few countries would consider one or even the threat of one. The use of force is always a risky, unpredictable business, and, in any case, a country's reputation might suffer if its government turned a minor matter into a major confrontation. The second factor concerns the identity of and the relations among the relevant states involved. If they are long-standing partners or allies, for example the United States and Canada or Britain and New Zealand, the question of a military riposte is unlikely to arise no matter how thorny the issue between them. Where, on the other hand, the dispute is between two traditionally hostile powers, the weaker is only likely to contemplate violence if there are weighty matters at stake and if it has the backing of a formidable combination of powers or else the where-withal to resort to less conventional forms of struggle such as assassination, political intrigue, subversion or guerrilla warfare. Third, there is the country's orientation. A much respected somewhat conservative status quo power with a considerable investment in international law and order is likely to be more reluctant to instigate hostilities than a radical power with unfulfilled ambitions and little stake in the existing international system. A fourth factor is the degree to which a country enjoys the substance as well as the status of sovereignty. The greater a country's dependence on others, the less it is likely to be in a position to issue unilateral threats or mobilise for a campaign of hostilities. Finally, whether or not international violence is contemplated depends on the available alternatives to the military option. Coercive measures are not likely to be in prospect if there are several viable alternatives, and, in fact, most governments—the weak as well as the strong—have at their disposal a host of non-violent pressures and inducements.

Viable alternatives

Moral suasion

There is, first of all, the kind of pressure most likely to be used by the weak and between long-standing allies—moral suasion—an appeal to sentiment based on the existence of religious, ideological, historical, ethnic or some other common bond. When, for example, New Zealand was troubled by Britain's failure to take its economic interests into account following the Macmillan government's first application for entry into the European Community, its prime minister flew to Britain to issue a heartfelt appeal along the lines of: 'We fought and died for you in two world wars. We are your kith and kin. How can you let us down?' His bid proved successful in so far as Britain then asked for New Zealand 'sheep meat' and butter to be given special exemption from EC tariffs and received a favourable response.

Diplomatic pressure

Second, there are a range of diplomatic pressures. At the one end of the scale there is reasoned argument mediated behind the scenes through the usual diplomatic channels or through unofficial third parties. During what was called 'the second cold war', when Moscow found it difficult to get a sympathetic response in the West for even the most reasonable of suggestions, the writer was assured by people in the Soviet foreign office that Moscow would be willing to make significant concessions, including the release of many well-known dissidents, if the Western powers stopped lecturing the Soviet Union on how to behave and started negotiating with the country on terms of equality. But with President Reagan in the ascendant, the West was not at the time prepared to soft peddle its relentless anti-Soviet campaign, and the failure of that particular Soviet initiative may have sealed the fate of many incarcerated dissidents for a further four or five years.

When reasoned argument fails there is always the possibility of third-party representations, where officials of a country friendly to both disputants use their good offices as either sounding board or mediator: as when Pakistan put its services at the disposal of both the United States and Communist China in the early 1970s to bring about their *rapprochement*; when Romanian, Moroccan and US diplomats prepared the ground for Egypt's President Sadat to make his historic visit to Israel in 1977; or when the Norwegians used their good offices in the secret talks between Israelis and the PLO prior to the 1993 agreement.

Should such diplomatic pressures fail, there are more formal compellants such as mobilising critical or hostile resolutions in international forums (especially favoured by weaker states whose ability to affect outcomes is enhanced by their membership of multilateral organisations), recalling ambassadors, withdrawing all or most of the embassy staff and *in extremis* total diplomatic rupture—as occurred between the United States and Cuba and the Soviet Union and Albania in 1961. There is also, though somewhat more rare, the possibility of a multilateral breach of diplomatic ties, sometimes co-ordinated through an international organisation—as when the UN sanctioned the boycott of Franco's Spain or when the Organisation of African Unity (OAU) sanctioned the isolation of South Africa following its withdrawal from the Commonwealth in 1961—quite a year for the diplomatic rupture! Other countries which have been international pariahs at various times have been the Soviet Union, China, Libya, Iraq, Yugoslavia and Haiti, while Israel, East Germany, North Korea, Rhodesia and the Republic of Northern Cyprus have all suffered the indignity of widespread non-recognition.

Judicial pressure

There are, third, judicial pressures, which would include resort to an international tribunal in the hope of obtaining a favourable authoritative judgment which could then be used as part of a political campaign to win support and to discredit an opponent. This happened, for example, in the Corfu Channel case when the Albanians were ordered by the International Court to pay compensation for the mining of a British warship off the Albanian coast—a claim, incidentally which was only settled after more than 40 years of wrangling and the collapse of the Communist regime.

Political pressure: propaganda of word and deed

Fourth, there are a host of pressures that could be classified as political. These differ from diplomatic pressures in that they are designed to appeal in the first instance to the public or to influential interest groups and lobbies of the target state, though its government remains the ultimate quarry.[5] Such appeals may be made in external broadcasts, syndicated articles, books, leaflets and the like or they may take the form of TV productions, films and videos. In its heyday, the Communist Third International (Comintern) used to sanction publication of a vast array of books, periodicals and journals as well as films to suggest the inevitability of Communism. Later, the CIA with an even larger budget developed an even more impressive array of materials, often, as in the case of many of the Comintern's titles, attempting to disguise the source. Even the British got into the act. Ampersand, the publisher that commissioned the author's first book, *Fifty Years of Communism*, turns out to have been a front for the Foreign Office. Perhaps mention should also be made of what is becoming known as 'the media event', as when a tearful Kuwaiti appeared before the UN General Assembly with a heartrending eyewitness account of how, following Baghdad's invasion of Kuwait in 1990, Iraqi troops had killed dozens of Kuwaiti babies by removing their incubators from the hospitals. The tale had the effect of galvanising American popular support for hostilities, though we now know that the 'eyewitness' was the daughter of the Kuwaiti ambassador to the UN and her account a complete fabrication.

In addition to propaganda of the word there is what has been called 'propaganda of the deed', from which it is hoped that appropriate inferences will be drawn. At its most benign it would include such things as a

Reagan 'walkabout' in Moscow or a Gorbachev 'walkabout' in Washington to suggest that neither superpower had anything to fear from the other. Rather more chilling was Saddam Hussein's denial of exit visas to the several hundred foreigners in Baghdad who received his 'hospitality', following the invasion of Kuwait, implying that in the event of hostilities they would be in the firing line. This latter example brings us to the psycho-political 'war of nerves' in which the language of gesture takes on an unmistakably threatening hue. Examples would include weapons testing, manoeuvres, putting forces on the alert, mobilisation—all of which occurred in the Soviet Union prior to the establishment in Poland in December 1981 of martial law, and many see a direct connection between these events. At its most extreme, 'propaganda of the deed' can take the form of the kidnapping or assassination of prominent personalities, the firebombing of embassies, hostage-taking and the killing of innocent civilians, though such actions run the risk of stiffening rather than reducing the will of the people of the target states to resist. A further form of political pressure, dating back to the time of the Trojan horse, is the infiltration or encouragement in the target state of a subversive faction whose actions might include spreading alarm, sabotaging communications and seizing key installations on behalf of the applicant state.

Economic pressures and inducements

Finally, governments can employ a variety of economic, financial and commercial inducements as well as pressures. The former range from the promise or grant of financial and technical assistance, massive commercial investment and most-favoured nation trading status; the latter include the threat or imposition of aid cut-offs, disinvestment, revocation of trade advantages, discriminatory tariffs and quotas, the freezing of assets and, ultimately, economic boycott and embargo. The distinction between threat and actual imposition of economic pressure is important since the threat can sometimes be sufficient to produce compliance, as when Britain withdrew its troops from Egypt in 1956 at the time of the Suez Crisis following Washington's threat to deny Britain an IMF loan, with the real possibility of a run on sterling; or when Finland revamped its administration in 1958 following a Soviet threat to exclude the country's exports.

The actual imposition of economic pressure can often have disappointing, even counter-productive results, as when the Soviet Union curtailed its trade with China in 1960, and the United States cut its economic ties with Cuba in 1961. Sanctions may be marginally more effective when applied multilaterally, but if they are to work, it generally takes time. The imposition by the Soviet bloc of sanctions against Yugoslavia in 1948 merely propelled the country first into the Western orbit then among the non-aligned, while the Western powers' strategic embargo against the

Soviet Union and its Eastern European allies merely served to solidify the Soviet bloc as the embargoed Eastern European countries became increasingly dependent on the Soviet Union as a market and source of supply. Possibly the West's more recent sanctions against Libya have fared better, since they seem to have had the effect of reining in Colonel Ghaddafi's penchant for terrorism. In general, however, the record of sanctions imposed by international organisations has been less than satisfactory. Though the threat of League sanctions may have helped to avert a war between Greece and Bulgaria in 1925, the actual imposition of sanctions failed to end Italy's occupation of Abyssinia in 1935, while the role of UN sanctions in ending white minority rule in Rhodesia in 1980, in bringing Namibia (formerly South West Africa) to independence and in virtually ending apartheid in South Africa is the subject of much controversy. Even if a significant influence, sanctions certainly took a long time to produce the desired effect, while the sanctions against Saddam Hussein's Iraq and Slobodan Milosevic's Yugoslavia seem only to have adverse effects on their people. The fact is that if it has sufficient warning of the possible imposition of sanctions, a country can stockpile goods in advance, alter domestic production and consumption patterns, bribe countries or international trading organisations into acting as sanctions busters and apply counter sanctions against some of the sanctioning states.[6]

Lack of capacity, opportunity and fear of consequences

The availability of such moral, diplomatic, judicial, political and economic pressures are a reminder that governments do not have to react to a perceived injury with military pressure, even if tempted to. If an administration faces a severe test of its resolve on an issue deemed of vital importance, it may still rule out physical measures—on one of three grounds: first, lack of capability. It may consider it lacks the means to guarantee success and that a military enterprise would be too risky. Second, there may be lack of opportunity. Though it may believe it has the requisite means, it might be unwilling or unable to bring them into play at a particular time. After all, timing is of the essence in any military operation, and a country may want to postpone a particular engagement—as the Western allies repeatedly did in opening up a second front in France during the second world war—until it believes the time is ripe. Alternatively, a country may be unable to utilise its military potential to the full because of political turmoil at home, as in Russia during the first world war, France during the second. A third constraint may be fear of the consequences. Success in these matters is never guaranteed, and even the successful employment of force can have serious unintended consequences. For example the Soviet-led intervention in Czechoslovakia in 1968 successfully suppressed 'the Prague Spring' but at the same time cemented an anti-

Soviet alignment among Communists, created serious rifts within the Communist Warsaw Pact, propelled the Americans and the Communist Chinese into an *entente,* created a mass of frustration and dissidence within the intervening countries as well as within Czechoslovakia, the target. It also required generous infusions of assistance to Prague which the Soviet exchequeur could ill-afford and provoked the kind of despair and disillusion that was in the end to destroy both the bloc and its creator, the Soviet Union—a high price to pay for a temporary success! Thus, among feared consequences of the use of force would be loss of prestige among allies as well as habitual foes which might have disastrous 'knock-on' effects on the country's ability to function effectively.

9.5 INTERNATIONAL CONSTRAINTS

So far the analysis has focused on the constraints within a state's discretion. However, there are also rules, norms and general principles of conduct pervading the entire international system, providing mechanisms—albeit modest—for containing the incidence or intensity of inter-state hostilities and facilitating co-existence. What, then, are these mechanisms and how effective are they?

International law

In an international society lacking government, common culture or sense of kinship and in which power is dispersed, the framing and operation of rules will be different from those in an orderly civil society where there is central authority, a common culture and a sense of solidarity. On the other hand by comparison with countries such as Afghanistan, Angola, Rwanda or Somalia, where there has been a complete absence of civil discipline and control, international society would seem to be reasonably well ordered.

Even though its relevance has been queried both by classical Realists and by many municipal lawyers, international law is probably the most dependable and discernible manifestation of order in international society. Like municipal law, it comprises a body of rules prescribing and proscribing certain methods of conduct, though these are not in a form similar to that of municipal law, nor is there an international legislature or central police force, while the international judiciary is only an imperfect instrument for settling conflicts. But those claiming that law has no place in international relations have to answer why governments crave legal recognition, why they are so anxious to provide legal justification for what they do, why they are so keen to participate in the process of creating new law and why those who expressly repudiate the international system—as did the Soviet Union in 1917 or Communist China in 1966—soon opt back in again.

But if international law is not irrelevant to the international political process, what are its sources? First, there is custom, comprising rules emanating from repeated patterns of behaviour which take on a binding quality over time. An example would be freedom of the seas. However, in an era of rapid political, economic and technological change, a second source—international agreements, treaties and conventions—takes on a greater significance. Though till recently they were considered binding only on their signatories, the recent proliferation of multilateral treaties has begun to suggest to some though not all legal theorists a broadening of the concept of international obligation. Firstly, the provisions of multilateral treaties such as those covering exploration of the Antarctic region or of outer space are increasingly being regarded as binding on non-signatory states that might wish to become co-signatories in the future. Secondly, according to Richard Falk, the notion of law by consensus ie 'something more than a simple majority, but something less than unanimity' could be about to supersede the idea of law by specific consent,[7] as when the provisions of the UN are deemed to be binding on non-members such as Switzerland; though the tendency in the European Union now seems to be in the opposite direction as Denmark, France and Britain try to repatriate some of the powers assumed by Brussels.

In addition to custom and treaty, there is another, relatively minor source, the so-called 'general principles of law' which may be inferred from the writings of legal scholars and decisions previously reached by the courts. The 'general principles' owe their presence in the lexicon of international legal sources to the fact that given the range of controversy, judges tend to need a basis other than custom and treaty for their adjudications.

Thus, despite the absence of centralised legislative machinery, there are none the less recognised rules of international conduct and also the rudiments of a judicial structure. Though national courts can adjudicate matters of international law, recourse to them tends to be limited, but regional courts, such as the European Court, are increasingly resorted to, while the International Court of Justice and other international tribunals are frequently asked for an adjudication or advisory opinion. No state, however, can be compelled to submit its disputes to or give evidence before the courts, and there is no enforcement machinery to ensure that an adjudication will be strictly adhered to.

If lack of an international legislature, compulsory international adjudication and enforcement procedures are serious shortcomings, so, some argue, is the lack of precision regarding the laws relating to war and peace. The term 'aggression' still lacks clear and agreed legal definition, making it possible for any country which instigates hostilities, as did Japan against China in 1931 or Iraq against Iran in 1979, to claim that it is a retortion for a wrong already inflicted, which is a policy perfectly justified in law. Alternatively, consider the appearance of one country's troops in the territory of another in answer to that government's invitation, as the Soviet Union claimed in Hungary in 1956 and in Afghanistan in 1979. If the claims were true, both Red Army interventions would have been perfectly consistent with the law. Others would suggest that such vagueness, which allows the law to be bent rather than broken, is the price we have to pay for a legal system which is much more precise in most other respects and which is generally observed. Indeed, it is only when it is broken that we tend to hear about it.

Just why the system works has much to do with convenience. Though individual governments may object to particular laws, they tend to accept the system as such, since even the most revolutionary in the end prefer order, which is what law tries to safeguard, to chaos. It is a system, moreover, which confers reciprocal benefits in terms of sovereign recognition, non-interference, diplomatic immunity and so on, and in honoring their legal obligations, governments may have a mixture of motives: moral conviction, habit, inertia, convenience, concern for their reputation, the hope of reward for good behaviour, the fear of sanctions.[8]

International institutions

The strengths and weaknesses of international law as a mechanism for constraining and controlling international activity apply in almost equal measure to international organisations: global, like the UN; regional, like the European Union; and functional, like the IMF or NATO. There are broadly two views as to their role in regard to international order—the Rationalist or Pluralist view that they are the harbingers and custodians of a potential community of humankind; the other, the Realist view, is that they are the instruments of their members, generally of their leading members, to be used as they see fit. There is something to be said for both views, since in providing a meeting place and a forum for technical representatives as well as diplomats and politicians who might not otherwise get together, such organisations may facilitate the kind of co-operation and regulation that might not otherwise occur. In addition, the UN has played a role in peacemaking as well as peacekeeping, speeding the process of decolonisation, transmitting the concerns of 'the have nots' to 'the haves' and in the creation of new law. Meanwhile, bodies such as the EU and the North American Free Trade Area (NAFTA) have helped to moderate the claims of narrow national interest, though not without protest.[9]

'Rules of the game'

In addition to the formal rules attaining the status of law and the decisions or recommendations of international institutions, there are informal understandings, tacit agreements, what might be termed 'rules of the game' between governments. Here considerations of prudence and discretion rather than legal obligation demarcate the permissible from the forbidden. The existence of such 'rules' may be inferred from such things as the experience of international societies prior to the establishment of international law, when diplomatic envoys were considered inviolable; from non-binding declarations such as those during the cold war referring to 'peaceful co-existence' between states with different social systems; from the general willingness of adversary states to keep confidential any secret discussions between them, from the inclination of rival powers to exchange prisoners of war and spies and to preserve unchallenged for lengthy periods of time spheres of influence. A good illustration would be the failure of the Western powers to dismantle the flimsy wall the East Germans built in August 1961 and which could at the time have been knocked down by a few West German bulldozers.[10]

Regimes

Both legal formality and the informality of the prudential 'rules of the game' play their part in the establishment and maintenence of what are called 'regimes'. These comprise bodies of regulations, implicit as well as explicit, not all of them binding, laying down norms of conduct and prescriptions for the management and control of actions in specific issue areas such as trade, commerce, transport, fishing, the sea bed, conservation, arms control and space exploration. The Common Agricultural Policy, the Exchange Rate Mechanism, the General Agreement on Tariffs and Trade may be considered examples. Though the term 'regime' is of comparatively recent origin, it refers to a phenomenon long in existence. For example the regulations concerning international postal services and the navigation of international waterways a century and a half ago were in the nature of regimes, as was the gold standard. What distinguishes a 'regime' from the body of legal ordinances and 'the rules of the game' is not just its combination of formality and informality but also the fact that the framework of allowances, dispensations, prescriptions, limitations, restrictions and prohibitions owe as much to international and transnational bodies, non-government organisations and specialised agencies as to governments. And of course those establishing them are expected to abide by them.[11]

International morality

If international law, institutions, 'rules of the game' and regimes contribute to international order, should what is called 'international morality' also be included in the list? The problem is that even if one is prepared to beg a host of questions by defining international morality as a concern with certain kinds of obligations, duties and rights, identifying the moral agent as the state and the object of its moral endeavours as other states, some other state, group, individual or even humankind, two other thorny questions arise. First, do states in fact have moral obligations? Second, if they do, would respect for them enhance or undermine international order? As to the first of these, there are conflicting opinions. Classical Realists like Machiavelli and Hobbes would have dismissed the idea entirely. In their view serving the state was the highest moral duty, and no state had any moral obligation to any other. Natural law theorists from the Roman Cicero down to the Spanish Jesuit Suarez and their modern followers, including E.B.F. Midgley and Michael Donelan, would hold that there is a universal law with a moral dimension binding on all individuals, peoples and states.[12] Ideologues and revolutionaries including Kant, Marx, Lenin down to the Ayatollah Khomenei would take a bifurcated, polarised approach, arguing that those who worked on behalf of states had moral obligations only to those of like mind, not to 'the reactionary', 'class enemy' or 'infidel' who stood in the way of a 'just' order. Finally there are the modern Realists such as Reinhold Niebuhr, Herbert Butterfield and Arnold Wolfers who would argue that morality arises in context and that the moral requirements of a state in a context of states each of which is potentially a violent criminal and above which there is no political superior to enforce law and order must be different from those of an individual in an orderly civil society.[13]

For students of International Relations the question is not whether states in fact incur such obligations, since the state is only a personified abstraction, but whether in the realm of discourse in which states are deemed to exist, they are also deemed to incur such obligations—and the obvious answer is 'yes'. Most recent discussion about, say, the turmoil in Bosnia is likely to have centred around what governments ought or ought not to have done about the war, sanctions, refugees and so forth. Again, there are many different moral standpoints, and even among those holding to the contextual ethic there will have been divergent views on both the nature of the circumstances and on what could best be done. For some the 'right' thing would have been to have become involved in the fray, even if it meant adding a further element of turmoil to an already disordered situation. Here the argument would be that the Serbs are expansionist, that no international order could be secure while such expansionism continued unchecked and that the short-term disorder that would come from a widening of the war would be a small price to pay for long-term stability. Others argued that the Serbs who know their mountainous terrain better than any conceivable foe would not be easily intimidated into surrender and that the casualties from a widening of the war would in any case be too high. Nor could there be any guarantee that the Serbs would lose. Here are two arguments with a moral dimension but with contradictory implications for international order.

On the other hand even if there is no necessary accord on whether morality requires intervention or non-intervention in such a case, there does exist some limited consensus, at least verbally, on what constitutes internationally acceptable behaviour. It would include, for instance, the provision of aid to the victims of natural and man-made disasters and of asylum to the persecuted, respect for the 'rights' of minorities and of accredited diplomatic representatives. Unacceptable behaviour would now include imperialism, the wanton destruction of the biosphere and the infliction of unnecessary suffering during and after hostilities. Though such principles are frequently violated, it would be wrong to suppose that decision making automatically excludes any sense of international moral obligation. For when governments constantly reiterate their concern for moral values, their conduct is unlikely to be wholly unaffected. The classical dichotomy between ethics and interests is probably nearer fiction than reality: for moral scruple, sensitivity and sensibility, combined with a shrewd sense of political realities, have always played a part in sustaining that modicum of order which makes possible the continued functioning of international society.

NOTES

1. Schwarzenberger, G., *Power Politics*, New York, Praeger, 1941 and Wight, M., *Power Politics*, Harmondsworth, Penguin, 1978.
2. For a comprehensive elucidation of 'power' see, Minogue, K., 'Power in Politics', *Political Studies*, October 1959, pp. 269–89.
3. See, for example, Miller, J.D.B., *The Nature of Politics*, London, Duckworth, 1965, pp. 13–23.
4. For an analysis of those rules and institutions, see Bull, H., *The Anarchical Society*, London, Macmillan, 1977.
5. See, for example, Roetter, C., *Psychological Warfare*, London, Batsford, 1974.
6. For an excellent introduction to the subject, see, Doxey, M., *International Sanctions in Contemporary Perspective*, London, Macmillan, 1987.
7. *The Status of Law in International Society*, Princeton University Press, 1970, p. 177.
8. Brierly, J.R. in Lauterpacht, H. and Waldock, C.H. (eds), *The Basis of Obligation in International Law*, Oxford, Clarendon Press, 1958, p. 69.
9. See, for example, Maddock, R., 'The Global Political Economy' in Bayliss, J. and Rengger, N. (eds), *Dilemmas of World Politics*, Oxford, Clarendon Press, especially pp. 126–8.
10. On 'rules of the game' and their implications, see, Cohen, R., *International Politics, the Rules of the Game*, London, Longman, 1981.
11. Krasner, S. (ed.), *International Regimes*, New York, Cornell University Press, 1983.

12. See, for example, Midgley, E.B.F., *The Natural Law Tradition and the Theory of International Relations*, London, Elek, 1975 and Donelan, M., *Elements of International Political Theory*, Oxford, Clarendon Press, 1990, pp. 7–21. Also Bull, H., 'Natural law and international relations' in *British Journal of International Studies* vol. 5, July 1979, pp. 171–81.
13. See, for example, Niebuhr, R., *Moral Man and Immoral Society*, New York, Scribner, 1952; Butterfield, H., 'Morality and an International Order' in Porter, B. (ed.), *The Aberystwyth Papers*, London, Oxford University Press, 1972, pp. 336–57; Wolfers, A., *Discord and Collaboration*, Baltimore, Johns Hopkins University Press, 1966, and Stern, G., 'Morality and international order' in James, A. (ed.), *The Bases of International Order*, London, Oxford University Press, 1973, pp. 133–55.

CHAPTER 10

POWER BALANCES AND ALIGNMENTS

In one pithy sentence the 19th-century British apostle of free trade, Richard Cobden, dismissed the balance of power as: 'a phantasm, without definition, form or tangible existence—a mere conjunction of syllables, forming words which convey sound without meaning'.[1] For him the concept was not merely nonsensical. It was dangerous nonsense since even if it had no clear meaning it implied government intervention in the affairs of other countries, presupposing a world of division rather than of harmony in the pursuit of interests.

Yet ever since the dawn of history, some such concept has been a preoccupation of men of power. In his magisterial analysis of the Peloponnesian war, Thucydides concludes that 'what made war inevitable was the growth of Athenian power and the fear which this caused in Sparta'.[2] Later in the text he speaks of the Spartans voting 'that war should be declared because they were afraid of the further growth of Athenian power, seeing as they did, that already the greater part of Hellas was under the control of Athens'.[3] The implication, clearly, was that the only way to prevent Athens from taking over the whole of Hellas and to be able to establish some sort of balance was through war. But if Athens already controlled so much of Hellas, what kind of balance was possible? Containment...holding the line. But if Athens was that strong, how was Sparta going to be able to deter or defeat her? Thucydides suggests the answer in attributing to one Spartan leader: 'Others may have a lot of money and ships and horses, but we have good allies'[4] ie that shrewd diplomacy can compensate for economic or technological weakness.

As in Thucydides, so in Machiavelli there are several alternative formulations of 'the balance'. For example in *The Prince*, he warns, among other things, of the need for vigilance in a political context that he sees as 'zero sum' ie in which one person's gain is another's loss. 'Whoever is the cause of another becoming powerful is ruined himself.'[5]

Thus whereas Cobden appeared to think that the balance of power was meaningless, perhaps the main problem for scholars of International Relations is that it has too many meanings. As Inis Claude put it, even the teachers of the subject tend to 'slide blissfully from one usage of the term to another and back again, frequently without posting any warnings that plural meanings exist'.[6] What are its possible meanings? Two scholars in particular have done some valuable linguistic spadework. The first is Ernst Haas, who in a celebrated article: 'Balance of Power: prescription, concept or propaganda'[7] details eight possible connotations, all mutually exclusive. The second is the above-mentioned Professor Inis Claude, who in his book *Power and International Relations* produces a further useful inventory of possible definitions.

10.1 BALANCE OF POWER AS A DESCRIPTION

Significant indicators

Basically balance of power would appear to have three important connotations, the first being a purely descriptive term to denote any distribution of power, balanced or unbalanced—a kind of intellectual snapshot of the condition of international relations at any particular time. In the picture, so to speak, would be some perceived inventory of capabilities which the countries concerned could mobilise and utilise in support of objectives. But even as a descriptive term there can be controversy about the significant indicators in the balance and the nature of the situation to which it refers. Regarding the significant indicators, defence analysts at the Pentagon during the cold war tended to argue, as defence analysts often do, that the answer depended largely on relative military capabilities. For them the disposition of the balance was to be found in the military hardware and software available to the superpowers and also the force levels and deployments, command and control systems, payloads, megatonnages and throwweights. However, even if one accepted the questionable supposition that the military factor was decisive, it was open to the objection that the military balance was not so easily measured, that many elements of critical importance to the success or failure of a military enterprise could not be easily quantified. There were, for example, crucial technical questions about the mechanical reliability of weapons systems, the capacity to improve on them if necessary and the supply of spare parts. There were some equally important questions about geography. How was one to quantify the military advantage or otherwise of a state's location, size, terrain etc.? In a country like Bosnia, for example, the possession of mountains and the ability to use them for guerrilla warfare can be of vital significance. Possibly even more critical are the politically related factors: the degree of accord between political and military leaders, their resolve, their judgment and, more broadly, their ability to carry the country with them. For it was the lack of cohesion and morale that contributed to the collapse of the French war effort in 1940, the American role in Vietnam in the 1970s and the Soviet effort in Afghanistan in the 1980s. There is also the all-important question of the cohesion of an alliance system. Yet none of these factors, which vitally affect a military enterprise, can be easily measured.

But if one means by 'power' the capacity to achieve objectives, is the military factor necessarily the decisive test? After all, we have seen the collapse of one Superpower, the Soviet Union; the humbling of the other by countries such as North Vietnam and Iran; the humiliation of France in Algeria and Indo-China and of Britain in Egypt in 1956. Clearly any analysis of power balances has to take into account constraints as well as capabilities, and in assessing capabilities consideration has to be paid to more than just the military option. For in our nuclear age, military strength is one thing; the ability to get one's way another; and any realistic account of the capacity of states to outwit, outmanoeuvre or defeat their rivals has to be based on a whole range of diplomatic, economic, political and other considerations, including the skill of leaders in being able to choose the appropriate pressures for the end in view. Perhaps the Soviet theorists had a point when they came up with the conception of 'the correlation of forces', where the balance was seen as the product of a wide variety of factors, with political and ideological orientation taking a key place.

Definition of the situation

But disagreements can arise not only regarding the significant indicators in the balance but over perceptions and definitions of the situation itself. What one observer sees as an example of equilibrium between two or more powers, another might view as disequilibrium. There can also be lack of accord as to the precise direction the balance is taking—whether it is tilting towards or away from a particular power or group of powers. During the cold war, for example, there was much talk of strategic parity between Moscow and Washington, though some harboured the suspicion that the United States enjoyed superiority in most fields and was grossly overestimating the Soviet 'threat'. Ironically there were many in the West who seemed to share Moscow's erroneous perception that the world 'correlation of forces' was tilting in favour of socialism, and they took as evidence the fact that in the 1970s and early 1980s more countries than ever before had Communist or crypto-Communist regimes. What they ignored, however, was that many of the more recent additions were 'basket cases'—weak, impoverished, divided and a constant drain on the resources of Moscow or Peking. Moreover, they were often in conflict either with one another (one need only think of the Sino–Vietnamese and the Vietnamese–Cambodian wars of the late 1970s) or with themselves, with different Communist factions fighting it out in Ethiopia, Cambodia and Grenada, and, of course, in South Yemen—where the war between Communists became so intense at one time that Soviet officials had to take shelter in the British royal yacht *Britannia* to avoid getting caught in the crossfire. Not even Afghanistan was spared. While the Communists battled it out with the Mujaheddin, different wings of the party were also

settling political scores with one another in the streets of Kabul. Thus at
the very time when the global balance was being portrayed by both
Western alarmists and Communist propagandists as having tilted in
favour of Communism, the movement was in fact debilitated, divided,
nearly destitute and, as we now know, in possibly terminal decline.[8]

But even if it is agreed that some kind of equilibrium exists, there may
be disagreement as to its precise nature. During the cold war some
described the balance as loose ie flexible and bipolar, others as tight ie
inflexible and bipolar; others, yet again, included in their description a
significant third force—either a potential independent Superpower such
as China; or a bloc such as the non-aligned; or a balancer holding the ring
between the Superpowers, the EC for instance, or even China. However,
some ventured beyond triangular conceptions to talk of a multipolar or
polycentric world, at least in diplomatic and economic terms. Before entering office as National Security Advisor in 1969, Henry Kissinger spoke of a
world which was 'bipolar militarily but multipolar politically'.[9] Five years
later the late Professor Alistair Buchan spoke of a world which was strategically tripolar—the United States, the Soviet Union and China—and
economically pentipolar ie balanced among five centres, which he detailed
as the United States, Soviet Union, China, Western Europe and Japan.[10] As
with descriptions of the central balance, so in depictions of regional power
balances, whether regarding southern Europe, the Middle East, the Horn
of Africa or South East Asia, the experts may disagree. Where controversy
rages over intentions as well as over the balance of capabilities, lasting
peace accords between rival powers are difficult to achieve.

10.2 BALANCE OF POWER AS A POLICY

But balance of power is not just a descriptive term. It has a second set of
meanings as a policy—a policy, incidentally central to Realism, for which
order generally has to take priority over justice. What kind of policy? In
the classical writings on the subject—from Machiavelli to Morgenthau,
from Hume to Holsti, from Burke to Bull and from Castlereagh to
Churchill—the statesman is enjoined to aim for one of three things. The
first might be an even distribution of 'power', where power means the
capacity to produce intended effects between his state and any potential
rival or group or rivals. An example would be the decision of Britain's
Foreign Secretary, Canning, to call, as he put it, 'the New World into existence to redress the balance of the old',[11] after both France and Spain had
come under Bourbon rule. It was a notion which found its American coun-
terpart in the Monroe Doctrine of non-intervention in Europe in return for
European non-intervention in the Americas. In addition to an equal distribution of power, the aim might be a margin of strength over any military

or political rival. Here the word 'balance' is used in the sense of having a balance in the bank ie a surplus not an equality of assets and debits. Pushed to extremes, possessing a margin of strength can come to mean predominance, and here 'balance' comes to mean the opposite of its original sense—*over* balance. Certainly many felt this was the understanding of many of those Pentagon defence analysts referred to earlier when they spoke both of a balance between the Superpowers and of negotiating from strength. A third possible aspiration might be to be able to act as balancer, holding the ring between rival states and changing alignments in response to perceived shifts in capabilities. This, for example, had been Britain's traditional position at least since Elizabethan times, which is why it was dubbed 'perfidious Albion'—perfidious because it could not be relied upon to maintain any alignment for long. As the 19th-century Prime Minister, Palmerston, put it, Britain had no 'eternal ally or...perpetual enemy'. Only 'interests' were 'eternal and perpetual';[12] and Britain's sizable navy, which at the end of the century had to be as large as any two rivals put together, stood at the ready to service them.

Such policies can be pursued unilaterally or multilaterally, the latter either through formal alliances or less formal alignments or even through institutions such as the 19th-century Concert of Europe, the Council of the League of Nations, the Security Council of the UN—all set up in part to manage the balance in the interests of peace and order.

Purposes

But what was this balance supposed to do? Again from the classical writers we can infer that its purpose was one or more of the following: (1) prevent the establishment of a universal empire; (2) preserve the existing international system and the independence of the political actors within it; (3) provide the conditions in which other institutions on which international order depends—international law, diplomacy, international institutions, regimes, great power management etc—could operate; (4) deter war by assuring overly ambitious powers that any attempt at hegemony would meet a determined and effective collective response; (5) emerge victorious from any hostilities if deterrence failed and reinstate the vanquished into international society.[13]

In order to maintain a balance of power or rectify one perceived to be shifting to its detriment, a state or group of states may employ a number of different techniques or mechanisms.

Techniques

Alliances

They may form alliances, bilateral or multilateral, counter-alliances, align-ments (lacking the formality of alliance systems) or mutual security arrangements. These can be of global or merely of local significance. They may comprise volunteers, as has been the case with NATO, or conscripts ie states entered often unwillingly into an alliance system by the most powerful state in the region. Several members of the former Soviet-domi-nated Warsaw Pact and of the US-dominated Organisation of American States probably come into this latter category. They may be wartime or peacetime, offensive or defensive ie aimed at changing the status quo or supporting it; long or short term ie established to deal with a continuing threat or a sudden emergency. For the most part they are based on perceived needs not emotions. They exist to enable their members to increase their overall bargaining and fighting power in relation to their rivals and persist as long as those perceived needs remain. They tend to weaken in cohesion when a perceived threat disappears or when some members—NATO's Greece and Turkey, perhaps—come to regard some of their fellow members as more inimical to their interests than the presumed common enemy.

Intervention

A second technique for maintaining a perceived balance is intervention—a term with, again, many different definitions—but one of the more useful comes from Oran Young in an article written in 1968. 'Intervention refers to organised and systematic activity across recognised boundaries aimed at affecting...political authority structures...designed either to replace existing structures or to shore up structures thought to be in danger of collapse.'[14] Thus it can be offensive—aimed at changing a policy, an orientation, a government or a country's independent status. In this sense it is usually, though not invariably, an act of a greater against a lesser power and is primarily, though not exclusively, military in character. Moreover, though aimed at stability, it can engender destabilising resentments and hostilities. No doubt the anti-Russian feeling pervading much of the former Soviet bloc, the anti-Yankee sentiments in much of Latin America, the anti-Western and anti-Russian feeling in Iran, the anti-China mood in Vietnam and the anti-Vietnamese emotions in Cambodia are the products of such interventions and may eventually serve to undermine the capacity or the will of the perceived intruder to intervene again. There can also be defen-sive intervention or counter-intervention, aimed at preserving the status quo or restoring the status quo ante in face of a rival bid to establish politi-cal and economic control, as when 14 powers sent token forces to Russia in

1918 to try to restore the pre-Bolshevik regime; or when the Red Army shot its way to Budapest in 1956 and Kabul in 1979 to try to prevent the overthrow of a Communist regime; or, indeed, when American GIs entered South Korea, South Vietnam, Guatemala, the Dominican Republic and other Central and Latin American countries from 1950 onwards to shore up anti-Communist regimes. Such interventions may also eventually prove counter-productive, especially if they prop up unpopular regimes to the fury of their populations.

Since non-intervention has been a cardinal principle of international conduct, military interventions are almost always illegal unless in response to a request by a government or sanctioned by an international body such as the UN Security Council. On the other hand some political, economic and diplomatic pressures and inducements which can effectively make or unmake governments are lawful and sometimes stand a better chance of success than direct military intervention. For example, the collapse of Soviet power was not unrelated to the relentless political and economic pressure put on Moscow by its opponents in the West and beyond. By contrast, the continued existence of Israel in face of the hostility of its neighbours and many of its dispossessed Arab citizens may be said to have been due in part to the unfailing largesse of the United States.

Compensation

A third technique is what is called 'compensation', in which any increase in the components of power by one side is matched by some such increase on the part of its rival. In the 18th and 19th centuries for example, it was quite common for the balance to be regulated by means of agreed territorial adjustments. Sometimes it was in the nature of a straight swap—as when in 1720 the Duke of Savoy traded the kingdom of Sicily with the Holy Roman Emperor for the kingdom of Sardinia. Generally, however, the process was rather more haphazard and done without reference to the rulers or the inhabitants of the territories involved. Nobody asked the Poles at the end of the 18th century whether they wished their country to be partitioned among Russia, Prussia and Austria to maintain some kind of European balance; nor was the advice of Peking sought as the European powers plus Japan carved out large slices of Chinese territory ostensibly to stabilise some world balance. Nor is the process of compensation necessarily by agreement between rivals. Mussolini is supposed to have seized Albania in April 1939 in compensation for Hitler's seizure of Czechoslovakia the previous month and to have invaded Greece in October 1940 as a response to Hitler's occupation of Romania—though neither of the Duce's actions seem to have been worked out in consultation with the Führer. When Poland returned to the political map after the second world war, it had no control over the process by which as a country it was moved westward, the Russians taking much of what had been eastern Poland and, without consulting the Germans now under occupation, handing over to Poland a large slice of German territory up to the Oder–Neisse line.

But compensation can be claimed for something more intangible than territorial privation, for example loss of prestige—as when certain diplomats are declared *persona non grata* or foreign businessmen arrested on espionage charges. As often as not such actions will give rise to tit-for-tat expulsions and arrests if there is a cold war between the countries concerned. We saw this amply demonstrated in relations between Britain and the Soviet Union and between Britain and Iran in the 1980s, and when in 1992 fanatical Hindus demolished a mosque at Ayodyha in Uttar Pradesh, fanatical Moslems wreaked compensatory vengeance against Hindu temples not just in the Indian subcontinent but even in Britain, in turn generating further retaliatory action by Hindus.

But compensation can also have a more positive side—as in recent arms control negotiations based on the principle of balance. In the Strategic Arms Limitation Treaty of 1971 (SALT I), the Soviet Union was permitted to build more strategic weapons than the United States in a manifest attempt to stabilise the balance. In more recent disarmament arrangements involving intermediate-range nuclear missiles, it was on the whole the Soviet Union which made the greater sacrifices, again in the presumed interests of balance.

Spheres of influence

A fourth balance of power technique is that of spheres of influence, by which competing great powers delineate their areas of hegemony; in the hope of minimising friction each undertakes to respect what the other claims as its rights within its zone. From the mid-19th century, for example, much of northern and western Africa was divided between the British and the French, and on the whole each respected the spheres of the other. Much the same can be said for the Soviet and American spheres from the 1940s till the collapse of Eastern European Communism at the end of the 1980s—though the establishment of Communist and crypto-Communist regimes in Cuba, Nicaragua and Grenada and President Reagan's crusade in the early 1980s against the 'evil empire' threatened to erode these spheres. In general, however, they were maintained, and we can each have our own idea as to whether the overall effect was positive or negative.

There are, however, two anomalies that need to be explained: one relating to Greece in the 1940s, the other to Afghanistan in the 1970s. At the time of the Communist insurrection in Greece in 1944 and the subsequent Greek civil war, many Western commentators maintained that Stalin had breached the spheres of influence arrangement he had entered into with

Roosevelt and Churchill during the war. However, the evidence now available suggests that the Communists in Greece were acting on their own initiative and though Communists in Yugoslavia and Bulgaria supplied them for a time, they received little or no direct support from Moscow. Thus, Stalin more or less stuck to the agreements by which Greece was in the Western sphere. As for Afghanistan, the evidence, leaving aside the moral question of whether there ought to be spheres of influence at all, indicates that the Soviet Union had had a close relationship with Kabul ever since 1919 and had been developing Afghanistan's industry and infrastructure since 1954. During those years the West showed little or no interest in the country, and in this sense the implication was that Afghanistan, at least since 1954, was within the Soviet sphere.

Buffer zones

A fifth technique for managing the international balance and incidentally trying to reduce conflict between antagonists is the establishment of buffer zones, generally small or weak powers situated between two or more greater powers. The underlying assumption is that it is in the interests of each great power to prevent the others from controlling the buffer, that preserving the integrity of the small state in the middle is preferable to its falling prey to a rival. Switzerland, Luxembourg, Belgium, Austria, Afghanistan, Nepal and Korea have all at one stage or another been called upon to play this role. Often for this purpose they are neutralised ie accorded neutral status in law by which they are prohibited from joining alliances, their neutrality being guaranteed by the powers. In time of war, however, there is in fact no guarantee that that guarantee will be respected—and in the case of Belgium and Luxembourg during both world wars and in Korea from 1910 to recent times, it was not.

Divide and rule

A sixth technique is one associated with ancient Rome—*divide et impera*, divide and rule—in which a great power tries either to split its opponents, potential opponents and competitors into hostile camps or to sharpen their disagreements, often by siding with an enemy's enemy in a dispute and then changing sides as the power situation seems to demand. Clearly, various Western powers have used recent hostilities between Iran and Iraq for this purpose. On the other hand any short-term advantage may be outweighed by the discredit it can bring in the long term, as when some British Ministers are discovered to have encouraged arms sales to Iraq contrary to declared government policy.

Other techniques

Among other techniques in maintaining or restoring some kind of equilibrium are on the one hand diplomatic bargaining (usually in secret), the
legal or judicial settlement of disputes and partial and selective disarmament and on the other hand arms sales, arms races, space races and,
arguably, war (if, that is, resort to war can be considered a technique in the
maintainance of balance rather than its breakdown). What is clear is that in
the interests of balance, vanquished powers tend to be reinstated to international society following hostilities as, for example, France after 1815,
Germany after 1918, Germany and Japan after 1945.

10.3 BALANCE OF POWER AS A STATISTICAL TENDENCY

Having examined balance of power as a descriptive term and as a policy, it
is time to consider a third connotation, which is of a supposed fundamental law of history or statistical tendency. This suggests that any power
seemingly bent on establishing international hegemony will sooner or
later provoke a hostile and countervailing coalition. Here the theory can
be compared to a Newtonian conception of a universe in equilibrium, to a
biological balance of nature between organism and environment, to an
economic law, with its interest in a balance of countervailing forces such as
supply and demand. In this sense it arises without conscious effort. It just
happens, as when a Xerxes, Attila the Hun, Genghis Khan, Napoleon,
Hitler, Stalin or even a Saddam Hussein are perceived to be aiming at
some kind of hegemony—local, regional or global. On the other hand the
fact that some leaders often succeed in securing major territorial advantages suggests that if the balance is to be considered as a mechanism for
limiting excessive power, it tends to come into operation later rather than
sooner. As suggested in the previous chapter, in the short run governments will often try to avoid involvement, as was the case with Bosnian
Serb and Bosnian Croat expansionism.

Such balance of power theories are structural or systemic and imply
that (1) if the structure of the system as perceived alters, then the behaviour of governments tends to change too, as new alignments are forged
and old ones go into disuse; (2) the system as perceived with its emphasis
on *raison d'état* tends to impose a considerable degree of uniformity of
behaviour upon states regardless of their ideology, political culture,
economic system or class structure. For this reason an official or state ideology, whether Marxism–Leninism, Islamic Fundamentalism or even
Cobdenite liberal universalism tends to be seen by the theorists as a function or rationalisation of interest; (3) the system as perceived places limits
on the policy choices available to governments, and (4) as a consequence
even radical or revolutionary governments are often obliged after an initial

period of turmoil to act in part according to the foreign political agendas of their predecessors and of their neighbours. One need only think of the deradicalisation of the original revolutionary agenda of the Soviet Union and of China and their quest for recognition, credits and technological knowhow.

10.4 CRITIQUES OF THE CONCEPT

If for Cobden the balance of power concept was intellectually barren, many 20th-century Pluralists—among them John Burton and James Rosenau—would take the intellectual critique a little further: if balance of power had any meaning at all it rested on generalisations both untested and untestable about the relentless pursuit by governments of power;[15] further, that it presented a static, deterministic world based on 'zero-sum' reasoning in which all outcomes are determined by threat, display or use of force. Since the end of the first world war, however, it has been not so much its alleged intellectual poverty as its presumed moral and practical weaknesses that have disturbed the critics, particularly in relation to techniques of managing the balance. People like Woodrow Wilson placed on those techniques the responsibility for the first world war,[16] and in recent times there has been no shortage of critics. What are their grounds of complaint? (1) That the politics of balance of power put a premium on order over justice; (2) that they serve the interests of the greater over those of the smaller powers; (3) that they disregard international law; (4) that they are a source of war; (5) that in a thermonuclear world they are obsolete; (6) that in an interdependent world they are inappropriate. Some of those objections are more powerful than others, but they all merit an answer.

10.5 CRITIQUES OF THE CRITIQUES

As to balance-of-power thinking being intellectually barren, there is always a problem with any concept that is ambiguous. On the other hand if we students of IR were to be intolerant of ambiguity, we would hardly have a subject at all. But with the help of linguistic analysis we can sort out some of the applications of such terms, which have meaning and value to those who use them. Throughout the ages balance of power terminology has been employed: first, to characterise the state of international affairs— locally, regionally and globally; second, as a guide to policy—in particular to tackling the security dilemma that faces every government and to realising the need to make provision for future contingencies and, third, as a method of explaining cyclical patterns in international relationships—the challenges and responses, the assertions and denials of sovereign status and the checks and balances on expansionism.

Regarding the claim that balance of power theories are untested and untestable, it is true that they cannot be validated in the way that one can verify, say, the boiling or freezing point of water. But then, for reasons essayed in the first chapter, the nature of proof is always problematic in the social sciences. However, while there is no proof, there is ample histor-ical evidence to support many balance of power propositions. On the other hand such propositions need to be clearly understood, and, sadly, they are often not. First, balance of power theorists do not as a rule hold that governments are motivated solely by the acquisition and maintenance of power. Governments generally have a broad agenda of aims, but the claim of balance of power theorists is that administrations need to concern themselves with power capabilities and relations if they are to stand a chance of securing some of their ambitions. Second, such theorists do not posit an unchanging and unchangable world. Though they suggest a world of continued constraints and limitations, they can point, among other things, to shifting patterns of power from the 17th century onwards and to watershed periods—such as the French revolutionary wars, the end of the first and second world wars and the collapse of East European Communism—when one political configuration appears to end and another to begin. Third, balance of power theorists do not necessarily take a 'zero-sum' approach. Men like George Kennan, Hans Morgenthau and Henry Kissinger were constantly searching for balances which might serve the interests simultaneously of a large number of states, including small states. Finally, while such theorists at one time tended to stress the military factor, today they examine a wide spectrum of capabilities—economic, political, diplomatic etc—that govern relations and enable states to survive and prosper.

The claim that balance of power theorists tend to stress order over justice is probably true, though most would claim that unless there is a modicum of order, 'justice', in any of the guises essayed by Hedley Bull in *The Anarchical Society*, cannot in any case be secured. After all, where there is anarchy, few benefit apart from the bandits.

The claim that balance of power policies serve the interests of the great powers is, again, probably true. However, that those interests are always at variance with those of the smaller powers would seem to introduce an unwarranted 'zero-sum' dimension into the equation. Whether smaller powers suffer or not would depend on the circumstances. True, during the cold war several East European and Latin American countries for a time appeared to lose the capacity to exercise effective sovereignty, but on the other hand it could be argued that the interests of many a Third World country benefited from bipolarity as they were able to play off one set of hostile powers against another.

The notion that balance of power theory disregards international law is at best a half-truth. Yes, 'balance' thinking has led to particular breaches of law. On the other hand it could be argued that without the kind of international order which balance of power is supposed to preserve, the system of international law could not properly function at all.

What of the oft-heard claim after the outbreak of war in 1914 that balance of power thinking was largely responsible? One could, in fact, assert with equal justification that if only there had been some kind of balance, say, an arms race, before 1939, instead of a one-sided military build-up by the Fascist powers, Hitler might have been deterred from some of his conquests and a second world war might have been averted. Equally, if the Bosnian government had had the weaponry of their opponents, the Bosnian conflict might have been much shorter. The point is that though a particular war might result from a particular application of balance precepts, war avoidance might be the resultant of other applications. For much of the post-war period the theorists debated among themselves which international political configuration best served the interests of peace, multipolarity (Deutsch and Singer)[17] or bipolarity (Waltz), while Organski suggested that peace was best served when those with preponderant power were interested in the status quo.[18] If historical experience is anything to go by, bipolar configurations probably preserve peace longest. On the other hand the implications of breakdown are particularly serious. In multipolar configurations, as in the 18th century, wars tend to be more frequent but less catastrophic.

The argument that balance of power policies are obsolete in a thermonuclear world seems to depend on a very narrow interpretation of world politics. Clearly the possession of such weapons by some half-dozen countries introduces a novel dimension into balance mechanisms—as new weapons always do—but it does not necessarily render balance of power thinking obsolete. The idea of a balance of terror, which may be said to date back at least to the ancient Greeks, is but another variation of the balance of power, and it can be argued that between non-nuclear powers and between nuclear and non-nuclear powers at the local and regional level—whether in the Middle East, southern Africa, southern Asia or wherever—power considerations are no less relevant today than they were before. The same argument may be used in answer to those claiming that interdependence renders balance notions inappropriate or inapposite. Admittedly the emerging patterns of economic and political integration in Western Europe, North America and South East Asia somewhat inhibit the degree of policy flexibility normally required for an effective balancing process. On the other hand with sovereign status still sought, attained, nurtured and prized, notions of power balances would appear to be no more inapposite today than the notion of the state, the nation and of international society—all mental constructs which continue to exert enormous influence on our thinking and behaviour.

NOTES

1. Cobden, R., 'Russia' (1836) in *Political Writings*, Vol. I, Ridgway, London, 1868, p. 263.
2. *The Peloponnesian War*, translated by Rex Warner, Harmondsworth, Penguin, p. 49.
3. *Ibid.*, p. 87.
4. Ibid., p. 86.
5. Quoted in Padelford, N. and Lincoln, G., *International Politics: Foundations of International Relations*, New York, Macmillan, 1954, p. 198.
6. Claude, I, *Power and International Relations*, New York, Random House, 1962, p. 22.
7. *World Politics*, vol. 5, July 1953, pp. 442–77.
8. Stern, G., *The Rise and Decline of International Communism*, Aldershot, Elgar, 1990, pp. 234–48.
9. 'Central issues of American Foreign Policy' in *Agenda for the Nation*, Washington DC, Brookings Institution, 1968.
10. *The End of the Postwar Era*, London, Weidenfeld and Nicolson, 1974.
11. Therry, R., *The Speeches of George Canning*, Vol. VI, London, Ridgeway, 1828, p. 111.
12. Speech in the House of Commons, 1 March 1848, *Parliamentary Debates*, Third Series, Vol. 97, Col 122.
13. Bull, H., *The Anarchical Society*, London, Methuen, 1977, pp. 101–26.
14. 'Intervention and the international system', *International Journal*, vol. 22, no. 2, 1968, pp. 177–87.
15. For example, Burton, J., *World Society*, Cambridge, Cambridge University Press, 1972 and Rosenau, J., *The Study of Global Interdependence*, London, Pinter, 1980.
16. In his speech to Congress, 11 February 1918, Wilson spoke of the balance as 'the great game, now for ever discredited'.
17. See, for example, Jones, W.J., *The Logic of International Relations*, 6th ed., Glenview, Scott and Co, 1988, pp. 315–16.
18. Organski A.F.K., *World Politics*, 2nd ed., New York, Knopf, 1968, pp. 282–99.

CHAPTER 11

DIPLOMACY: OLD AND NEW

In the previous two chapters we began to explore some of the elements comprising that modicum of order obtaining internationally—the constraints and rules, written and unwritten and the various dimensions of the power balance. In this chapter we examine a further element—an institution which has lubricated the intercourse between communities since the dawn of history—diplomacy. But first, what precisely is it, and why, if diplomacy plays an important role in the orderly relations between states, have its practitioners so often been derided?

11.1 CONNOTATIONS

Though the term 'diplomacy' would appear to be one of the least controversial in this study, like the other key concepts it has a number of different, if related applications, one of which need not concern us here. That is the use of the expression as a synonym for foreign policy, a subject which was considered in an earlier chapter. A second and much older conception concerns the orderly conduct of relations between one political community and another, following the despatch from one tribe to another of an envoy or messenger indicating an intention to parley on matters of common concern. A third connotation concentrates on the factor of negotiations between one community and another, while a fourth focuses specifically on negotiations between one state and another. A fifth and more recent application is concerned with negotiations between politically significant entities, which would include so-called 'liberation groups', MNCs, international organisations as well as sovereign states. In a further construction diplomacy is understood in terms of the bureaucratic machinery underpinning the process of international negotiations ie the offices, divisions and bureaus of the home establishment, the embassies and legations abroad, the rules of procedure, diplomatic protocol and immunities.

In a further guise, diplomacy is a term widely employed to describe the kinds of skills—intelligence, tact, patience and empathy—writers often claim are required for successful negotiations. Thus when a college tutor commends a none too penetrating essay by a not especially brilliant tutee with some such cant phrase as 'shows a steady grasp of essentials', he is clearly being diplomatic. If he writes, 'with a brain like yours you can never hope to succeed', he is not. There are two further uses of the term:

diplomacy as a branch of the foreign service; and diplomacy as what professional diplomats do. In this chapter particular attention will be paid to the last of these.

11.2 EVOLUTION

Though in some guise or other diplomatic activity is thousands of years old, as applied to the conduct of international business by professional diplomats the term is comparatively recent. The Latin word 'diploma', derived from a Greek word meaning 'to fold', originally referred to metal plates, stamped and folded, issued by the Roman authorities to those travelling along imperial roads or going abroad on official business. The 'diploma' was thus a pass or a passport, and when the term was extended to cover virtually any official document, there was soon a need for a cluster of clerks to decipher, index and preserve such documents in the imperial archives. The ascription 'diplomatist' was the word given to the archivist, and diplomatic business was the business of dealing with archives. But the archivist works on precedence and experience, as does the modern diplomat, and many medieval and Renaissance envoys, especially those despatched by the Pope in Rome, were either archivists themselves or had been tutored by them. Hence the connection between the older and more modern usage of the term 'diplomacy'.[1]

Pre-historic

According to medieval legend, the first diplomats known to humankind were archangels because they had acted as messengers between heaven and earth. None the less, envoys probably existed long before people were receiving angelic visions. The former diplomat Harold Nicolson in a classic study suggests a pre-historic origin, in which hostile tribes, tired of slaughtering one another over hunting boundaries, stolen cattle, abducted womenfolk or whatever and anxious for a truce to bury their dead, decided to try to reach some accommodation. But for the process to begin, one side would have had to have taken the initiative and to have chosen a suitable envoy to approach the enemy unarmed. To both allay suspicion and suggest seriousness of purpose, it will have been necessary to garb the envoy in a distinctive non-military dress, to adorn his or her body with religious symbols or recognised emblems of peace and to have chosen for the purpose people of an impressive and dignified demeanour. In addition the envoys will have required courage, a good constitution, a retentive memory and, above all, a loud voice, since they were, after all, heralds and messengers. But for negotiations to follow, the envoys will have had to have been accorded certain privileges denied to warriors, including the right to return unmolested to their people. In this respect diplomatic immunity will have been among the earliest of the man-made rights.[2]

Greek

By the time of the ancient Greek city states the envoy's tasks were more demanding, since he or she was required to argue before the assembly of the host state ie to be a skilled orator, adept at conducting negotiations and in the full glare of publicity. As a diplomatic system it was, however, fatally flawed. For the missions tended to consist of several envoys, each representing a particular political faction, and as such they would be inclined to spend more time in surveillance of fellow envoys than in pleading the cause of their city. And because an incautious remark or indiscreet phrase could be taken out of context by a rival emissary and used back home as evidence of corruption or even treachery, the envoys soon developed the art of talking without saying anything. Thus, the empty rhetoric of the 'let me make it absolutely clear', 'at the end of the day', 'if you will', 'in real terms', 'with respect', 'if I may say so', variety has a long history. Perhaps this was only to be expected given that the ancient Greeks chose as patron of ambassadors and heralds the god Hermes, who was also the patron of vagabonds, thieves and liars.[3]

Roman

Under the Romans, diplomacy had to fit into the imperial pattern. And though it meant the development of treaty law, it was on a basis almost always advantageous to the Romans. Foreign envoys would be handed the Roman draft of a treaty, and if there was too much argument they would be given a deadline. Should the deadline be reached without agreement, they would often be stripped of their immunity, denounced as spies or speculators and escorted back to the frontiers of their own country as virtual prisoners. Moreover, in order to secure the other side's respect for the 'sanctity' of treaties, the Romans would often insist on the surrender of diplomatic hostages as a guarantee of good behaviour—a practice which, mercifully, later fell into disuse. But the Roman contribution to legal procedure was certainly not matched by any corresponding contribution to the art of diplomacy.[4]

Papal

If imperial Rome was strong enough to be somewhat cavalier about diplomacy, papal Rome was different. For by its position as simultaneously Italy's largest state and the fount of Christendom, the papacy had to enter into relations with the governments of Europe if only to keep them doctrinally in line and to deal with contentions between church and state. Though the first such representatives were 'legates', people sent on temporary missions, by the 13th century they were being supplemented by 'nuncios', whose missions were more prolonged and whose tasks were not dissimilar from those later entrusted to ambassadors in a secular state ie to represent and implement the policies of their sovereign. In theory they were governed in their conduct of relations by ecclesiastical rules known as canon law; in practice they were soon to adopt the gamut of practices characterising the diplomacy of the rest of the Italian peninsula ranging from arbitration, negotiation, treaty-making and alliances down to intelligence-gathering, espionage, subversion, conspiracy and the adroit use of poison and the stiletto.[5]

Byzantine

If to papal Rome diplomacy was a valuable adjunct to policy, for the Byzantine empire it was essential. Without it, the empire probably could not have survived so long. With scores of 'barbarian' tribes on its borders, its only hope lay in either playing off one potential enemy against another or in bribing or converting them to Christianity, and that called for another diplomatic dimension—accurate information about the state of mind of neighbouring rulers. The Byzantine emperors met the problem by appointing to other courts on a semi-permanent basis envoys with trained powers of observation and sound judgement who would regularly report back to a department for external affairs based in Constantinople. There all reports were carefully sifted, a policy thrashed out and instructions despatched telling the ambassadors what line they should take; the first time diplomacy had been regarded as anything more than an improvised, *ad hoc* activity. On the other hand because of their evident role as informers, the ambassadors were generally mistrusted by both sides. They were sometimes virtually interned by the host country, while the Byzantine emperors would ensure that anyone not on official business would be denied access to foreign envoys. At the same time to impress the foreign diplomats (and by implication the governments they served), the emperors would mount endless military parades, often with the same troops entering by one gate, passing out by another, running round the back, changing uniforms and marching past again. Meanwhile, many an ambassador coming within the Imperial Presence was greeted with an elaborate ceremonial that would have outdone in theatricality even the most outlandish Andrew Lloyd Webber extravaganza. For on rising from their kneelings and prostrations before the emperor, an ambassador would have discovered that the throne of his Imperial Majesty had risen up in the air as if by magic, while the carved gilt lions at the side of the chair of state were belching forth fire and smoke and giving out the most terrifying roars. It was all, of course, done by an elaborate system of pulleys and with an inordinate number of slaves, but it evidently impressed the more credulous envoys to the Imperial Court.[6]

Renaissance Italian

Even though both Rome and Byzantium were centres of what diplomatic interchange there was, diplomacy could hardly yet be called a profession, nor was there any system of regular, diplomatic interchange with permanent embassies, rules of procedure and precedence. Diplomacy was still fitful and sporadic rather than habitual and residential. Such diplomats as existed were generally expected to pay out of their own pocket for their travel and entertainment, the upkeep of their foreign residence and any staff which meant that the diplomat generally had to be a wealthy aristocrat or else a travelling salesman who could pay for his keep by unloading commodities and materials on to local markets. Not surprisingly, therefore, diplomacy was an occupation not exactly overburdened with potential recruits, and till it became a regularly paid profession in the 18th century governments often resorted to methods not unlike those of the naval press gang to induce the wealthy to take up a diplomatic post. In the Florence of Machiavelli, reluctant ambassadors designate would sometimes be conducted to their post by what in theory was a guard of honour, in practice an armed escort. On the other hand, it was in Italy that diplomacy as both organised system and profession may be said to have taken root. The papacy had long ago pointed the way, and at about the time of the Renaissance, the Italian city states—with their interconnecting economic and security interests as well as their rivalries—turned their temporary missions into permanent legations and embassies.

If modern diplomacy as a permanent and not *ad hoc* proceeding can be said to have an origin, it may have begun in Genoa in 1455 when the Duke of Milan established the first recorded permanent mission. By the end of the 15th century most of the capitals of the Italian city states hosted the permanent missions of their Italian neighbours, and by the beginning of the 16th century the Italian states had established permanent embassies in London and Paris and at the court of the Holy Roman Emperor. Thereafter it was only a matter of time before the other governments followed suit. It would still, however, be another century before diplomacy became regarded as a profession worthy of some kind of payment, another two centuries before the profession was governed by a system of precedence consistent with the doctrine of legal equality. Meanwhile several countries continued to exercise close supervision of foreign envoys or to resist their presence altogether. And no wonder, because the diplomats of the 16th and 17th centuries often provided good grounds for the suspicion from which their successors have often suffered. They bribed courtiers, financed rebellions, encouraged opposition parties; they subverted, seduced, lied, spied and stole official documents, convinced that private and public morality were two different things. Hence, when Soviet and American intelligence bugged each other's embassies during the cold war, they were doing nothing new. They were merely applying new technology to an old practice.[7]

Post-Westphalian

In the post-Westphalian world, which was neither in a Hobbesian state of nature nor in process of moving towards a Kantian perpetual peace, diplomacy had to change if it was to serve as one of the major pillars for upholding such international order as there was. And change it did. At this time diplomacy began to be organised as a profession, if not always a paying one. In the process, the diplomatic resources of the state began to be arranged between separate ministries; official despatches began to be regarded as state property rather than the personal possession of the envoy; and in time the diplomats began to develop their own social manners and rules of procedure, styled largely on French diplomatic etiquette. By the beginning of the 18th century the profession appeared to possess a kind of corporate identity. Members of the *corps diplomatique* came from similar aristocratic backgrounds, spoke the same language, French, having by now discarded Latin as the language of diplomacy, shared similar tastes and, like boys from a select public school, 'understood' one another. They could argue, bargain and intrigue usually without banging the table. They could swap gossip and mistresses generally without raising their voices. It was all very gentlemanly, polite, civilised, exclusive and secret. The only role for the citizenry, who played no part in the proceedings, was to gape at the magnificent diplomatic coaches as they drove from one palace to another in a seemingly endless round of banquets, balls and conferences.

Moreover, from 1716, when the French diplomat François de Callières published his treatise *De la Manière de negoçier avec les Souverains*, (On the Manner of Negotiating with Princes), the profession now had a kind of Bible—a manual, incidentally, which could hardly be further removed from the spirit of *The Prince*. For example:

> The good negotiator will never base the success of his negotiations upon false promises or breaches of faith; it is an error to suppose, as public opinion supposes, that it is necessary for an efficient Ambassador to be a past master at the art of deception. Dishonesty is in fact little more than a proof of the smallness of mind of him who resorts to it and shows that he is too meagrely equipped to gain his purposes by just and reasonable methods.[8]

With such sentiments, de Callières probably did more than anyone to counteract the long-held view that diplomacy was a somewhat discreditable profession and the ambassador, in the famous words of the 17th-century British diplomat Sir Henry Wootten, 'an honest man who is sent to lie abroad for the good of his country'.

On the other hand diplomacy never entirely lost its discreditable side. The age of 'boudoir diplomacy', largely focused on Catherine the Great's much frequented bedroom in St Petersburg and involving some of the handsomest men in the diplomatic service, was yet to come. There were also to be numerous unseemly wrangles over rank and precedence. At one time the Pope had tried to have the last word on the subject. In a memorandum of 1504 he had placed himself first among the monarchs of the earth, nominated the Holy Roman Emperor and his heir apparent as second and third, followed by the kings of France, Spain, Portugal and Britain. The king of Denmark was last in the papal pecking order, though not surprisingly the list fell into disuse as more and more states abandoned Roman Catholicism, and even Catholic monarchs increasingly questioned a proceeding that could reflect adversely on their own honour and prestige. But the jostling of their representatives to be at or near the head of any ceremonial procession would often lead to violence, to be followed by duels or threats of diplomatic rupture unless honour was satisfied in the shape of an apology or financial reparation.[9] It was not until 1815 at the Congress of Vienna, following the French Revolutionary wars, that a formula was finally arrived at for establishing rules of precedence and protocol. Even so, the presiding monarchs had to be assured prior to the meeting that the conference hall would have five equal doors so that they could enter and depart simultaneously without anyone yielding precedence and that the conference table would be circular, thereby eliminating the problem of who should sit at its head.[10]

Post-Vienna

Vienna established that ambassadors and papal nuncios would be accorded the highest rank, to be followed by envoys extraordinary and ministers plenipotentiary, then ministers resident and, finally, the chargé d'affaires, the official temporarily in charge in the absence of the ambassador or minister. At a subsequent conference, in Aix-la-Chapelle in 1818, it was agreed that among members of the same rank, precedence should be established not on the prestige or power of the diplomat's government but solely on the length of time the diplomat had served in the country—the longest-serving ambassador being referred to as the 'doyen' or dean of the diplomatic corps and taking precedence over all the other ambassadors. With the rules of precedence now standardised, henceforth the diplomat could devote much more attention to matters of substance instead of worrying about his place in the pecking order.

11.3 DIPLOMATIC FUNCTIONS

Until recently a single envoy might have had to fulfil several different functions simultaneously. Nowadays diplomacy is a much more specialised affair, yet in the course of duty a diplomat may be called upon to serve in a variety of capacities, among them:

1. *Representation* Once the representative of a monarch, the diplomat is now the agent of a country; and the courtesies, privileges and immunities accorded him or her are on a par with those normally extended to visiting heads of state. In this representative capacity the diplomat usually has an associated function—historically as old as diplomacy itself;

2. *Communication* The most elementary function of the diplomat is to be a messenger, to reflect the government's views in accordance with instructions. If the views change overnight, as they have tended to do in times of absolutist kings or authoritarian rulers, the diplomat has to reflect and defend that change. For some diplomats this has not been easy. It is quite clear, for example, that diplomats under Fascist and Communist rulers (and sometimes under democracies as well) have suffered crises of conscience in having to justify policies in which they do not believe. To quote a recent example. The former minister counsellor of one of the Yugoslav embassies was obliged to defend Belgrade's policy of supporting the activities of the Bosnian Serbs. It later transpired that he was himself a Bosnian Serb, born in Sarajevo where his family still lived, and where his brother was in charge of one of the hospitals. In utter despair at the antics of some of his more militant fellow countrymen, he endorsed in an interview the policy of sanctions against the very government he was supposed to be representing. Needless to say, having failed to maintain the line he was paid to defend, he was recalled to take up a far less prestigious post.

3. *Negotiation* The late Harold Nicolson, himself a diplomat, called diplomacy 'the art of negotiating between conflicting interests'. This is an over-simplification, not least in that it presupposes that interests always conflict and that it is the diplomat's task to reconcile them. In fact, interests often overlap or coincide, and part of the diplomat's function is to explore the degree of common ground that exists. Naturally when interests do conflict it is normally the diplomat's function to see whether there is any possibility of reconciliation, and this is a process that can continue even during a war. On the other hand at a time of cold war, it may be part of the diplomat's function to make

impossible demands and then put the onus for rejection on the negotiating partner. This, for example, was the fate of many a disarmament or arms control proposal in the fifties and sixties. The diplomats of one superpower would put forward a draft that contained a unilateral advantage to that power which would, of course, prove unacceptable to the other side. Once the other side had, as expected, rejected the proposal, it would be immediately branded 'a war monger'. In effect, disarmament and arms control negotiations had then become part of the fabric of the cold war.[11] None the less, in general, negotiators are charged with securing positive rather than negative results.

4. *Ingratiation*—winning friends and influencing people—and in an age of mass communications this often means media people, who, like politicians, civil servants and academics, are in a position to shape minds and attitudes. Many an academic will have enjoyed the hospitality of envoys who thought we were worth cultivating. The writer, once a specialist on the Communist world, found the Eastern European and the Chinese embassies especially attentive. Significantly, the more unpopular the country the more excessive seemed to be the hospitality. In the case of the Czech embassy in London, receptions, once so lavish, were drastically reduced in scale in 1968 and early 1969, during the 'Prague Spring' when the late Alexander Dubcek was the toast of the Western world, only to become much more extravagant when the country again came under hardline Communist control. But attempts at ingratiation are not just about courting popularity. They also have to do with a fifth function of diplomacy.

5. *The extraction of information* The gathering of intelligence has long been a key function of diplomatic activity, and in an age of rapidly developing industrial and military technology when knowledge is power, access to classified government or commercial material becomes particularly important. Once asked to explain the difference between a political attaché and a spy, a political attaché at the former Yugoslav embassy in London gave a revealing answer: 'There is an invisible line between normal intelligence gathering (which comes from open sources) and espionage that you cross at your peril. If you go over that line and are a foreign national, you get arrested. If you are a diplomat and cross the line, you are declared *persona non grata* and thrown out.' It was an answer all the more interesting for the fact that shortly after that conversation the attaché in question was declared *persona non grata* and expelled. But as is clear from both the 'Iran-' and the 'Iraq-gate' scandals, the quest for information can be a deadly and vicious game.

6. *Recommendation* ie tendering advice to the home government on the basis of the diplomat's appreciation of the situation in the country to which he or she is accredited. As will be revealed later, such advice can

still be critical in helping a government frame its policy towards the country in question.

Among other diplomatic functions are the protection of nationals resident in the country to which he or she is accredited and the registration of their births, marriages and deaths.

11.4 CRITIQUE OF 'OLD' DIPLOMACY

Diplomacy serves as both an instrument of state policy and a major agency in the maintenance of international order. Why then did it come into such disrepute earlier this century? Many held what they regarded as the 'old diplomacy' to be responsible for the first world war. In particular, people like Woodrow Wilson castigated it for its secrecy, duplicity, unrepresentativeness, lack of political accountability and archaic language and proceedings.[12] But in their reproofs they were confusing the formulation of policy with its execution. The diplomats were themselves no more responsible for the secret treaties prior to and during the first world war than they were for the spheres of influence arrangements of the second world war. It was not the diplomats but the politicians who decided on the non-publication of such agreements. The diplomats were merely called upon to make the necessary arrangmements. It is true that diplomatic discussions generally take place in secret, but then it is hard to see how negotiations can ever be successfully concluded if constantly subjected to the glare of publicity. After all, an accord generally requires concession and compromise, something not easily made in the public gaze. In any case, if the expectations aroused by publicity are not met there is always the danger of public recrimination, which can hamper future diplomatic dialogue. It is doubtful, for example, whether the compromises necessary to pave the way for Kissinger's visit to Peking in the early 1970s, President Sadat's trip to Israel in the late 1970s or Arafat's provisional deal with the Israelis in 1993 could have been made without the strictest secrecy between the parties and their diplomatic intermediaries.

Significantly, Woodrow Wilson, who had called for 'Open covenants, openly arrived at' himself became a convert to secret diplomacy. When the peace treaty was being negotiated after the first world war he had two American marines with fixed bayonets standing guard outside the Palace at Versailles. He had come to believe in open covenants secretly arrived at, suggesting once again that criticism of the 'old diplomacy', so-called, should have been addressed to the politicians who refused to publicise their treaty arrangements rather than the diplomats who did their masters' bidding.

Moreover, though many believe that with the growth of multilateral diplomacy through international, regional and transnational bodies, secret diplomacy is now a thing of the past, this is an illusion. True, the deliberations of the UN General Assembly and of the European parliament are available to press and television. But what happens in such forums is often far less important than what goes on behind the scenes—in the delegate's lounges, the lobbies and even in the lavatories. It appears, for example, that the matter of the Berlin Blockade was more or less resolved in one of the urinals where the Russian and American Ambassadors happened to have a chance encounter.[13] But it is as well that the stratagem they worked out together never hit the headlines at the time, since any premature disclosure might have led to the shelving of the plan. The fact is that though international organisations may have changed the form, they do not necessarily alter the content of diplomacy. Diplomatic skills are needed as much in a multilateral as in a bilateral context.

As for duplicity, when it occurs it generally has to do with instructions from political masters. A diplomat may be required to be 'economical with the truth' either if his or her government is involved in highly questionable activities or if he or she is on a delicate mission. It is said, for example, that shortly after President Kennedy arrived in Berlin in 1963 to raise morale in that divided city, one of his aides was dismissed for having publicly ventured the opinion that the US 'would never fight for Berlin'. Whether the statement was true or false, it was clearly undiplomatic and could only undermine what the president had been trying to achieve. In diplomacy, candour cannot always be considered a virtue.

As to the criticism that the diplomatic service is both unrepresentative and lacking in political accountability, here there may be valid grounds for complaint. Certainly till recently in Western Europe the profession tended to be drawn from the upper middle class, in the United States it tended to be drawn from the wealthy and in the Communist and Third World countries the recruits tended to be the trusties of the ruling party or establishment. However in many countries it is changing. In Britain, at one time overwhelmingly 'Oxbridge', the diplomatic service now contains many from the newer universities, not least graduates from the LSE's International Relations department. True, the service does its own recruiting and may have a traditional brand image of the kind of character it is looking for. But at least it draws them from a much broader spectrum, even though women and the ethnic minorities are still decidedly underrepresented. And if the profession lacks direct public accountability, just as the armed forces are ultimately responsible to the Ministry of Defence, so the diplomatic services are ultimately responsible to Foreign Office or State Department, and at the head of each, at least in a parliamentary or congressional democracy, is an elected official subject to parliamentary scrutiny. Whether diplomatic activity should be shielded from the public gaze is a matter for debate. On the one hand it is argued that the public is neither knowledgable nor interested enough to be able to determine what is wise and prudent in foreign policy and can be easily led astray by blind prejudice reinforced by propaganda from the less scrupulous tabloids. Against this there is the argument that such a view is elitist and out of keeping with the spirit of the age. The debate continues.

Finally, the point that diplomatic language and proceedings are somewhat archaic is itself rather out of date. Certainly, much of the more arcane phraseology has gone. On the other hand a number of expressions remain that are unmistakable in their implications and possibly all the more effective for their undertone of politeness. Thus if 'Her Majesty's Government cannot remain indifferent to', or 'views with concern', or 'views with grave concern' some policy of a rival state, the implication is that Britain will take a strong line. If 'Her Majesty's Government will be obliged to consider its own interests', or 'to claim a free hand', and 'declines to be responsible for the consequences' it is clear that diplomatic rupture or even hostilities could be contemplated. The advantage of such conventional forms of communication is that they maintain an atmosphere of calm while conveying warnings unlikely to be misunderstood; and clarity in diplomatic signalling is always important, unless the government decides for whatever reason that its messages should be deliberately ambiguous.

11.5 A 'NEW' DIPLOMACY?

If these are the charges against what was called the 'old diplomacy', is there a 'new diplomacy', and if so what are its characteristics? Contrary to what some may claim, there was in 1918 no abrupt transition from one to another. Secret diplomacy did not suddenly yield to open diplomacy, bilateral to multilateral diplomacy, elitism to something less patrician. On the other hand, the vast increase in the number of states and of international institutions, combined with technological innovations in modern communications could not but have had a powerful effect on diplomacy. In the first place it has led to a proliferation in the number both of embassy posts and of specialised attachés with a particular interest in the military, the economy, the press or legal procedure. Second, it has led to a steady shift from discussions of security issues to trade and economic problems. Third, negotiations have to take place against a background of burgeoning information networks, of international press, radio and television and of direct discussions either face-to-face or fax-to-fax or phone-to-phone between heads of government which may complicate diplomatic proceedings. Fourth, there is perhaps not the same reverance for diplomatic institutions as hitherto. Diplomatic immunity is abused more often than before; diplomats all too frequently engage in propaganda, infiltration and spying; and too many diplomats have become targets for the hostage-taker.

11.6 THE ROLE OF THE DIPLOMAT TODAY

But have political, social and above all technological changes in the 20th century relegated the diplomat to that of mere errand boy or girl for the administration? If the diplomat had declined into almost insignificance, it is doubtful whether there would have been such a burgeoning of diplomatic posts. In any case none of the diplomatic functions itemised earlier have lost their salience. For a new state, the symbolic ceremonial functions of the diplomat are regarded as of especial importance, and the numbers of diplomats expelled for 'conduct unbecoming' suggests that intelligence remains an important consideration. Indeed, given the potentially catastrophic consequences of political miscalculation in a thermonuclear age, it could be argued that the communication activities, information gathering and advice that the diplomat can tender are more important than ever. After all, diplomacy often involves matters of considerable sensitivity which cannot be suitably discharged by political summitry or by fax. Significantly, Presidents Kennedy and Johnson repeatedly recalled their ambassadors from Moscow for consultations, and during the Cuban Missile Crisis in 1962 the American ambassador in Moscow was one of the main communications links between the White House and the Kremlin.[14] Moreover, when two countries have little understanding of one another or have lost contact over the years, what the diplomat says can be very influential. From a former student who had gone into the diplomatic service, the writer discovered that when Canada and Communist China established relations in the early 1970s, the diplomats on the spot more or less made Canadian policy towards Peking.

It had been much the same story when US diplomats were sent to Indo-China in the 1960s and 1970s. Here, lack of expertise in Washington obliged the White House to rely heavily on the reports of American officials in Hanoi, Pnomh Penh and Vientiane. Unfortunately all too few spoke the relevant languages or were authorities on the region—the real experts having been pensioned off in the 1950s during Senator McCarthy's anti-Communist purges—and their reports often showed an appalling ignorance of the country to which they were accredited.[15] But this is an argument for well-informed diplomats, and in itself it gives the lie to the idea that the diplomat has become a mere lackey. At the same time it suggests that if only America's diplomats in Vietnam had studied 'Structure of International Society', it might all have ended differently. At least they might have asked more searching questions before giving their woefully inadequate answers.

NOTES

1. Nicolson, H., *Diplomacy*, 3rd ed., London, Oxford University Press, 1969, pp. 9–11.
2. See Numelin, R., *The Beginnings of Diplomacy*, Oxford, Oxford University Press, 1950, p. 124.
3. Roetter, C., *The Diplomatic Art*, London, Sidgwick and Jackson, 1965, pp. 9–11.
4. Ibid., pp. 11–12.
5. Ullman, W., *The Growth of Papal Government in the Middle Ages*, London, Methuen, 1955, p. 292.
6. Roetter, C., op. cit., p. 14.
7. Nicolson, H., op. cit., pp. 20–2.
8. Quoted in Nicolson, H., op. cit., p. 57.
9. Ibid., pp. 98–100.
10. Hartmann, W.H., *The Relations of Nations*, 2nd ed., New York, Macmillan, 1964, p. 93.
11. See Spanier, J. and Nogee, J., *The Politics of Disarmament*, New York, Praeger, 1962.
12. For an informed discussion of the 'old' diplomacy and the 'new', see Watson, A., *Diplomacy: The Dialogue Between States*, London, Eyre Methuen, 1982, pp. 132–57 and 212–26.
13. This is implicit in the account in Truman, H.S., *Memoirs*, Vol. 2, New York, Doubleday, 1956, pp. 30–1.
14. Beschloss, M.R., *Kennedy versus Khrushchev: The crisis years 1960–3*, London, Faber, 1991.
15. See, for example, Halberstam, D., *The Best and the Brightest*, New York, Random House, 1972.

CHAPTER 12

IMPERIALISM

Until a few years ago, most textbooks on International Relations or World Politics would contain an enlarged section on imperialism. Though the writers may not have agreed on the definition or on their approach—some would see imperialism as a product of a particular historical epoch, others as a product of a particular social system, some would regard it as a propensity inherent in the state while others, more partisan, would see it as a propensity inherent in states of which they disapproved—imperialism was regarded as sufficiently central to the subject as to deserve comprehensive treatment. Nowadays most of the books tend to have far less to say about the subject and some do not bother to mention it at all. This suggests that too many compilers of IR texts think that the study deals almost exclusively with contemporary events and that imperialism is largely a thing of the past.

Since, as was made clear at the start of the volume, the approach here is not confined to current affairs or to the modish and the fashionable, even if it had no current relevance, 'imperialism' would deserve a chapter to itself. But, in fact, it has a contemporary resonance. For many living in the vicinity of such countries as the United States, Iraq, Syria, Israel, Libya, South Africa, India, Vietnam, Indonesia, Serbia and Croatia, 'imperialism' still represents something very real. At the same time, many in some of the world's poorest and most strife-torn countries tend to seize on 'imperialism' as 'the source' of their plight. To discover whether or not such claims have validity, it is necessary, as usual, to tease out the different strands of meaning in the concept at issue.

12.1 CONNOTATIONS

A philosophy

In the first place, 'imperialism' has long been a philosophy: the idea that certain kinds of states should undertake the burden, the responsibility, the duty or perhaps the satisfaction of extending their rule to other lands. Sometimes this was justified by some such phrase as 'shouldering the white man's burden', a phrase coined by the English writer Rudyard Kipling in referring to America's annexation of the Philippines. In similar fashion, the French would refer to their quest for colonies as a *'mission civilisatrice'*, to bring, as it were, the benefits of French culture to backward peoples. It has also been justified at various times by the devout, especially among Christians and Muslims in seeking the 'salvation of souls'. When, for example, the Americas first came within the ambit of Europeans, they presented a field not only for trade but also for spiritual conquest, which is why a host of Jesuit and Dominican priests and Protestant missionaries followed in the wake of the European explorers. In the 19th century empire builders provided ample opportunity for the spread of the Gospel in Africa, India and China. Accordingly, Western missionaries played a leading part in obtaining extra-territorial rights in China after 1858. Missionary societies were active in promoting the German colonisation of South West Africa, while British Protestant missionaries were highly vocal in their hope that British rule, which they took to be synonymous with Christian civilisation, might be expanded to what they regarded as the 'dark continent'.[1]

But imperialist philosophies were the preserve not merely of the right and of the religious. They also found favour with some on the left, and in particular with the Fabian Socialists, including Sidney and Beatrice Webb (who founded the LSE). Like Karl Marx, who had once praised British imperialism for 'laying the material foundations of Western society in Asia' and for being 'the subconscious instrument of history in bringing about [social] revolution in Asia'[2], the Webbs saw imperialism as a progressive force, bringing the benefits of Western civilisation, efficient government and democratic structures to backward peoples while raising their political consciousness. In addition, with their 'scientism', ie faith in science in general and the social sciences in particular, the Webbs relished the creation of large, well-governed multinational units in which technology would be both used and controlled in the name of progress. This is presumably one of the reasons why in one of their more dotty discourses they were to give their blessing to what they called the Soviet 'civilisation' of Stalin,[3] whom they appeared to regard as an experimental social scientist worthy of an M.Sc. with Distinction.

Others, however, made no secret of their ethnocentric and frankly racist justifications for imperialism. The more extreme were Social Darwinists who believed that it was the destiny of certain races, ethnic groups or civilisations to rule over those they deemed inferior or weak. Well before Hitler seized on the idea, there were French and British as well as German 'scribblers'—one hesitates to use the word 'thinkers'—who talked of the inequality of the human races; some like Wagner speaking as if the fate of the 'inferior' races was of no account; others like Cecil Rhodes persuading themselves that there was a kind of harmony of interests when the superior governed the inferior. Rhodes summed it up by declaring in that high voice of his: 'I contend that we British are the first people in the world and the more of the world we inhabit the better it is for the human race.'[4] Such a sentiment was, of course, entirely in keeping with the idea of Britain presiding over 'an Empire on which the sun never sets'—a sentiment boosted by the new cheap popular press and which found favour with factory workers for whom tales of heroic exploits in strange lands offered something of an escape from the drabness of their living and working conditions. It should, however, be noted that those with powerful reasons for extending the domain of their particular state often find equally powerful reasons for seeking to deny the same impulse to others. Indeed, theorists of empire tend to go in for special pleading, one of the least attractive forms of political hypocrisy.

A policy

But 'imperialism' has a second connotation, where it becomes a policy as distinct from a philosophy of expansion because it is possible to have one without the other. A government may fail to realise the expansionism commended by the theorists. Alternatively, it can acquire territory and dominion, as China did so often in the past, not as a result of any theory of expansion but in consequence of attacks against it which go wrong and end in the invaders being absorbed by their potential victim. As a policy it may be passive, conserving an imperium already in existence, or active, involving the extension of dominion or rule; and if the latter it may be a planned or else a pragmatic operation, a reaction to circumstances. As a plan it may involve a general disposition to expand territorially or else a title to a specific territory, strategic waterway or resource. Further, it may embrace expansion overseas or overland, though because it is obviously more noticeable when it happens overseas, many Americans during the height of the cold war were able to persuade themselves that, as distinct from the Soviet Union, the United States had never been imperialistic. Ironically, many of those Americans, with an evident disdain for or ignorance of history, hailed from California or New Mexico. Further, imperialist expansion may involve the acquisition of land and/or the extension of control, and its exercise may be direct or indirect. Direct control is always political in nature, the result of outright conquest or of political absorption. Generally speaking the exercise of such control involves a transfer of sovereignty, though its implementation may be mitigated by legal arrangements providing for a measure of self-government for the newly acquired dependent.

Direct control

There is, for example, the protectorate, in which most of the residual rights of sovereignty revert to the metropolitan power, which normally assumes a legal obligation to defend the protected country from external attack and to determine property relationships and the treatment of foreign subjects within its borders. Examples would include Basutoland (Lesotho),

Bechuanaland (Botswana) and Swaziland, which came under British protection from the 1880s to the 1960s; Manchuria, which the Japanese renamed Manchukuo in 1932; Albania, which came under Italian protection in the 1920s and 1930s; and Slovakia and Croatia, which became German-sponsored protectorates in the 1940s. Although foreign control in such countries did not wholly eradicate vestigial elements of self-government, what remained was largely in the gift of the protecting power.

So-called 'mandated territories' under the League of Nations or 'trusteeships' under the UN were among other forms of modified imperial control. Here territories, most of which had never enjoyed independence before, came under the aegis of an administrative power acting in the name of an international institution and charged with preparing them for self-government and eventual sovereignty; Namibia, formerly South West Africa, was the last of these territories to gain independence.

Indirect control

The indirect method of imperial domination may or may not involve the acquisition of terrain or disturbance to the political structure of a country. The most visible indicator of this form of control is the 'sphere of influence', by which competing great powers delineate their area of hegemony. Among the better-known examples would be the 1494 treaty between Spain and Portugal dividing the world more or less between them (a suitably modest endeavour!); the Monroe Doctrine, promulgated by the American president in 1823 by which the Americas were to be free from European colonisation and by implication free for American intervention; the various arrangements between the 19th-century European powers for the partitions of Africa and of the Near East; and between the European powers and Japan for the semi-partition of the Far East. In addition, there were the agreements between Churchill and Stalin in 1944 mapping out the post-war division of Eastern and South Eastern Europe, and the so-called 'Brezhnev Doctrine' of 1968 whereby Moscow and its Warsaw Pact allies claimed the right to intervene in any Eastern European country where they deemed Socialism to be at risk. In theory, no such agreements infringe sovereign rights. In practice, however, a country's ability to exercise its sovereign power may be severely undermined. It becomes in effect a client state, though the changing political fortunes of the countries of the Americas, Eastern Europe, North Africa and East Asia indicate that its subordinate position need not necessarily be maintained indefinitely.

Less visible, perhaps, but often equally subversive of the ability to exercise sovereign power, is what the late Ghanaian President, Kwame Nkrumah, called 'neo-colonialism',[5] and which creates what many Latin American theorists call a situation of *dependencia* (dependency) in which the possibilities for political action become constrained. What, then, characterises the neo-colonialist relationship? The declaration of the 3rd Afro–Asian Peoples' Conference in Cairo in 1961 spelled it out.

(a) Puppet governments represented by stooges, and based on some chiefs, reactionary elements, anti-popular politicians, big bourgeois compradors, or corrupted civil or military functionaries.

(b) Regrouping of states, before or after independence, by an imperial power in federation or communities linked to that imperial power.

(c) Balkanisation as a deliberate political fragmentation of states by the creation of artificial entities, such as, for example, the case of Katanga, Mauritania, Buganda etc.

(d) The economic entrenchment of the colonial power before independence and the continuity of economic dependence after formal recognition of national sovereignty.

(e) Integration into colonial economic blocks which maintain the under-developed character of African economy.

(f) Economic infiltration by a foreign power after independence, through capital investments, loans, and monetary aids or technical experts, of unequal concessions, particularly those extending for long periods.

(g) Direct monetary dependence, as in those emergent independent states whose finances remain in the hands of and directly controlled by colonial powers.

(h) Military bases sometimes introduced as scientific research stations or training schools, introduced either before independence or as a condition for independence.[6]

If, indeed, many LDCs are prey to more than one of these they are hardly likely to enjoy to any significant extent the substance as well as the form of independence.

A further and even less visible type of informal imperialist penetration relates to communications exchange and technology. Though the LDCs are beginning to develop news agencies of their own, such as IRNA, the Iranian news agency, those entirely independent of Western sources are comparatively few and far between. In the meantime Western agencies, many owned, controlled and staffed by Americans, have tended to dominate LDC news networks. And while the bulk of LDC trade tends to be with the developed countries, so the bulk of their press coverage has also tended to focus on the developed world. Moreover, since indigenous journalists who write about the affairs of the LDCs are generally Western trained, they often view LDC events through, as it were, the distorting mirror of Western perceptions. It is partly for this reason that sub-Saharan Africa rarely gets a good press and that no feature on the Middle East seems complete without at least a reference to 'fundamentalism', 'fanaticism', 'corruption' or 'terrorism'. With the development of satellite transmission, Western domination of the news networks is likely to be further accentuated, and even if the LDCs follow Beijing's example and develop their own communications satellites they may still find, as China's own journalists have found, that the American offer of technical as well as training facilities is too good to miss. No wonder many speak of the need for a new, presumably non-Western-dominated, information order!

Combined with this subtle form of informal penetration, there is another. It has been called 'Coca Colonialism' or 'Pepsicology', in which the transmission of ideas through education, secular and religious, technological transfer and trade serves to inculcate a range of Western ideas into non-Western minds. While some would see this as a two-way process in which the delights of the kebab, curry, chow mein and sukiyaki as well as the bliss of oriental forms of meditation can become as familiar in the West as McDonalds, Marks and Spencer and Mickey Mouse are in the Orient, the transfer from East to West seems somehow less destructive of traditional values than the transfer from West to East. If this is a reflection of the dominance of the Western economy, the situation could presumably change as the Far Eastern economies boom while some in Europe and North America have remained in recession. In this connection, the recent rise in the number of European converts to Islam is arguably not unconnected with the recent rise in the economic fortunes of the oil-bearing countries of the Middle East.

A structural relationship

But 'imperialism' is not just a philosophy and a policy, since for Structuralists, and especially Marxist Structuralists, like Lenin and Immanuel Wallerstein, it is essentially an unequal relationship between dominant and dependent. In the Structuralist view such a relationship need not be the result of conscious planning or of anyone's conscious desire to dominate anyone else. It is something that happens in all social situations and not just in international relationships. Thus a Structuralist can speak of imperialist structures in, say, the family between parents and children, between men and women, teachers and pupils, governments and governed. And according to Marxists, there are particular economic patterns which reinforce the structural relationship of dominance and dependency in an international arena dominated by world capitalism and which survive formal empires. So what are these patterns? They comprise relations of unequal exchange between a dominant centre ie that of developed capitalism and a dependent periphery ie that of the LDCs in which there are common interests between 'the centre of the centre' and 'the centre of the periphery' ie the elites of the LDCs. The subordinate status of the LDC, according to such Marxist methodology, is perpetuated by hierarchical structures which

(1) Weight terms of trade heavily in favour of the industrialised states;
(2) Facilitate foreign penetration of development projects in the peripheral states through credit and technical expertise which generally work to the long-term benefit of the industrialised states;

(3) Accelerate internal inequalities within the LDCs as their elites are bribed or else co-opted to serve foreign interests;
(4) Sap indigenous cultures of their vitality by subjecting them to a creeping tide of Western cultural penetration; and
(5) Help reinforce ties of dependency through the discouragement of regional co-operation among the LDCs themselves.[7]

Increasingly, the structural relationship of dominance and dependency is being applied by ethnic, religious or national minority groups to refer to the political arrangements of states in which they feel their capacity for self-realisation, self-expression or self-determination is being denied. It is this sense of being dominated by an alien presence residing in Moscow, Belgrade or Prague that led to the disintegration, respectively, of the Soviet Union, Czechoslovakia and Yugoslavia. It is the same sense that leads to secessionist movements in many of the successor states, as well as in multi-ethnic states such as Iraq, India, China, Spain and even Britain. Here 'imperialism' is equated with a relationship which is perceived as denying the realisation of national, ethnic or religious aspirations. But if 'imperialism' is a philosophy, a policy and a structural relationship of inequality, are not expansionism and resistance to it part and parcel of the fabric of international relations?

12.2 EXPLANATIONS

Psychological

In attempting to account for the frequent incidence of war, Martin Wight in his book *Power Politics* makes the following observation.

> There are many kinds of wars...But it is convenient to classify them into three chief motivations:...gain;...fear,...doctrine. This grouping corresponds to the causes of war suggested by Hobbes, who was himself adapting the motives of Athenian imperialism described by Thucydides.[8]

Though Wight does not make it entirely clear whether the relevant motivations are those of individual statesmen, of the ruling body or can be imputed to the state itself, his classification suggests conscious motivation and a mode of analysis applicable as much to the causes of imperialism as to those of war.

Gain

When a statesman talks of the need for 'a place in the sun', 'living space', 'warm water outlets', 'natural frontiers' and 'frontier rectifications', he is using the language of acquisition, of seeking to extend control or dominion for the benefits it can supposedly bring. And what are these benefits? They can take the form of guaranteed markets and of sources of raw materials such as oil, uranium, chrome and the like, precious metals such as gold and silver, precious minerals such as diamonds, geo-strategic areas—waterways, sheltered harbours, hilly vantage points, railway junctions—good agricultural land and, of course, populations which can be seen as a reservoir of man- and woman-power for military, industrial and agricultural purposes. Finally they can involve the acquisition of terrain for the settlement of surplus populations, as in the case of Japanese expansionism in the 1930s and 1940s or to satisfy the hunger of the young and restless for adventure or a sense of purpose. ('A vast system of outdoor relief for the younger sons of the upper class' is how John Stuart Mill characterised the colonies.)[9]

Nor is such expansionism necessarily confined to the greater powers. After all, many of today's minor powers once went through an imperialist phase: Spain and Portugal from the 15th to the 18th centuries; Switzerland at the end of the 15th and beginning of the 16th centuries; Sweden and Holland in the 17th century; Belgium in the 19th century; Norway in this century after splitting from Sweden. More recently Poland, India, Indonesia, Egypt, Ghana, Libya and Iraq among others have all made bids for territory not originally theirs.

Fear

Martin Wight's second motivation for imperialism is fear. If at first sight this seems a curious stimulus, one has only to recall such oft-repeated adages as 'attack is the best form of defence', 'kill or be killed' and to consider the notion of the pre-emptive strike ie of 'getting them before they get you'. Part of the 'scramble for Africa' at the end of the 19th century may be said to have been motivated not so much by gain as by the fear of getting left behind and, hence, of having to face an adverse world balance. This would seem to have been the case, for example, with Germany, which came into 'the game' late, after Bismarck had declared that Germany was 'satiated' and which did very little to develop, exploit or even populate its African colonies. Alternatively a country might acquire territory where it can as its rival acquires territory elsewhere. It is sometimes said, for example, that Italy's acquisition of Albania in April 1939 was a direct result of the perceived power imbalance occasioned by Germany's final thrust into Czechoslovakia the month before.

Sometimes, the impetus can be strategic or defensive—in order to safeguard existing possessions. The British, for example, were constantly involved in overseas intrigues to protect trade-routes to India. More recently the strategic urge has been largely to defend the home territory, as when the Soviet Union invaded Finland and took over the Baltic

States—Latvia, Lithuania and Estonia—in part to safeguard the area around Leningrad at a time when Germany was advancing into Southern and Eastern Europe; or when South Africa made its repeated incursions into Mozambique, Angola and the other black states of southern Africa where the African National Congress (ANC) had their guerrilla bases; or when Israel moved to carve out a slice of southern Lebanon and to occupy the West Bank and the Gaza strip in time of hostilities and decided to stay there. Incidently, it is fear that the Bosnian Serbs often give as their reason for the acquisition of terrain and what has been termed 'ethnic cleansing'. As in the other cases cited, we can all make our own judgement as to whether or not fear has been the real impulse.

Doctrine

Doctrine is Martin Wight's third category, and ever since biblical times, if not before, people have sought to spread their cherished beliefs by peaceful means if possible, by the sword if not. The salvation of souls has long provided the pretext for crusades of one kind or another; and other creeds, both left and right wing, internationalist as well as nationalist, have provided the stimulus for the extension of domain. But 'scientism' can also be the spur for the acquisition of territory. For the scientifically inclined are often obsessed with the conquest of nature, and this can involve the control of the very terrain that will enable them to conduct their experiments, just as it provides the incentive for the exploration of space and of the ocean bed.

Prestige

Two more motivations should perhaps be added to those of Martin Wight. The first is prestige or reputation. The quest for either personal fame or national glory, *la gloire*, is often sought through the acquisition of terrain by those assuming that the more extensive the land mass, the higher the standing and status internationally. Alternatively, it may be undertaken in order to avenge a past humiliation, as when Mussolini seized Abyssinia in 1935 in part as a belated reprisal for the defeat of Italian troops by Abyssinian forces in Adowa in 1896.

Distraction

The second addition to Martin Wight's categorisation is that of distraction, as when a leader or a ruling body embarks on an expansionist adventure in order to direct attention away from domestic discontents. It can be argued that this was the mainspring of President Sukarno of Indonesia's confrontation policy with Malaysia in the early 1960s, Cambodia's repeated incursions into Vietnam under Pol Pot in the mid-1970s, or General Galtieri's attempt at seizing the Falklands/Malvinas for Argentina in the 1980s.

The kind of classification suggested by Wight is of value so long as the suggested motivations are not regarded as mutually exclusive. After all, for an understanding of, say, the Iraqi occupation of Kuwait, it would be necessary to draw on virtually all five: gain—given Kuwait's oil reserves and outlet to the sea; fear—given Kuwait's reported over-production of oil thereby driving down the price and its habit of syphoning off oil from Iraqi territory; doctrine—in this case nationalism combined with anti-imperialism in that Kuwait was regarded as an appendage of the West (Saddam Hussein also drew, but far less convincingly, on Islamic as well as Arab nationalism); reputation (if ever a man sought *la gloire* it was Saddam Hussein, especially after a prolonged, expensive and unsuccessful war against Iran); and, finally, distraction—a clear motivation given that in little more than a decade Iraq had gone from riches to rags, its healthy economic surplus being turned into crippling debt.

As the Iraqi example shows, the long-term effects of expansionism can often be counter-productive, as other countries or combinations of countries decide to launch a counter-offensive. In the case of the struggle against Iraq, it might be interesting to consider how far each country in the Gulf war coalition was motivated by gain, fear, doctrine, reputation or distraction.

But, of course, explanations of imperialism, like those of war, are to be found not merely in psychological accounts but also in structural theories that make no reference to conscious choice or motivation.

Structural

Political

One of the most pervasive theories is political and based on the simple proposition, to quote Martin Wight, that 'it is in the nature of powers to expand. The energies of their members radiate culturally, economically and politically, and unless there are strong obstacles these tendencies will be summed up in territorial growth.'[10] The historian Lord Acton put it this way: 'Power tends to expand indefinitely, and will transcend all barriers, abroad and at home, until met by superior forces.'[11] In his essay on *Perpetual Peace*, Kant wrote ironically that 'it is the desire of every state or of its ruler to attain to a condition of perpetual peace ... by subjecting the whole world, as far as possible, to its sway'.[12] One of the most recent scholars to develop this theme was the late F.S. Northedge who in *The International Political System* suggests that the propensity of states to expand their territory, interests or influence abroad is but one example of a cycle that in his view characterises all social organisms, in which birth is followed by growth, and then eventually decay and demise. And he sums up the position with the simile that 'the state ... is an imperialistic animal, just as the beaver is a dam-building animal'.[13]

Sociological

A second structuralist theory is sociological, and based on the analysis of particular kinds of social systems. From Kant to Woodrow Wilson and probably down to Ronald Reagan people have viewed imperialism as an outcome of elitist, authoritarian and despotic governments. For Plato, through Burke, down to the Webbs, the most potent source of imperialism would be where demagogues and populists rule. And whereas the late Elie Kedourie would have seen imperialism as an outcome of nationalism, Mazzini in the 19th century would have seen it as stemming from the denial of nationalist sentiment. Only when states and nations coincided would there be an end to imperialism and war. Why did Kedourie dispute this? Basically, he held that nationalism, which begins as a demand for separation and secession from a multinational state, diverts the spiritual vitality which inspired the original independence struggle into expansion after the new state is formed, since the force released by the quest for national liberation cannot be contained within the new national entity. But when nationalism becomes imperialism it engenders resistance among those whose own national identity is threatened by it, and so there is an endless cycle of thrust and counter-thrust. Those subscribing to this theory could select a host of examples from the Roman Empire down to the more recent actions of Russia, Germany, Italy and Japan (though no doubt those who take an alternative view would select examples of imperialism in which the nationalist dimension was missing).

Economic

Third, there are a host of structural economic theories, many directed at an explanation of what its proponents call 'modern' imperialism. The reason the term 'modern' is appended is that though they see in capitalism the cause of imperialism, they are well aware that the phenomenon is far older than the capitalist system. Among the better-known theories are, first, that of the English economist J. A. Hobson whose study of *Imperialism*, written in 1902, attributes the phenomenon to the existence of maladjustments in European capitalism and suggests that imperialism might be avoided if corrections were made within the capitalist system itself. Another treatise is that of Lenin who in his *Imperialism, the Highest Stage of Capitalism* of 1916 transformed Hobson's thesis into a determinist theory, suggesting that imperialism was an inevitable outcome of capitalism in what he called its 'monopoly stage' ie when the system is dominated by business cartels and when finance houses have an overwhelming need to export surplus capital. At this stage, he says, 'the division of the world by the international trusts has begun and in which the partition of all the territory of the earth by the greatest capitalist countries has been completed'.[14] Though Lenin's was an influential theory, it is, like some of the other such theories, flawed not only in that it fails to explain imperialism before the age of capitalism but also in that history does not invariably show a coincidence of surplus capital and imperialist venture, nor that imperialist powers have found it necessary to possess foreign territory in order to export capital. Indeed, it could be argued that the imperialist countries of Western Europe and Japan were never so prosperous as when they had divested themselves of their colonies. However, a neo-Marxist of the *dependencia* school would counter that such an argument is not relevant since imperialism continues to exist wherever there is a structural relationship of dominance and dependency.

International systemic

One final theory, which goes by the name of 'Structural Realism', is expounded by Kenneth Waltz in his *Theory of International Relations*. It suggests that states tend to expand not because of any psychological impetus but because of the fact of their existence in a world without government, in which power is dispersed, life is precarious and there is no sense of international solidarity. In such a world, each country faces a security dilemma, and expansionism may be conceived as a way of coping with the logic of the situation.

12.3 CAVEATS

Earlier, reference was made to the Northedge contention that states are inherently imperialistic, and it merits serious discussion by way of conclusion. There is a sense in which states are inherently nothing but mental constructs and personified abstractions. On the other hand they have an existence in our minds and as such they shape our behaviour, and when we think of the state we see it as something capable of and often involved in expansion. We can also conceive of states which have contracted and not expanded over the years. Most of the Western countries have divested themselves of formal empire, as has Russia. In 1993 Czechoslovakia separated into two independent states more or less amicably, not unlike an earlier political divorce this century—that of Norway from Sweden. Nor is the voluntary cession of territory necessarily a 20th-century phenomenon, as in the 18th century at the end of the Seven Years' war, Britain handed to France several West Indian islands it had captured in a highly successful colonial and maritime campaign, and in the 19th century Britain transferred the Ionian isles to Greece. There have been many other examples, too.

Do such concessions occur only in response to external pressure? They generally happen in response to pressure, but the operative pressures may be internal rather than external and the result may be a leaner and possibly fitter country, better prepared than before for the cut and thrust of power politics, like France after being forced to cede Algeria. Conceivably Britain would be better off without Northern Ireland, though pulling out the British troops is made almost impossible by the violence of the extremists on both sides. Nor is it always the case that powers attempt to stem their decline in territory and status. Venice, Portugal, Denmark, Sweden and Holland were eventually to resign themselves to a lesser role than in the historic past. So was Turkey, even if there are signs now of a desire to exert greater influence than in the past half century or so. But such are the vicissitudes of international politics that it would appear to serve little purpose to define imperialism in a narrowly restrictive way, to seek a single factor or monocausal explanation for it or to suggest that all states are imperialistic all the time, even if it may sometimes look like it. True, all states seek to expand their influence, but to expand their terrain and to do so all the time is surely a dubious proposition, and to call the desire for influence 'imperialistic' is to stretch the meaning of the term too far.

NOTES

1. Moon, P.J., *Imperialism and World Politics*, New York, 1926, p. 64; Langer, W.L., *The Diplomacy of Imperialism*, New York, 1951.
2. Marx, K., *The First Indian War of Independence 1857–1859*, Moscow, 1959, p. 33.
3. Webb, S. and B., *Soviet Communism: A New Civilisation*, 3rd ed., London, 1944.
4. Quoted in Carr, E.H., *The Twenty Years Crisis*, London, Macmillan, 1962, p. 76.
5. His views were spelled out in *Neocolonialism*, London, Nelson, 1965.
6. 'Neocolonialism' in *Voice of Africa*, Vol. 1, No. 4, April 1961, p. 4.
7. Though not a Marxist, Galtung, J. in his 'A Structural Theory of Imperialism', *Journal of Peace Research*, Vol. 13, No. 2, 1971, pp. 81–94 puts the argument very clearly.
8. Op. cit. p. 138.
9. Quoted in Zilliacus, K., *The Mirror of the Past*, London, Gollanz, 1944, p. 32.
10. Wight, M., *Power Politics*, Harmondsworth, Penguin, 1979, p. 144.
11. Lord Acton, *Lectures on Modern History*, London, Macmillan, 1952, p. 156.
12. Quoted in Wight, M., op. cit., p. 144.
13. Op. cit. p. 203.
14. English translation, New York, 1933, pp. 80–1.

CHAPTER 13

WAR

13.1 ATTITUDES TO WAR

On 4 November 1918, a young man was killed in the trenches barely a week before the Armistice that ended the first world war. He was just 25 years old and was to become posthumously one of the most celebrated of Britain's war poets. His name was Wilfred Owen, and shortly before his death, he had written a preface to go with a volume of his poetry he hoped to have published. 'This book is not about heroes...Nor is it about deeds or lands, or anything about glory, honour, might, majesty, dominion or power...My subject is war and the pity of war...All that a poet can do is to warn.'[1] And in his verse Owen speaks of war's legacy as 'the eternal reciprocity of tears' and with uncanny prescience predicts his own death. 'I am the enemy you killed, my friend...Let us sleep now.'[2]

Considering the countless lives lost not just in the fields of Flanders but in the plains of Central Europe, the waters of the Atlantic and the Pacific, in the once bustling cities of Hiroshima and Nagasaki, the frozen wastes of Korea, the jungles of Vietnam, the mountains of Bosnia, the deserts of Ethiopia, Sudan and Somalia and in so many other theatres of war throughout the five continents, it is tempting to conclude that Owen got it about right. That war is not about glory or honour or might, majesty, dominion, power or, for that matter, about winning an award for gallantry, which the poet did, just before his death. It is about death, destruction, mutilation, separation, sorrow, pity, grief.

Yet two years before Wilfred Owen penned his preface, another British poet, Robert Bridges, had put an entirely different gloss on the hostilities.

> Britons have ever fought well for their country and their country's Cause is the high Cause of Freedom and Honour...We can therefore be happy in our sorrows, happy even in the death of our beloved who fall in the fight; for they die nobly, as heroes and saints die, with hearts and hands unstained by hatred or wrong.[3]

Admittedly the elderly Bridges was holding forth there as Poet Laureate ie the king's appointee, but it may be that kind of bombast rather than the agonising of his much younger contemporary that typify much popular thinking about war.

After all, even now many will still speak nostalgically about life in the trenches or in the bomb shelters and recall fondly past battles when adversity, distress and hardship were shared and there was a heightened sense of solidarity and comradeship. And most of us will be familiar with people who eagerly wrap themselves in the national flag or else take up the cudgels on behalf of some religious, ethnic, class or even gender-based cause to be able to fight, metaphorically or literally, and with a clear conscience, another round or two with their presumed enemy.

Nor is this anything new. After all, the ancients worshipped, among other deities, the gods of violence, if only to placate them. The Hindus of India had Shiva, the often malevolent King of the Beasts and his even more destructive spouse Kali. The Scandinavians had Odin (Wotan of the Wagnerian *Ring* cycle) and Thor, who hurled thunderbolts at his enemies. In Greece, Ares, and in Rome, Mars, were celebrated as the deities of war. At least three of our weekdays—Tuesday (in French, *Mardi*), Wednesday (Wotan's day), and Thursday (Thor's day)—are named after these fierce divinities. The sacred texts of the world's three monotheistic religions are full of imagery drawn from war and combat. The Jewish Lord of Hosts 'smites' his enemies, the Christian is directed to put on 'the breastplate of righteousness', 'the helmet of salvation' and 'the sword of the Spirit', while the Moslem is promised a reward in heaven if he dies in the defence of Allah and his cause.

Between the two contrasting attitudes to war—one seeing it as destructive of so much of value, the other regarding it as somehow necessary that values may be upheld—the historical record reveals a variety of conflicting views. For some warfare was an adventure, even a kind of recreation, and, indeed, both the Crimean and the American Civil wars became something of a spectator sport as families and friends of the combatants made their way to the front to watch the contest, thus giving a novel meaning to the notion of a 'theatre of war'. But since time immemorial warfare had been regarded as a kind of virility test in which victory becomes, as it were, proof of physical superiority. In fact, the warrior has always cut a rather glamorous figure, invested with the symbols and attributes of splendour, and even now military parades and ceremonials tend to be spectacular demonstrations of glory and magnificence.

Disinfectant

The old idea that war sorted out 'the men from the boys' was to find more recent expression in Social Darwinism, with its emphasis on the survival of the fittest. Ironically, it was often the weak who were most attracted. For example, at the end of the 19th century, Friedrich Nietzsche, who had been ill for most of his life, finally drugging himself into insanity, suggested that: 'For nations that are growing weak and contemptible, war may be prescribed as a remedy, if indeed they really want to go on living.'[4] What may be called 'the disinfectant theory of war', the notion that warfare purifies society, purging the body politic of its ailments, was given still more robust expression in the writings of the German General von Bernhardi. In his *Germany and the Next War*, written in 1912, the General claimed that 'War is a biological necessity which cannot be dispensed with...Without war, inferior or decaying races would easily choke the growth of healthy budding elements and a universal decadence would follow.'[5]

In case it should be thought that this was an attitude peculiar to Germans, it must be recalled that similar views were held by people like the British writer Robert Louis Stevenson (another chronic invalid) and who had created Mr Hyde as well as Dr Jekyll; by the Italian poet d'Annunzio, who had inspired Mussolini; and by the British aristocrat Lord Elton who in 1942 claimed that 'war, however much we may regret it, is still the supreme agent of the evolutionary process...It remains the final arbiter, the one test mankind has yet contrived of a nation's fitness to survive.'[6]

Expedient

Fortunately, most politicians do not think in these terms, at least not nowadays. For them war is not so much a biological necessity as about securing objectives so far unattained and is, as often as not, a last resort. Their guru, in so far as they have one, tends not to be Nietzsche but von Clausewitz who in his classic study *On War* of 1832 speaks of it as 'a continuation of policy by other means', and as being intended 'to compel our opponent to fulfil our will'.[7] It is thus a means of influence, never an end in itself, and its modalities have to be tailored to the objective.

Religious duty

For yet others the justification is not so much instrumental as ideological or even theological. In both Bible and Koran, war is represented as in some sense a manifestation of the Divine purpose, either as a punishment for sin or as an appropriate means for spreading the Word. It was partly as a consequence of his understanding of the New Testament that the Emperor Charlemagne in the ninth century took it upon himself to try to expel the Muslims from Spain, thereby blazing the trail for the forthcoming Crusades, and already the priests were beginning to bless the weapons of the warrior who would defend Christianity against the so-called 'heathen'. Soon the Crusading spirit had become identified with the cause of liberating Jerusalem from Islam. Not surprisingly the Muslims had their answer in the form of a counter-Crusade or jihad.

Political duty

If some saw war or a particular war as a religious duty, others were to see it as a political duty. For example, though the overthrow of capitalism was for the Marxists inevitable, exactly when that would take place was to an extent to be determined by the exercise of collective willpower, and it was up to Marxists to 'give history a push'. For Lenin that meant doing whatever was necessary to hasten capitalism's demise, and since he believed that post-capitalist society would be morally and politically superior to any preceding social system, the Marxist had a political duty to wage unceasing struggle and by any means, including violence, to destroy the citadels of capitalism.

Moral duty

If the Marxists saw war as a political obligation in the creation of a new and, by definition, better world order, others saw it as a moral obligation in the preservation of a nation's independence. For example, though that ardent 19th-century liberal, J.S. Mill, believed that nations had to secure their own self-determination, he also held that where a country's very existence was at risk from the activities of a foreign invader, other states had a duty to counter-intervene, if necessary by force. As he put it: 'Intervention to enforce non-intervention is always rightful, always moral, if not always prudent.'[8] It was a similar sentiment which led a US-dominated Security Council to order UN troops in 1991 to repel Baghdad's invasion of Kuwait.

Irrationality

While threat, display or use of force has always had its defenders, there have always been pacifists, who object to all war, and conscientious objectors who object to particular wars; and in recent times, especially in the West, anti-war sentiment has grown. One reason, no doubt, is the influence of television, which brings war, in all its horror, into our living room; another is the fear of nuclear escalation with its potential threat to the planet. It would be gratifying if it also had something to do with the spread of education, though given that some of the most highly educated people have also been among the most brutal, one cannot be sure. It was, however, among the politically aware in the 19th century that the animus against war first began to make an appeal. For liberals such as Cobden and Bright, both apostles of free trade, war was not so much wicked as irrational. Although it might suit arms dealers and manufacturers, it was injurious to almost every other kind of commercial activity, since it disrupted the kinds of orderly procedures on which commerce depended. But it was in the 20th century with the writings of Norman Angell that the idea that war was irrational received its most articulate expression. For him war was 'the Great Illusion'—the illusion being that it would be to anyone's long-term benefit.[9] Though it might bring short-term commercial and political results, it could only contain the seeds of further conflict; and by the time of the second world war, he felt that his warnings of 30 years before had been only too justified.

A variant of this idea gained ground in the First and Second Socialist Internationals of the 19th century, among people like Eduard Bernstein representing the Social Democratic wing of the Labour movement. But whereas the liberal internationalists held that almost nobody benefited from war, the Social Democrats suggested that what has become known as 'the military–industrial complex' profited handsomely and that it was simply irrational for the working class to engage in an activity from which only 'the bosses' could benefit.

Evil

Finally, there were the thoroughgoing pacifists who held that all war was wrong. Some were of a religious disposition, such as the Quaker followers of William Penn, whose notion of the Divine Will differed from that of many of their Christian predecessors; people like Leo Tolstoy, who condemned both violence and the conditions giving rise to it and Mahatma Gandhi for whom Hinduism was incompatible with the shedding of innocent blood. But there were secular pacifists, too. Some were life-long advocates such as the writer Aldous Huxley and the composers Benjamin Britten and Michael Tippett; others were pacifists for a time like the philosopher Bertrand Russell, who abandoned his pacifism during the second world war at about the time that writer Christopher Isherwood, who had had a German lover, acquired his. Though they had different starting points, all held that no cause was worth killing for, though not all believed that their stand would have any practical political effect. It should perhaps be added that the Campaign for Nuclear Disarmament (CND), which some have called a pacifist organisation, is nothing of the kind. CND's aim has been to secure the abolition of nuclear weapons, and though many members would abolish all war as well, others would fight for what they considered a just cause provided the means were proportionate. But they would all hold that as an instrument of war a nuclear weapon can never be proportionate to any cause, just or otherwise.

13.2 TYPES OF WARFARE

Civil

That some people can countenance non-nuclear but not nuclear war is a reminder that there are different kinds of organised and protracted armed conflicts (which is what war may be taken to be). There are civil wars, and though these are sometimes limited in scope and scale to hostilities between rival factions within a ruling clique, as has happened so frequently in Central and Latin America, more often than not they polarise whole populations. They tend to begin with street violence, graduate to acts of terrorism—random or against selected targets—then to insurgency and guerrilla warfare and finally protracted civil conflict. When this happens, as in Spain in the 1930s, Vietnam in the 1960s and 1970s or Bosnia and Croatia in the 1990s, such conflicts tend to be particularly brutal. For civilians do not merely get caught in the crossfire. They are often prime targets in a struggle which pits whole ethnic, religious or political communities against one another and makes combatants out of anyone capable of holding a gun. And where the outcome could potentially affect the overall international situation, outside powers tend to get involved, either as protagonists, as in Spain and Vietnam, or as peacekeeping mediators, as in Bosnia and Somalia—though as these examples show, the external presence, even if designed to bring hostilities to a speedy conclusion, may merely succeed in prolonging them.

Liberation

When the conflict is between those attempting to secure some kind of national liberation and the existing authorities who try to resist, it can, again, involve much brutality, and when it takes the form of attempted secession from a larger contiguous entity, as in Tibet, Kashmir, Kurdistan or even the Serb-dominated parts of Bosnia, the geographical proximity of the protagonists probably makes it even bloodier than a struggle for liberation from an overseas colonist. Moreover, in countries where national liberation fails to bring greater individual fulfilment—as in Iraq, Afghanistan, Georgia or Bosnia—the seeds of serious post-independence conflict may lie. Consider the Indian sub-continent—first India, then Pakistan, then Bangladesh—what next? An independent Sindh or Punjab? And what of Sri Lanka—once an island paradise, now a quagmire of communal hatreds and violence as Tamil and Sinhalese extremists butcher one another in Jaffna, Colombo and elsewhere? Where there is bitterness on such a scale, any viable multicultural and multiracial political community becomes almost impossible to sustain.

Limited

One of the more ambiguous terms in the inventory of conflict is that of 'limited war'. Though it implies constraints on the scope, scale, arena and intensity of hostilities, there appears to be no consensus on when a war ceases to be limited. After all, though the Thirty Years war of 1618–48 was limited largely to Central Europe, the devastation and destruction during this protracted and vicious conflict were colossal. An estimated six million people are believed to have lost their lives, representing about 40 per cent of the Central European population of the time.[10] If one considers the Second Indo-China war of 1961–75—'the Vietnam war'—again, though limited in geographical area, in the number of participants and in the scale of violence (in that the United States resisted the temptation to take it to the nuclear threshold), American planes none the less dropped some 20 million high-explosive fragmentation bombs—far more than in the second world war, which no one regards as a limited war. Moreover, the American strategy involved chemical agents and defoliants never used during the second world war, devastating much of the country's agricultural land and forestry and taking Washington to within an inch of breaching the 1925 Geneva Conventions on chemical warfare. By the end of hostilities some two million had been killed, an additional four million seriously injured and a further 17 million or so (one third of the entire Indo-Chinese people) displaced.[11] Such examples appear to indicate, therefore, that the term 'limited' as in the phrase 'limited war' needs qualification. 'Limited' in what sense?

Proxy

The notion of 'war by proxy' is more easily defined than exemplified. It occurs when state A encourages the people of state C to take up arms against state B, which happens to be its own adversary. It is claimed, for example, that both the Korean and Vietnam wars come into this category, for the real instigators were the Soviet Union—the patron of North Korea and North Vietnam—and the United States—the patron of South Korea and South Vietnam; and that the 'Third Indo-China war' between Cambodia and Vietnam in 1978 was really a Sino–Soviet war by proxy. The trouble with this kind of ascription is that even if true at one level, there is generally another level at which the war is a local affair dealing with local concerns. In the case of Korea, given that the then South Korean leader Syngman Rhee had been clinging to power despite his massive defeat in a recent election, the North Koreans would have been tempted to attack either because they believed the South to be divided and therefore vulnerable or alternatively because they feared the South might strike northwards in order to give Syngman Rhee a pretext to remain in power.[12]

Total

If there are problems about the notion of 'limited war', there are far fewer difficulties with the contrasting concept of 'total war'. Given currency during the first world war, it indicated a conflict in which the total resources of the states involved—their man- and woman-power, manufacturing and extractive industries, agriculture, shipping, road and rail transport, communications networks etc—were mobilised for the purpose of achieving victory. In the meantime, millions were conscripted into the forces or drafted into the war industries, and even in the most *laissez-faire* economies, governments tended to take virtual control of industry, farming and labour, in effect laying the framework for both state socialism and Fascism. As the scale and intensity of the war mounted, the conflict was increasingly portrayed as a Manichean struggle between good and evil, light and darkness, civilisation and barbarism, in which a whole way of life was deemed to be at stake. In this sense victory, too, had to be total, involving unconditional surrender and the disarmament and demobilisation of the vanquished—all very different from, say, the Bismarckian wars of the 19th century or the Russo–Japanese conflict of 1904–5 fought by limited means for limited objectives. Though both world wars were 'total' in the sense described, the seeds had been sown during the French revolutionary wars when the authorities in Paris introduced the *levée en masse* (conscription), conducted an intense propaganda campaign and yoked the country's productive capacity and its civil service to the war effort.

Nuclear

One final category—nuclear war—remains, mercifully, hypothetical, though the atom bomb was used to end the second world war and an increasing number of states either have nuclear weapons or else access to nuclear knowhow. Though a nuclear capacity appears to have a sobering effect on the policies of those in possession and a strategic nuclear exchange, given the threat of mutual destruction, seems unlikely, it is interesting that in the 1950s and 1960s far less lethal tactical and battlefield nuclear weapons were introduced, giving rise to the theory of 'limited nuclear war'.[13] Sceptics wondered whether the theorists were serious or merely trying to boost the credibility of the nuclear deterrent which was already beginning to be regarded as 'the weapon none dare use'.

On the other hand the improbability of strategic nuclear war suggests mutual rationality, but what, say the pessimists, if there is a lack of rationality on one side or the other? Might not a nuclear war come about by miscalculation or misunderstanding? Alternatively, what if there is a critical mechanical failure? Could not a nuclear exchange occur inadvertently? It is, of course, true that mechanical failures have occured in nuclear-related technology. At one time, for example, a flock of starlings appeared on a computer screen as a cluster of airborne missiles. And in 1983 when Soviet intelligence detected an alien intruder over the USSR's vital Far East nuclear installations, it was shot down, though the intruder turned out to be a Korean passenger plane that had strayed off course. On the other hand as political and military establishments acquire greater understanding of the possible errors that nuclear-related computers can make, they build greater 'fail safe' mechanisms into them; while the numbers of fingers on the safety catch ensure that the nuclear trigger is rarely at the disposal of a single, fallible and perhaps irrational leader. This is not to say that strategic nuclear war could never come about through inadvertence or miscalculation. It is, however, to say that in the course of time such a war becomes increasingly unlikely.

13.3 WAR: A CALCULATED ACT?

In fact, as Geoffrey Blainey has argued, war rarely occurs by chance, though it can arise by miscalculation.[14] For example military manoeuvres designed to put pressure on an opponent may be understood as indicating an intention to attack. An ultimatum which begins as an elaborate bluff may have to be followed by military action if that bluff is called, otherwise credibility suffers. Certainly, in both the first world war and the more recent Falklands and Gulf wars there were elements of miscalculation. Normally, however, wars come about as a result of the calculation of one side or another, though occasionally they are provoked by a third-party catalyst with an interest in seeing 'the tigers fight'. It is said, for instance, that the 1967 'Six-Day war' in the Middle East was provoked as a consequence of false information about Israeli intentions supplied to both Syria and Egypt by Moscow.[15]

13.4 SOURCES

Human nature

As organised and protracted conflict between rival groups has been endemic in human organisation since the dawn of history, thinking people have long speculated on its cause. In his *Man, the State and War*[16], Kenneth Waltz examines the literature on the subject and identifies three main bodies of theory. The oldest attributes war to some defect in human nature. In any school playground, sports field, boardroom or even senior common room discussion, competition, contention and conflict are the norm. If such emotions are transferred to political groups and get out of control, say the Hobbesians, violence results. For war is what is likely to happen when the aggressive and self-seeking fail to keep their passions in check. Variants of the Hobbesian position are to be found in the psychological theories of Freud and of William James, who point out that even well-balanced individuals, if frustrated, provoked and enraged will commit acts which under less extreme circumstances they would deplore, as when after losing so many comrades in battle, ordinary GIs gunned down innocent women, children and even babies at My Lai during the Vietnam war. Some theorists of a more religious disposition, from St Augustine to the psychoanalyst Jung, trace the source of the defect in the human psyche to the biblical story of the fall of man and tend to see war, therefore, as a manifestation of sinfulness—of turning away from God. The more apocalyptic, like the Jehovah's Witnesses, envision sinful man as moving towards a final world conflagration—Armageddon—before God establishes his kingdom on earth. Other theorists, following Darwin, Thomas Huxley and the writer Bernard Shaw take an anthropological view and regard war as a disreputable relic of an earlier age when we were savages. Some trace it even further back to our supposed animal ancestry, though some animal 'liberationists', ironically not averse to using violence themselves in defence of their cause, contend that calculated and purposeful violence is a human institution and not to be found in the animal kingdom at all.

Socio-political systems

If war is inherent in human nature, why are there not organised hostilities all the time? Why do wars occur at certain times and not at other times? The idea that human nature is the cause leaves crucial questions unanswered. An alternative theory—at least as old as Aristotle—holds that the cause is not so much in man as in the way society is organised. In the 20th century, with the vast increase in the scope and scale of hostilities, such an interpretation has seemed especially relevant. Certainly after the first world war, for which many held the Kaiser and his fellow autocrats responsible, there were numerous diatribes concerning the war-making propensity of autocracies. In the view of Woodrow Wilson, the voice of the people was the voice of reason, and governments responsive to what he called 'the organised opinion of mankind' would desist from war. Even if such an idea seems at variance with the kind of war nostalgia referred to earlier, it gained fresh impetus with the rise of the dictators in the 1930s, though, ironically, it did not produce any feasible solution to the perceived threat from the new despots.

If liberals traced the origin of war to a lack of democracy, less liberal thinkers, like Plato, through Burke down to the Webbs, tended to see the cause in an excess of it, as when a gullible public puts its trust in demagogues who then lead it to international disaster. For Marx and Lenin it was not so much in leadership styles as in socio-economic systems that the cause of war lay; and only when capitalism had dug its own grave would it finally be abolished. For Mazzini, a contemporary of Marx, war was the consequence not of capitalism or despotism but of the denial of national

self-determination. His contention was that those nations denied international legitimacy in the form of a sovereign state representing and enshrin-
ing their sense of group identity would go on struggling until they realised
their objective. Only when states and nations coincided would war be
abolished. However, the 20th-century thinker, Elie Kedourie, held the
reverse to be true. Nationalism was the problem.[17] However enlightened
and noble its origins, it had become a harbinger of hatred and hostility,
and only when its aspirations were kept under control could we envisage
an end to inter- and intra-state conflict.

But if Professor Kedourie is right, what of the wars long before nationalism ever existed? If Marx and Lenin are on the right track, what of the
many conflicts between Communists? As for the idea that despotism,
Fascism or Communism represent the main danger, is the record of liberal
democracy so much more impressive? After all, the Amritsar and My Lai
massacres, the brutality towards indigenous Algerians of the French
empire and the mistreatment of the indigenous peoples of the Americas
and Australia were all committed by the agents of liberal democracy.
Sadly, no political or economic system to date appears to have avoided
bloodshed on the grand scale; and for this reason some theorists have
offered yet a further mode of explanation as to the causes of war. They
look not to any particular political or economic arrangement within the
state but to the system of states itself, seeing war as a product of collective
insecurity in a divided world lacking government or moral consensus.

International system

It was probably Thucydides who first saw war not so much in terms of
human or societal failings but rather as a product of the security dilemma
facing all states in conditions of international anarchy. Since then, many
others have made their contribution—from Hobbes to Rousseau and more
recently from Norman Angell, through Hans Morgenthau to Kenneth
Waltz. Perhaps the predicament was best summed up by a man who basically deplored the international system he wrote about, the Christian pacifist Martin Wight. In *Power Politics* he suggests:

> The fundamental cause of war is not historical rivalries, nor unjust peace settle-
> ments, nor nationalist grievances, nor competitions in armaments, nor poverty,
> nor the economic struggle for markets and raw materials, nor the contradictions
> of capitalism, nor the aggressiveness of Fascism or Communism; though some of
> these may have occasioned particular wars. The fundamental cause is the absence
> of international government; in other words the anarchy of sovereign states.

But Wight goes on to link what he sees as the prime systemic cause of war
to secondary psychological and sociological factors.

The patriotism of ordinary people can have its ugly side, if it is joined to suspicion and ignorance of other countries. The growth of democracy and socialism has probably tended to accentuate this, by spreading among the middle classes and the masses the sentiments of national pride that used to be confined to kings and courts; and in most countries there is a powerful section of journalism that thrives by promoting distrust of foreigners and the illusion of self sufficiency.

And he concludes with predictable pessimism. 'In a world of independent sovereign powers, war is the only means by which each of them can in the last resort defend its vital interests.'[18] It was left to Martin Wight's student, Hedley Bull, to add that war might also be undertaken either to transform the international system, as in some revolutionary agendas or else to preserve the system as against those who would transform it.[19]

13.5 TERMINATION OF HOSTILITIES

It is usually much easier to start hostilities than to end them, and one of the problems for both combatants and observers is to determine whether they have, indeed, ended. After all, we have all become painfully aware from the experience of Bosnia and Angola that cease-fires, peace negotiations and even peace treaties do not necessarily resolve a conflict. Even when the guns are silent and the armies have withdrawn to barracks, we can have no guarantee that the conflict is finally over. For whether war ends in the physical victory of one side as in the second world war, the political victory of one side as in the cold war, mutual exhaustion and stalemate as in Korea, in compromise as between Israel and the PLO or in third-party intervention as in the 1991 Gulf war, the dissatisfaction or resentment of one side or the other can always lead to further hostilities at a later date. Can we quite certain that the conflict, say, between Iraq and Kuwait is finally over? What is clear is that wars often produce results unintended by those who launch them. Certainly none of those responsible for the first world war would have envisaged either the Bolshevik revolution, a direct result of the conflict, or the birth of Israel, an indirect long-term consequence. Hitler no doubt turns in his grave at the thought that his invasion of the Soviet Union ended in the establishment of Communist rule in Eastern Europe, not least in the east of Germany.

13.6 CONSEQUENCES

In fact whether lost or won, war does tend to produce unexpected results. It has always been an expensive business, but the costs of modern warfare can be astronomical, which is presumably why many governments are increasingly reluctant to resort to it. What is involved nowadays is not only direct military expenditure but also the costs in terms of devastated land, real estate and capital equipment; lost production and trade; depleted resources; the requirements of reconstruction; welfare payments for veterans, widows and orphans; the expenses incurred in maintaining public services and so on. Such massive costs leave even many a victorious country indebted and impoverished, creating the conditions for economic depression, political instability, civil strife and even revolution, as in the 1920s and 1930s.

Politically, the after effects of an exhausting war can be to weaken resistance to national secessionism, leading to the creation of new, possibly unviable states whose very instability can become the harbinger of further international strife, as in 1939. At the same time the very precariousness of the post-war order may lead, as in 1919, 1945, 1947 (when Marshall Aid was proffered) and 1957 (when the Treaty of Rome establishing the EC was signed) to the creation of new international institutions designed to stabilise the system and encourage mutual aid and co-operation. However, such order as there is may depend on new alliance systems and on the powers with the resources to support them; and until recently, in the post 1945 period, the United States and the Soviet Union were the main arbiters in the matter of international order.

Psychologically, the end of a prolonged and costly war tends to produce paradoxical effects. On the one hand the bitter memories of the recent past and apprehension for the future may prolong historic animosities and lead to a heightened state of war preparedness. On the other hand they can also have a moderating influence, dampening whatever enthusiasm might have once existed for resuming hostilities at a later stage. In terms of ideology and religious principle, the effect of victory is often to strengthen conviction, the effect of defeat to weaken it. It is after a lost war, particularly one perceived as having been mismanaged, that revolutions and counter-revolutions tend to occur. Witness the spate of Communist, nationalist and Fascist revolutions in the countries of Central and Eastern Europe following world wars one and two.

Do wars ever settle anything? The term 'settle' suggests the end of a process, and just as we can never say for certain that a war has reached its final termination, we can never be sure that a problem is resolved for all time. On the other hand some wars do result in the creation of new states, changed borders and transfers of population which seem to stand the test of time, even if still resented by those connected with the losing side. Other wars, however, settle nothing and merely fuel the grievances that result in further hostilities.

13.7 IS WAR INEVITABLE?

Is war inevitable? Realists have tended to think so, even though Martin Wight held that 'particular wars could be avoided',[20] presumably by deterrence, diplomacy, third-party mediation or a reappraisal of priorities by one or other side. It all depends on what is meant by 'inevitable'. If it is to suggest a continuous process, then clearly it is not inevitable. Wars occur at some times in some places and not at other times in other places. If on the other hand it is to suggest a phenomenon likely to recur at various times in the future as in the past, then this seems much more plausible. But is the past always a guide to the future? Since habits and institutions can change, it is often hazardous to project the past into the future. Indeed, we can have no warrant for believing that anything is inevitable, except, as someone once said: 'death and taxes'. What we can say is that war occurs with sickening statistical frequency, and that though there have been useful suggestions for reducing its incidence, scope and scale, no one has yet come up with a convincing way of abolishing it.

NOTES

1. Owen's 'Preface' is quoted in Giddings, R., *The War Poets*, London, Bloomsbury, 1988, p. 102.
2. From 'Strange Meeting' in *Poems by Wilfred Owen*, London, Chatto and Windus, 1920.
3. Written in 1916 and quoted in *Old and True*, London, English University Press, undated, pp. 133–4.
4. Quoted in Joad, C.E.M., *The Bookmark*, London, Westhouse, May 1945, p. 99.
5. Quoted in Brend, W., *Foundations of Human Conflicts*, London, Chapman and Hall, 1944, p. 89.
6. Quoted in ibid., pp. 89–90.
7. Penguin edition, 1982, p. 101.
8. 'A few words on non-intervention' in *Dissertations and Discourses*, New York, 1873, pp. 261–2.
9. *The Great Illusion*, [1910], New York, Arno, 1972.
10. See, for example, Wegwood, C.V., *The Thirty Years War*, New Haven, Yale, 1939, p. 516.
11. Barnaby, F., *Future War*, London, Michael Joseph, 1884, pp. 116–17.
12. Nathan, J. and Oliver, J., *United States Foreign Policy and World Order*, Boston, Little, Brown, 1976, pp. 143–4.
13. A cogent exposition of the theory is to be found in Kissinger, H., *Nuclear Weapons and Foreign Policy*, New York, Harper, 1957.
14. *The Causes of War*, London, Macmillan, 1973.
15. Yapp, M.E., *The Near East since the First World War*, London, Longman, 1991, p. 417.
16. New York, Columbia University Press, 1959.
17. *Nationalism*, 3rd ed., London, Hutchinson's University Library, 1966.
18. Wight, M., op. cit., pp. 101, 103 and 104.
19. Bull, H., *The Anarchical Society*, London, 1977, pp. 184–99.
20. Op. cit., p. 137.

PART V
NON-STATE ACTORS

CHAPTER 14

INTERNATIONAL ORGANISATIONS: REGIONAL AND GLOBAL

Throughout the centuries priests, philosophers, poets and potentates have dreamed dreams and drawn up blueprints for a more just and better-ordered world. In biblical times, in between the endless skirmishes, wars and massacres, there were hopes for such a change in the human condition as to lead people to beat their 'swords into ploughshares and their spears into pruning hooks'. But how would such a transformation occur? For the people of the Book it had to do with divine intervention in the form of a Messiah, a Messianic Age or a Second Coming. But the Hebrews and early Christians had no monopoly on idealism, and ever since the Greeks began to philosophise about the 'good society', there have been broadly three schools of thought as to how a strife-torn world might be reformed and regenerated: one, envisaging a change in human nature, another looking forward to a recasting of society and a third visualising a radical alteration in the organisation of international society. What generally lends urgency to the search for the ultimate panacea is the experience of a particularly bloody and brutal conflict within or between tribes or states. Certainly the senseless slaughter of the first world war was the stimulus for a profusion of plans, proposals and projects, and people like Woodrow Wilson, Alfred Zimmern, Philip Noel-Baker and Norman Angell came to believe that in the idea of a League of Nations they had found that elusive formula long engaging the idealists.

14.1 BEFORE THE LEAGUE

Visionaries

In fact, the League had not been conjured out of thin air. It represented a refinement of ideas and institutions that had been around for centuries. As early as 1313 the Italian poet Dante in his *de Monarchia* had outlined a proposal for a unified *imperium mundi*, an empire of the world, or, rather, of the Christian world. In effect, Dante was looking backwards to the time of the Roman Empire rather than forwards to something entirely novel. By the time of the Renaissance, blueprints for a better world were proliferating, several anticipating some of the detailed arrangements of the League. The Frenchman Éméric Crucé in *The New Cyneas*, in 1623, proposed a small neutral country to house a 'general assembly' to which the states of Europe would send ambassadors, there to vote on the merits or otherwise of the claims of countries in dispute. Fifteen years later, another Frenchman, the Duc de Sully, who had been minister to the recently assassinated French king, Henry IV, produced a *Grand Design* for the permanent pacification of Europe in which the frontiers are redrawn so as to create 15 states—five Catholic, five Lutheran, five Calvinistic—of comparable strength and a council arbitrates conflicts of interest. Fifty years later, in 1688, the English Quaker, William Penn, in his *Towards the Present and Future Peace of Europe* advocated a European confederation with a parliament and a council chosen in proportion to annual national revenue to help resolve differences between states on the basis of what he called 'rules of justice'. Like Penn, the French Abbé de St Pierre in his *Project* of 1713 *for Making Peace Permanent in Europe* advocated the renunciation of war and a confederal union. In addition, he devised a variety of bureaux for the union to deal with such matters as commercial jurisprudence, a common currency and standard weights and measures—ideas which were to find resonance in this century not so much in the League as in the European Union.

Perhaps the best known of these historical designs is Kant's *Perpetual Peace* of 1795,[1] an essay anticipating in substance and in style Karl Marx as well as Woodrow Wilson. Like Wilson, Kant believed that war was an inevitable product of authoritarian or absolutist rule. In his view, the rationale for such political systems was material gain; and to this end they were constantly involved in war preparations, if not actual hostilities. But like Marx he believed that what was required was a transnational struggle to overthrow absolutism world-wide, envisaging the creation in one country after another of assemblies in which the common people would have a real say in policy-making. In his view, such assemblies would refuse to sanction or finance war, except under threat of some foreign despot. Like a Marxist, too, he believed there was an inexorable law of history that made the goal—in this case perpetual peace—as inevitable as it was desirable but that through the global overthrow of absolutism, history could be given a push. This was expected to be followed by a confederal union of states, eventually to lead, as communism is supposed to lead, to the withering away of the state and the establishment of a community of humankind.

Schemes, mechanisms and agencies

The chief architect of the League of Nations, Woodrow Wilson, had been a Professor of Politics, and since many of his advisers were also intellectuals with an interest in politics, philosophy, history and the classics, they may have been influenced by such blueprints, of which they will have been well aware. There will, however, have been other influences.[2] First, the historical legacy of confederal schemes, from the Swiss Confederation of the late 13th century, through the American Confederation of the late 18th century and beyond. A second influence was the already existing mechanisms for sustaining order internationally and on which the post-Westphalian system rested—international law, diplomacy and balance of power. Third, there was the legacy of the Congress or Concert system established at Vienna in 1815 in which the five acknowledged great powers of Europe met periodically to discuss and if possible resolve some of the world's major political and military problems. Though it had no permanent organs or powers of enforcement, the Concert system had established the idea of great power responsibility for international order, and this created the precedent for both the principle of regular meetings of the League's Council and Assembly and the collective security principle of the Covenant.

Fourth were the specialised international agencies, such as the European Commission for the Danube, the Universal Postal Union and the International Red Cross, established in the wake of the massive growth of international trade and communications in the 19th century. By the time of the first world war there were nearly 50 such organisations existing, dealing with a host of political, economic, technological and humanitarian activities, most providing for periodic conferences and with a permanent secretariat to handle information, statistics and administration.

Finally, there were additional international mechanisms on which the framers of the League Covenant could build. There had been increasing resort to various forms of peaceful settlement, and towards the end of the 19th century, arbitration had become fashionable. More than a hundred arbitration treaties had been concluded between 1881 and 1900, and the Hague Conferences of 1899 and 1907 had established a Permanent Court of Arbitration with a panel of judges for dealing with disputes.

14.2 THE LEAGUE

Organs

Basically, therefore, the League, which emerged from the peace conference terminating the first world war and was to promote 'international peace and security' and 'international co-operation' was built on a legacy of ideas and experience. On the other hand since it was also bred of a popular desire to make future wars impossible, it was a pity that President Wilson insisted that the League be an integral part of the Peace Treaty, since Germany, Italy and Japan resentful of a peace accord they felt unjust were almost bound to transfer their hostility to the League itself. Since its fate was much in the minds of those who were to create a successor—the

UN—25 years later, it is important to examine its structure. It had four principle organs: an Assembly in which all participating states were represented; a Council containing the five major victors of world war one plus 10 others elected by the Assembly; a Secretariat, and a Court with nine judges at its disposal. But throughout, the League's major problem was lack of 'teeth'. Both Assembly and Council could only make recommendations not binding resolutions, and it was left to member states to interpret the recommendations as they chose. In any case recommendations had to be unanimous, and this greatly hampered the ability of Assembly or Council to come to agreed resolutions. As for the Secretariat, it had no executive functions of any kind, while the Permanent Court of International Justice could only adjudicate if members submitted their disputes to it or asked for an advisory opinion.

Agenda

True, the League agenda was not confined to dealing with threats to the peace. It also spawned a number of organisations to promote inter-state co-operation in the fields of labour, finance, transport and communications, public health and welfare. It concerned itself with the slave trade and with traffic in women, children and narcotics. Under the Mandates system it promoted the development of the former colonial territories of the Ottoman Empire and of Germany, in effect preventing their annexation by the victorious powers. In spite of such activities, grudgingly financed by the member states, the principle aim of the organisation was the establishment of a new world order. The old, decentralised balance of power mechanism was to be replaced by something more centralised and institutionalised—collective security through collective deterrence, disarmament and the peaceful settlement of disputes.[3]

Record

During its 19 years of active operation, the League was called on to deal with 44 crises concerning threats to peace and security, from minor misunderstandings and frontier incidents to disputes over treaty rights and more endemic conflicts. Since in the 1920s the League was not faced with any direct challenge from a major power, it was able to chalk up one or two successes to its credit. Through mediation it defused tensions on the Albanian/Yugoslav frontier in 1921; in 1927 it steered Poland and Lithuania towards ending their 'state of war' over possession of Vilna, and by threatening sanctions against both sides it deterred a war between Greece and Bulgaria in 1925. But in the 1930s, the successes were few and far between, as the challenges to the League came not from minor countries but from the greatest military powers of the day and for whom rapid rearmament, not disarmament took priority.

First to lay down the gauntlet was Japan, which felt entitled to far more of the spoils of war than the peacemakers had granted in 1919. By the time Hirohito had ascended the throne in the mid-1920s, the militarisation of the country was already underway and in 1931 Tokyo embarked on a plan of territorial expansion in Asia and beyond. In September, after an incident directed against a Japanese patrol guarding the South Manchurian railway, Japanese troops sacked the local Chinese barracks and proceeded to occupy the whole of Manchuria, China's vast and most prosperous province. Clearly the League's deterrent posture had failed to prevent a blatant act of aggression. Yet the League had nothing to offer China beyond a mere rebuke to Tokyo. No military action was in prospect, and there was nothing to deter a further Japanese attack. In effect, Tokyo had fired the first shots in its 14-year assault on China, while the League's dedication to collective security stood exposed as a sham. Its only act of significance was to issue a report branding Japan as an aggressor. Even this modest endeavour was too much for Tokyo, and the Japanese delegate stormed out of the League Assembly.

As he angrily withdrew, another envoy was soon to pack his bags—the representative of Germany, now under Nazi rule. In fact Adolf Hitler, who had come to power in 1933, had never made any secret of his intention to restore his country to greatness and avenge those he claimed had humiliated Germany in the peace of 1919. As German rearmament and expansionism were incompatible with League membership, Hitler pulled his country out. While he finalised his expansionist plans, another dictator took action.

In Italy Mussolini, the architect of Fascism, saw himself also as the architect of a new Roman empire, hoping to make the Mediterranean once more an Italian lake. But first he turned his attention to Abyssinia, a country which had humiliated an Italian force in the 1890s. In October 1935, following an incident he was able to turn to advantage—just as the Japanese had done in Manchuria—Mussolini sent in the troops. Against defenceless civilians and soldiers whose only weapons were spears, bows and arrows and bare knuckles Mussolini sent in the air force, tanks, machine guns and poison gas. It was an unfair fight, and the Emperor of Abyssinia took the country's only plane and in Geneva pleaded with the League to take effective action. Though the League did agree to impose economic sanctions, their implementation was so half-hearted as to make little difference to the Italian war effort. As in Manchuria, there was to be no military rescue, and the Abyssinians went under.

The League's failure yet again to take decisive action was noted with satisfaction in Berlin as well as in Rome. And in 1936 Hitler's Germany was ready. In defiance of the post-war agreements, Germany reoccupied the Rhineland. In 1938 it occupied and forcibly absorbed Austria. Then the

Führer turned to Czechoslovakia, demanding from the Czechs the German-speaking area known as the Sudetenland. In the ensuing crisis, the leaders of Britain, France and Italy met Hitler at Munich, and in return for a German pledge not to annexe the rest of Czechoslovakia, gave the green light for Hitler's takeover of the Sudetenland. Britain's prime minister, Neville Chamberlain, claimed, on his return from Munich that he had brought 'peace in our time'. Others, however, called it 'appeasement', giving in to blackmail. And in March 1939, the bankruptcy of this policy became only too clear. Betraying the assurances he had given only six months before, Hitler seized the rest of Czechoslovakia.

While Germany was digesting its fresh acquisitions, Italy in April 1939 turned its guns on one of Europe's smallest and most backward states— Albania. In a matter of days what had been a virtual protectorate had now become an integral part of Italy. Meanwhile in Spain, three years of civil war were ending in a Fascist victory, thanks to the military help given General Franco by Germany and Italy. Belatedly, the members of the League began to take their responsibilities seriously. With Poland under threat of a German attack, Britain and France offered their joint protection. Given the dismal record of the upholders of the League, Hitler discounted that guarantee but to his cost. For two days after 1 September when Hitler's army marched into Poland, Chamberlain, who had tried so hard to avert war, found himself declaring it. Other declarations followed. And so the second world war (which some saw as a direct consequence of Japan's unhindered conquest of Manchuria, a lesson not lost on some of those who 60 years later decided that Saddam Hussein must not be allowed to get away with the conquest of Kuwait) had now begun in earnest. But while Britain and France struggled to contain the Nazi threat, they were soon confronted with a further series of aggressions, but from an entirely unexpected source.

Less than a month after concluding a non-aggression pact with Nazi Germany, its ideological foe, Stalin's Russia occupied eastern Poland. Whether or not a defensive measure, the Soviet action, so soon after the Nazi onslaught, served to wipe Poland off the political map. Three months later, Moscow seemed to have the same fate in store for Finland. The Red Army's unprovoked attack against a country, once an integral part of the Russian Empire, led to the Soviet Union's expulsion from the League—by now a more or less meaningless gesture since after a decade of creeping paralysis the League was effectively dead. Whether the League had failed the nations or the nations the League is debatable.[4] What is clear is that it had been deeply flawed in both theory and practice.

Flaws

(1) It had been part and parcel of a peace settlement that several countries thought unfair, and were determined, when strong enough, to overturn.

(2) It had been crippled from the first by America's refusal to join—an irony this, since it was largely the brainchild of the country's own president. And although the Concert at Geneva went ahead, as it were, without the composer who was to have conducted, it was deprived of the one country that had the economic power, the physical vitality and the detachment from the tangled affairs of Europe to give the League the drive and larger vision it needed.

(3) The powers of the various bodies had been far too limited for effective action. Council and Assembly could only make recommendations, not binding decisions, and any government was free to reject or resist any proposed operation.

(4) It was, in any case, often difficult to get agreement on whether or not an aggression had occurred, so necessitating a League response. For 'aggression' itself is not clearly defined, and an action which appears to some as aggression may be regarded by others as a retortion to an aggression against it and, therefore, perfectly legal. When, for example, Iraq attacked Iran in 1979 ostensibly over passage along the Shatt-Al-Arab waterway, it claimed it was a reprisal for wrongs inflicted against it in the 1970s when the Shah had forced Baghdad to make territorial concessions. Of course, in determining whether an aggression has occurred or not, states tend to be partisan. They are reluctant to admit that, say, an ally might be an aggressor or a foe the victim of their ally's aggression.

(5) Even if it were agreed that an aggression had occurred, it was one thing to take action when the aggressor was a small power, another when the aggression had been committed by one or more great powers, which was the situation the League faced more than once in the 1930s, and in such circumstances many were especially reluctant to act.

(6) In any case the League had been largely Eurocentric, and its members were rather less interested when the arena of aggression was in Asia, as in Manchuria; Africa, as in Abyssinia; or Latin America, as when Bolivia and Paraguay fought a full-scale war between 1932 and 1935 over the uninhabited river basin known as the Chaco.

(7) Several governments, having joined the League not out of conviction but of fear of popular disapproval if they had not, were in fact opposed to the very principle of combining for collective security. As Quintin Hogg, later Lord Hailsham, said: 'I believe it is right to fight for...King and country. But it's against nature...to be called to die for someone else's King and country.'[5] But it was precisely because too few had been prepared to fight for someone else's 'King and country' that so many states succumbed to aggression. And it was for similar reasons that the League failed to acquire its own armed forces.

(8) The League was insufficiently focused on the kinds of economic and social conditions that might be a contributary cause of inter-state war.

14.3 THE UNITED NATIONS

Learning the lessons

Having felt they had understood the essential flaws in the make-up and performance of the League, the framers of the UN Charter were determined to learn the lessons.[6]

(1) Though the UN had begun during the second world war as an anti-Fascist coalition, it was not tied to any particular peace settlement after it, and never gave the appearance of being an association of status quo powers anxious to preserve the post-war arrangements at all costs.

(2) Though the UN has never been entirely inclusive of all states, it is near to being so, and included the United States, and for that matter the Soviet Union, from the start. In addition, being far more representative than the Eurocentric 'club' of 1919 it was, as intended, to become increasingly global in orientation as decolonisation proceeded apace.

(3) The Charter was designed to give the UN powers lacking in the League. It was to have armed forces at its disposal, the veto was to be denied to all save the five Permanent Members of the Security Council, and the Council was itself to determine whether or not an aggression had occurred. If, in its opinion, it had, it could call for collective action against the offending power ranging from verbal condemnation, through economic sanctions to military force.

(4) In both stated purposes and organisation, the UN was to have a broad agenda, in keeping with its wide-ranging membership, many far more interested in the problems of development than in the security dilemma. Though peace and security remained a priority, the UN was also to try to harmonise action in solving economic, social, cultural and humanitarian problems affecting inter-state relations. Unless, however, peace was deemed at risk, it has tended to avoid intervention in matters of domestic jurisdiction.

Organs

As is well known the UN has a General Assembly, comprising all member states (185 in 1994), but with the power only to make recommendations, and a Security Council of 15 members which can make binding decisions, provided the five powers with the veto can agree. There are, in addition, four further organs. The Economic and Social Council, (ECOSOC), whose members are elected every three years by the General Assembly, can do a

variety of things: initiate studies and reports, call international conferences, make recommendations, establish regional economic or functional
commissions on such subjects as human rights, narcotics, population
growth, the status of women, industrial development and trade. Moreover
it works closely with the UN's specialised agencies such as the Food and
Agricultural Organisation (FAO), the World Health Organisation (WHO),
the International Labour Organisation (ILO), the United Nations
Educational, Scientific and Cultural Organisation (UNESCO) and the
World Bank.

A fourth UN body, the Trusteeship Council, was to be the successor to
the League committee dealing with the mandated territories, though it
became responsible for additional territories, mainly in the Pacific, once
the responsibility of Germany and Japan. In fact, it has more or less
successfully completed its mission as most of its charges now have their
independence. A fifth UN body, the International Court of Justice, was to
be the successor of the PCIJ, but now plays an important role in the codifi-
cation and development of international law in conjunction with the
International Law Commission, also established under the UN's auspices.
Finally, there is the UN Secretariat, a much more substantial body than
under the League, with a large staff of international civil servants whose
tasks range from gathering, publishing and distributing essential data to
preparing special studies on international problems and servicing the
multitude of meetings under the UN's auspices. More importantly,
perhaps, its Secretary General has become an important figure in his own
right, taking independent initiatives which in his view advance the principles of the Charter—one has only to think of Dr Boutros-Ghalli's prompt-
ings on Bosnia, Somalia, Iraq and Haiti.

Difficulties

No matter how the UN has in fact developed, not for the first time experience has failed to match up to expectations.[7]

(1) Though the very location of the organisation in New York and the veto
ensured that this time the United States would be a member from the
start, the onset of the cold war greatly hampered the ability of the
Security Council to authorise effective action and made virtually
impossible the creation of a permanent UN standing army. For whenever the major interests of either superpower was involved, it would
resort to the veto, and neither would sanction an international force
over which it would lack exclusive control. The one exception—the
creation of a UN force in 1950 to fight in Korea—proves the rule since
the crucial decision was taken at a Security Council meeting from
which the Soviet Union was absent. Had it been present it would

206 THE STRUCTURE OF INTERNATIONAL SOCIETY

doubtless have rejected the claim that North Korea had been the aggressor.

(2) When the Soviet Union and the United States did have matters of common interest to discuss, they would often deal with them outside the aegis of the UN—secretly, in either Moscow, Washington or some other venue: more openly at summit conferences.

(3) Many of the more thorny issues concerning peace and security have not easily lent themselves to UN action because of the question of domestic jurisdiction. Though there have been several hundred wars since 1945,[8] most have been civil rather than international and, unless a beleagured government itself called for UN action or there was deemed to be a general threat to peace, the organisation would or could not get militarily involved. In consequence, several such conflicts were never even brought to the attention of the Security Council.

(4) Since many of the issues in contention have related to questions of human rights and in particular the treatment of minorities, such as the Palestinians in Israel, the Kashmiris in India, and the Kurds in Iraq and Turkey, the impulse to intervene on humanitarian grounds has always had to be balanced against the UN's commitment to preserve national sovereignty. But in the case of the white regimes of Southern Africa—Rhodesia and South Africa—where the treatment of majorities was at issue, the UN had few qualms about imposing economic sanctions since the former lacked sovereign recognition, while the very policies of both were deemed to constitute a threat to peace under the terms of the Charter.

(5) On welfare, and the UN's commitment to try to reduce the disparity between rich and poor, the picture has been decidedly patchy. On the one hand the deliberations of the General Assembly and the various bodies under ECOSOC have served to dramatise the plight of the poor, the malnourished, the persecuted and the dispossessed. In addition, through the UN's various agencies, considerable funds have been disbursed for the relief of suffering in various parts of the world. Smallpox has been eradicated and epidemics of cholera, typhoid and malaria controlled thanks to the work of the WHO, which has also been in the forefront of the drive to inform people about the different methods of birth control and the danger of AIDS. In many parts of the world, too, agricultural practices have been improved, together with local diets, thanks to the work of the FAO. And, of course, the Trusteeship Council completed its job successfully in preparing territories for self-government and eventual independence. On the other hand, for all the UN's good work, it has not been able to reduce to any extent the extremes of wealth and poverty either within or between states. If anything, the gap has tended to widen, not least in many of the LDCs, where economic progress has been hampered all too

frequently by domestic corruption, inefficiency and civil strife, combined with a heavy burden of foreign debt made all the more onerous by often adverse international trading conditions. To make matters worse, whatever economic advance there is can be imperiled by massive population pressure.

Moreover, Third World demands for a New International Economic Order (NIEO) in the form of more development and technical assistance, duty-free access to Western markets, long-term commodity agreements at stable prices and the cancellation or reduction of debt have tended to get an unsympathetic response. Nor can the wealthy and powerful states be compelled to concede on the matter since the UN, like any other political institution, has to reflect the competing objectives of its members and can only do what in the end the more prosperous are prepared to pay for.

(6) Finally, a whole range of new issues have appeared on the international agenda that were never in contemplation when the UN was founded. Such problems as the pollution of the international environment, the depletion of economic resources, the population explosion, terrorism, the spread of AIDS, nuclear proliferation, global warming, the debt crisis and so on are matters for the treatment of which the UN has yet to develop appropriate mechanisms. One has only to consider, for example, the meagre results of the 1992 'Earth Summit' in Rio, under the UN's auspices.[9]

Facilities

Yet, despite shortcomings, the UN's very existence provides a valuable framework for the handling of international crises. For one thing, the fact that representatives from countries hostile or indifferent to one another can be in continuous contact in the lobbies and lounges behind the scenes is important.[10] In an earlier chapter mention was made of how a formula for ending the Berlin Blockade was hammered out as a result of a chance encounter between the Soviet and American ambassadors in one of the 'men's rooms'. What happens in private, therefore, may be far more significant than what the public perceives. And if conflicts are not being resolved by rational discussion, they can sometimes be deflected when the UN is used as a kind of safety valve by those who can discharge verbally the accumulated resentment and anger of a people or government. In this sense the organisation has a quasi-psychiatric function in which the protagonists act out their quarrel in lieu, as it were, of physical combat. But the UN has, in addition, a further quasi-psychiatric function. It can serve as a face-saving mechanism for states which have to make a policy climbdown. For example Britain and France probably called off their 1956 Suez adventure because the United States had issued a number of veiled economic and other threats. However, that they could say it was in response to pressure from the UN made withdrawal easier. Again, Premier Khrushchev's decision in 1962 to remove Soviet missiles from Cuba was probably because Kennedy threatened to go to the brink of nuclear war if they were not withdrawn. But because the UN had also requested their removal, it made it just that little bit easier for the Soviet leader to do a U-turn.[11]

Developments

Surprisingly perhaps, the UN may be said in certain respects to have exceeded the hopes of its founders in that it has developed techniques for what a former Secretary General, Dag Hammarskjold, called 'preventive diplomacy', in which it attempts to settle local conflicts without the involvement of the most powerful states and at an early stage before they escalate. Basically small and medium powers are asked to contribute forces for a variety of peacekeeping roles, and at least till recently they have been happy to oblige. More importantly, perhaps, the duties of such peacekeeping forces have been greatly expanded over the years, as have their number of operations.[12] At first it was a matter of an interposition between combatants in an inter-state war, as when in 1956, on the retreat of British and French troops from Egypt, the UN Emergency Force (UNEF) was placed in the Sinai peninsula to keep Egyptian and Israeli troops apart. However, any such deployment has to be approved by the state or states on whose territory it is situated, and if that approval is subsequently withdrawn, as it was by Egypt's President Nasser in 1967, it has to go. In this particular case the departure of UNEF was followed shortly after by another round of Middle Eastern hostilities in the shape of the Six-Day war.

The next UN peace-keeping force found itself in a different kind of situation—one with which, strictly speaking, the UN was not supposed to deal—a civil war in a newly independent country. The country in question was the Congo (now Zaire), and the government, which had assumed power as the Belgian colonists beat a hasty retreat, was unable to keep control. When, however, it looked as if the Belgians and the Russians who were supporting different factions in the conflict might become deeply embroiled, the UN declared the situation 'a threat to peace' and with the acquiescence of members of the Congolese government which had in effect been toppled, voted to send in UN troops. Known as ONUC (Operation des Nations Unies—Congo), it played a controversial role, sometimes firing before being fired on, but by 1964 it had succeeded in restoring law and order. It had not, however, restored the original left-wing administration, but a right-wing government of which the country's long-serving dictator, President Mobutu (one of those immensely rich rulers of a potentially wealthy country he has impoverished), was the direct successor.

A third UN peacekeeping force was again involved in a domestic dispute, but this time with the explicit backing of all the protagonists. The venue was Cyprus, the date 1964, and the unit known as UNFICYP (UN force in Cyprus) was to police the lines between the hostile Greek and Turkish communities. Despite the presence on the island since 1974 of a quite separate Turkish force, after a coup designed to bring about the union of Cyprus with Greece in the teeth of Turkish Cypriot hostility, the UN force remains and may be said to have played a generally constructive role in defusing tension and maintaining the peace, even though the island remains divided.

Since then peacekeepers have again been sent to Sinai, to the Golan Heights between Israel and Syria, to Southern Lebanon and elsewhere; they have become involved in monitoring cease-fire lines in places such as Afghanistan and on the Iran/Iraq border; they have also become involved in disarming insurgents, as in Nicaragua and El Salvador; in mine clearance, as in Cambodia and Angola; in preparing for elections, as in Cambodia; in monitoring elections, as in Namibia, Haiti and Angola; in securing humanitarian assistance, as in Bosnia and Somalia; in resettling refugees, as in Mozambique; in protecting enclaves of minorities, as in Croatia; in pre-empting the possibility of hostilities, as in Macedonia; in documenting war crimes, as in Bosnia and in a variety of capacities following the 1991 Gulf war when the UN, having first sanctioned a military force to remove the Iraqis from Kuwait, then needed various bodies to monitor the ceasefire and to dismantle the country's nuclear, chemical and bacteriological war-making capacities.

But peacekeeping is one thing, peacemaking another;[13] and if the former is often a risky and not always successful enterprise, the latter is even more hazardous. It is precisely because there is so little peace for it to keep that the UN has been very wary of getting too enmeshed in the Bosnian mêlée, which, in any case, is more of a civil than an international conflict and in which those who know their mountains have a considerable military advantage over those who do not. None the less it would appear that the peacekeeping services of the UN, though often the butt of criticism, are still much in demand. Indeed, as Boutros-Ghali once put it: the UN seems to be suffering from success, in the sense that far too many people want it to do far too many things, but are not prepared to give it the financial backing it needs to do them properly. In short, the UN peacekeepers are overstretched and underfunded.

It is a somewhat patchy record then, but by no means unimpressive. Moreover, since the end of the cold war, the Security Council has found a degree of cohesion hitherto lacking, with all that that implies for future peacekeeping operations and the possibility of creating a new world order, even if partly dependent on the whims and fancies of the United States.

14.4 REGIONAL ORGANISATIONS

Where does this leave the regional organisations? Though there is in theory no necessary contradiction between regional and global integration, in practice the more united the regions, the more fragmented international society could become.[14] The General Agreement on Tariffs and Trade (GATT) notwithstanding, the European Union, the North American Free Trade Area and the Association of South East Asian Nations have acquired distinctly protectionist overtones. On the other hand it is not yet clear how solid are these economic blocs. In the case of the European Union, the strains are unmistakable. It is not just that national sentiment tends to reassert itself the more the exercise of sovereignty seems to diminish. It is also that already some of the Union's objectives have been outdated by events. Its role as a bridge between the superpowers is clearly obsolete now that the cold war is over, and those who had hoped to use it to keep Germany divided have already seen their worst fears realised. And despite the introduction in 1993 of the Internal Market, several years of recession affecting virtually all its members to a greater or lesser degree have produced a measure of disenchantment further complicating attempts at a unified currency and a common social, defence and foreign policy. Though integration proceeds, it is at a slower pace than many anticipated and in the meantime a kind of dialectic is being played out between integrative and disintegrative tendencies. Such contradictory impulses are also, however, to be found in most other inter-governmental organisations (IGOs) as well, and in turn they tend to affect not merely the institutions in question but also the global political and economic instutions which form the broader canvass within which IGOs and, for that matter, INGOs (international non-governmental organisations) operate.

NOTES

1. [1795] translated by Lewis Beck, New York, Bobbs-Merrill, 1957.
2. See Hemleben, S.J., *Plans for World Peace through Six Centuries*, Chicago, Chicago University Press, 1943; York, E., *League of Nations, Ancient, Medieval and Modern*, Swarthmore Press, London, 1928; Woolf, L., *International Government*, Brentane's, New York, 1916 and Bartlett, R.J., *The League to Enforce Peace*, Chapel Hill, 1945.
3. See, for example, Wight, M., *Power Politics*, Harmondsworth, Penguin, 1979, pp. 200–15.

4. See Manning, C.A.W., 'The "failure" of the League' in Cosgrove, C. and Twitchett, K. (eds), *The New International Actors*, London, Macmillan, 1970, pp. 105–23.
5. From a BBC broadcast of June 1934.
6. Goodrich, L.M. and Simons, A.P., *The Charter of the United Nations—Commentary and Documents*, 3rd ed., New York, Columbia University Press, 1970. Also Nicholas, H., 'From League to UN', *International Affairs*, November 1970, Special issue.
7. See, for example, Nicholas, H., *The United Nations as a Political Institution*, 5th ed., Oxford, Oxford University Press, 1975.
8. Kidron, M. and Smith, D., *The War Atlas*, London, Pan, 1983.
9. Tickell, C., 'The World after the Summit Meeting at Rio', *The Washington Quarterly*, Spring 1993.
10. Alger, C.F., 'Personal Contact in International Exchanges' in Kelman, H.C. (ed.), *International Behaviour*, New York, Holt, Rinehart and Winston, 1965, p. 527.
11. See, for example, O'Brien, C.C. and Topolski, F., *The United Nations: Sacred Drama*, London, Hutchinson, 1968.
12. See Morphet, S., 'UN peacekeeping and election monitoring' in Roberts, A. and Kingsbury, B., *The United Nations: Divided World*, 2nd ed., Oxford, Oxford University Press, 1993, pp. 183–239.
13. 'Rikhye, I.J., 'Peace keeping and Peace making' in Wiseman, H., *Peace-keeping: Appraisals and Proposals*, Oxford, Oxford University Press, 1983, pp. 5–18.
14. See Jones, W.S., *The Logic of International Relations*, 6th ed., Glenview, Ill., Scott and Co, 1988, pp. 226–8.

CHAPTER 15

TRANSNATIONAL MOVEMENTS AND ORGANISATIONS

15.1 TRANSNATIONALISM PRIOR TO WESTPHALIA

So far the text has been not only traditional in content, it has been positively old-fashioned in that the main concentration has been on states. Yet as will have been made clear, if only in passing, the sovereign state was never the sole actor in world politics.[1] Long before it appeared, there were non-state actors of political significance. These included city states, feudal fiefdoms, principalities, duchies, kingdoms and empires; social groups such as the clan and the tribe; corporate economic bodies such as the Hanseatic League and the Merchant Adventurers, the large scale banking enterprises of Venice, Lombardy, Hamburg and Antwerp and the finance houses of families like the Medicis; and there were the religious authorities which generally established the rules by which political administrators were bound—the Papacy, the Holy Roman Empire, the Byzantine Church, the dominion of Islam and, further East, the power of Confucianism, Buddhism and Hinduism to transcend frontiers and to conquer minds. Before the age of the sovereign state, when the frontiers of existing political units were often both impermanent and porous, much political, social and economic activity was transnational ('trans' meaning across) in the sense that it took and needed to take no account of existing frontiers.

Moreover, ideas and inventions had always been transnational. As soon as social or political bodies interacted, there was always the possibility that axioms and assumptions, concepts and creeds, doctrines and dogmas, precepts and principles, routines and regulations would be transmitted from one to another, in effect serving, as did the ideas of the Reformation and Renaissance, to revolutionise political and social configurations. It was never possible to confine the impact of inventions such as gunpowder and the mariner's compass or of new technologies in construction, production and the extraction of minerals to their countries of origin. Meanwhile the discoveries of voyagers like Columbus and Vasco da Gama, their explorations encouraged and financed by one or other of the economic corporations with the necessary capital, were helping to shape and reshape the intellectual, geographical and political contours of the medieval world. However, for the indigenous populations, the transnational effects of such discoveries had often been disastrous as some of the diseases, viruses, bacteria and parasites of the old world were released into the new, taking a heavy toll of lives.

Prior to the age of the sovereign state, loyalties, too, had tended to be largely transnational. If asked to define the collective entity to which they belonged, most Europeans of the 15th and 16th centries would probably have said Christendom and would have meant by it not a society occupying a defined space but a community of persons sharing the same faith, whether in its Catholic, Orthodox, Lutheran or Calvinist form and whether or not they lived under Christian rulers. A few might also have considered themselves 'European', a comparatively novel concept, again not so much rooted in a geographical area as indicating a culture forged by a Church claiming to be the inheritor of Graeco–Roman as well as Christian civilisation. In a sense, Europe would have been defined in terms of what was regarded as non-European, and increasingly the boundary was held to lie at the point where Christian civilisation encountered Islam.[2] That that 'boundary' persists in many a European mind is indicated by the considerable surprise generated by the recent 'discovery' of the existence in the Balkans of so many European Muslims of Slav or Albanian origin.

Where allegiances were not transnational they were often subnational—to individuals and groups, cities and other localities within existing political frontiers. Due deference was paid to the feudal lord or baron, the seigneur of the parish, the local squire or the abbot of a particular monastery. Craftsmen tended to give their loyalty to their guild—a kind of friendly society of masons, goldsmiths, watchmakers or whatever—that took care of the elderly, the sick and even the unemployed members of the craft. Yet others found their sense of identity in a kind of local patriotism, of attachment to their region or province or, more narrowly, to their town. Widespread allegiance to king and country was to come later, and in the meantime wars were often fought with the aid of mercenaries or soldiers of fortune whose loyalty depended on whoever happened to be the paymaster at the time.

15.2 TRANSNATIONALISM SINCE WESTPHALIA

Religious and political affiliations

Even after the 16th and 17th centuries when the sovereign state in its modern form began to crystallise, non-state actors continued to play significant political roles. In fact the state system was always part of a wider system of political, economic and social interaction.[3] Long after Westphalia, for instance, the papacy and the Holy Roman empire continued to command widespread loyalty, and within the newly consolidated kingdoms there were semi-autonomous principalities, duchies and archbishoprics to which many give their primary allegiance.

14 THE STRUCTURE OF INTERNATIONAL SOCIETY

Class and cultural affiliations

There were still class, ideological and other kinds of ties transcending frontiers. For all their insistence on sovereign independence, the rulers of post-Westphalian Europe were often bound to one another by strong cosmopolitan links, by a common culture, by religious affinities and often, because of dynastic marriages, by ties of blood. Indeed, so cosmopolitan was the royal profession that often the rulers were not even nationals or native speakers of the countries they governed. In 1688, for example, a Dutchman became King of England, and a Hanoverian in 1714—the latter, incidentally, hardly spoke English at all. As for the servants of the royal households and of the state, they, too, were often people with no particular national stake in the system on whose behalf they operated. Much of the entourage of Peter the Great and of his successors in Russia was German, while for generations Italians helped in the running of the French royal household, and Spain's military and diplomatic services were saturated with English, Irish and German nationals.

Ideological ties and movements

There were other kinds of transnational allegiances too, including those of the theorists and activists whose inclinations were revolutionary and whose sympathies could not be confined to any particular state. The philosophers of the Enlightenment, for example, were to have a marked impact on the course of both American and French revolutions, in turn promoting the paradox of transnational nationalism, as militant nationalists in 1830 and 1848 used the new railway networks to go from capital to capital fomenting revolutionary nationalist insurrection. And, of course, there were the contagious ideas of the French socialists and communists which inspired Marx and Engels. These contributed to the climate of ideas that led to the development of trade unions, co-operatives and welfare legislation throughout much of Western Europe and spawned the Socialist Internationals of the 19th century and the Communist (Third) International of the 20th century. Meanwhile, before the age of the passport, the work permit and the immigration quota, it was possible for people attracted to a political culture other than their own to settle abroad without too much difficulty.

Economic non-state actors

Trading companies

Generating not so much allegiance as power were a host of economic non-state actors, foremost among which were the transnational trading organisations. The political and economic influence of such 17th- to 19th-century mercantile trading organisations as the British East India Company, the Dutch East India Company, the various West India companies, the sundry 'Levant' and 'Africa' companies, the 'Plymouth', the 'Virginia' and other companies concerned with trade with the Americas and the Hudson's Bay company were often enormous. The East India Co, which in effect ruled the greater part of India and South East Asia for much of the 17th and 18th centuries, employed its own armed forces to secure exclusive trading rights and trained native armies to keep out missionaries as well as competitors in trade.[4] Company rules served to restrict exports of tea from countries not under its control, including America, and it was this above all that led to the sabotage in Boston harbour of a Company tea cargo, in turn precipitating the revolt of the American colonies. The Company also introduced opium to China, which led, ultimately, to the opium wars. How many modern MNCs can boast a comparable record of the use and abuse of power?

Finance houses

A second set of significant non-state economic actors were the finance houses. It was, for example, the great Fugger banking house that largely determined whether Charles V of Spain or Francis I of France would wear the crown of the Holy Roman empire in 1530. In the end the crown went to Charles, largely because the bank lent him 543,000 florins to enable him to buy it. By 1546, the Fugger balance sheet was recording debts from a German emperor, the city of Antwerp, the kings of England and Portugal and the queen of the Netherlands.[5] Though strictly speaking such transactions predate the sovereign state as such, the Fuggers together with the other great banking houses went on to provide the financial backing to meet the expanding needs of international commerce and enterprise in the 17th and 18th centuries, and when loans were not repaid, they took over the vast estates, crown lands, mines, or whatever pledged as security.

Craftsmen

A third and increasingly important economic actor, especially in the age of mercantilism—the system designed to protect native manufactures in the newly consolidated states of the 17th and 18th centuries—was the transnational craftsman. Many governments enticed foreign inventors and skilled workers from distant lands with tax exemptions, free dwellings, loans of capital with which to establish an enterprise and a monopoly on the product manufactured, and in fact there were thousands of such entrepreneurs to take up the offer.[6]

The international economy

A fourth non-state actor was the international economy itself, whose power to influence policies and events seemed to grow as some of the restraints, regulations and restrictions of mercantilism gradually withered before the onslaught on them by Adam Smith and the other leading *laissez-faire* economists. They had argued (1) that increased productivity comes about through the division of labour; (2) that the division of labour grows or diminishes according to the extent of the market; (3) that the market is extended to its widest limits by free trade; (4) that, therefore, free trade brings about increased productivity; (5) that with the extensive division of labour accompanying free trade, each country can specialise in whatever it can produce most cheaply; and (6) that this process increases the total wealth of the world.[7] It was a seductive doctrine, especially among merchants and manufacturers in the 'have' as against the 'have not' countries. But as an increasing number of governments began to act upon it, the effect was to make each domestic market sensitive to what was happening in the international market. As the revolutions in British commerce, industry, agriculture and transportion had 'knock-on' effects in the international economy, so the international economy began to develop the power to constrain the actions of governments.

For example, the unemployment, poverty and destitution which so impressed Marx and Engels during the 1840s was clearly not confined to any one state. During that decade manifestations of the slump were to be found in all the countries in which Marx found himself—Prussia, France, Belgium and Britain—and many more besides. By the same token the massive boom which lasted from the 1850s until the late 1870s, and which had so surprised Marx and Engels, also affected most trading countries simultaneously. During this century it has been much the same story: a world-wide boom in the first decade; a global depression in the 1930s; a global boom in the 1960s; world recession affecting all but the protected markets of the Far East in the 1980s and early 1990s. Though not every country is equally affected and some manage to buck the trend, the international economy can be said to be an actor in its own right, constraining choices and affecting outcomes.

Benevolent organisations

Mention should also be made in this connection of certain influential non-state actors with a decidedly anti-commercial bias—for example the anti-slavery movements of the late 18th, early 19th centuries. For having captured the public imagination in Britain, they found champions among distinguished parliamentarians and helped to create a climate leading to the abolition of the slave trade in Britain in 1807 and throughout the empire in 1833. Britain's example was to prick the consciences of many slave owners and slave traders elsewhere, though it took some time and not a little violence for the plantation owners of America's southern states or of the Arab traders in East Africa to get the message.

Other non-national allegiances

If we turn our attention to Africa and Asia where till recently the conception of the sovereign state was largely unknown, allegiances were of necessity non-national. Here Western colonialism often made little difference to indigenous loyalties which continued to be based on the tribe, on traditional political and cultural entities and on tributary relationships; and in this sense the Hausa, the Zulu, the Kikuyu, the Baganda or the Ashanti continued to be politically significant even after the independence respectively of Nigeria, South Africa, Kenya, Uganda or Ghana. By the same token, wherever the Chinese were to be found there was a strong attachment to the *Chung Kuo*, the Central Land, or the *Chung Hua*, the Central Splendour ie China, with its peculiar vassal state system and the rituals, ceremonials, celebrations and festivities that went with being Chinese.

Individuals

Finally, no account of traditional non-state actors would be complete without reference to individuals whose actions singly or collectively helped, as it were, to make history. In the end, it is individuals who make policy, individuals who carry them out—the state being no more than a personified abstraction on behalf of which they govern and cause other people to act.

15.3 CHALLENGE TO STATE PRIMACY?

If non-state actors have played such a significant role throughout history, why do so many teachers of the subject continue to talk about the primacy of the sovereign state?[8] The answer depends on how one interprets the expression 'the primacy of the sovereign state' and on the realm of discourse to which it is applied. The term 'primacy' suggests the existence of a range of entities, one of which takes precedence and is in some sense pre-eminent. The term 'sovereign state' refers to a political entity which has obtained full recognition as a legal person and is thereby the bearer of legal rights and obligations. Here the question of state primacy will be considered in three separate contexts—the legal, the political and the instrumental ie as an instrument for promoting world order.

Moral

First, however, it is necessary to dispose briefly of the question in one further realm of discourse—the moral. What is or is not moral rests on a subjective judgement, not an objective fact, even though one can discuss objectively the moral suppositions of others. There is a school of thought, traceable to Machiavelli through Spinoza, Hobbes, Hegel and eventually Morgenthau that the state is the ultimate source of moral authority and that as such it should be regarded as having claims morally prior to those of other bodies or individuals. But such an argument is to endorse the notion that the dictates of even authoritarian or totalitarian state must be obeyed not merely because it may be expedient or politic to do so but because they have moral priority. Once again it must be stressed that the state is no more than a personified abstraction; unless those who exercise power in its name are accountable in some sense, such a system, so the liberal-minded would maintain, can have no claim to moral primacy. If one has to obey the authoritarian state it is because one is compelled to do so, not because it is morally right.

Legal

As to whether the state can be considered to have primacy in a legal sense, there used to be not much doubt as to the answer. For the system of international law bequeathed by Grotius in the 17th century and further elucidated by Vattel in the 18th century made the state the sole bearer of international legal rights and duties. Individuals, groups, corporations and collective entities other than states might have had moral but not international legal entitlements and obligations. They might have been objects but could not be subjects of international law. They could not enjoy sovereign status with the right to be constitutionally and juridically free from outside interference, to be able to make treaties, to be represented by an ambassador, to make war, to be able to sue in the International Courts and so forth.

On the other hand, in this century the position of state as sole international legal actor has begun to be eroded. In the first place, inter-governmental organisations of a global, regional or functional character such as the League, the UN, NATO, the Warsaw Pact, the EU, the WHO and the FAO have begun to acquire corporate international legal personality, with substantial title to rights and duties, though not yet on a par with those available to the sovereign state. The same goes for the international non-governmental organisations, ranging from the vast commercial conglomerates like IBM, EXXON or IT&T to the non-profit-making bodies such as the Save the Children Fund, Friends of the Earth or Amnesty International.

Woodrow Wilson's promulgation of the right to national self-determination raised the question of whether the nation as distinct from the state was entitled to legal status. For a time the legal, as distinct from the moral answer was in the negative, but the UN Charter seems to suggest otherwise; since when several legal theorists, particularly from the Communist and Third World countries, have begun to expound on the National Liberation Movement as an international legal personality. On the other hand that such theorists have often been highly selective about the movements to which they attribute legal personality—Soviet legal writers, for example, recognising the PLO and the ANC as legal persons but not Latvia, Lithuania and Estonia (former sovereign states forcibly incorporated into the Soviet Union)—does not make for clarity; and the exact legal status of 'nation' and 'liberation movement' remains contested.

What of realms, provinces or states that are not sovereign—Scotland, say, or Quebec or California? Are they beginning to develop a legal personality hitherto lacking? For years Scotland and Wales have had their own rugby and ice hockey teams, and if they play England the game is regarded as an 'international'. But that, strictly speaking, gives neither Scotland nor Wales significant legal character. On the other hand now that Quebec has what it regards as 'national' offices in Paris and in the Francophone countries of Africa, some international lawyers are beginning to think that some legal threshold may have been crossed. Again, however, it is a contentious issue.

Finally, since the second world war it has been increasingly held among international lawyers that individuals may be subjects as well as objects of international law. When the Universal Declaration of Human Rights was first agreed in 1948, most lawyers assumed it was just a statement of moral principle, not a set of binding ordinances. When, however, the European Convention of Human Rights was signed in 1950, an increasing number of lawyers began to suggest it might have legal validity, a view reinforced by the time of the Covenants of 1966, the one concerning civil and political rights, the other economic, social and cultural rights. Today it is accepted that individuals claiming to have been wronged by some European institution or national legal body may ask for a definitive ruling by the European Court of Human Rights or the European Court of Justice.

On the other hand ever since the post-war Nuremberg and Tokyo war crimes trials, in which it was claimed that individuals had a duty to disobey those state authorities that issued monstrous and inhuman commands such as the killing of innocents, mass murder and genocide, human rights issues have remained a legal minefield. Part of the problem lies in the fact that such matters seem to invite essentially partisan judgments. After all, Nuremberg and Tokyo were the products of an Allied victory, the judgment of each Court the verdict of the winning side. And in the cold war which followed, controversies concerning human rights were too often rooted in alliance politics, with each side using the notion as a stick to beat its cold war opponent: the Western powers chiding the Communist countries for their lack of civil liberties; the Socialist countries condemning the Western record on employment, housing and social-welfare provisions; the newly independent countries often rebuking their former colonial masters for the denial of full collective rights ie for their failure to deliver the substance as well as the form of independence.

Thus since controversy seems to surround virtually every ascription of legal personality to non-state actors, it can hardly be said that the state has lost its legal primacy. The most one can argue is that it is no longer regarded as the sole bearer of rights and duties under international law.[9]

Political

What of the political as distinct from the legal realm? Can it be demonstrated that the state had a primacy it has now lost? Numerous Pluralist writers, from Richard Mansbach, James Rosenau, and John Burton to Robert Keohane and Joseph Nye seem to suggest that it can—that the state, once regarded as impermeable and impregnable, has become so penetrated transnationally, supranationally, subnationally and internationally that to think of it as in some sense politically supreme is wholly misconceived. Leaving aside the question of whether the state ever was impermeable and impregnable—a dubious proposition!—it can hardly be denied that the number of non-governmental organisations, both profit- and non-profit-making, have greatly multiplied in the 20th century, that the impact of the MNC on the world economy has been dramatic, that vast networks of exchanges, contacts and connections have been developing at the transnational level and that the revolution in global communications has created an unprecedented degree of mutual awareness among the diverse elements in the human community. In consequence, political organisations of all kinds, states included, are probably more sensitive and vulnerable to one another than before. On the other hand while non-state actors may have significantly increased their claim to attention, the role of the state in world politics may also be said to have been growing dramatically.

In the first place, whereas a century or so ago as a form of political organisation the sovereign state was confined largely to Europe, its numerical and geographical spread in the 20th century has been remarkable. Today there are nearly four times as many such states as there were only 50 years ago; and the demands of peoples such as the Palestinians, Kashmiris, Sikhs of the Punjab, Kurds, Quebeçois, Basques and Scots suggest that the number and geographical dispersion are likely to expand still further. True, there are mini- and micro-states such as Nauru and Vanuatu as well as states in apparent decomposition such as Afghanistan, Bosnia, Cambodia, Liberia, Rwanda and Somalia, hardly capable of exercising the sovereignty they in theory possess. As some states show signs of disintegration, so others show an interest in confederation or even federation. Even so, the existence of neither the disintegrating nor the confederal state suggests the obsolescence of the state as such, merely an alteration in their total number and size. Sovereignty remains a status eagerly sought after throughout the world.

Second, while before the 20th century governments tended to leave such matters as international trade and commerce, migration, social and ideological relations between peoples to the private sector, these have now tended to become increasingly the province of government. In a sense the state may be said to be progressively eroding the independence of initiative once enjoyed by the international businessman and banker, the labour organisation, the sporting body, the churches and political parties. In other words, while the Pluralists see transnationalism as moving into the preserve of the state, the Realists can argue that the reverse is also true, and that the functions of the state have so expanded in the 20th century as to erode much of the previous autonomy of the non-state actor. Perhaps the truth is of an overall expansion of the international dimension of policy in which both the state and non-state organisations have an increasing share. Certainly there is no zero-sum relationship between state and non-state actor, and the expansion of the one does not necessarily mean a contraction of the other.

By the mid-1970s when, for example, the transnational creed of Communism was the ruling ideology of more countries than ever before or since, leading Moscow and possibly Washington, too, to believe that the 'correlation of forces' was moving towards Socialism, the Communist movement was probably more divided by rival nationalisms than it had been before. There was serious tension between the Soviets and the Chinese, a war between the Chinese and the Vietnamese, hostilities between the Vietnamese and the Cambodians, and a civil war between Communist factions in Cambodia, Afghanistan and Ethiopia. Later there were to be serious factional struggles between Communists in the Yemen and in Grenada. Thus the transnational and the national interpenetrated. The same dialectic is to be found in Islam. As with Christianity, Islam has a global mission. It is universal in aspiration, and when the world of Islam feels itself under threat, either from Hindu militants in India, Jewish extremists in Israel and Christian fanatics in the Balkans, the rhetoric is of unity and community. Yet, like Christianity, and for that matter Communism, the solidarity which exists in theory is often belied in practice, and the Muslim way of life is so often seen in national or parochial terms, leading to strife and conflict, as is only too evident in, say, Afghanistan or Somalia today.

As with religions, so with MNCs, the transnational implications are not in practice incompatible with nationalism and the notion of national interest. There are abundant examples, to be explored later, of relations between states and MNCs which are to the benefit of both.

Instrumental

Many looking at the degree of disorder, economic injustice and ecological mismanagement in the world would blame these by and large on the state. They would see the state as a harbinger of war and therefore an obstacle to peace. They would see it as pandering to the greed of the peoples of the developed North and as a shield behind which corrupt rulers of the South can hang on to their multiple investments, hunting lodges and Mercedes while the mass of the people starve. Finally, they would charge the state with merely encouraging the waste, pollution, depletion of resources and other assaults on the environment which make any sensible ecological balance almost impossible to attain. To this extent they would deny the state primacy in the quest for world order. On the other hand since violence, economic injustice and disharmony between humankind and nature have a much longer history than that of the modern state system, the state can hardly be held entirely responsible for them. Were conflicts more acceptable when they involved people like Xerxes, Attila the Hun and Ghenghis Khan ie before the age of the modern state system? Was there a fairer distribution of global wealth and greater respect for the global commons and the environment when transnational ties and parochial loyalties were supreme?

Such an analysis, moreover, neglects what Hedley Bull has called the 'positive functions of the state', first in imposing order domestically, the importance of which is immediately obvious when the state—as in Afghanistan, Somalia or what was Yugoslavia—can no longer fulfil those functions; second, in co-operating with one another in preserving a framework of co-existence through legal and other rules and constraints, imperfect though they be; third, in providing the kinds of instititutional and other structures within which international co-operation can grow, and, fourth (and this would be a relatively novel function), in considering measures which previously would never have reached the international agenda regarding the management of the world economy, the promotion of racial equality and women's rights, the control of population, the raising of educational standards, the accountability of governments and so forth. Bull concludes that the state system can sustain not only co-existence but co-operation in the pursuit of a vast array of shared goals, and that even in the promotion of world order the state may have some claim to primacy.

Economic

If all this is at variance with much current thinking, concerning the decline or obsolescence of the sovereign state, it may also throw into sharp relief current nostrums regarding the role of the multi-national corporation—a non-state actor widely believed to have demolished the final vestiges of state primacy. Doubtless many advanced industrial states are undergoing a kind of post-industrial revolution essentially international in scope and technological in basis. For the revolution in communications and the ease with which investment, production and marketing can take place internationally have produced the conditions for the rapid growth of enterprises which can integrate whole sections of economies across state frontiers. Such enterprises, moreover, increasingly employ a multinational team, respond to a common strategy, draw on a common pool of financial and human resources and are run by managers whose primary loyalty is to the corporation as a whole and not to the states in which they are based. Though many such enterprises are of comparatively modest size, the top one hundred or so are massive. Because of the economies of scale and the obvious advantage of producing in a country where skilled labour is cheap, foreign exchange in short supply and imported goods subject to high tariffs, the more powerful enterprises will tend to enlarge their spheres of operation both at home and abroad with the result that the annual sales turnover of a corporate giant such as General Motors, Exxon, Ford, the Royal Dutch Shell Group, IBM, etc. exceed the GNPs of most states. To give one example; in 1973 the annual sales of General Motors were greater than the combined GNPs of Switzerland, Pakistan and South Africa. In the process the balance of authority may be said to have shifted somewhat from state to market. But such massive operations have produced anxieties both in the countries which host the operations of the MNC and in the countries in which the parent companies reside.[10]

The hosts have two basic fears: (1) that the companies will intervene in politics, as the Anglo-Iranian oil company (later BP) did in Iran in restoring the Shah to power after his expulsion in the early 1950s, or the United Food Company in so blatantly helping to remove a left-wing regime in Guatamala in 1954 or IT&T in helping to destabilise Allende's Chile in the 1970s; and (2) that they will severely damage the economies of these states by taking decisions in one country that adversely affect workers in another, as when Hoover suddenly decided to switch production facilities from France to Scotland. As a developed country, France can be reasonably resilient in the face of such a set back. When a Third World country is affected, so the argument goes, the effects can be catastrophic.

But the source countries also have certain anxieties, especially when it comes to investment overseas and relocating production. For they not only stand to lose jobs, they may also lose markets if the technology transferred abroad by the MNC is used to create overseas competitors. How justified are such fears?

In fact much of the high-handed political behaviour associated with the MNCs in the 1950s, 1960s and 1970s had less to do with the enterprises themselves than with the political interests of Washington, for often they acted as a hidden arm of US foreign policy. In the case of IT&T, which helped to bring down the Allende regime in Chile, its links to the Oval Office were barely disguised, with so many 'ex'-CIA, 'ex'-Pentagon, 'ex'-State Department officials on its Board of Directors. On the other hand such intrusion, combined with the MNCs' capacity to make sudden decisions as to funding, employment or marketing, which can even unwittingly destabilise a country's economy, has produced an inevitable reaction, and the competition among MNCs to find suitable host countries has provided the latter with powerful bargaining levers many have tried to exploit to the full. By the late 1970s, therefore, many potential host countries sought to insist on their own terms, say, taking capital from one main source, technology from another and management from a third, depending on where they could obtain the most at the least possible cost. Where the so-called 'trickle down' benefits of MNC operations are limited or non-existent, governments can impose restrictions on MNC activities—the 1994 General Agreement on Tariffs and Trade (GATT), notwithstanding—and ultimately nationalise, expropriate or expel the offending corporation. On the other hand the developed countries are better able than the LDCs to cope with the political or economic dislocation which tends to result at least in the short term, even though Egypt did not fare too disastrously after nationalising the Suez Canal Company nor Guyana after taking over Booker's Brothers.

By the 1990s, therefore, a kind of balance has been restored whereby the state and the MNC can exercise leverage against one another, but there is no reason why both should not benefit mutually from their relationship. After all, no state is forced to host any MNC, and without the permission of a government, the MNC cannot operate.

15.4 THE ROLE OF THE STATE

So what are we to conclude? (1) that non-state actors are and always were a fact of life in world politics; (2) that while many see them as making a nonsense of state sovereignty, others see the state as posing a powerful challenge to those non-state actors which were once able to perform more or less without government interference; (3) that though the primacy of the state is under challenge legally, politically, instrumentally and in the economic sphere, as yet it cannot be convincingly shown that the state has had to yield primacy to any other body; and (4) that no matter how penetrated the state, transnationally, subnationally, supranationally and internationally, its continued existence appears to fulfil a kind of psychological need, and far from disappearing the state seems destined to continue to be a rallying cry for those who feel that their current aspirations for national self-determination are being denied.

NOTES

1. See, for example, Wolfers, A., 'The actors in world politics' in Fox, W.T.R., (ed.), *Theoretical Aspects of International Relations*, Notre Dame, University of Notre Dame press, 1959.
2. Roberts, J., *The Triumph of the West*, London, BBC, 1985, pp. 96–7.
3. See Keohane, R. and Nye, J. (eds), *Transnational Relations and World Politics*, Cambridge, Mass, Harvard University Press, 1971.
4. Trevelyan, G.M., *English Social History*, London, The Reprint Society, 1948, pp. 216–22.
5. Huberman, L., *Man's Worldly Goods*, London, Gollancz, 1937, pp. 95–6.
6. Ibid., pp. 127–9.
7. Smith, A. *Wealth of Nations* [1776], ed. and introduced by E. Cannan, London, Methuen, 1930.
8. See Bull, H., 'The state's positive role in world affairs', *Daedalus*, vol. 108, no. 4, pp. 111–23.
9. The question of legal personality receives cogent exposition in Higgins, R., *Problems and Process: International Law and How we use it*, Oxford, The Clarendon Press, 1994, pp. 39–55.
10. Spero, J., *The Politics of International Economic Relations*, 3rd ed., New York, St Martin's Press, 1985, pp. 131–51.

PART VI
THE INTERNATIONAL
POLITICAL ECONOMY

CHAPTER 16

INTERNATIONAL ECONOMIC ORDER AND DISORDER

In the standard International Relations texts of up to 20 years ago, the international economy tended to get scarcely a mention. Though there were references to economic pressure, aid and sanctions, and passing mention of the Common Market, IMF and ECOSOC, little attempt was made to explore in any systematic way the dynamics of the international economy and how they impacted on international political structures. Nor were there many column inches on the way the changing fabric of international politics shaped the international economy. However, at about the time that 'imperialism' was dropping out of the textbooks, 'the international political economy' was creeping in, and today, no self-respecting IR course could ignore it.

16.1 ORIGINS OF THE INTERNATIONAL ECONOMY

The earliest economic transactions were those of primitive barter in which groups of individuals with a surplus of a certain commodity—salt, shells, skins, women or whatever—would trade them for commodities they lacked. At a later stage the notion of a medium of exchange, ie of a store or measure of value, was introduced—something generally in demand. For thousands of years the commonest medium of exchange in many countries was cattle (in Latin, *pecus*, from which are derived the words 'pecuniary' and 'impecunious'). Then in more sophisticated societies, in some of the ancient Chinese provinces, ancient Egypt and Greece for example, the medium of exchange was to take more durable form. It was to be something that would outlast the life span of a cow, bull, ox or water buffalo but be treasured both for the effort in producing it and the varied uses to which it could be put—precious metals such as gold, silver or copper. The Greek philosopher Aristotle, in suggesting that such measures of value should be not merely durable but also easy to handle, easy to recognise and divisible into smaller units, was commending the idea of coinage, which was already in use by traders with regular and extensive transactions. And along the famous medieval Silk Road from Xian in north-west China, through Central Asia down to the borders of European Turkey, it was not just silks and fine linen, cattle and camels that were traded but also precious metals, some in the form of coins with the embossed heads of the more distinguished leaders of the time.[1]

16.2 MEDIEVAL TRADE AND COMMERCE

In medieval Europe the Church, then wielding secular as well as spiritual power, prescribed in minute detail the conditions under which trade and commercial transactions were to take place, and when its power declined, the guilds determined the ground rules. But given the mountain of regulation, the many regional customs barriers, the lack of sophisticated transport and the unsafe highways of the time, the level of international trade remained comparatively low until the end of the Middle Ages. But as Europe's monarchs began to assert their new found power and to make use of such inventions as the mariner's compass and the sextant, the situation changed. The seas, which had always provided cheap if dangerous transportation, could now be utilised as never before; and as the 'king's men' began to make the highways safer, to abolish local tariffs and establish uniform royal currencies, the scene was set for a vast increase in international trade and commerce.[2]

16.3 17TH-CENTURY MERCANTILISM

Though the Silk Road had gone into disuse, the use of sea power insured that European trade with the Orient developed apace in the 17th century, and for some time it was more profitable and extensive than trade within Europe. On the other hand the Europeans tended to import more silks, spices, sugar, coffee and tea than they could pay for with the textiles and other products they sold in return, and, as a result, the Europeans had to pay in precious metals like gold and silver to make up the deficit. Given that these were precisely the commodities needed to pay for the incessant wars on the continent, the European states, emerging from medieval universalism and parochial allegiances, were soon in financial crisis. Anxious to extend and consolidate their political dominion while overcoming their economic difficulties, they began to impose strict controls on commercial activity. Believing wealth and power to be associated with the acquisition of precious metals, their governments organised their domestic and international trade to achieve the favourable balance they deemed necessary to attain their objectives.

In the first place, in an attempt to protect domestic enterprise, they imposed quotas and tariffs on imports, excluding altogether goods in direct competition with home industries such as hats, manufactured woollens and products made of iron. Though some commodities were allowed to enter the country duty free, these tended to be either luxury items, foodstuffs and spices which could not be produced in the home country or else raw materials needed for domestic industry. One industry that many governments were anxious to develop at the time was shipbuilding; and by the 17th-century Navigation Acts Britain asserted that transportation of goods was to be by ships owned and operated exclusively by nationals of the exporting state. In consequence Britain rapidly developed a mercantile marine and for the purpose subsidised the production of ships and encouraged the duty-free import of pitch, tar, masts and stout timbers. Second, though trade remained largely in private hands, the state began to take a share, giving bounties to certain export and import substitution industries and attempting, often successfully, to poach skilled craftsmen and inventors from other countries. Third, to maintain a trading surplus, the acquisition of colonies was encouraged. These were supposed to provide much needed raw materials cheaply as well as markets for the manufactures of the mother country at a price which it usually determined. Fourth, there were strict controls on the international movement of precious metals. Such, in brief, was the system known as mercantilism, a system which took a 'zero sum' approach to trade, presupposing that one country's economic gain is another's economic loss.[3] That trade could be mutually advantageous seemed to have little place in this conception, and from the early 16th until the early 19th centuries the mercantilist system dominated Europe's production, distribution and exchange.

16.4 FREE TRADE VERSUS MERCANTILISM

By the 18th century, however, mercantilism began to be criticised from many different quarters, sometimes with momentous consequences. The restrictive practices with which it was associated led to the revolt of the American colonies, eventuating in a successful bid for independence. Significantly 1776, the year of the American rebellion, was also the publication date for the treatise which was to revolutionise thinking about production and trade, domestic and overseas—*Wealth of Nations* by Adam Smith. In it he gives intellectual force to the growing sense of frustration being felt, first, among those producers, manufacturers and traders not favoured by government subsidies and insensed by the Corn Laws which kept the price of wheat artificially high and, second, among the financiers, disadvantaged by the restrictions and regulations of mercantilism and irritated by the army of inspectors to see that the rules were enforced. As it happens, it was a French businessman, de Gournay, who in the 1750s had coined the phrase that was to become the rallying cry of all those opposed to mercantilist restriction—*laissez-faire!*,[4] which roughly translates as 'leave us alone', but it was a theme that was to permeate Smith's treatise.[5]

Basically his starting point is that gold and silver are of little value in themselves. They could not be eaten or worn, and unless they were used to produce commodities which people could consume and enjoy, overall living standards were likely to fall rather than rise. Specifically he claims that any trade imbalance if left to what we now call 'market forces' would automatically correct itself, as if by 'an invisible hand'. His argument is that under *laissez-faire* conditions, first, any sizeable influx of gold into a country would tend to raise that country's price level as currency increases relative to the supply of goods; second, that such a situation would lead both to growing imports of cheaper goods from abroad and to falling exports because of their comparatively high price and, third, that to pay for the excess of imports over exports it would be necessary to export gold and in this way restore the balance of trade.

In arguing that the shackles on trade should be removed Smith propounds two key principles, both still in common currency. First, that where a country has an absolute advantage over others in producing a particular commodity because of the availability of cheap raw materials, markets and skills, it should specialise in producing it. Similarly, if a particular commodity costs a country more to produce at home than abroad, then it should import it. This is what Smith calls the doctrine of Absolute Advantage. Second, that where a country has an absolute advantage in the production of everything, it should none the less concentrate on producing where its comparative advantage is greatest so that other countries can concentrate on production where their inefficiency is comparatively low. This is what Smith calls the doctrine of Comparative Advantage. Underlying this reasoning was the belief that specialisation—the division of labour—was an indicator of efficiency and that the wider the market, the greater the degree of specialisation. It followed, therefore, that a free and unfettered world market (ie free trade) would produce maximum efficiency, adding greatly thereby to the wealth of nations—a Pluralist argument, if ever there was one.

But Smith condemns not just the restrictive practices of mercantilism. He also attacks the whole colonial system so integral to mercantilist thinking, and in a pithy passage he declares:

> the monopoly of the colony trade...like all the other mean and malignant expedients of the mercantile system, depresses the industry of all other countries but chiefly that of the colonies, without in the least increasing, but on the contrary diminishing, that of the country in whose favour it is established.[6]

While Smith's call for a political economy freed of mercantilist restraints may have come like a breath of fresh air to the enterprising—those already in the money and the prospective capitalists who stood to do well out of the industrial revolution—as well as to the educated—the writers, teachers, doctors, lawyers, judges and civil servants—it had potentially ominous overtones for the class of artisans and labourers just beginning to emerge in both mother country and colony. As Smith himself says:

> The workmen desire to get as much, the masters to give as little as possible. The former are disposed to combine in order to raise, the latter in order to lower, the wages of labour...It is not, however, difficult to foresee which of the two parties must, upon all ordinary occasions, have the advantage in the dispute...The masters being fewer in number, can combine far more easily, and the law, besides, authorises, or at least does not prohibit, their combinations, while it prohibits those of the workmen. We have no acts of parliament against combining to lower the price of work: but many against combining to raise it.[7]

As an apostle of *laissez-faire*, Smith was not commending the laws making it illegal for workers to join together to protect their interests. However, he was accurately depicting a situation which was to obtain in the early years of virtually every society which empowered the rising bourgeoisie. And it was what Marx saw as a conspiracy against the political and economic aspirations of labour wherever capitalism existed that led him in *The Communist Manifesto* of 1848 to conclude that the class interests of workers were the same everywhere and that only a transnationally organised global revolution to wrest power from the bourgeois power holders would free them from what he called their 'increasing misery'. In fact, of course, the anti-labour legislation and the inhuman working conditions characterising the early years of capitalism were to be greatly modified even during Marx's lifetime, with the advent of trade unions, co-operatives, labour parties and social legislation. And as, contrary to Marx's predictions but possibly in part because of them, the worker's quality and standard of living began to rise—at least in Western and Central Europe—he would tend to identify with nationalist aspirations rather than the cause of 'proletarian internationalism' as envisaged by Marx. Even so, how secure were the political and economic gains of labour? Given the repeated recessions and slumps, the backlash against union power in Thatcher's Britain, the decline of traditional manufacturing industries and economic blight in the towns of many developed countries, it is hardly surprising that organised labour never feels entirely assured of its role in society. On the other hand perhaps recent anti-union legislation stemmed from a perception of a pendulum that had swung too far in the direction of organised labour and that some sort of Adam Smith-style balance between capital and labour needed to be restored.

16.5 THE 19TH CENTURY AND THE ECONOMICS OF IMPERIALISM

Despite the popularity and forceful logic of Adam Smith's writings, mercantilism survived until well into the 19th century as the predominant philosophy of international trade, and even when the system began to lose ground in the 1840s following the repeal of Britain's restrictive Corn Laws, it was never completely abandoned. Whether or not a country espoused free trade depended, ironically, not so much on business men as on governments, and the fact is that free trade was simply not acceptable to a number of them. In countries such as Britain, Belgium, Holland and France where industrialisation was proceeding apace and whose products enjoyed considerable prestige abroad, the movement towards free trade went furthest because it appeared to offer considerable economic benefit. However, in a country such as Russia, where industrialisation was still in its infancy, high tariffs tended to be maintained, if only as a means of protecting newly established enterprises. The argument was, and incidentally still is in many quarters, that to abandon protection too soon would be to open the floodgates to a host of imports, making industrialisation almost impossible. As Bismarck once pithily observed: 'England abolished protection after she had benefited from it to the fullest extent...Free trade is the weapon of the strongest nation',[8] a notion, incidentally, endorsed by E.H. Carr in his *Twenty Years' Crisis*. Finally, in the semi-industrialised countries of Central Europe and the United States, a half-way policy was usually adopted in which protectionist tariffs tended to remain but at a comparatively low level of duty.

As industrialised Europe moved towards free trade, official enthusiasm for empire began to diminish, even if missionaries, adventurers and certain trading concerns retained an interest. It was the British statesman Benjamin Disraeli, ironically later to become an apostle of empire, who summed up the case for retreat from it. In 1852 he dismissed Britain's overseas possessions as 'those wretched colonies', those 'millstones round our necks', and 15 years later, in 1867, he again queried the value of what he called these 'colonial deadweights'.[9] In the case of Portugal and Holland, which retained their colonies, there was neither the will nor the means to further extend control. France, having established itself in Algeria in the 1830s, was too preoccupied with repeated revolutionary disturbances and changes in the European map to try to recover the vast areas of North America and India it had lost to Britain. Spain was in process of losing all her vast dominions in the Americas, and while Britain still possessed vast holdings in North America, Asia and Australasia, disillusioned by the loss of the American colonies and preoccupied with domestic money-making and industrialisation, she had little incentive to add to her existing possessions. Though the colonial powers would sometimes fight one another over territories already claimed or occupied, by the beginning of the 19th century official encouragement for colonisation had all but ceased. During the time that international trade was bringing vast profits and prospects to Western and Central Europe, the further acquisition of colonial empire was thought to be passé.

On the other hand towards the mid-1870s, throughout Europe and North America production began to outstrip the available markets, in part because of the intensity of the competition between enterprises domestic and foreign. As Marx had predicted, many of the goods pouring out of the factories were failing to find sales outlets, and enthusiasm for free trade began to evaporate. As businessmen saw their profit margins dwindle, they moved to restrict domestic competition, hoping thereby to benefit from the economies of scale. The result was the growth of large combines through amalgamations and take-over bids. Soon the attempt to bring order out of competitive chaos resulted in a multiplicity of trusts, syndicates, pools, combines, cartels and associations seeking to fix the production and prices of commodities such as oil, steel, coal, sugar, and whisky—a far cry from Adam Smith's free enterprise, *laissez-faire* capitalism.[10] As with domestic trade, so in international trade competition began to be restricted and by the end of the 1870s the way was open for a return to protectionism.

In 1879 Bismarck levied heavy duties on the import of both industrial and agricultural products. In 1881, France followed suit, raising tariffs at first modestly and then much more steeply. Across the Atlantic the very steep McKinley Tariff of 1890 marked the abandonment of America's traditional low-tariff policy. Other states did likewise, Britain almost alone clinging to the wreckage of free trade until 1931. However, as a general approach to international intercourse, it was virtually dead well before the end of the 19th century, and in the economic chaos left by the first world war it did not seem possible to revive it.

The revival of protectionism at the end of the 1870s corresponded closely with the renewal of imperialism after an official pause of more than half a century. Just as mercantilism had been the harbinger of colonial acquisition, so the new protectionist trend resurrected the demand for extra-European colonies—the European continent itself having reached a kind of temporary stabilisation following the Franco–Prussian war of 1870-1, the creation of the Bismarckian system of alliances and the deliberations at the 1878 Congress of Berlin which appeared to settle the affairs of the Balkans for a generation.[11]

On the other hand this second wave of imperialism was both more rapid than and at least as extensive as the first phase. By the time of the first world war all of Africa save Liberia, Ethiopia and South Africa was under the control of seven European powers (Belgium, Britain, France, Germany, Italy, Portugal and Spain). In the Far East and the Pacific only Siam (Thailand), China and Japan remained outside the direct control of Europe or the United States. In fact China had been divided into spheres of influence by foreign powers, and Japan, having wrung certain concessions out of China, had joined the imperialist wave with the acquisition of Korea and Formosa (Taiwan). In the Western hemisphere the United

States expanded across its continent, acquired Puerto Rico from Spain, extended its colonial reach westwards to Hawaii and the Philippines (whom God had expressly told President McKinley to annexe),[12] leased the Panama Canal 'in perpetuity' from the new state of Panama, also an American creation, and came to exercise considerable political leverage over Cuba and several other Caribbean islands. As for the British Empire, by 1900 it covered nearly a fifth of the land surface of the globe and comprised nearly a quarter of the world's population. When the orgy of expansionism had been exhausted shortly before the outbreak of the first world war, there was very little territory left to colonise.

Although imperial possessions had become important symbols of national power and prestige and were justified as such, a group of radical thinkers writing at the turn of the century began to see the phenomenon in strictly economic terms and as an emanation of capitalism. For some, imperialism was the product of the malfunctioning of the capitalist system; for others it was the inevitable outcome. For some, imperialism served the interests of the capitalist system as a whole; for others it served the interests of particular groups within the system. Yet others saw imperialism in terms not so much of interest as of ideology, an ideology of expansionism as closely identified with capitalism as it had been with mercantilism.

Two such economic theories were especially influential in the first half of the 20th century, the first of which was the pioneering study on *Imperialism* by J. A. Hobson, written in 1902. Like E. H. Carr, Hobson was a polymath—economist, university lecturer, essayist and journalist—who managed to bring his many talents to bear in his riveting study. What makes his analysis all the more compelling is that he incorporates insights gained in South Africa, where as a correspondent for *The Manchester Guardian* he reported on the course and consequences of the Boer War. Basically his argument was that the unequal distribution of income and wealth in capitalist countries had left large sections of the population without the wherewithal to consume very much, forcing capitalists to invest abroad and to compete with others to control foreign markets—most easily achieved with the acquisition of colonies. On the other hand, according to Hobson, there was no inevitability about the process. If the surplus wealth of the richer capitalists were creamed off and redistributed among the poorer sections of the community, the greater domestic consumption that would result would make imperialism unnecessary.

Prior to Hobson's treatise, the politically aware in Britain had tended to glory in imperialism or, at any rate, British imperialism. As far as they were concerned it was contributing towards the civilisation of the world through the spread of education, the rule of law, parliamentary institutions, rational administration and so forth. It is a mark of the sheer force of Hobson's prose that he not only more or less initiated the economic theory of imperialism, he also did much to create a feeling of revulsion against imperialism in the English-speaking world. But for him it was not simply immoral, it was also irrational and generally economically disadvantageous for the country as a whole, even if certain groups—shipbuilders, arms manufacturers, engineers and those who filled the ranks of the colonial civil service—benefited. In short, the meagre results in the form of increased trade and a modest return on capital were out of all proportion to the enormous risks and costs to the nation in pursuing an imperialist policy. In an attack on capitalist profiteering, which had certain anti-Semitic overtones later to be picked up by Hitler but not Lenin, whose intellectual debt to Hobson was considerable, Hobson claimed 'there is not a war, a revolution, an anarchist assassination or any other public shock which is not gainful to these men; they are harpies who suck their gains from every new forced expediture and every sudden disturbance of public credit'.[13] What you hear in that passage is not the scholarly tone of the academic, which he was to become, but the sense of moral outrage of a journalist/philosopher who, like Lenin, believed that something had to be done.

In his analysis of *Imperialism: The Highest Stage of Capitalism*, written in 1916, Lenin, seeking to explain how it was that nationalism rather than world revolution had triumphed in 1914, drew heavily on the ideas of Hobson but reached a different conclusion. In his view imperialism was the inevitable outcome of what he called 'monopoly capitalism', when the rate of return on domestic investment is low, when production is concentrated in combines and cartels and when financial interests predominate over the commercial, underwriting the loans to backward countries, the capital issues of the railway and steamship lines and extending credit to colonial plantation owners, importers, manufacturers and distributors. For the monopoly capitalists, according to Lenin, were seeking to gain undue economic advantage from the export of surplus capital to backward countries where 'profits are usually high, for capital is scarce, the price of land is relatively low, wages are low, raw materials are cheap'.[14] The effect was to divide the world *de facto* into various spheres of influence, making capitalism a world phenomenon, despite the uneven economic development of the various countries. But it also drew a wedge between the workers in the metropolitan countries and those in the colonies, the former benefiting at the expense of the latter. Hence the former's support of leaders who 'bribed' them with the spoils of imperialism while betraying their real interests as proletarians. If Hobson saw the answer in a redistribution of wealth under capitalism, Lenin saw it as lying in capitalism's overthrow, believing that as the coffins came home from the war which the treacherous leaders of labour had decided to support, the workers would realise they had been betrayed and in their anger turn to revolution.

16.6 CRITIQUES OF ECONOMIC THEORIES OF IMPERIALISM

As will be evident by now, theses tend to generate counter-theses and such economic theories of imperialism were to be the subject of intense criticism.[15] What were the objections?

(1) That Hobson, Lenin and their disciples ignore the history of imperialism prior to the advent of capitalism. Further, that they err in identifying a single economic cause for a complex and recurrent international phenomenon and in neglecting the political, military and social dimensions of the problem;

(2) That their theories fail to explain what they purport to explain since it is not businessmen but politicians who make the decisions in respect of imperial expansion, war and the like; and that in any case, as Marx himself pointed out, capitalism for all its alienating qualities requires order, predicability and rationality and therefore peace to be able to pursue profit maximisation; and most seriously;

(3) That their theories rest more on inflammatory and inflated rhetoric than on empirical evidence.

What was the counter evidence?

(1) That the notion that the most advanced capitalist countries would be the most expansionist was simply not borne out by the facts. For example Sweden and Switzerland exhibited no interest whatever in colonial ventures, while Portugal, one of the most under-capitalised states in Europe, was a leading colonial power;

(2) That far from being enslaved, many recipients of European capital, such as Japan, the United States, Australia and Argentina profited handsomely and became independent and formidable powers;

(3) That contrary to the economic theorists, more capital moved into most of the metropolitan countries than out of them during the period from the 1870s to 1914;

(4) That the bulk of the capital exported from the metropolitan countries came not from monopoly concerns but from governments and government-guaranteed public utilities;

(5) That most colonies during this period were open to international trade on a more or less equal basis with the mother countries and that, therefore, it was not necessary to have colonies to extend trade with the backward nations;

(6) That the colonies were not nearly as important in the trade and investment patterns of the capitalist countries as the theories suggested. Most of the capital exported from the advanced economies, then as now, went to other advanced economies, or else to a less-developed country, like Russia, which another country, in this case France, was anxious to build up as a counterweight to a third country, Germany. The bulk of

German capital went to the United States and Latin America, and only about 3 per cent to its African colonies, and while about a half of British capital did, indeed, go to the Empire, almost all went to the white dominions—South Africa, Rhodesia, Canada, Australia and New Zealand—the rest going to the advanced capitalist countries not plagued by surplus capital conditions.[16] In fact both capital and trade, as if in accord with the law of comparative advantage, tended to be directed outside the colonies;

(7) That although the Boer and Chaco wars may have been fought largely for economic reasons, it is hard to see economics as the major motive for most of the other wars of the past century or so. Where, for example, was the economic motivation in the two world wars, the Arab–Israeli wars, the Korean war, the several Indo–Chinese wars, the Indo–Pakistani wars over Kashmir and Bangladesh, the current civil wars in Bosnia, Somalia, Sudan, Rwanda and so forth?

This is not to say that there is no connection between capitalism, imperialism and war. Clearly, some capitalists profit handsomely from both the arms trade and the waging of wars, and in the conflict which Hobson covered for *the Manchester Guardian*, the Boer war, the economic motivations of the British, in particular, were only too evident. Moreover, as a corrective to the excessive concentration on the political and strategic dimensions of imperialism and warfare, the economic theories are very useful. A permanent supply of cheap primary products from the colonies seemed a logical answer to the problem of keeping down the costs of, say, British exports at the end of the 19th century. Moreover, opening up the new colonies to international trade doubtless had a tonic effect on the world economy as a whole. Regardless of the motives involved, the new markets and sources of supply did give considerable impetus to international exchange, and but for the colonial imposition, the participation of the colonies in the world trading nexus would almost certainly have been much slower. As it was, world trade leapt ahead in the years before the first world war: from a mere $4 billion in 1850 to $10.6 billion in 1870, $17.5 billion in 1890, $33.6 billion by 1910, and on the eve of war $40.4 billion.[17] By this time, despite high tariffs, the industrialised states continued to be one another's best customers; yet their increased trade with one another rested upon the bounty of raw materials which imperialism made possible.

16.7 THE INTERNATIONAL ECONOMY POST-1918

The war shattered the structure of international trade that had existed before, and its aftermath dealt even greater shocks to the system. First, the collapse of the continental empires—the Ottoman, the Austro-Hungarian and the Russian—meant the break-up of long-established integrated economies and the creation of new states, many, like Austria, barely viable and an easy prey to extremist ideologies—and, indeed, the pattern has been repeated following the break-up of the Soviet Union. Second, the vast public debts incurred during the war distorted both domestic and international economies as the supply of money in circulation was vastly increased so that when the countries attempted to return to the gold standard after the hiatus of hostilities, they had to do so with currencies that had lost their value. In any case with the United States, the major creditor, pursuing a deliberately deflationary policy in the early 1920s and levying the highest-ever tariffs on imports by the end of the decade, repayment of debt was made difficult, if not impossible. Third, there was the problem of the excessive reparations levied on Germany. At 132 billion gold marks ($33billion), it was an impossibly high figure given that total world trade on the eve of war had been $40.4 billion of which Germany's share had been about $5.3 billion.[18] In fact, of course, Germany's initial efforts to cope soon destroyed the value of the mark, and by the middle of August 1923 the mark stood at 20 million to the pound sterling, its value comparable to the Serbian dinar in 1993. Attempts to re-establish the German currency in the 1920s through the so-called 'Dawes' and 'Young' plans failed to scale down the amount due to any realistic figure, and Germany was obliged to take out new short-term loans to pay off its older longer-term debts. But the Depression of the 1930s punctured any fragile financial boom and forced the Americans to put a moratorium on debts and reparations.

Finally, the need to export gold to pay for debts led to a gross imbalance in stocks: by 1929 the United States had 38 per cent of the world's gold, while the whole of Europe put together had only 41 per cent. This haemhorrage of precious metal from Europe revived mercantilist ideas, leading Britain to abandon the gold standard in 1931 and other countries to follow suit. By 1936 not a single state had a convertible currency, a number of banks had collapsed, stock markets had crashed, unemployment was soaring and many financiers had committed suicide (despite the adage that 'old moneylenders never die, they just lose interest'!).

In the era of the Great Depression, economic nationalism brought in its train the whole panoply of high tariffs, import quotas, exchange controls and managed currency. Such restrictive practices reduced much international trade to the level of primitive barter, and there seems little doubt that there was a direct connection between the economic chaos of the inter-war period and the rise of Fascism. Interestingly enough this was for many on the left a signal that capitalism was in its death throes and that the world was teetering on the edge of Socialist revolution. But the Marxists and Leninists of the time were wrong. What was in prospect was not a world revolution but a world war. The monetarists may also be said to have been in error, for those who stood firm against government spending on arms or anything else merely contributed to a climate of rising unemployment and the appeasement of aggressors. Those who probably did have their finger on the pulse of events were, first, the followers of John Maynard Keynes, whose *General Theory of Employment, Interest and Money* of 1936 argued that given falling demand the states should abandon classical economic theory and spend their way back into prosperity—something that Roosevelt and Hitler in their different ways were already doing, and, second, those like E.H. Carr and Georg Schwarzenberger who were writing of the politics of not being overpowered, though it has to be said that in the *Twenty Years' Crisis*, Carr also seemed all too ready to appease, at least in the short term.

Just as the founders of the UN were determined to avoid the mistakes of the League, so those who met in Bretton Woods in 1944 to fashion a new international economic system for the post-war period were also determined to learn the lessons of the previous 30 years. What they decided, how successful was the system that they fashioned and what it all meant for the new countries emerging from empire will be essayed in the following chapter.

NOTES

1. Bozeman, A.B., *Politics and Culture in International History*, Princeton, Princeton University Press, 1960, pp. 39–43, 152 and 167–71.
2. Trevelyan, G.M., *English Social History*, London, The Reprint Society, 1948, pp. 187–97.
3. Huberman, L., *Man's Worldly Goods*, London, Gollancz, 1937, p. 135.
4. Ibid., p. 43.
5. Ibid., pp. 137–49.
6. Smith, A., *Wealth of Nations* (edited and introduced by E. Cannan), Vol. II, London, Methuen, 1930, p. 111.
7. Ibid., vol. I, pp. 68–9.
8. Quoted in Culbertson, W.S., *International Economic Policies*, New York, Appleton, 1925, p. 13.
9. Quoted in Northedge, F.S. and Grieve, M.J., *One Hundred Years of International Relations*, London, Duckworth, 1971, pp. 49–50.
10. The moves to restrict economic competition are traced in Hodges, C., *The Background of International Relations*, New York, Wiley, 1931, pp. 333–9; Hobson, J., *The Evolution of Modern Capitalism*, London, Macmillan, 1914; and Moon, P., *Imperialism and World Politics*, London, Methuen, 1926.
11. The connection between protectionism and imperialism is traced in Moon, P., op. cit. and also Woolf, L., *Empire and Commerce in Africa*, London, Allen & Unwin, 1920.
12. Carr, E.H., *The Twenty Years' Crisis*, London, Macmillan, 1962, p. 78.
13. London, Nisbet, 1902, p. 65.
14. London, Lawrence and Wishart, 1948, p. 76.

15. See, for example, Schumpeter, J., *Imperialism and Social Classes*, New York, 1951; Staley, E., *War and the Private Investor*, New York, 1935; and Langer, W.L., *The Diplomacy of Imperialism*, 2nd ed., New York, 1951.
16. Feis, H., *Europe, the World's Banker: 1870–1914*, Yale, 1930.
17. Hartmann, F.H., *The Relations of Nations*, 2nd ed., New York, Macmillan, 1964, p. 142.
18. Ibid., pp. 143–9.

CHAPTER 17

UNDERDEVELOPMENT: CAUSES AND PROPOSED CURES

17.1 BRETTON WOODS

In July 1944, as the Allied Forces were sweeping across northern France and northern Italy, the Soviet Union's Red Army was cutting a swathe through Eastern Europe and the Americans were landing on the Japanese Naval Base on Saipan Island in the Pacific, officials from 44 mainly Western countries were gathering for discussions at a beautiful and secluded estate in New England. The venue was Bretton Woods in America's New Hampshire, and their self-imposed task was to plan for a post-war international financial order that would avoid becoming prey to all those forces which in the 1920s and 1930s had brought about economic and political collapse and a second world war.

That most of the participants were from the West was because this was not yet the age of the LDCs, while in Moscow Stalin had made it clear that though his country was prepared to join the UN, it was unwilling to support any international economic institution he saw as aimed at preserving capitalism and imperialism. Given Moscow's scant representation, the discussions were dominated by the two major economic powers of the day—the United States and Britain. However, differences of economic outlook between these powers and an increasing disparity of production and resources complicated the deliberations. Like Britain when it was economic 'top dog' a century before, the United States' basic goal was of a return, albeit gradual, to free trade, which, in its view, would produce world prosperity. But the British government had inherited a discriminatory tariff in the form of Empire or Commonwealth preference which it was unwilling to jettison. In any case John Maynard Keynes, who, as Britain's chief negotiator at Bretton Woods, represented a wartime coalition soon to be shorn of its right-of-centre members, maintained that trade liberalisation, if too rapid, could leave a country vulnerable to economic turbulence and instability. Cheap imports were all very well, but if they led to large-scale unemployment in particular regions and industries, the social costs could outweigh the economic benefits. And though he agreed that economic nationalism had been a cause of the second world war, for the time being, he argued, tariffs and quotas were necessary safeguards against slump and depression.

Whatever their differences both the Americans and the British, as well as their Bretton Woods colleagues, accepted that for some time after the war they could not leave international economic matters to chance, or even the market. Some degree of international regulation or intervention was essential. During the war there had been a number of bilateral agreements to regulate currency and exchange rates; these could serve as a basis for the multilateral management of finance and trade.

Learning the lessons

The first priority was to learn the lessons of the past, in particular the causes of the breakdown of the pre-war international economy.[1] By common consent, one of the major factors contributing to its collapse was the failure of US leadership. Washington had kept aloof not just from world politics but from world economic developments as well, and an international plan to stabilise currency, which might have blunted the effects of the Depression, had had to be aborted because of Washington's refusal to participate. If the post-war world were to avoid the mistakes of the 1920s and 1930s, the United States would have to play a leading role in fashioning suitable international economic institutions for the 1940s and 1950s, not least because of its unprecedented economic power.

The fact is that while most other countries had suffered economic disorder, dislocation and decline as a result of the war, mainland USA, shielded from the main theatres of conflict, had profited. At more than 15 per cent a year, its industrial advance between 1940 and 1944 had been faster than at any time before or since. Moreover, the country's production plant had expanded by nearly 50 per cent and the physical output of goods by more than 50 per cent. Again, in contrast to other combatants, American manufactures had been barely affected by the need to invest in armaments, and standards of living actually rose during the war. As Paul Kennedy suggests in *The Rise and Fall of the Great Powers*:

> Among the Great Powers, the US was the only country which became richer—in fact much richer—rather than poorer because of the war. At its conclusion Washington possessed gold reserves of $20 b, about two thirds of the world's total...Again, more than half the total manufacturing of the world took place within the USA, which in fact turned out a third of the world production of goods of all types. This also made it by far the greatest exporter of goods at the war's end and ... because of the massive expansion of its shipbuilding facilities it now owned a half of the world supply of shipping. Economically the world was its oyster.[2]

Paul Kennedy's startling statistics explain why the participants at Bretton Woods looked to what was in effect the world's only economic superpower to manage the post-war international economy.

The second lesson was the need to avoid the kind of reparations tangle that had led in the 1920s to the collapse of the German mark and ultimately of the inter-war economy. True, there were those in the West who sought to keep the level of German industry down to a bare minimum; and in the Soviet Union, which had lost some 27 million people—one in nine of its population—as a result of the Nazi invasion, Stalin had a plan for a sizeable reparations bill, half of which was to go, understandably, to his own country. But though Germany had in fact borne a much greater responsibility for the second than for the first world war, the emerging consensus at Bretton Woods was that the reparations levied on Germany and the defeated powers should be considerably smaller than in the 1920s. Further, that they were for the most part to take the form of the return by the vanquished powers of assets they had seized abroad and in goods to be dispatched over a period of years to countries whose lands they had devastated.

The third lesson—the need to keep war debt within measurable proportions—had been eased from the start by America's use of a device called 'Lend Lease'. According to Lend Lease, any credit or commodities made available by Washington to its allies during the war were to be regarded as 'Uncle Sam's' contribution towards winning it, and any repayments were not to interfere with the revival of world trade.

The fourth lesson was to become the principle concern at Bretton Woods—the need to correct the monetary imbalances caused by the gold drain to the US and the chaos of competitive devaluations, floating exchange rates, multiple exchange rates (where there are different rates according to the purpose for which the currency is to be used) and what were called 'cross exchange rates' where a currency like sterling is traded for more dollars in Britain than in, say, France or Italy. The remedy for financial imbalance was to plan for fixed exchange rates among the major currencies and the use of gold as a reserve asset, which the United States, who now possessed some 70 per cent of the world's stocks, promised to sell at a fixed price of $35 an ounce. Since the American government committed itself to exchanging gold for dollars at any time, the dollar became literally as good as gold, indeed better, for, unlike gold, dollars earned interest and did not entail storage and insurance costs. In return for the American pledge to maintain the value of the dollar, other countries agreed to keep fluctuations in their exchange rates within very narrow limits. To maintain the value of their currencies they were to take measures to control inflation and increase productivity, and their central banks agreed that when necessary they would either buy or sell the country's own currency using the US dollar to raise or depress the currency value.

Institutions

To manage and lubricate the system agreed at Bretton Woods, the participants established two institutions: the first known as the International
Monetary Fund (IMF); the second the International Bank for
Reconstruction and Development (IBRD), to be known as the World Bank,
which would in effect perform central bank functions for the international
economy. The IMF was to provide overdraft facilities and advance short-
term credits to countries with balance-of-payments' problems. Further, it
was to act as adviser and umpire regarding the movement of national
exchange rates, and its approval was necessary before any alteration of
these could be made, as when Britain devalued in 1947. The World Bank
was to furnish longer-term loans to underwrite private lending and to
issue securities to raise new funds for speeding a return to economic
normality. Both institutions were to be funded by the member countries in
the form of quota contributions in gold and national currency; under the
system of weighted voting the United States was able to exert a dominant
influence in both.

17.2 UNFORESEEN DIFFICULTIES

In fact the world into which the IMF and World Bank emerged proved
very different from what had been envisaged at Bretton Woods.[3] In the
first place, the ultimate objective of a single global economic community
based on multilateral trade and currency convertibility was unrealisable as
long as the world remained polarised between East and West. Second,
within the Western world the economic imbalance between Europe and
North America was far greater than had been anticipated. Before the war,
Europe's deficits in its balance of trade with the US had always been offset
by a healthy surplus on what are called 'invisible' items in the balance of
payments such as banking, insurance, shipping and freight services, interest on loans and so forth. After the war, however, the immense carnage
and devastation, the bombed-out housing, the decaying machinery, the
need to resettle refugees, the lost markets and so on created enormous
economic problems which could not easily be solved, and the consequent
fall in production of consumer goods made the deficit on visible exports all
the greater. The disruption of trade with Eastern Europe on the onset of
the cold war only made matters worse. At the same time the pre-war
surplus on so-called 'invisibles' was replaced by a deficit because of the
sales of overseas investments to finance the war, the loss of shipping
during it and the need to maintain a high level of military expenditure
abroad after it. As a result, European imports from the US were soon seven
times its exports to that country, engendering a massive 'dollar gap' with
which the IMF and World Bank were unable to cope.

By 1947 Washington had decided that it would have to take drastic action to remedy the situation because it was in a financial position to do so but also out of economic and political self-interest. Economically, the impoverishment of Europe was bound to affect US trade adversely because the Europeans could not afford to buy American goods. Politically, it seemed in Washington that Moscow might take advantage of the West's economic plight to add to the list of countries it had recently inducted into the Communist system. Already it was pressurising Iran and Turkey for territorial concessions, Communist guerrillas were making significant headway in Greece and the mass Communist parties of Italy and France were seen as threatening the democratic system. Washington's fears were perhaps exaggerated, but what matters in this subject is what people think is the case; and the perception in the State Department and Pentagon was that the Soviet leaders were both promoting and waiting for the economic collapse of Western Europe. Were Moscow to fill the vacuum the US would be dangerously isolated, and therefore Washington could claim to have sound economic and political reasons for what appeared to be a series of acts of almost unparalleled generosity as it stepped in to fill the economic gap. How did it fill the vacuum?

17.3 THE US RESPONSE

In March 1947 President Truman outlined to Congress what was to become known as the 'Truman Doctrine', offering financial support to what he called 'free peoples who are resisting attempted subjugation by armed minorities or by outside persons'.[4] The first countries to benefit were Greece and Turkey. They were allocated $400 million in the first instance and a further sum for American civilians and military personnel who would assist them in reconstruction and defence. It was a watershed in the history of America which for a century and a quarter had stood aloof from European politics. Within three months Washington was giving its new found concern for the European balance a much broader application, when Secretary of State George Marshall announced a plan of assistance to speed post-war recovery and, as he put it, 'permit the emergence of political and social conditions in which free institutions can exist'.[5] In theory Marshall aid was available to Communist and non-Communist alike—indeed, to every European country except Spain, whose leader General Franco had been helped to power by the military support of Hitler and Mussolini. The only stated condition was that the recipients should co-operate together in an Organisation for European Economic Co-operation (OEEC) to reduce trade and monetary barriers between themselves, even if it meant their discrimination against American exports (again, a remarkably generous gesture!), but the implications were enough to bring about a rejection by Moscow—probably as intended. Though Communist leaders in Czechoslovakia and Poland were interested in the Marshall aid programme, Stalin exercised his veto on their behalf, and in economic terms Eastern and Western Europe drifted further apart.

17.4 ECONOMIC EFFECTS

Initially some $6,000 million of Marshall aid flowed into Europe, and in April 1948 the 16-member OEEC met in Paris to decide on how to allocate it. By 1951 when the Marshall Plan had run its course, Western Europe had benefited to the tune of $17,000 million, only a fraction of which was repayable, and was well on the way to recovery. With mounting economic success came the idea of closer economic integration. In the European Coal and Steel Community, established in 1951, the region had a pilot project to point the way. Moreover, thanks to continuing American assistance and the assurance of US military protection, the region soon began to experience record growth rates in manufactures, exports, employment, investment capital and disposable income. To quote Paul Kennedy again:

> Between 1950 and 1970 European gross domestic product grew on average about 5.5% per annum and 4.4% on a per capita basis as against world average rates of 5% and 3% respectively. Industrial production rose even faster—at 7.1% corresponding to a world rate of 5.9%. Thus by the latter date output per head in Europe was about 2 and a half times greater than in 1950...The European Community possessed a larger share of gross world product than even the US and [was]...twice as large as the Soviet Union's.[6]

In the process several of the objectives of Bretton Woods were being realised in the Western European theatre. Trade liberalisation had proceeded apace as the members of OEEC reduced or removed quotas and tariffs on trade in relation to one another, and monetary stabilisation and convertibility were facilitated by the establishment of an institution called the European Payments Union (EPU) which acted as a clearing house for the region's commercial transactions.

While Western European economic development proceeded apace, so apparently did that of Eastern Europe, though the extent of its progress is rather difficult to gauge because of the notorious unreliability of Communist statistics at the time. But even if the statistical 'evidence' was only half true, it pointed to a massive expansion of productive capacity, an expansion ironically assisted, in no small measure, by Western trade embargoes and boycotts. For Western sanctions merely encouraged, as sanctions so often do, the target states to produce for themselves what they had formerly imported. Thus, by the perverse logic of history, we in the West, by refusing to have normal economic contacts with the Eastern European Communist countries once Marshall aid had been rejected, helped to create the Soviet bloc. On the other hand the economic system created in the East was too inflexible to reward initiative, innovation or efficiency, too uncompetitive to keep enterprises up to the mark, too centralised and inordinately wasteful in the use of human and material resources; and in consequence quality was continually being sacrificed for quantity. As a result, Communist factories poured out a profusion of often unusable goods: leaky hot water bottles, fridges that gave an electric shock as they were opened, spin driers that slopped water on to the floor, to say nothing of the constructions that had to be rebuilt within two or three years because they were in danger of collapse.

Part of the problem was that the Eastern European Communist countries never developed any proper mechanism for economic co-operation. True, there was COMECON, the Council for Mutual Economic Assistance, but for a long time it was no more than a forum for attacking the economic arrangements of the West and a cover for Moscow's exploitation of the economies of its Communist neighbours. When in the late 1950s it did attempt to develop joint investment projects, specialisation and the co-ordination of national plans, the results rarely seemed to match up to expectations. Lacking any obvious basis for multilateral trade or payments, COMECON's economic exchanges tended to remain largely bilateral; and in their search for managerial skills, technology and foodstuffs its members were increasingly drawn to the West as cold war conditions eased.[7]

If there was rather less economic co-operation in Eastern Europe than was suggested by their common Communist ideology, Western Europe, too, remained somewhat divided. Though each country had experienced to a greater or lesser degree some kind of economic miracle up to 1970, in institutional terms Western Europe was literally at 'sixes and sevens'. In fact as a response to the establishment in 1957 of the Treaty of Rome setting up the European Community, seven non-Common Market countries had formed the European Free Trade Area (EFTA), which shared with its Common Market neighbours the objective of eliminating tariffs and quotas but, unlike them, made no provision for a common external tariff.

Led by Britain, EFTA was a kind of experiment in balance of power economics. As a counterweight to the EC, it was able to accommodate Commonwealth economic interests in a way that the EC would not. Even though by 1959 there was an economic fault line dividing Western Europe, and the OEEC was deemed to have reached its 'sell-by' date, the region as a whole continued to prosper. Furthermore, like Japan, which had also prospered in part due to the largesse of the Americans, it was able to benefit from the US market while being able to restrict US imports.[8]

17.5 THE US ECONOMY IN TROUBLE

While the economies of Western Europe and Japan performed their American-induced miracles, by about 1960 the US economy was itself in trouble. For Washington's policy of providing enough dollars to facilitate international trade had turned a dollar shortage into a glut; for the first time there were more dollars in circulation than the United States had gold to redeem them. If every foreign bank had then asked the US for an ounce of gold for every $35 in its possession, Washington could not have paid. Moreover, its continued assistance, foreign investments and overseas military expenditure were creating a balance of payments deficit that threatened to get out of control, and in November 1960 the US experienced its first-ever run on the dollar as international speculators began to convert dollars into gold.

Soon it was apparent that the US could no longer manage the monetary system alone and had to call on the assistance of a multilateral elite of bankers and finance ministers from the leading Bretton Woods' countries. But sudden massive movements of capital and the internationalisation of banking and production facilities through the MNCs made every currency, including the dollar, sensitive and vulnerable to such transnational monetary flows. At the same time President Johnson's unwillingness to raise taxes to finance either his domestic anti-poverty programme called 'the Great Society' or the ruinously expensive Vietnam conflict induced serious inflation. This combined with the fact that America's MNCs were modernising their overseas enterprises, often to the neglect of domestic production, in turn contributed to a loss in the competitiveness of American exports. Hitherto Washington had used favourable trade balances to offset unfavourable payments balances, but by 1971 the US economy suffered its first trade deficit this century, indicating just how precarious was the country's economic situation. In short, while the EC and Japan were rapidly increasing their share of world trade, the US share was fast declining.

17.6 WASHINGTON TAKES DRASTIC ACTION

Faced with mounting economic crisis, President Nixon in August 1971 took drastic action. Without consulting the other members of the IMF, he inaugurated what he called a New Economic Policy.[9] This meant wage and price controls, the suspension of the convertibility of dollars into gold and a 10 per cent surcharge on all imports. Eventually the dollar was devalued by some 18 per cent, effected by increasing the price of an ounce of gold. By December 1971 a system of free-floating currency rates had emerged, with values to be determined, or so it was assumed, by market forces rather than by government regulation. In effect the financial disciplines of the Bretton Woods' system lay in ruins, and the shared interests that had once bound its members together were fast disappearing. Since then the attempt to fashion a new international monetary system has been undermined by a series of further shocks to the system.

17.7 FURTHER SHOCKS

The food crisis

The first blow was the world food crisis of the early 1970s—precipitated by climatological calamities affecting Africa, the Soviet Union, China and the Asian sub-continent; compounded by the largest commercial transaction in foodstuffs ever, as the Soviet Union purchased 28 million tonnes of grain, mainly from the United States. This had the effect of depleting reserves and hence driving up the world price; the resulting crisis was further exacerbated by a sudden fall in the world catch of fish, in part due to over-fishing by countries like the Soviet Union and Japan using the latest technology. A sudden drop in the supply of staple foodstuffs was bound to cause especial problems in the part of the world where growth in population was beginning to outstrip growth in readily available food supplies—the Third World.[10]

The oil price shocks

Hardly had the impact of the food crisis been absorbed when the world economy suffered an even greater shock—the first massive oil price hike—a rise of some 400 per cent generated by the oil-exporting countries (OPEC) in the wake of the renewal of Arab–Israeli hostilities in 1973. The fact is that with more countries switching from coal to oil, for supposedly environmental as well as economic reasons, the producers of petroleum, who had hitherto been restrained in their pricing, thought this a golden opportunity to secure both economic and political advantage as they made money while putting Islamic and, in particular, Arab grievances on the map. The effect was to destabilise the world economy, putting severe pressure on the balance of payments of the 'NOPEC' countries ie the non-oil producers and precipitating an inflationary spiral that was to end in a world recession in demand, output and trade. Though some believed that OPEC's success in 1974 had been some kind of victory for the LDCs collectively, since most of the producers were in the Third World, it was nothing of the kind. For many Third World countries have little or no oil, and since oil is used in almost every sector of the economy, including industry, agriculture, transport, defence and domestic heating, many a 'NOPEC' country had to face the prospect of foregoing industrialisation, searching for alternative fuels or borrowing heavily. A further oil shock at the end of the 1970s, occasioned by the turmoil in Iran following the fall of the Shah and the expectation of a drop in oil production in the Gulf, merely compounded the problem, engendering into the vocabulary of economics a new word—'stagflation'—when stagnation in output is combined with massive inflation. For in six years the price of petroleum had soared from just over two and a half dollars per barrel to 40—a 16-fold rise.[11]

The fall in oil prices

Ironically, a sudden drop in oil prices in 1983 precipitated by falling demand brought a further shock to the system because now even the oil producers were beginning to feel the pinch. But, far more traumatic had been the impact of the successive oil crises on the circulation of money. Since payments to oil producers had been considerably more than their economies could absorb they had tended to deposit their vast surpluses in the banks. Some had found their way into the state banks or to the IMF and World Bank, but the bulk had ended up in the private banks. Soon the whole banking system was awash with petro-dollars ie dollars obtained from the sale of petrol, and naturally the banks had been anxious to dispose of them in the form of loans. As it happens, there had been no shortage of borrowers, especially among those oil-importing countries unable to increase their exports or reduce their oil consumption sufficiently to balance the books. In this way petro-dollars had been recycled from oil exporter to oil importer. By far the biggest borrowers were the LDCs, but with a number of Eastern European Communist countries following suit, hoping to use Western loans to modernise their economies.[12]

The debt crisis

At first all seemed well, because LDC exports grew along with the debt, but with the second oil shock the picture changed dramatically. For the LDC debtor countries in particular this was an unmitigated disaster as they faced simultaneously rising interest rates, severe increases in the cost of servicing their debts and declining terms of trade as the volume and value of their exports plummetted. None the less, the LDCs continued to borrow and the banks to lend, in the hope of an imminent world recovery, which the leading economists of the day, with their enormous talent for getting things wrong, were constantly predicting. But instead of recovery the world was in for a severe financial crisis—in part the consequence of a rise in international tension in several different areas simultaneously. The Iran–Iraq war became a kind of vortex sucking an increasing number of

nations into its path of destruction. At the same time, the Soviet intervention into Afghanistan had brought unaccustomed US military support in
the region for Islamic fundamentalists, while the introduction of martial
law in Poland was treated by Washington with a sense of outrage never in
evidence when far more ruthless military men established pro-Western
military regimes. Since President Reagan had found in both Afghanistan
and Poland 'evidence' for his 'evil empire' postulate, East–West relations
took another serious turn for the worse. Then came the crisis in the South
Atlantic as Britain and Argentina fought for the islands the former calls the
Falklands, the latter Las Malvinas.

That Poland having failed to modernise its economy nearly defaulted
and that Argentina after its defeat by Britain decided to suspend payment
on its external debt indicate the intimate connection between political
turmoil and economic dislocation. Both reactions lowered confidence in
capital markets, and there were calls for immediate repayment of some
short-term loans. However, when Mexico, among other countries, proved
unable to come up with the required cash, it triggered off what was to
become known as 'the debt crisis'.[13]

In a sense Mexico's economic problems were but a paradigm or proto-
type for what was happening elsewhere. Like many a developing country
it had had an impressive period of growth from the 1940s to the 1960s. But
even though the country was an oil producer, the cumulative impact of
the various shocks of the 1970s combined with a population growth far too
rapid to be able to preserve agricultural self-sufficiency put the country
into economic reverse. By August 1982 the Mexican government was
forced to declare that it no longer had the means to cover payment on its
foreign debt, which at just over $80,000 million was second only to that of
Brazil. How had it amassed such a huge deficit?

In the early 1970s the banks had been as eager to lend to Mexico as to
any other country, and at negligible rates of interest; by 1978 its debt stood
at a potentially repayable $21,400 million. But the rapid rise of interest
rates world-wide which followed and the combined effects of domestic
inflation, a mounting imports bill, a decline in the value of exports, a flight
from capital and dwindling foreign exchange reserves brought Mexico to
the point where it could no longer afford even to service its debt. For a
time there was talk, encouraged by Cuba's Fidel Castro, of a 'cartel' of
Latin American debtors, which would refuse as a group to pay the $400
billion or so they owed. Others like Peru's President Alan Garcia were
thinking of refusing to use more than 10 per cent of export earnings for
debt repayment. Either course could conceivably have contributed to a
collapse of confidence in the international banking system, driving even
secure financial institutions to the verge of bankruptcy. But such proposals
were then dismissed on the grounds that a collective default might meet
collective punishment, as a result of which developed and underdevel-

oped alike would suffer. The preferred alternative was for Mexico to amend its economic policy to reach agreement with the private foreign banks and with the IMF, suitably replenished with additional funds by the wealthier states. As a result the banks, fearful of the consequences of a threat of collective default, were inclined to be somewhat forbearing, writing off some debts, agreeing to reschedule others and offering bridging loans in return for what is called a 'structural adjustment package'—an austerity programme developed in the West largely for Western conditions (and which are often far more difficult to implement in non-Western conditions), involving massive cuts in government spending. It is, incidentally, largely because the banks found their profit margins declining over this period that some of their customers today face often exorbitant charges for services that once warranted a nominal fee or were even free.

Mexico became the model for managing debt crises, but there were other crises in the financial markets for which most professional economists were not prepared and to which there seems as yet no easy remedy. It will be recalled that when the system of fixed exchange rates had to give way to one of floating rates in the early 1970s, the economists, with their usual flair for deriving preconceived conclusions from unwarranted assumptions, supposed that the rate would be a reflection of purchasing power and related to real economic conditions. They were, of course, wrong. In practice, exchange rates, as illustrated so graphically with the problems of Europe's Exchange Rate Mechanism (ERM), can be easily undermined by financial speculators who on a whim or a rumour can move vast sums across frontiers physical or notional (as from one side of a computer screen to another). Furthermore, currency values can be manipulated by governments, as policy priorities shift between devaluation (the Keynesian solution, which tends to stimulate exports but promotes inflation) or revaluation (the monetarists answer, which tends to cheapen imports but causes unemployment). This combination of speculative capital transfers and policy-induced shifts in exchange rates have together created a very volatile and unstable international monetary system since the 1970s.

In part as a result of these repeated shocks to the international system and the perceived decline in Washington's economic leadership ('hegemony', in the jargon), people of influence in those LDCs and Communist countries who fared especially badly put accepted economic orthodoxies—capitalist and socialist—under critical scrutiny.

17.8 CRITIQUE OF ECONOMIC ORTHODOXIES

Reformist

In many LDCs the conviction grew that the implementation of orthodox liberal theories concerning world trade had produced not balance but a kind of two-tier system whereby some countries were enriched and rather more were impoverished.[14] In the early 1950s Raoul Prebisch, a reformist but non-Marxist Argentinian economist, had suggested that the world was divided economically into 'centre' countries—fully developed and indus-trialised—and 'periphery' countries—non-industrialised and the casualties of a trading system whose terms were permanently loaded against them. For Prebisch the only way of breaking out of this structural vicious circle was for the elites of the 'periphery' countries to embark on a programme of forced industrialisation to reduce dependence on imports and the acquisition of debt. But how was this to be achieved? Domestically, by what he called 'healthy protectionism' ie controlling imports in order to speed the development of a domestic manufacturing base. Internationally, by pressurising the developed countries to show greater regard for the interests of the periphery.[15] Prebisch's ideas were to become increasingly influential. They provided much of the intellectual inspiration for the UN Conference on Trade and Development (UNCTAD), created in 1964, and the New International Economic Order expounded 10 years later. Basically what was called for was: (1) preferential treatment in the markets of the developed countries for LDC manufactures, combined with measures to create financial stability through long-term contracts and the building of international buffer stocks of commodities likely to change in price in the event of a sudden glut or scarcity; (2) long-term development assistance and debt relief programmes for the LDCs; and (3) changes in international economic institutions to give the LDCs a greater if not an equal voice in their deliberations.[16]

Radical

The developed countries' resistance to even these relatively modest reforms was to give currency to more radical theories. The former prime minister of Jamaica, Michael Manley, basically agreed with the Prebisch analysis, but felt that it did not go far enough. He held that for many LDCs the domestic market was too small to support the development of efficient industries and that answer must lie in regional common markets such as CARICOM, involving the Caribbean countries, and the Andean pact.[17]

Another radical perspective was provided by the American professor Thomas Weisskopf who advocated that the LDCs should selectively delink from the world economy in favour of a policy of self-reliant development. Basically it was a strategy of diversifying overseas sources of supply and markets, prohibiting luxury imports, stockpiling essentials, dispersing and diversifying domestic production, increasing the share of investment financed from indigenous savings and replacing foreign experts where possible.[18]

Revolutionary

As against the reformists and the radicals there were the revolutionaries who believed that the world structure of dominance and dependency was more complex than Prebisch had suggested and that the structural rigidities included precisely those classes Prebisch was relying upon to transform the LDCs' domestic economies. In the view of such theorists as Gunder Frank and Samir Amin the elites of each dependent economy represented the interests not of their peoples but of the 'centre' states and that nothing would be basically changed without the use of peoples' armed power to destroy the old order.[19] Such revolutionary theorists were further divided into two schools: the neo-Marxists like Frank who believed that by national revolution and selective or comprehensive delinking from the capitalist world economy, a people could achieve true national liberation; and the more orthodox Marxists such as Immanuel Wallerstein who believed that nothing short of world revolution would suffice.

17.9 MORE ORTHODOX SOLUTIONS

Throughout the 1970s and most of the 1980s reformist, radical and revolutionary nostrums were in vogue in the LDCs and many leaders, especially in Africa and Latin America, tried to put one or other into effect. However, the collapse of Eastern European Communism, China's successful move into the world market and the enormous economic problems experienced by Cuba, Vietnam and most of the other countries still under Communist rule somewhat dampened enthusiasm in the LDCs for the more radical solutions to the problems of debt and underdevelopment. Increasingly, supporters of a more classical economic approach who saw the 'little dragons' of Asia such as Taiwan, South Korea, Singapore and Hong Kong and the bigger 'dragons' such as Thailand, Indonesia and Malaysia as indicating that liberal solutions can work for the LDCs were listened to with respect. And there was also some sympathy for the kind of neo-classical thinking of the World Bank's *World Development Report* of 1982 which argued that there was no particular merit in industrialisation, and that like Switzerland, Denmark and New Zealand, many LDCs would be wiser to concentrate on non-industrial production such as agriculture and the service industries.

17.10 THE FOLLY OF UNIFORMITY

But with market mechanisms already in difficulty in many of those post-Communist countries of Eastern Europe, Africa and Latin America where Western economists with a blithe disregard of history had encouraged the belief that through 'shock therapy' a planned Socialist command economy could be turned rapidly into a liberal free-enterprise economy, it may not be too long before reformist, radical and revolutionary solutions are again *de rigeur*. However, if the history of the post-war international economy has taught us anything, it is surely that what works in one country does not necessarily work in another, that to try and thrust capitalism on to a people not geared to it is as foolish as to try to thrust Socialism on a people not wanting it, and that ultimately what is needed is something that accords with experience as well as aspiration.

NOTES

1. See, for example, Hartmann, F.H., *The Relations of Nations*, 2nd ed., New York, Macmillan, 1964, pp. 149–54.
2. London, Fontana, 1989, p. 461.
3. See Scammel, W., *The International Economy since 1945* 2nd ed., London, Macmillan, 1983 and Spero, J., *The Politics of International Economic Relations*, 4th ed., London, Unwin Hyman, 1990.
4. 'The Truman Doctrine' in *Public Papers of the Presidents of the United States, Harry S Truman*, Washington, US Government Printing Office, 1947, pp. 178–9.
5. 'European Initiative Essential to Economic Recovery' in *Department of State Bulletin*, Vol. 16, 15 June 1947, p. 1160.
6. Kennedy, P., op. cit., p. 543.
7. Stern, G., *The Rise and Decline of International Communism*, Aldershot, Elgar, 1990, pp. 209–12.
8. On Japan's 'economic miracle' see Kennedy, P., op. cit., pp. 537–40 and 591–608.
9. Spero, J., op. cit., pp. 4–5 and 109–11.
10. For an admirable survey of the problems involved see Kegley, C. and Wittkopf, E., *World Politics: Trend and Transformation*, New York, St Martin's Press, 1981, pp. 220–59.
11. Spero, J., op. cit., pp. 58–94 and 311–14.
12. Ibid., pp. 74–8.
13. Ibid., pp. 78–99.
14. Kegley, C. and Wittkopf, E., op. cit., pp. 72–102 and 182–204.
15. *The Economic Development of Latin America and its Principal Problems*, New York, The United Nations, 1950.
16. See, Reubens, E., *The Challenge of the N.I.E.O.*, Boulder, Colorado, Westview, 1981, especially pp. 1–17.
17. Interview with Michael Manley in Stern, G., *Leaders and Leadership*, London, LSE/BBC World Service, 1993, p. 98.
18. Weisskopf, T., 'Self reliance and Development Strategy' in Ngo Manh-Lau (ed.), *Unreal Growth*, Delhi, Hindustan Publishing Co., 1984, pp. 845–61.
19. See, for example, Frank, G., 'The Development of Underdevelopment', *Monthly Review*, September 1966, pp. 17–30 and Amin, S., *Imperialism and Unequal Development*, New York, Monthly Review Press, 1977.

PART VII
WORLD SOCIETY?

CHAPTER 18

PLANETARY DANGERS AND OPPORTUNITIES

In a recent address at an American university, the comic Woody Allen warned the students that from now on there were only two roads open to them: one leading to extinction, and the other merely to catastrophe; and he added that now more than ever it was very important to choose the right road. It was a joke, of course, but it strikes a chord precisely because it seems to be in keeping with a kind of cosmic pessimism which has become increasingly fashionable and which suggests that we will be lucky to get to the end of this century, let alone the next.

18.1 19TH-CENTURY OPTIMISM

The pessimism of the age is in marked contrast to the 19th century when, certainly in the West, optimism was in vogue. This was, after all, a time of rapid scientific and technological advance, when scientists were revered as people of incontrovertible knowledge and the harbingers of progress— people whose training and understanding had given them the potential for solving the world's problems, satisfying all needs and transforming the moral as well as the material conditions of existence. It was the age of Hegel and Marx, of Darwin and John Stuart Mill, each in his own way suggesting that people could look forward to self-improvement as well as social and economic advance. Although the 20th century has also produced its optimists, not least among those who in 1917, 1919, 1945 and 1991 talked of new world orders, the prevailing mood among creative artists, scientists, intellectuals and academics has been, on the whole, much more sombre. So where, when and why did the vision of a science based nirvana begin to be replaced by the concept of a technological Valhalla? Why did the prospect of a 'utopia' in which ideals are realised give way to the nightmare of what has been called 'dystopia', in which all ideals are shattered?

18.2 20TH-CENTURY PESSIMISM

The first hints of a change of attitude were to be found around the turn of the century when a number of creative artists began to exhibit signs of doubt, disillusion and even despair regarding the state of society. In Britain, for example, the exiled Polish writer Joseph Conrad wrote a series of novels in the first decade of the century, including *The Secret Agent* and *Under Western Eyes*, depicting the isolation of the individual in mass society and expressing what he called his 'deep sense of fatality governing this man-inhabited world'.[1] At about this time the composer Edward Elgar started to plough a similar kind of lonely furrow in his music but with the sense of desolation tinged with nostalgia. On the continent artists were beginning to express themselves in new forms. The composers Schoenberg, Berg and Webern broke with tonality altogether, and in art such movements as cubism, futurism, surrealism and Dadaism suggested a questioning of accepted standards and an imminent breakdown in social values.

In effect these artists were intimating that traditional social, economic and political structures were crumbling and that humankind was entering collectively into an 'unstructured situation' they could not properly comprehend. This mood was only reinforced in 1914 when the world was engulfed in war, at the end of which the German philosopher Osvald Spengler produced a text encapsulating this mood of despair. It was called, appropriately enough, *The Decline of the West*.

18.3 THEMES

Machines a threat to liberty

The irony is that it was very largely those elements that had made for such optimism in the 19th century that were beginning to generate feelings of despondency, alarm and revulsion in the 20th. First, there was the revolution in technology. Though new technologies deriving from steam power, the manufacture of mass-produced steels, the internal combustion engine, the invention of man-made dyes and plastics, the use of electrical energy and the like were already making a positive contribution to the sum of human happiness, some creative artists were beginning to realise that there was a price to be paid for these developments. The main danger then seemed to lie in the potential threat to individual initiative posed by the machine. For while some might have liberating qualities, others seemed to have the power to enslave. After all, the negative side of technology was already to be seen in assembly-line production, where an individual's whole day might be taken up with repetitive work involving simply tightening a screw, clamping a lid, affixing a label or stoking a fire—all totally soul-destroying and dehumanising. At the same time, the very technologies that were taking the drudgery out of life could also lead to its extinction, as was so graphically illustrated in both the Boer and first world wars, and also, though in different vein, in the sinking of the 'unsinkable' *Titanic*.

Science a threat to spiritual values

The second element that was beginning to be re-evaluated at the turn of the century was the very scientism of the previous half-century or so—the self-confidence and assurance of the scientists and the idea that science could solve all problems. In a kind of rehearsal for post-modernism, the scientific attitude was increasingly seen, possibly mistakenly, as being in conflict with spiritual values: with religion, metaphysics and with the kinds of irrational forces and drives which Freud and the psychoanalysts had indicated were of the very stuff of human existence and experience. This gave rise to a feeling of revulsion against the precision and logic of science and took the form of a predisposition, especially among creative artists, in favour of the mystical and the mythical, the instinctive and the intuitive, the ambiguous, the enigmatic and the downright bizarre.

Capitalism a threat to health and welfare

The third element for reassessment was the nature of the economic system—capitalism. True, in the 19th century the capitalist criteria of efficiency, market mechanisms and profit motives had been largely responsible for the phenomenal rise in the supply and distribution of consumer goods and the development of communications, making countries far more accessible to one another. None the less, the negative psychological features of capitalism—its alienating characteristics which Marx had warned about—had largely gone unchecked. It was becoming increasingly evident that capitalism could have a pernicious effect on the health and welfare of society:

(a) Because of the noxious fumes, hazardous wastes and often insanitary working conditions;
(b) Because of the drudgery involved in much of the work; and
(c) Because of the even greater drudgery of suddenly being jobless and homeless as a result of one of capitalism's many recessions.

Hypocrisy a threat to civilised behaviour

A further element that began to come under critical scrutiny at the turn of the century was the moral certainty of the so-called 'Age of Progress'. One of the dominant myths of the 19th century was that material advance had also brought with it moral progress and that science and technology had fostered a kind of higher ethic. However, several of the critics examining the rhetoric and then the reality of, say, the Victorian family or the colonial experience began to feel that the whole system was riddled with double standards, and again psychoanalysis revealed that there was a divergence between what was supposed to be happening and what was really going on. In the matter of religion, politics, economics and sex, public virtue tended to conceal private vice—'respectable' married men impregnating their housekeepers, businessmen seducing their secretaries, public benefactors defrauding their beneficiaries, pillars of the military and religious establishment engaging in the 'vice that dare not speak its name'—and the critics were, so to speak, in moral revulsion against such hypocrisy.

Antidotes to 'scientism' deeply flawed

With the unleashing of the ever more awesome destructive power of science culminating in the second half of the century with the H-bomb, together with the ability of corrupt rulers to use such power in the service of totalitarian ideologies, what had begun as a minority concern within the creative community soon became a much more pervasive preoccupation. But by this time there were additional reasons for gloom and despondency. For some of the suppositions, theories and belief systems many had taken up as an antidote to 19th-century scientism—Anarchism, Communism, Expressionism, asceticism and the like—had turned out to be worse than the disease. For example in *The Lotus and the Robot*, Arthur Koestler describes the failure of his spiritual journey to find a better alternative to Western materialism. He flirts first with Communism, only to become disillusioned following the murderous anti-left antics of Stalin's secret police during the Spanish civil war. He then seeks solace in Eastern mysticism, and after prolonged exposure to the activities of certain Indian ascetics he decides that their self-denial is a form of self-indulgence. In what way, he asks, does sticking nails into one's body, burying oneself underground for hours at a time or taking food through one's rectum and expelling it through one's mouth represent an improvement on the acquisitiveness of Western society? In the end he decides that they do not and that Western materialism probably adds more to the sum of human happiness than his two chosen alternatives.

Humans as robots

Once again it is in the arts that we can trace the widely shared descent into dejection and despondency following the first world war. In the silent classic *Metropolis* of 1926, Fritz Lang visualises a future city in which humans work like robots in the service of machines. A decade later in the film *Things to Come* based on a story by H.G. Wells the potentially suffocating propensities of science are again to the fore. Here humans, rather less robotic than in Fritz Lang's film, are entirely dwarfed by gargantuan architectural forms from which it is difficult to escape. Earlier, in 1932, Aldous

Huxley had produced his novel *Brave New World* depicting a future in which humans behave like automata, albeit cheerful automata under the influence of mind-numbing drugs which take away human creativity.

Society under totalitarian control

After the second world war, by which time the creative artist had been able to take stock of the nature of totalitarianism—both of the Hitler right and of the Stalinist left variety—the images became darker and starker. George Orwell's *1984*, written in 1948, sets the tone, with its grim picture of a fully developed police state in which the individual's every word and action are kept under surveillance through TV monitors which cannot be switched off, and the thought police stand ready to stamp out any behaviour deemed subversive. With the ubiquitous message, 'Big Brother is watching you', and ominous slogans emblazoned on the white façade of the Ministry of Truth: 'War is Peace'; 'Freedom is Slavery'; 'Ignorance is Strength'—all examples of what Orwell calls 'double-think'—it was an immensely powerful and influential text. The representation of the boot trampling on a human face has served as a powerful metaphor for oppression ever since.

NUCLEAR WAR

The ultimate technological nightmare—nuclear warfare and its aftermath—was the theme of a whole series of films in the 1950s and 1960s. This was the heyday of CND, of the slogan 'disarm or perish', of events in Berlin, Cuba and Vietnam that produced fearful reactions throughout the world. In 1959 there was *On the Beach*, based on Neville Shute's novel about people in Australia awaiting death by fall-out after the rest of the world has been destroyed. *Dr Strangelove* appeared in 1964, a black comedy about a power-crazed nuclear scientist which ends with a cowboy-hatted American accidentally falling out of a B-52 together with an H-bomb emblazoned with the words 'Nuclear warhead, handle with care, Hi there' that detonates the Soviet doomsday machine and destroys the world to the tune of 'We'll meet again'. In 1965 came the film *The War Game*, banned in Britain for some time because of its terrifying depiction of the after-effects of a nuclear conflict.

In the late 1960s there was a return to themes concerning abuse of power and oppressive regulation, including *Fahrenheit 451* about firemen whose job it is to burn books; Roger Vadim's *Barbarella* in which there is a lot of sexual ecstasy but not much fun since any erotic encounter has to be modulated by machine; and in 1971 *THX1138* about a society in which everyone looks alike and sex is prohibited.

The triumph of evil

In the late 1970s and 1980s came a whole series of films in which technology is used to dramatise age-old issues of right and wrong and in which the power of evil often triumphs. This is the period of the space fantasy offering nightmarish examples of possible future worlds. Darth Vader, destroyer of planets, makes his debut in *Star Wars* of 1976, and reappears in *The Empire Strikes Back* of 1980 and in *The Return of the Jedi* of 1983. Evil triumphs yet again in the shape of the boy Damien in *The Omen* and its sequels. And throughout the 1960s, 1970s and 1980s, the fight between good and evil was being waged on Britain's television screens for the benefit of children of all ages in the various episodes of *Dr Who*.

18.4 ENVIRONMENT IN CRISIS

It was in the context of a world widely portrayed as facing either Armageddon or technological purgatory that another kind of doom-laden scenario began to surface in the 1970s. As before, it was based on perceptions of reality, but in the process the realities and potentialities have sometimes been obscured by those who are convinced, to return to Woody Allen, that we face either extinction or catastrophe. Though this latest scenario goes under various headings, it stems from the perception of a world in ecological crisis whose implications are potentially no less devastating than those of nuclear war. However, some of the more extreme exponents of the global environmental predicament seem to exude not just pessimism but paranoia, induced, possibly by over-exposure to computer simulations, colour graphics and selective statistics.

For example in his *Enquiry into the Human Prospect* of 1975, Robert Heilbroner suggests that we live in a world of not merely unparalleled violence and brutality, mass poverty, hunger and disease but of calamitous environmental degradation. Further, those who could stem the process have failed to mount an appropriate response and show little sign of willingness to do so. The human prospect is, therefore, dim. The science-fiction writer Isaac Asimov goes even further. He calls his essay of 1979 *A Choice of Catastrophes* and suggests that the dispersion of nuclear weapons and knowledge, the depletion of the world's resources, the wanton destruction of the ecosphere and the phenomenal growth of the world's population in relation to available resources are now at a stage when they impact on one another and are virtually impossible to reverse. In short, such global trends constitute a time bomb that is ticking away and which threatens to destroy what Richard Falk in a book of 1972 called *This Endangered Planet* and others have called *Spaceship Earth, Lifeboat Earth* or *The Global Village*. And every time there is a man-made environmental disaster, usually summed up in one place name—Seveso, Bhopal,

Chernobyl—the doomsday scenario sounds that much more plausible. What then is the nature of the planetary crisis as depicted in the writings of those deeply or even mildly Green?[2]

DEPLETION OF RESOURCES

At the core of virtually every Green analysis is the idea that on present form the human race will soon have exhausted the capacity of the planet's resources and environment to support it, and that it has reached this predicament as a belated consequence of the industrial revolution. The argument is that in attempting to satisfy an ever-expanding growth of consumer demand, industry has seriously depleted the fossil fuels—coal, oil and latterly natural gas—and the other non-renewable material resources on which they depend. At the same time it has created the conditions for a population explosion especially in the less-developed parts of the world which can least afford to sustain it. For a burgeoning population puts intolerable strains on already overburdened support systems, impoverishing the countryside, increasing urban squalor and threatening mass starvation as well as the collapse of social institutions. Nor can the social dislocation this causes be confined to the LDCs. This is because their plight contributes to the production and export of potentially lethal commodities such as cocaine and heroin that fetch a high price on world markets, while causing growing pressures for international food assistance. This, in turn, places ever more burdensome demands on the soils of the world's croplands to the detriment of the agricultural resource base. Furthermore, since food production increasingly relies on energy-intensive measures such as the use of chemical fertilisers, pesticides and irrigation equipment, the oil and gas on which they depend are bound to become scarce and hence more expensive, in turn driving up the price of foodstuffs.

Destruction of the ecosphere

Already, the chemicals used in the attempt to produce high crop yields are taking their toll in that they destroy natural soil fertility. As a consequence there is loss of organic matter, erosion, desertification and so forth, to say nothing of the hazards chemicals pose to water supplies and which produce health problems for livestock and humans alike, posing, so it is said, a serious threat to the sperm count. At the same time, the chemical pesticides are already beginning to prove counterproductive—encouraging the appearance of new and more ravenous insects that are immune to existing pesticides but not before these have themselves destroyed natural biological control mechanisms, introducing further perils into the food chain.

According to the environmentalists, our current habits threaten not only the land. We also pose daily hazards to the oceans. Already the harvesting of edible fish is in decline due to a mixture of overfishing and pollution—the product of the dumping into the seas of toxic wastes, sewage, refuse and other kinds of effluent. Meanwhile fresh water and bird-life are also at risk from pollutants, sewage, salinisation and the like.

At the same time we are also degrading the atmosphere. We pollute the air and cause acid rain through burning or otherwise releasing into the atmosphere fossil fuels and producing synthetic gases—so called CFCs. This in turn has adverse effects on our wildlife, crops, soils, lakes and buildings and takes a toll of our lungs. In addition, there is the dangerous depletion of the protective ozone layer in the earth's atmosphere which increases the amount of ultra-violet and other cosmic radiation reaching the surface of the planet and in turn causes a 'greenhouse' effect. This does serious damage to our food crops, increases the incidence of skin cancer and interferes with our genetic programming. Although the main culprits in causing acid rain are the developed countries which consume so much fossil fuel, the LDCs, the environmentalists claim, create a serious problem of their own by their heavy dependence on firewood to supply most of their energy needs. In order to maintain the supply they are obliged to destroy large areas of forest; but recently there has been an added incentive to cut down large areas of forest, including rainforest ie to make way for cattle ranches to satisfy export demands. Each year, according to environmentalist Norman Myers, an area of rainforest about the size of the UK is lost to the logger and the rancher.[3] The process of deforestation not only destroys plant and wildlife, it also interferes with the precarious balance of fragile tropical soils and soil nutrients. With tree cover gone, more heat is returned to the atmosphere, local moisture stocks are depleted and as a consequence wind and rainfall patterns and local temperatures are disturbed. All this threatens the environment in which trees, grasses or crops grow, and has a wider effect on world climatological patterns. Hence recent record droughts in Africa, the record floods in the American mid-West and so on.

Overpopulation

Indeed, it is the very interdependence of the problems of developing and developed countries that the environmentalists posit. As they see it, pollution and resource depletion are problems not just for the 'centre' countries. After all, lethal chemical cocktails adversely affect the whole planet. In any case, the consumption and production patterns of the northern hemisphere must contribute heavily to the stress on the environment throughout this overpopulated planet when the demand on the earth's scarce resources of an average American family is perhaps 20 or more times that of a peasant family in India. At the same time the problems of overpopulation cannot be confined just to the Third World since their economic, social and political effects are world-wide. A burgeoning population in any country puts pressure on food resources well beyond that country's frontiers and can also be a catalyst for either war, imperialism or mass migration.

In the case of Japan in the 1930s, the population explosion clearly provided the stimulus for both war and imperialism. As for migration, there is no doubt that growing numbers from the Third and Second Worlds (the former European Communist countries) are making their way to the First World, hoping to build a new life for themselves and their families. During the past two decades, for example, at least seven million Mexicans and Central Americans have migrated, legally or illegally, to the United States. The result is that today there are more Mexicans in Los Angeles than in any other city except the Mexican capital, while in Miami Spanish seems to have become the first language. There are increasing migrations of South-East Asians to Australasia; of Turks, North Africans, Sub-Saharan Africans, South Asians and Eastern Europeans to Western Europe; and a considerable influx of non-Europeans claiming some sort of Jewish ancestry to Israel—each migration producing significant socio-political changes and testing tolerance of foreign immigration to almost breaking point.

The fetish for industrialisation

Finally, most environmentalists would claim that the widespread belief among both First and Third World leaders that the solution to underdevelopment and Third World poverty lies in industrialisation is profoundly mistaken. In the view of those who contributed to the famous team efforts known as *The Limits to Growth* of 1972, and *The Global 2000 Report* to the President of 1981, as long as the poor nations seek to emulate the richer and the richer to continue on their present profligate path, the total collapse of civilisation through the depletion and destruction of the environment is virtually inevitable. The main problem they argue is one of what is called 'exponential growth'—a steady growth which in the end produces surprising and sometimes shocking results. For example even a comparatively modest annual rate of growth such as a 2 per cent rise in population or of economic activity or of ozone depletion can mean that they double their size in only 35 years. As the economist Kenneth Boulding observed: 'Anyone who believes that exponential growth can continue indefinitely in a finite world is either a madman or an economist.'

Not surprisingly such an argument sounds hollow to many Third World leaders. It has the ring of special pleading by the affluent, who have it all and want to keep it that way. But if the environmentalists have their way, then many of the LDCs could be trapped between the inequities of today's distribution of global wealth and the limits to growth which the Greens assert are imposed by the ecological crisis. What is more, many of the LDCs would have no way of building up a supply of capital to invest in industrialisation even if they wanted to. As importers of finished products they often find themselves having to pay ever higher prices for the manufactures they need. If the Green message is accepted is there nothing the people of the Third World countries can do to rid themselves of the cycle of poverty and deprivation?

18.5 SOME GREEN ANSWERS

Those Greens that still see a future for this planet—such as Johan Galtung, Kenneth Boulding, Herbert Girardet and the Gaia Movement—provide a number of different answers but all based on the notion that in both rich and poor nations there has to be a radical change in our view of ourselves in relation to nature, that we have to learn to see the human race as existing in a very fragile biosphere which we continue to abuse at our peril.[4] Beyond that what are the LDCs to do? First, they must sacrifice development of 'high-tech' industries in favour of more labour-intensive enterprise, using more modest intermediate and low technologies, as it is claimed China has done with success. Second, they will have to curb population growth through family planning advice and free contraceptives. But the developed countries have to make their contribution by providing food assistance, by being prepared to pay more for the resources imported from the LDCs and to allow far greater access to the export manufactures of the LDCs. If the LDCs are to change their patterns of reproduction and development, then the developed countries have to scale down their consumption. Finally, it is argued, the solution to the environmental crisis can only be found in a global context; if the world is to have a future it requires international cooperation and planning and the creation of new global institutions.

18.6 SOME CORRECTIVES

There in brief is the ecologist's argument. What we make of it is likely to depend on our existing presuppositions. It is, however, worth pointing out that prophets of doom are sometimes mistaken and that those who concentrate on the ills of self or society often fail to notice what is positive. It is clear that the world was never on the verge of the paradise which some, especially 19th-century theorists, envisaged. But has it ever been on the verge of destruction, as a host of mid- to late 20th-century creative artists, philosophers, strategists and environmentalists have suggested?

As against what CND was saying in the 1950s and 1960s, the world did not perish even though it failed to disarm. As against the political prophets of doom, 1984 came and went without the universal police state. And what many environmentalists have portrayed as 'irreversible' depletion of resources may well have to be revised in the light of recent discoveries: first, of manganese nodules and other such mineral deposits on the sea-bed which appear to be self-generating and therefore renewable; second, of fossil fuels which though not renewable are frequently being discovered in unexpected places, so that the indices of available supplies are constantly being revised upwards. Further, what many environmentalists regarded as irreversible degradation can, in fact, be reversed. Up until 40 years ago, London was known for its life-threatening 'pea-soupers', its 'smogs', its smoke-filled fogs. Not any longer, since the invention of smokeless fuels and the development of electric or gas central heating. Just as certain aspects of London's environment have been altered positively, so has its river. In T.S. Eliot's poem *The Wasteland*, 'The river sweats oil and tar'. When that was written, anyone who fell or ventured to swim in the Thames was at risk, so polluted had it become. Then in the 1960s it was cleaned up and salmon began to be discovered round about Richmond, Barnes and Hammersmith. Though it is fairly dirty again, we have learnt that it is perfectly possible to clean it up as long as someone is prepared to foot the bill. True, London suffers, as does Los Angeles, Athens, Istanbul and many other major cities from the carbon-monoxide gases emitted, among other things, by the motor car. But, again, the situation is not irreversible. When the electric car comes on stream the level of air pollution should fall, and already many cities have benefited from unleaded petrol, the catalytic converter, the kind of public transport policy the government has refused to finance in Britain, heavy taxes and tolls on private motoring and generous provision for the humble bicycle.

As with pollution, so with population: many of the doom-laden forecasts have turned out to be somewhat wide of the mark. A recent report in a leading scientific journal indicates that though world population is indeed growing apace, it is at a lower rate than had been widely predicted;[5] drastic curbs on population have been very much the government policy in China since Mao's death and for a time in India where Mrs Gandhi had promoted male vasectomy as a method of birth control. Finally the evidence of climatological change caused supposedly by carbon emissions is highly suspect. For one thing from the 1940s to the 1970s while carbon dioxide, methane and other 'greenhouse gases' were pouring into the atmosphere, global temperatures actually fell, and some in the scientific community were talking of the possibility of a new ice age. The 'greenhouse effect' is now said to be largely a natural phenomenon coming from water vapour in the atmosphere which warms the earth by trapping some of the heat from the sun. Without it the average temperature would be far below zero and the earth would probably resemble the planet Mars. In this sense, some measure of 'global warming' is an absolute necessity.[6]

As for the change of life-style sought by environmentalists, to a degree this has already begun to happen. How many dare wear a fox fur or a mink coat these days? How many would think of buying a 'gas-guzzling' car? What self-respecting middle-sized town does not have one or more bottle-banks? And who would have thought that it would become 'politically correct' not to smoke or to eat meat or chic to eat organically grown fruit and vegetables from bio-degradable containers?

Those who believe that in order to survive on this planet we need to dissolve the state system, which rests on the basis of collective selfishness, and totally to transform our political and economic existence have to face the fact that the state system is unlikely to be replaced in the forseeable future. Even the most modest attempts at international ecological co-operation, like the 'Earth Summit' in Rio in 1992, have had disappointing results.[7] There is probably much that can be done to improve the quality of life on this planet without having to alter unduly the present nature of the world political system. Nor is it necessary to look only to governments to make the requisite contribution since some beneficial changes can be made at the local level: some by business corporations, some by individuals. Here, then, are some modest proposals for saving the universe, but since the approach here resists policy science, few are addressed to governments and none is regarded as a pancea.

18.7 TO 'SAVE' THE UNIVERSE!

First as individuals we can walk more, cycle more, use our rivers more, insulate our houses better and invest more in solar energy. We can use energy-saving fluorescent lights more, recycle a great deal more, share cars and use our gardens and patios much more productively. If we have shares in multinationals we can turn up at shareholders' meetings and hold the directors to account if their enterprises are less than friendly environmentally. As a community we might invest more in public transport, lead-free petrol and catalytic converters, plant more trees and grasses, encourage organic farming and horticulture, cut back on cattle that eat and excrete too much and pesticides that also pollute too much, package less, conserve more water (possibly through a market approach), build smaller dams, give tax advantages to those with ingenious conservation schemes, decommission nuclear plants where they are found to be in danger of producing hazardous waste or emitting harmful rays, finance more small labour-intensive projects and encourage safe sex and family planning. Finally, we might propel into the stratosphere balloons filled with ozone to burst in low pressure where the ozone layer is particularly thin and project dust into the atmosphere if we think we need protection from the 'greenhouse effect'!

18.8 THE OPPORTUNITIES WE FACE

To conclude, even if some Green fears may be exaggerated, the basic theory concerning exponential growth is probably substantially valid and in this regard the rise of ecological awareness in the West and beyond is a positive development. For anything that helps to combat ignorance and carelessness with respect to our global commons and serves as an antidote to complacency can only do good. On the other hand what is also needed is an appreciation of the opportunities as well as the dangers the planet faces, in terms of the possibilities of mental, intellectual, emotional and spiritual growth through education and the technological revolution; if we can get the dangers and opportunities into perspective, the future should be reasonably secure.

NOTES

1. From a letter written to Bertrand Russell and quoted in Karl, F.R., *Joseph Conrad: the three lives*, New York, 1979, pp. 137–8.
2. The following analysis owes much to Myers, N., *The Gaia Atlas of Future Worlds*, London, Robertson McCarta, 1990.
3. Ibid., p. 28.
4. See, for example, Boulding, K., *Three Faces of Power*, San Fransisco, Sage, 1989 and Girardet, H., *Earthrise: How we can heal our injured planet*, London, Paladin, 1992.
5. Robey, B., Rotstein, S. and Morris, L., 'The fertility decline in developing countries', *Scientific American*, December 1993, pp. 30–7.
6. Salmon, J., 'Greenhouse Anxiety', *Commentary*, 12 July 1993 and Kenny, A., 'The earth is fine: the problem is the Greens', *The Spectator*, 12 March 1994.
7. Tickell, C., 'The world after the summit meeting at Rio', *The Washington Quarterly*, spring 1993.

CHAPTER 19

PRESCRIPTIONS AND PROSPECTS FOR PEACE

In the West we talk loosely of the 'post-war era', of the second world war as 'the last war' and of the present time as one of 'peace'. Yet for many people from Bosnia to Somalia, from Afghanistan to Angola and well beyond, war is still quite acceptable as a means of furthering political ends. And since 1945 there have been several hundred such conflagrations to prove it.

There are several ways of trying to account for this melancholy statistic. Many a sociologist might see it as a reflection of forces well beyond the control of those obliged to fight. Some, indeed, would view the soldier and the civilian that gets caught in the crossfire as mere cannon fodder for the ambitions of unscrupulous leaders. The international historian, on the other hand, might see those leaders themselves as being at the mercy of pressures international, transnational and domestic which may make the decision to go to war almost inescapable. Yet others— biologists, psychologists and anthropologists, perhaps—might explain the persistence of warfare not so much in terms of predicaments and situations as in a disposition inherent in human nature.

But surely people also want peace? Yes, of course, but not necessarily if the price is submission to the bully, the tyrant, the oppressor, to those who have threatened to kill our kith and kin and destroy our way of life. In the Near East, the Middle East, the Indian sub-continent, South-East Asia, Central America, Southern Africa and in Northern Ireland, there are many who would feel a sense of shame if they failed to confront what they see as the forces of injustice. Not even the tragedy of mass starvation on both sides of the barricades in Afghanistan, Angola, Somalia or Rwanda has been enough to bring an end to fratricidal strife. Even in places remote from any conceivable battlefield we find war veterans speaking with pride and nostalgia of past hostilities, when there was a sense of solidarity and common purpose, when even the dullest task was dignified in the name of the cause.

If the past is strewn with the corpses of the fallen, it is also, paradoxically, littered with the failed hopes and frustrated expectations of those who sought to limit the scope, scale and frequency of hostilities. But is the attempt to tame war doomed to futility?

Revolutionists like Marx would claim that short of the millennium, most anti-war panaceas must fail. For though they believe in the potential unity of humankind they tend also to be short-term pessimists, sceptical of palliatives which in their view deal only with symptoms and not fundamental causes. On the other hand, Rationalists like Grotius, Locke or Woodrow Wilson would have an array of answers, for they see war as essentially a kind of social disease for which the correct diagnosis might produce a number of remedies, antidotes or cures. In contrast, Realists from Thucydides to Morgenthau and Waltz would be far less optimistic, tending to see war as a contingency of the international system and fearing that even were we to locate its cause or causes, we might still encounter almost insuperable obstacles in trying to find a foolproof remedy. On the other hand they can also be short-term optimists, believing that particular wars might be avoided by stabilising the international system and finding the most appropriate conditions for defusing or neutralising the kinds of tensions that can escalate into war. Like Rationalists, they are also interested in trying to find ways of limiting the scope and effects of warfare.

19.1 REGULATING WARFARE THROUGH CODES OF CONDUCT

Since war is about achieving political purposes through violence, the idea of applying rules to tame it would appear to be a contradiction in terms. Yet there have been many such endeavours. The medieval codes of chivalry gave a measure of protection at least to knights, even if to no one else. Then the natural law theorists attempted to introduce the notion of proportionality into the means of pursuing hostilities—an eye for an eye, but no more. More recently there have been a number of international conventions relating to the Red Cross, prisoners of war, the treatment of the wounded, the protection of civilians in occupied lands and so forth.

Anyone surveying the vast tally of destruction and devastation from, say, the Thirty Years war down to the horrors of Bosnia might be forgiven for being sceptical about the value of such codes. Yet if millions have perished due to the failure of governments to honour them, millions more have been saved or assisted by those same codes. For example no matter how badly the Nazis treated their own citizens both before and during the second world war, Germany's treatment of British POWs was on the whole correct. The prisoners were able to exercise, to receive food parcels and letters from home and there was the occasional swap of POWs through the good offices of the Swiss. Moreover, prisoner exchanges which tend to occur in the aftermath of hostilities are often negotiated before they end. Whether implementation of codes of conduct in wartime is in deference to moral principle, to the thought of reciprocity or to its propaganda value need not concern us here. The fact is that such codes can, for whatever reason, affect the conduct of war.[1]

19.2 LIMITING THE SCOPE OF WARFARE

When two parties resort to violence, third parties can so easily get sucked into their conflict either by choice, as when they ally themselves with one or other protagonist, or by accident, as when their people, property and/or territory get caught in the crossfire. For centuries there was not much they could do about the latter, unless they had sufficient strength or diplomatic skill to deter the warring sides from incursion or else possessed a geographical advantage affording them protection: like Switzerland, surrounded by mountains; Iceland, small, remote and largely icebound; or the United States, an impregnable fortress distant from the main theatres of international conflict.

'Neutrality' and 'neutralisation'

The development of international law in the 17th century gave a new dimension to neutrality. 'Neutrality' was now a legal status in which the non-belligerent was to enjoy rights and duties pertaining to, among other things, trade, commerce, innocent passage for ships, as well as freedom from the fray. In the 19th century another term entered the diplomatic vocabulary—'neutralisation'—in which legal limits were set on the belligerent activities of certain states.[2] For Switzerland, Belgium and Luxembourg in the 19th century and the Vatican, Austria and Laos in the 20th, neutralisation meant permanent neutrality. They could maintain armed forces but enter no alliance commitments, while their neutral status was to be strictly respected and guaranteed by the powers. Sadly, during the second world war only five states succeeded in retaining the neutrality that 20 had declared in 1939. That today only Switzerland and Austria remain of the neutralised nations—the latter contemplating entry into the European Union—indicates how precarious in practice is the legal status of both neutral and neutralised. Generally speaking, where there are hostilities between small, weak states in a region of small, weak states—as was Central Europe in the 17th century—the rights of neutrals tend to be disregarded; it is likewise the case where there is a widespread and protracted war fought to validate a creed or to secure unconditional submission—as in the French Revolutionary wars and the first and second world conflagrations.

On the other hand where wars are fought for limited objectives or for the settlement of specific issues, with each belligerent fearful of converting non-belligerents into enemies, as during the 1870 Franco–Prussian war, neutral rights are more likely to be respected. Perhaps the circumstances are most favourable for neutrality when there is a multiple or complex balance of great powers, as in the period 1815–1914.

'Neutralism' and 'non-alignment'

If the preservation of neutrality depends on the character of warfare, what determines the success or otherwise of what is called 'neutralism' and 'non-alignment'? Here we need to define our terms. In fact both concepts are comparatively recent additions to the political vocabulary. Unlike 'neutrality' and 'neutralisation', they are not about legal status; they have to do with policy options. The term 'neutralism' emerged among the domestic critics of French policy in the late 1940s and indicated distrust of alliances in general and of membership of NATO in particular.[3] Though at the time its protagonists had little effect on policy, their ideas contributed to the development of the concept of 'non-alignment', taken up by a number of governments in the 1950s. Nowadays non-alignment has economic overtones. It has become a movement of LDCs seeking a new international economic order. In its original, now defunct, sense, however, it meant dissociation from the cold war, but whether or not that posture could be sustained depended largely on calculations in Moscow and Washington. Though both superpowers had global interests, each had to calibrate the political, economic and social costs of securing them by means of intervention. The higher the perceived cost the greater was their constraint, and correspondingly, the greater the capacity of countries to pursue non-alignment. Those most at risk were states like Laos, Afghanistan, Grenada and Nicaragua which happened to figure in what a great power claimed as its 'backyard', and at moments of extreme cold war tension their credibility as members of the non-aligned movement was seriously imperilled.

19.3 LIMITING THE INCIDENCE OF WAR

Given the evident lack of equality within and between states—the fact that there are countries large and small, rich and poor, developed and under-developed, satisfied and dissatisfied—it is not at all clear that peace has the same salience for all. But any suggested technique or procedure for curbing the resort to arms has to begin with an analysis of the causes of war, and, as indicated in Chapter 13, there are at least three broadly distinct modes of explanation,[4] one relating to human nature, a second to socio-political systems, a third having to do with the system of states. Those favouring the first method of explanation would go to work on human beings, either *en masse* or on key individuals in decision-making, trying either to change their nature or the way it finds expression. Those of the second school would attempt to remove or transform certain sorts of socio-political regimes. Adherents of the third would attempt to tackle the thorny question of collective insecurity in a world lacking government or moral consensus.

Combating anti-social drives

With regard to the first mode of explanation, favoured by many psychologists, biologists and theologians, if war is attributable ultimately to some defect in human nature, then it is to that same nature we have to look for the antidote. If, for example, humankind is characterised by self-interest, aggression and acquisitiveness or by irrational impulses fostered by perceived deprivation, then the remedy has to be sought by overcoming, redirecting or suppressing such drives.

World government

For Thomas Hobbes, life was likely to prove 'nasty, solitary, brutish and short' if the passions were allowed free rein, and his 'solution' was strong and effective government. But his concern was primarily with the domestic context. Not only does the introduction of such governments not solve the problem of international conflict, it may well make it worse, which is why some modern Realists, including Morgenthau, take the Hobbesian formula to its logical conclusion and advocate world government. But there are at least two problems with this formulation. First, how do you get it? The idea that states jealous of their sovereignty would willingly hand over their powers to a world authority would seem on present evidence to be highly implausible, save in the wake of some unforeseen tragedy—a nuclear or environmental holocaust or inter-planetary conflict. If the world authority were to be the product of world conquest, it would hardly be desirable. Furthermore, if we are talking of an effective world government, it would probably need a monopoly on weaponry and as such could become the most dictatorial as well as the most powerful body the world has ever seen, and possibly the harbinger of a world civil war.

Re-education

If not world government, then what about a world run more or less along lines prescribed by certain psychologists and behavioural scientists? People like John Burton and James Rosenau seem to believe that the best way to deal with the persistence of war is to re-educate the individual, to change the human conceptual apparatus, to bring about, in the jargon, a

'paradigm shift' ie a psycho-social adjustment.[5] Exactly how such intellectual therapy would be administered, financed and monitored, by and
upon whom is not exactly clear, but the prospectus is. It would, among
other things, encourage a greater understanding of the predicaments of
others, discourage a zero-sum approach to conflict, reduce expectations of
war by fostering thoughts of conflict avoidance, conflict management and
resolution and probably foster the use of 'politically correct' language. It
would also appeal directly to self-interest by suggesting that war was
unprofitable, even for the victors, given its effects on national budgets,
consumption patterns and employment prospects. And it would also offer
a variety of techniques for non-violent resistance in the event of an invasion by a foreign power whose forces have not been so re-educated. But of
what value would the enterprise be if taken up by countries like
Switzerland and Sweden but not by, say, Iraq and Serbia? And would it
work anyway? Does greater familiarity with the predicaments of others
necessarily increase either sympathy or willingness to compromise?
Conceivably if Chamberlain had understood Hitler a little bit better,
Britain would have declared war in 1938 instead of waiting till 1939. And
were the second world war or the cold war due to a failure of understanding or the very real understanding of the existence of a serious conflict of
interest and values?

Redirection

The psychologist William James suggests a third approach for tackling
those anti-social impulses that can result in war—to redirect them.[6] His
idea was to harness an individual's basic energies into socially useful
pursuits, fighting nature perhaps by building dams or dikes or making the
deserts bloom, undertaking exacting physical labour such as coal mining
(assuming there are any mines left open to exploit), or feats of endurance
from sports like boxing to pioneering activities such as scaling Mount
Everest or conquering the North Pole. James was also of the belief that
spectator sports were a useful safety valve. But since the kinds of tasks
James prescribes have long been a feature of societies both at war and at
peace, there is little reason to suppose that a few more miners, boxers,
Everest explorers and Everton supporters are likely to make any difference
to the incidence of war.

Transforming socio-political structures

Authoritarian regimes

Regarding the second mode of explanation, if war is an external manifestation of domestic circumstance—a projection internationally of certain sorts

of internal structures—then such structures have either to be dissolved, radically transformed or destroyed. There are, in other words, certain kinds of states, governments and social systems especially prone to acts of external violence. The most familiar theory is that elitist or authoritarian administrations put humankind most at risk, for such regimes are conflict-prone either because they put a premium on national glory or because they need an activist foreign policy to direct attention away from domestic discontents. It is an analysis, incidentally, which would unite philosophers as diverse as Kant and Marx, political analysts of many different hues and a motley crew of statesmen from Woodrow Wilson to Margaret Thatcher.

Demagogies

To such arguments there is a less familiar, though no less formidable answer. It is precisely the kind of internal discipline and order provided by hierarchical government structures that can keep in check those popular passions that can lead to war. Indeed, there is a tradition of thought from Plato, through Burke, probably including the Webbs and certainly many a Whitehall mandarin that holds that it is when established hierarchies decay through either inept leadership or demagogic agitation that the propensity to external violence is greatest.[7] If it is claimed that sane and decent people could not possibly hold to such a theory today, what about the view widely shared in the West that men like Tito and Gorbachev were to be preferred to their successors because they were far more adept at exercising firm and responsible leadership and thereby keeping a check on foreign adventurism?

Capitalism

Controversy rages over economic as well as political systems. Abolish capitalism, say the Marxists, and you abolish war. In one fell swoop you do away with the class system which projects conflict from the domestic to the international stage and rid the world of arms manufacturers and all those in the military–industrial complex with a vested interest in the production and distribution of weaponry. Not so, say the defenders of the free market. If you abolish capitalism you give governments far too much control over human affairs which is dangerous for world peace. As examples they could cite the troubled relations between most of the former Communist countries, and in particular the hostilities between China and Vietnam and between Vietnam and Cambodia and the legacy of bitterness between the Soviet Union and China. They could also, presumably, refer to Moscow's military interventions in East Berlin, Hungary, Czechoslovakia and Afghanistan. But to many a non-Communist Marxist such a critique would be largely irrelevant since in their view none of the countries just mentioned represented true socialism. Those more sympathetic to Marxism–Leninism (ie Communism) would argue that the anti-Communist mistakes crisis behaviour in a Communist ruled state for general policy and that to criticise the Socialist countries for their nationalism is to obscure the real contribution such states make to peace by eliminating booms and slumps, vast disparities of wealth and mass unemployment. The debate continues...

Nationalism: pros and cons

The relations between the 'state' and the 'nation' raise a further controversy about the foreign implications of certain national systems. If we take the state to be a territorial entity of legal and diplomatic consequence and the nation to comprise a group of people sharing a common bond of political or cultural kinship, then it is clear that state and nation frequently fail to coincide. But does this affect the cause of peace? The 19th-century Italian activist Mazzini thought it did, but when he proclaimed the peaceable propensities of national self-determination in the 1820s, the nation was seen as neither exclusive nor aggressive. At that time love for one's own country was still widely regarded as a prerequisite of service to humankind. Good liberal that he was, Mazzini believed in the virtues of diversity and in the harmony of interests between the nations.[8] Yet within two to three decades, a fellow Italian was taking a very different view. 'If only we did for ourselves what we do for our nation', said the statesman, Cavour, 'what rascals we should be.'[9] And in the 20th century men like Mussolini, Hitler and their foreign admirers began to manipulate the symbols of nationhood to destroy some of the liberal values nationalism had originally promoted. While giving large groups of people a sense of belonging, all too often the good of one society was sought at the expense of another. What began as a policy to unite within stable frontiers people sharing a sense of national solidarity could so easily develop into the most savage imperialism, justified by some such national slogan as *lebensraum* ('living space') or restoring 'the glory that was Rome'. Not for the first time was a noble ideal debased, and there seems little warrant for suggesting that the cause of peace is best served by either the grant of national self-determination or, as the late Professor Elie Kedourie claimed, by the containment of the nationalist sentiments on which it is based.[10]

Other prescriptions

In addition to the prescriptions already detailed, there are the claims of those who would commend to us a world of states united by a common religious bond. However, the record, past and present, of, say, Christianity, Islam, Judaism or Buddhism is hardly more edifying than the record of Marxism–Leninism, and the aspiration of universal brotherhood is all too often confounded by either human frailty or political irresponsibility.

What of the idea of some behavioural scientists that peace would be better served by a selection process which would exclude the unintelligent and the irrational from leadership? Apart from the question-begging nature of the exercise, who is to say whether any particular form of selection is better than any other? How and by whom are the processes of selection to be introduced? What if some of the leaders that some of the scientists regard as 'ill-chosen' and 'ill-informed' are popular and/or insist on clinging to office? Are they to be removed by force?

As for the feminist notion that there would be greater harmony if there were more women among the political elites, however seductive an idea, it is not always overwhelmingly obvious that when such formidable ladies as Golda Meier, Indira Gandhi, Sirimavo Bandaranaike, Isabelita Peron, Margaret Thatcher, Eugenia Charles, Benazir Bhutto, Tansu Ciller and the like take the helm there is a perceptible lessening of international tension. On the other hand since comparatively few women have made it to the top, where power and value structures tend in any case to be largely man-made, it is rather too early for a conclusive judgment.

Transforming the international system

But suppose it is not a particular kind of decision-making structure, but the whole structure of international society that is the problem. It is, after all, a society without government, in which power is dispersed and in which in the absence of any effective law enforcing authority, force often has to act as the arbiter in disputes. Professor Northedge's notion that war is 'a contingency or liability of the [international] system in much the same way as unemployment is a contingent liability of the market economy, divorce a contingency of married life'[11] brings us to the third mode of explanation. War occurs because there is basically nothing to prevent it. If its incidence is to be curbed, there must be some technique or stratagem to act as constraint or deterrent.

Transcendence or monopolisation of power

Once again, there is an array of pet schemes and nostrums, but at this particular level of analysis, many of the antidotes are rooted in concepts of power and what to do about it. One major difficulty, as has been repeatedly emphasised, is lack of agreement on the meaning of 'power'. Even if it is taken to mean, in Bertrand Russell's phrase, 'the capacity to produce

intended effects', and by implication, the capacity to deny to others whatever adverse effects they intend, what is to be done? The Revolutionists
look forward to the day when the instrumentality of power politics, the
state, withers away. Their solution, thus, is the transcendence of power. At
the other end of the spectrum the arch-Realists seek a monopoly of power
by a world government. In between there is a range of proposed solutions
for constraining power.

Erosion of power—disarmament

First, consider its erosion. The *Old Testament* reference to turning 'swords
into ploughshares and spears into pruning hooks' was an aspiration, not a
policy. However, in the 20th century, the Soviet foreign commissar,
Litvinov, among others, tried to bring it into practical politics, repeatedly
laying before the League of Nations his proposal for general and complete
disarmament—general, to embrace all states; complete, to include all
weapons save those needed for internal order. Needless to say it was a
non-starter. His argument that a world without arms would be a world
without war seemed, frankly, incredible. After all, long before modern
weapons were invented, humans had engaged in organised hostilities,
and clearly they could always do so as long as they had an array of sticks,
stones, iron bars, knives and broken bottles, to say nothing of their fists.
True, in a disarmed world war might become less frequent, less destructive and less extensive. None the less, in such a world some states would
still in effect have a military advantage over others since a nation's war
potential resides not simply in its armaments but in a whole complex of
economic, technological and demographic resources; and with the requisite know-how, the military capacity that had been disestablished could
soon be reestablished and discarded weaponry reinstated.

Yet all this is beside the point. For on present evidence there is no
prospect whatever of most states agreeing to forego what in the final
analysis they rely on to preserve their sovereignty. What of less drastic
proposals such as partial, selective or unilateral disarmament? Here, again,
the historical record is none too encouraging.[12] If we learned anything
from the 1920s and 1930s, it is that the world does not necessarily become
more secure when some powers agree, as in the Washington Conference
of 1922, to scrap weapons that are already obsolete, or to freeze deployment of some kinds of weapons, as in the Anglo–German Naval Treaty of
1935, leaving them free to concentrate on others. Nor is the cause of peace
necessarily served when the non-aggression pacts pile up (after all, the
Soviet Union signed over a dozen in the 1930s and was at war with most
of the signatories within the decade) or when the weak deprive themselves of weapons which the strong refuse to yield as Belgium, Holland,
Norway, Denmark and so on found to their cost in 1940. The danger is

that such partial schemes can create disequilibrium in favour of the most advanced militarily or else leave countries defenceless against predators. On the other hand recent agreements between the United States and what was the Soviet Union on military disengagement and on strategic and intermediate nuclear arms reductions suggest that a measure of meaningful disarmament is possible, but only after there is already a perceptible lessening of international tension.

Regulation of power—arms control

What of a much more modest ambition—arms control? Here the emphasis is not on arms reductions as such but on perceived balance and equilibrium where the states are asked to exercise restraint regarding the production, testing, deployment or use of certain weapons in order to keep in step with potential adversaries. If, as an example, we take the Geneva Protocol on poison gas, the record has been none too bad: the Italians used it in Abyssinia in 1935 and the Iraqis in the Gulf war against Iran, but most other states have been comparatively restrained. Within the past 30 years or so several more arms control accords have been initialled including the partial nuclear test ban treaty, the nuclear non-proliferation treaty, the ban on weapons in outer space and on the sea bed and the anti-ballistic missile treaty. On the whole these, too, have been observed. The main difficulties relate to negotiation rather than implementation. What are the problems that generally have to be overcome before agreement is possible?[13]

First, establishing a basis of trust is no easy matter, considering that the proliferation of arms is itself a manifestation of lack of trust among the nations. What often makes the creation of confidence all the more intractable is the memory of past arms negotiations in which each side would put forward a proposal with a built-in advantage for itself, thereby putting the onus for rejection on the other side, which is then accused of 'war mongering'. Even when the problem of trust is somehow overcome and substantive discussions begin, there is often a problem of definition. In the 1930s, for example, arms talks were constantly bedevilled by failure to agree on what constituted an 'offensive' and what a 'defensive' weapon. Many delegates would regard as 'offensive' and hence in need of control, any weapon their enemy possessed and they did not—hardly a promising basis for negotiations. More recently, nuclear discussions tended to get bogged down in arguments about what is or is not an 'intermediate' or a 'strategic' nuclear weapon. The West tended to regard anything that hit Europe but not the United States as 'intermediate'. The Soviet Union tended to regard anything that could hit it from whichever source as 'strategic'. A third problem relates to the extremely complex arithmetic any such agreement must involve. After all, power inventories are never symmetrical. One side may have more ground-launched, another more sea-based missiles; one side more launchers, another more warheads. One may have more potential enemies; another more advanced technology. Thus the attempt to balance out such considerations in a package to preserve equilibrium may be a lengthy process. If there is eventual accord, there then has to be some means of inspection and verification to prevent cheating—again, no easy matter when lethal weapons are becoming miniaturised and can be hidden away. Finally, how is any arms control arrangement to be enforced? What kinds of sanctions for the cheats, given that violation might well confer an unfair political advantage?

Perhaps the impetus to reduce or scrap arms rests on a misconception about the nature of arms and of arms races. Many assume that weapons are the basic cause of war. But they are not. They are mere instruments in the hands of people who feel they have cause to fight. If people decide against armed hostilities, they are not used. Another related and widely shared notion is that arms races cause war. Yet neither the Anglo–French arms race in the late 19th and early 20th century, nor the Anglo–American naval race in the first third of the 20th century, nor the superpower arms build-up from the 1940s to the 1990s resulted in hostilities. Further, had there been an Anglo–German arms race in the 1930s instead of unilateral rearmament by Germany, Hitler might conceivably have been deterred by Britain's warning not to invade Poland. The fact is that arms races can be as much a guarantor of peace as a harbinger of war. Largely a reflection or symptom rather than a cause of international tension, arms races will tend to subside when tensions ease.[14] In this sense, it is perhaps the tensions rather than the weapons that should merit more urgent specialist consideration.

Community of power—collective security

As to proposals for a community of power in the guise of 'collective security', in which the states join together to deter and if necessary defeat aggression, it has a number of weaknesses, some of which were rehearsed in Chapter 14. First there is the problem of involving every state in the scheme; then there is the difficulty of getting agreement on whether an aggression has indeed occurred, and here governments tend to be partisan, reluctant to admit that an ally might be an aggressor or a foe the victim of their ally's aggression. Further, even where there is agreement that an aggression has occurred, it is one thing to take action if the perpetrator is a small power, quite another when one or more great powers are involved. In any case, as we have constantly been reminded in the case of Bosnia, even when there is general agreement that the aggressor is a relatively minor power and that something has to be done to stop it sending signals that 'aggression pays', there may still be genuine doubt as to what to do—whether a concerted response would improve matters or possibly make things worse.

Pooling of power—federalism

As for proposals for pooling power through 'federalism',[15] given the evident persistence of people's attachment to their state, nation, tribe or locality, world federal union would nowadays appear to be on virtually nobody's agenda; while East Africa, the Caribbean and the Middle East are littered with examples of failed attempts at regional integration. Even though the EU is supposed to be a shining example of regional integration, the strains today are unmistakable. As we see from the all too frequent rows in France and Spain over fishing rights, the machinations over Maastricht and the differences over a common currency and defence policy, national sentiment tends to reassert itself the more that the exercise of sovereignty seems to be diminished. In any case, even if integration proceeded apace in Europe and in other regions, the kinds of inter-state conflicts that arise now would hardly disappear in a world of fewer but larger sovereign units.

Pooling of power—functionalism

With regard to the pooling of power through functional integration,[16] though resource or environmental problems may encourage governments to hand over some of their sovereign powers to international bodies of technical experts, it by no means follows that this must create a transfer of loyalties away from the national community or state. Nor, sadly, is there any warrant for the suggestion that the reduction of political conflict must flow from increased co-operation in trade and other non-political fields. After all, Germany was among Britain's best trading partners in 1939 and among the Soviet Union's in 1941 immediately prior to hostilities, while Washington and Tokyo had close economic ties before Japan's attack on Pearl Harbor. Furthermore, if modern technologies accentuate a sense of interdependence, they also facilitate the extension of government power within states. Hence the oft-noted paradox that the world is becoming simultaneously more unified and more fragmented. Certainly mutual awareness internationally does not necessarily engender mutual liking or respect, and, regrettably, some minds seem to narrow rather than broaden through foreign travel.

Balance of power

In respect of the balance of power as a proposed solution to the problem of war, the obvious question is what does one put into the equation? Is it merely a matter of megatonnages, throw weights and payloads or does it include the non-measurable like leadership skills, morale, cohesion and non-military assets such as technological skill and diplomatic expertise? If one does include all or some of these factors, how exactly does one assess whether or not some sort of balance or equilibrium has been struck? How, if some rough parity is deemed to exist, is the balance to be maintained in a world of rapid technological change? Do decisions relating to war and peace depend solely on calculations of power balances? What about national or leadership attitudes and aspirations?

Power hierarchy

Consider next power hierarchy, in the form of either a great power directorate—as after the Napoleonic wars—or a more subtle gradation of powers based on protection of the weak and deference to the strong—as in medieval times. Apart from the obvious question as to how in a dynamic world the hierarchy is to be sustained, there is the matter of the demand of the less privileged for justice. For all such hierarchies are likely at some stage to thwart the claim of the subordinate to equal treatment, and it is difficult to imagine the underprivileged, who constitute a majority in international society, allowing their interests to be indefinitely relegated for the sake of world order. The argument that peace depends on a preponderance of power, as in the case of the Roman Empire, would be open to similar objections.

Power dispersal

Finally, let us turn to perhaps the most bizarre of these power-based theories, subscribed to among others by Kenneth Waltz[17]—that of nuclear dispersal among virtually all the nations, giving each the capacity to inflict unacceptable damage on the others, and hence, so the argument goes, deterring attack from every other state. Apart from the obvious question of whether every state would in fact choose to have a nuclear capability, would all nuclear-endowed nations always be proof against attack—nuclear or conventional? What if there were technological breakthroughs—SDI-style—which led one power to believe it could attack another and fend off all possible retaliation from any source? What if one power were able to sabotage the nuclear installations of another? What if a less than rational leader were prepared to risk retaliation and launch a war for the sake of a religious or some other principle? The possibilitiess and permutations in a world of general and complete nuclear proliferation are endless.

19.4 THAT ELUSIVE FORMULA!

The almost inescapable conclusion is that a prescription for perpetual peace remains as elusive as ever. But any critical analysis of the proffered panaceas obliges us to crystallise our thoughts in response. Although this study is not concerned with policy recommendations or problem-solving, it can at least provide guidelines as to how, if not what, to think about limiting the incidence and effects of warfare. Those still searching for that elusive formula might care to consider the following suggestions:

(i)   That for any such formula to be viable, a consideration of the feasible must inform any discussion about the desirable.

(ii) That perhaps it is more feasible to look for palliatives rather than panaceas.

(iii) That an understanding of the kinds of tensions that can, but do not necessarily, escalate into war might yield valuable insights into how they might be deflected or defused.

(iv) That the diplomatic bargaining, third-party mediation and arbitration that have been among the time-honoured techniques for defusing or deflecting international tensions need to be supplemented by more novel procedures. These would include a technique used to considerable effect by both Henry Kissinger and Eduard Shevardnadze when in charge of the foreign affairs of their respective countries. Known as 'the pre-emptive concession', it involves giving away something prior to substantive discussions to sweeten the atmosphere and indicate seriousness of purpose. Another procedure is what is called 'graduated reciprocation in tension-reduction' (GRIT) which involves unilateral and unambiguous initiatives of a confidence-building character—small at first but of increasing import given a measure of reciprocity. If there are no reciprocal concessions, the process comes to an end, though it can be renewed at any time.

(v)   That the process of confidence-building does not have to be confined to diplomats and Foreign Office officials. A positive role as either adviser or participant can be played by research institutes and 'think tanks', informed bodies of journalists, financiers, bankers and entrepreneurs, special interest groups and lobbies as well as concerned individuals.

(vi) That confidence-building activity need not proceed on the basis of common ideals. After all, even the notion of 'peace' can mean different things to different people, ranging from the mere absence of war to a state of affairs in which 'justice' or 'harmony' in some sense prevails. It is sufficient, in a strategy to defuse or deflect tension, that the protagonists recognise common concerns, interests and perils (including the perceived danger of an escalation of their conflict if resentments and grievances are allowed to fester).

(vii) That the auguries are not unfavourable when increasingly and in many capitals of the world, IR graduates replace influential advisers and decision-makers whose insensitivity and ignorance of international politics are exceeded only by their persuasive power.

NOTES

1. For a comprehensive account of such codes and their implementation since the mid-18th century see Best, G., *Humanity in Warfare*, London, Methuen, 1983.
2. See, for example, Karsh, E., *Neutrality and Small States*, London, 1988 and Andren, N., 'On the meaning and uses of neutrality', *Cooperation and Conflict*, Volume 26, No. 2, 1991, pp. 67–83.
3. See Martin, L. (ed.), *Neutralism and Non-Alignment*, New York, Praeger, 1962.
4. As essayed in Waltz, K., *Man, the State and War*, New York, Columbia University Press, 1959.
5. Their arguments are analysed by Waltz, K., op. cit., pp. 42–79.
6. 'The moral equivalent of war' in *Memories and Studies*, New York, Longmans, 1912, pp. 262–72.
7. Kisker, G. (ed.), *World Tension*, New York, Prentice-Hall, 1951.
8. *Selected Writings*, Gangulee, N. (ed.) London, Lindsay Drummond, 1945.
9. See Salvadori, M., *Cavour and the Unification of Italy*, Princeton, Princeton University Press, 1961.
10. *Nationalism*, 3rd ed., London, Hutchinsons University Library, 1966.
11. *The International Political System*, London, 1976, p. 280.
12. See, for example, Bull, H., *The Control of the Arms Race*, London, Weidenfeld and Nicolson, 1961, especially pp. 30–64.
13. Ibid., pp. 65–76.
14. See, for example, Huntingdon, J.P., 'Arms Races: Pre-requisites and results', *Public Policy*, Harvard University, 1958.
15. See, Johnson J. (ed.), *Federal World Government*, New York, H.W. Wilson, 1948.
16. For a penetrating analysis of the integration theories (of which 'functionalism' is one) see Taylor, P., 'A conceptual typology of international organisation' in Groom, A.J.R. and Taylor, P., *Frameworks for International Cooperation*, London, Pinter, 1991, pp. 12–26.
17. As evidenced by his lecture on 'war' delivered at the LSE on 28 January 1993.

CHAPTER 20

AGENDA FOR THE TWENTY-FIRST CENTURY

Common observation has it that the repercussions of any explosion grow weaker the further they are from the point of origin. However, the 'knowledge explosion' seems to follow a different logic. Futurologists such as John Platt suggest that if by the end of the 18th century the sum total of human knowledge was doubling roughly every 50 years, by 1950 the interval had been shortened to some 10 years and by 1970 to five.[1] By this reasoning more than 90 per cent of our current scientific knowledge has accumulated since 1945. While such analyses beg the question of what is meant by 'scientific knowledge' and how precisely the appropriate calculations can be made, it is, none the less, indisputable that we are living in an age of enormously accelerated innovation and discovery.

Anyone aged 50 and over will have been born before the age of nuclear fusion, of jet engines and space rockets, of solar power, fibre optics and lasers, of molecular biology and genetic engineering, of transistors, satellite communications, fax machines, word processors and, of course, super-smart computers. But such innovations have had a profound effect on almost every aspect of contemporary life—economic, political, demographic, ecological and cultural—and it is against this background that the complex interlinkages that constitute international society have to be fashioned and understood.

Trying to make sense of such tumultuous developments and understand their implications will be a priority for the politicians, economists, financiers, ecologists, creative artists and other agenda-setters for the 21st century. What is already patently clear is that the agenda for the year 2000 will be vastly different from that of 1900. At the beginning of the century informed discussion in the world's major capitals centred around imperialism, monarchy and protectionism, European domination and national self-absorption expressed in the form of, for example, British 'jingoism', German naval expansion and American isolationism. But 'imperialism' is now a dirty word, as is 'protectionism', though, as explained earlier, both are still probably more widespread than generally realised. As for monarchy, it has lost its mystique nearly everywhere and where it still exists, even its symbolic, ceremonial functions tend to be little more than nominal. And even if the performance and potential of the European Union are being studied with interest in different parts of the globe, Europe no longer dominates world politics. Paradoxically, though much of the national self-assertiveness once so characteristic of the Western European state has been blunted, it has become one of the region's least attractive exports.

No matter how different the two agendas, they could share at least one common thread. As was pointed out in Chapter 18, at about the turn of the century there was some reassessment of the role science was playing in our lives, and it seems that the matter is again likely to be under review in the 21st century. In the light of some of the more controversial developments in weapons technology, nuclear physics, genetic engineering and the like, people are already asking: where is science taking us, will we want to go there and will its effects be generally beneficial or detrimental to the human race and the planet that has to sustain it?

Altogether it is reasonable to suppose that the agenda for the new century will be a mixture of the novel and the well worn, but four major and interlinked themes are likely to dominate. First, there is international security, a notion informed by the realisation that at the end of the 20th century the typical armed conflict is based on religious or ethnic antagonism and occurs within rather than between societies, and that instability, conflict and perceptions of threat in one part of the globe may have serious repercussions in another. After all, like a vortex, the bitter conflagration in what was Yugoslavia sucked in NATO, the European Union, the Conference on Security and Co-operation in Europe (CSCE), the Islamic Conference as well as the UN, and generated in turn a flood of refugees to countries both near and far. At the same time, with hopes of a 'new world order' confounded by the reality of a world seemingly in exceptional disorder as the familiar landscape of the cold war fades into history, the question of nuclear proliferation and in particular the dispersal of nuclear weapons through unofficial, possibly criminal channels, must loom large. The future role of the UN is virtually certain to be another key consideration. Is it to continue to be overstretched, underfunded and, in consequence, periodically humiliated in its inability to cope adequately with the multiplicity of tasks it is required to perform? Will it be properly financed or, alternatively, allowed, like its predecessor, the League, to decline into impotence and insignificance? Whatever the international community decides will affect the perception and treatment of other issues on the agenda, especially those regarding economic and social welfare, the environment and human rights.

The international economy is likely to constitute a second major item for the forthcoming agenda. Almost entirely unregulated a century or so ago, it became, for reasons elaborated in Chapter 17, an arena for 'global management' at the end of the second world war. However, the 'managers' have tended to come from the more affluent and industrialised countries, many of which practice a form of neo-mercantilism (how else could one characterise the European Union's Common External Tariff or Common Agricultural Policy?) while extolling the virtues of the market, and have been less than sympathetic to the pleas of the underprivileged for a New International Economic Order. As the economic gulf between the increasingly interdependent developed countries and the increasingly dependent and debt-ridden LDCs tends to widen, the question of whether or not something can or should be done to close the gap is likely to preoccupy the pundits. Though some may argue that 'charity begins at home', others, possibly worried about the implications of allowing the resentment and anger of the world's poor to fester, may find the answer in terms of subsidised loans, government-to-government grants, most-favoured nation trading agreements, technical assistance and/or the cancellation of debt, bi- or multi-laterally. On the other hand there must always be the fear that without some check on population growth, many trapped in a vicious circle of poverty and deprivation may find no way out beyond the cultivation, use and sale of narcotics—an international trade which the global 'managers' have been conspicuously unsuccessful in curtailing.

But there will be other economic problems for the agenda-setters to deliberate. In particular, the opportunities and challenges presented by the relative decline of Washington's economic hegemony, its absorption into NAFTA and the development of new centres of economic power, including Japan, the countries of ASEAN and, of course, the European Union, expanding to include new members and with special trading arrangements with upwards of 60 countries of Asia, the Caribbean and the Pacific. Apart from anything else, the creation of regional blocs tends to fragment rather than integrate the world economy, often causing acute problems for states that either by choice or mischance belong to none of the regional trading associations. Moreover where, as in the EU, there are both discriminatory policies against certain imports and also subsidies for agricultural products, which create massive surpluses which are then released on to the world market, their effect is seriously to undermine the earning power of those Eastern European countries and LDCs especially dependent on the export of foodstuffs.

A further problem likely to be on the economic agenda for decades to come relates to the growing power and lack of accountability of many transnational enterprises. All too frequently they find ways of evading taxation in their countries of operation and of eluding official control in their pricing, marketing and employment policies. Moreover, by being able suddenly to switch operations from one country to another, they are prone to leaving trails of economic and political dissatisfaction as the promised credits, knowhow, employment and export opportunities fail to be sustained.

The contest over economic systems is likely to constitute an additional issue for deliberation. Though the virtual collapse of Communist rule and the successful conclusion of the 1994 GATT agreement appeared to suggest that the debate between the 'free marketeers' and the 'social engineers' had been settled in favour of the former, Eastern Europe's soaring crime and unemployment rates, collapsing welfare, health and other social services, plummeting living standards and the spread of disillusion and despair in the wake of the attempt to turn a command economy into a free-market economy through 'shock therapy' should occasion much rethinking about the universal applicability or otherwise of the market approach. This is where the economic dimension ties in with other issues on the agenda. For political and demographic stability are increasingly dependent on the ability of governments to satisfy expectations, and if they fail to deliver there is always the danger of civil strife, rampant criminality and /or mass migration.

Of all the possible items on the agenda for the 21st century, the international environment will be the most novel, for till recently states, multinationals and even tribes tended to exploit and deplete the earth's resources with little consideration for their neighbours or, indeed, for future generations. In the process, land, sea and air became polluted, irradiated and toxified, posing dangers to health which, like the medieval plagues, are no respecters of frontiers. Yet since the first global initiative—the UN Environmental Programme established in Stockholm in 1972—and the appearance of a variety of international, regional and transnational bodies specifically designed to tackle environmental issues, cross frontier co-operation on the ecosphere has been all too slow and half-hearted. By the year 2000, however, the wider implications of environmental hazard and the dangers posed to the planet of such lethal diseases as AIDS should be better understood, with notions of prevention, preservation, conservation and restoration much to the fore. Once again a leading item on the agenda is likely to be linked to the others—to the international economy in so far as environmental degredation is connected in part with the level and direction of economic development, to international security in so far as the threat of an ecological catastrophe in one country potentially jeopardises the security of all the others.

As with the international environment so with human rights: here is a comparatively recent concern likely to be a key item on the agenda for the new century. Certainly Iraq's treatment of the Kurds in the north of the country together with recent conflicts in Somalia, Rwanda and what was Yugoslavia have raised fundamental questions as to whether or not international society should legitimise 'humanitarian intervention' where a total breakdown of civilised life or else gross violations of human rights are perceived to be occurring. One obvious problem is that such a conception challenges fundamental norms of sovereignty and non-intervention in the internal affairs of states. A further problem concerns the politicisation of the very concept of 'human rights', which for all the declarations and conventions on the subject remains a somewhat nebulous concept often used, as was explained in Chapter 15, in a partisan way by governments wishing to expand their influence or to strengthen resistance to regimes to which they are already opposed. In any case, armed intervention, as in Vietnam, may prove counter-productive. Since there are ways short of military intervention by which a country can express its disapproval of the activities of another—moral censure, diplomatic rupture, economic sanctions and political subversion among them—there is a predisposition among the international community to try these first.

None the less, the electronic media tends to sensitise people to the suffering of others, and ever since the Nuremberg and Tokyo trials after the second world war the gross abuse of human rights in the form of genocide, 'ethnic cleansing' or mass oppression has aroused international concern. More recently the notion of what constitutes a human right has been extended to encompass a social and economic dimension, including the 'right' to a job, a home, a decent standard of living and equality of opportunity and status between men and women, majorities and minorities, the able-bodied and the disabled and so forth. As such it ties in with other items on the international agenda because the use of arbitrary power or the condition of mass and unalleviated poverty can provide the pretext for international terrorism or lead to mass migrations, affecting the security and economic well-being of other societies.

So far we have considered what might be on the practical agenda for the next century. But what might constitute the academic agenda for the following century? As indicated earlier, International Relations has been steeped in controversy ever since it was first taught. For much of the time the debate was between Realists, Pluralists and Structuralists, and no doubt that contention will continue until well into the 21st century. But like many other studies, IR is beginning to feel the influence of both post-modernism and critical theory. The post-modernist scepticism of universal values and its embrace of new social movements has already been expressed in the form of international studies stressing feminist, gay, environmental, ethnic and religious issues; and no doubt the new century will see additions to the list, including, perhaps, the politics of disability. The future for critical theory is, however, less clear. Presaged on a particular conception of human emancipation, it is in danger, as one of its detractors recently pointed out, of being 'open to the charge of not being a "theory" at all, but a form of propaganda or persuasion masquerading as science'.[2] An even more serious objection is the opaque and sometimes well-nigh incomprehensible prose of some of its leading protagonists. Clearly, therefore, if it is to have an academic future it has to acquire a more empirical base and a more congenial mode of exposition. More assured of a future are IR texts with a proven track record and with a foundation in international economics, international law or strategic studies or some prescription for a better-ordered international society.

Is the discipline at a turning point? Those who believe that International Relations has to be restructured along the lines now fashionable in some of the other social and philosophical disciplines will say that it is. Those accepting the logic of this text may well feel that it is not. After all, throughout the centuries societies have been characterised by an encounter between elements of continuity and the forces of change, and international society is no exception. Moreover, the dialectic between continuity and change has also informed the discipline. If, therefore, the state were to be pronounced clinically dead, and IR was to lose touch with its traditional subject matter and methods of enquiry, the study would, indeed, be at a turning point. In that event there would be little or no call for a text of this kind, save as an intellectual curiosity. But if this volume and others of a similar character continue to be on the academic agenda in the 21st century rather than being left to gather dust on the library shelves, it would suggest that the subject had not yet completely outgrown its original preoccupations and was not about to turn itself into an abstruse, arcane and mildly pretentious sub-branch of social science theory. For this writer the hope is that both 'traddies' and 'trendies' may continue to make their contribution to the subject and perhaps be better disposed than in the past to learn from one another. Perhaps the solution is, as Mao once put it, though in a rather different context, to: 'let a hundred flowers bloom: let a hundred schools contend'.

NOTES

1. 'The acceleration of evolution', *The Futurist*, 14 February 1981.
2. Moon, J.D., 'Political ethics and critical theory', in Sabia, D.R. and Wallulis, J. (eds), *Changing Social Science*, New York, State University of New York Press, 1983, p. 176.

SELECTED BIBLIOGRAPHY

General introductory texts

J. Baylis and N. Rengger (eds), *Dilemmas of World Politics*, Oxford, Clarendon Press, 1992.

H. Bull, *The Anarchical Society*, London, Macmillan, 1977.

B. Hocking and M. Smith, *World Politics: An Introduction to International Relations*, Hemel Hempstead, Harvester Wheatsheaf, 1990.

B. Hollis and S. Smith, *Explaining and Understanding International Relations*, Oxford, Clarendon, 1990.

K.J. Holsti, *International Politics*, 6th ed., Englewood Cliffs, Prentice Hall, 1992.

R. Little and M. Smith, *Perspectives on World Politics*, 2nd ed., London, Routledge, 1992.

E. Luard, *Basic Texts in International Relations*, London, Macmillan, 1992.

F.S. Northedge, *The International Political System*, London, Faber, 1976.

R. Purnell, *The Society of States: An Introduction to International Politics*, London, Weidenfeld and Nicolson, 1973.

P.A. Reynolds, *An Introduction to International Relations*, 3rd ed., London, Longman, 1994.

M. Williams (ed.), *International Relations in the Twentieth Century: a Reader*, Macmillan, 1989.

A. Wolfers, *Discord and Collaboration*, Baltimore, Johns Hopkins University Press, 1966.

Contending theories

J. Burton, *World Society*, London, Cambridge University Press, 1972.

E.H. Carr, *The Twenty Years' Crisis*, London, Macmillan, 1939.

M. Donelan, *Elements of International Political Theory*, Oxford, Oxford University Press, 1990.

J. Dougherty and R. Pfaltzgraff, *Contending Theories in International Relations*, 3rd ed., New York, Harper Collins, 1990.

J.C. Garnett, *Commonsense and the Theory of International Politics*, London, Macmillan, 1984.

K.J. Holsti, *The Dividing Discipline*, London, Allen and Unwin, 1985.

R. Keohane and J. Nye, *Power and Interdependence*, Boston, Little, Brown, 1977.

M. Light and A.J.R. Groom (eds), *International Relations: A Handbook of Current Theory*, London, Pinter, 1985.

R. Little and M. Smith, *Perspectives on World Politics*, 2nd ed., London, Routledge, 1992.

H. Morgenthau, *Politics Among Nations*, New York, Knopf, 1948.

J. Rosenau, *The Scientific Study of Foreign Policy*, London, Pinter, 1980.

J. Rosenberg, *The Empire of Civil Society*, Verso, 1994.

G. Schwarzenberger, *Power Politics*, 3rd ed., London, Stevens, 1964.

I. Wallerstein, *The Capitalist World Economy*, London, Cambridge University Press, 1979.
M. Wight, *International Theory: The Three Traditions*, London, Pinter, 1990.

The evolution of international society

G. Barraclough, *An Introduction to Contemporary History*, Harmondsworth, Penguin, 1967.
I. Clark, *The Hierarchy of States*, Cambridge, Cambridge University Press, 1989.
H. Bull and A. Watson (eds), *The Expansion of International Society*, Oxford, Oxford University Press, 1984.
F.H. Hinsley, *Power and The Pursuit of Peace*, London, Cambridge University Press, 1963.
E. Luard, *Types of International Society*, New York, Macmillan, 1977.
R. N. Rosecrance, *Action and Reaction in World Politics*, Boston, Little, Brown, 1963.
A. Watson, *The Evolution of International Society*, London, Routledge, 1992.
M. Wight, *Systems of States*, Leicester, Leicester University Press, 1977.

The state

G. Allison, *Essence of Decision*, Boston, Little, Brown, 1971.
J. Barber and M. Smith, *The Nature of Foreign Policy: A Reader*, Edinburgh, Holmes McDougall, 1974.
M. Clarke and B. White (eds), *Understanding Foreign Policy*, Aldershot, Elgar, 1989.
I. Duchacek, *Nations and Men*, 3rd ed., New York, University Press of America, 1975.
F.H. Hinsley, *Sovereignty*, Cambridge, Cambridge University Press, 1986.
E. Hobsbawm and T. Ranger (eds), *The Invention of Tradition*, Cambridge, Cambridge University Press, 1983.
E. Hobsbawm, *Nations and Nationalism Since 1780*, Cambridge, Cambridge University Press, 1990.
G. Ionescu (ed.), *Between Sovereignty and Integration*, New York, Wiley, 1974.
A. James, *Sovereign Statehood: The Basis of International Society*, London, Allen & Unwin, 1986.
J. Mayall, *Nationalism and International Society*, Cambridge, Cambridge University Press, 1990.
A.D. Smith, *The Ethnic Revival in the Modern World*, Cambridge, Cambridge University Press, 1981.
G. Stern, *Leaders and Leadership*, London, LSE/BBC World Service, 1993.

Inter-state behaviour

G. Blainey, *The Causes of War*, 3rd ed., Basingstoke, Macmillan, 1988.
H. Bull, *The Anarchical Society*, London, Macmillan, 1977.
I. Claude, *Power and International Relations*, New York, Random House, 1962.
B.C. Cohen, *The Question of Imperialism*, London, Weidenfeld & Nicolson, 1980.

J.C. Hare and C.B. Joynt, *Ethics and International Affairs*, London, Macmillan, 1982.

R. Higgins, *Problems and Process: International Law and How We Use it*, Oxford, Clarendon, 1994.

M. Howard (ed.), *Restraints on War*, Oxford, Oxford University Press, 1979.

A. James (ed.), *The Bases of International Order*, London, Oxford University Press, 1973.

K. Nelson and S. Olin, *Why War?*, California, University of California Press, 1979.

H. Nicolson, *Diplomacy*, London, Oxford University Press, 1963.

R. Niebuhr, *Moral Man and Immoral Society*, New York, Scribner's, 1952.

R. Pettman, *Moral Claims in World Affairs*, London, Croom Helm, 1979.

R. Rothstein, *The Weak in the World of the Strong*, New York, Columbia University Press, 1977.

R.J. Vincent, *Non-Intervention and International Order*, Princeton, Princeton University Press, 1974.

J. M. Walt, *The Origins of Alliances*, Ithaca, Cornell University Press, 1987.

K. Waltz, *Man, the State and War*, New York, Columbia University Press, 1959.

A. Watson, *Diplomacy: The Dialogue between States*, London, Methuen, 1982.

M. Wight, *Power Politics*, Harmondsworth, Penguin, 1979.

Non-state actors

A.L. Bennett, *International Organisations*, 5th ed., Englewood Cliffs, Prentice Hall, 1989.

M.S. and L.S. Finkelstein (eds), *Collective Security*, San Francisco, Chandler, 1966.

A. James, *Peacekeeping in International Politics*, Basingstoke, Macmillan, 1990.

C. Kedley (ed.), *International Terrorism*, New York, St Martin's Press, 1990.

R. Keohane and J. Nye (eds), *Transnational Relations and World Politics*, London, Harvard University Press, 1971.

S. Krasner (ed.), *International Regimes*, New York, Cornell University Press, 1982.

E. Luard (ed.), *The Evolution of International Organisations*, London, Thames and Hudson, 1966.

R.W. Mansbach et al., *The Web of World Politics*, Englewood Cliffs, Prentice Hall, 1976.

J. Piscatori, *Islam in a World of Nation States*, Cambridge, Cambridge University Press, 1986.

A. Roberts and B. Kingsbury (eds), *The U.N: Divided World*, 2nd ed., Oxford, Clarendon Press, 1993.

G. Stern, *The Rise and Decline of International Communism*, Aldershot, Elgar, 1990.

S. Strange, *States and Markets*, London, Pinter, 1988.

P. Taylor and A.J.R. Groom, *International Institutions at Work*, London, Pinter, 1988.

P. Taylor, *Non-State Actors in International Politics*, Boulder, Westview, 1984.

The international political economy

P. Bauer, *Reality and Rhetoric*, London, Wideenfeld & Nicolson, 1984.

W. Brandt et al., *North–South: A Programme for Survival*, London, Commonwealth Secretariat, 1981.

E. Brett, *The World Economy since the War: The Politics of Uneven Development*, London, Macmillan, 1985.

R. Cassen, *Does Aid Work?*, Oxford, Oxford University Press, 1985.

S. George, *A Fate Worse than Debt*, Harmondsworth, Penguin, 1988.

S. Gill and D. Law, *The Global Political Economy*, Hemel Hempstead, Harvester, 1988.

R. Gilpin, *The Political Economy of International Relations*, Princeton, Princeton University Press, 1987.

N. Harris, *The End of the Third World*, Harmondsworth, Penguin, 1986.

G.K. Helleiner, *International Economic Disorder*, London, Macmillan, 1980.

S. Krasner, *Structural Conflict: The Third World Against Global Liberalism*, Berkeley, California, 1985.

R. Lipschutz, *When Nations Clash*, Ballinger, 1989.

J. Spero, *The Politics of International Economic Relations*, 4th ed., London, Hyman Unwin, 1990.

S. Strange (ed.), *Paths to International Political Economy*, London, Allen & Unwin, 1984.

World society?

M. Banks (ed.), *Conflict and World Society*, Brighton, Wheatsheaf, 1984.

H. Bull, *The Control of the Arms Race*, London, Weidenfeld & Nicolson, 1961.

J. Burton, *World Society*, London, Cambridge University Press, 1972.

F. Cairncross, *Costing the Earth*, London, Economists Books, 1991.

R. Falk, *The Promise of World Order*, Brighton, Wheatsheaf, 1987.

M. Finkelstein, *Collective Security*, San Francisco, Chandler, 1966.

J. Galtung, *There are Alternatives: Four Roads to Peace and Security*, Nottingham, Spokesman Books, 1984.

A. Hurrell and B. Kingsley, *The International Politics of the Environment*, Oxford, Oxford University Press, 1992.

E. Luard, *The Globalisation of Politics*, London, Macmillan, 1990.

R.L. Mansbach *et al.*, *The Web of World Politics*, Englewood Cliffs, Prentice Hall, 1976.

R. Pettman, *Human Behavior and World Politics*, New York, St Martins Press, 1975.

T. Skocpol, *States and Social Revolutions*, London, Cambridge University Press, 1979.

J. Spanier and J. Nogee, *The Politics of Disarmament*, New York, Praeger, 1962.

C. Thomas, *The Environment in International Relations*, London, Royal Institute of International Affairs, 1992.

NAME INDEX

Acton, Lord, 176
Alexander the Great, 52–4, 126
Allen, Woody, 261, 266
Allende, Salvador, 223–4
Allison, Graham, 116
Amin, Samir, 256
Anderson, Benedict, 93–4, 100
Angell, Norman, 183, 190, 197
Arafat, Yasser, 162
Aristotle, 33, 41, 189, 229
Aron, Raymond, 20
Ashoka, 49
Asimov, Isaac, 266
Ataturk, Kemal, 118
Attila the Hun, 126, 148, 222
Augustine, St., 189
Augustus Caesar, 54
Austin, John, 78
Ayer, A.J., 6

Bandaranaike, Sirimavo, 282
Banks, Michael, 10, 26
Bauer, Peter, 87
Bentham, Jeremy, 12, 16, 96
Berg, Alban, 262
Bernhardi, General von, 182
Bernstein, Eduard, 184
Bhutto, Benazir, 282
Bismarck, Otto von, 118, 174, 234–5
Blainey, Geoffrey, 188
Bodin, Jean, 78–9
Boulding, Kenneth, 269, 270
Boutros-Ghali, Boutros, 205, 209
Brandt, Willy, 37, 87
Bridges, Robert, 180
Bright, John, 183
Britten, Benjamin, 184
Buchan, Alistair, 142
Bull, Hedley, 10, 25, 65, 142, 150, 191,
    222
Burke, Edmund, 10, 12, 142, 177, 189,
    280
Burton, John, 26, 27, 28, 106, 149, 220,
    278
Bush, George, 40, 106, 107
Butterfield, Herbert, 136

Callieres, Francois de, 158
Canning, George, 142
Carlyle, Thomas, 118
Carr, E.H., 19, 20, 25, 31, 103, 123, 125,
    234, 236, 241
Castlereagh, Viscount, 142
Castro, Fidel, 253
Catherine the Great, 159
Cavour, Count, 281
Chamberlain, Neville, 115, 118, 202, 279
Chandragupta Maurya, 49
Charlemagne, 61, 182
Charles, Eugenia, 282
Charles V, 215
Chou En-lai, 45
Churchill, Winston, 118, 142, 147, 170
Cicero, 136
Ciller, Tansu, 282
Clarke, Michael, 116–7
Claude, Inis, 139–40
Clausewitz, Carl von, 182
Clinton, Bill, 106, 113, 119
Clinton, Hillary, 112
Cobden, Richard, 139, 149, 183
Columbus, Christopher, 45, 212
Conrad, Joseph, 262
Constantine, Emperor, 55
Cruce, Emeric, 197

Danilevsky, Nikolai, 97
D'Annunzio, Gabriele, 182
Dante, 77, 197
Darwin, Charles, 189, 261
Denktash, Rauf, 79
Deutsch, Karl, 151
Dicey, A.V., 78
Dickens, Charles, 92
Disraeli, Benjamin, 234
Donelan, Michael, 136
Dubcek, Alexander, 161

Easton, David, 32
Elgar, Edward, 262
Eliot, T.S., 271
Elton, Lord, 182
Engels, Friedrich, 214, 216

Falk, Richard, 133, 266
Fichte, Johann Gottlieb, 97
Francis, I., 215
Franco, Fransisco, 128, 202, 247
Frank, Andre Gundar, 37, 256
Freud, Sigmund, 41, 126, 188, 263

Galtieri, General, 27, 176
Galtung, Johan, 270
da Gama, Vasco, 212
Gandhi, Indira, 271, 282
Gandhi, Mahatma, 118, 184
Garcia, Alan, 253
Garnett, John, 118
George I., 69
Ghaddafi, Muammur, 131
Ghengis Khan, 126, 148, 222
Girardet, Herbert, 270
Gorbachev, Mikhail, 71, 80, 107, 118, 130, 280
Gromyko, Andrei, 110
Grotius, Hugo, 9, 12, 67, 218, 275

Haas, Ernst, 140
Hammarskjold, Dag, 208
Heath, Edward, 37, 87
Hegel, G.W.F., 10, 34, 218, 261
Heilbronner, Robert, 266
Hinsley, F.H., 70
Hirohito, Emperor, 110
Hitler, Adolf, 19, 21, 22, 41, 98, 105, 115, 118, 126, 145, 148, 168, 201, 202, 237, 241, 247, 281
Hobbes, Thomas, 9, 10, 12, 21, 65, 123, 125, 126, 136, 173, 190, 218, 278
Hobsbawm, Eric, 92–5
Hobson, J.A., 177–8, 236–9
Hogg, Quinton (Lord Hailsham), 203
Holsti, K.J., 142
Hume, David, 9, 142
Hussein, Saddam, 109, 130, 131, 148, 176, 202
Huxley, Aldous, 184, 265
Huxley, Thomas, 189

Ibn Khaldun, 57
Isherwood, Christopher, 184

James, Alan, 83
James, William, 188, 279
Johnson, Lyndon B., 165, 250
Johnson, Samuel, 95
Jung, Carl Gustav, 41, 189
Justinian, Emperor, 61

Kant, Immanuel, 9, 33, 136, 176, 177, 198, 280
Kautilya, 8, 10, 49–50
Kedourie, Elie, 177, 190, 281
Kennan, George, 150
Kennedy, John F., 45, 114, 118, 163, 165, 208
Kennedy, Paul, 244, 248
Keohane, Robert, 26, 220
Keynes, John Maynard, 241, 243
Khomenei, Ayatollah, 14, 136
Khrushchev, Nikita, 110, 208
Kipling, Rudyard, 167
Kissinger, Henry, 20, 23, 110, 113, 114, 115, 142, 150, 162, 288
Koestler, Arthur, 264

Lang, Fritz, 264
Lenin, V.I., 14, 35, 45, 118, 136, 172, 177–8, 183, 189–90, 237–8
Lincoln, Abraham, 109
Litvinov, Maxim, 283
Locke, John, 12, 78, 275
Louis XI, 78
Luard, Evan, 72–3

McCarthy, Senator Joseph, 165
Mackinder, Halford, 40–1
McKinley, William, 235–6
Macmillan, Harold, 118
Machiavelli, Niccolo, 8, 10, 49, 64, 77, 123, 136, 139, 142, 218
Magdoff, Harry, 35
Mahan, A.T., 40–1
Manley, Michael, 255
Manning, C.A.W., 5, 6, 7, 67
Mansbach, Richard, 220
Mao Tse-tung, 8, 118, 295
Marshall, George, 247

Marx, Karl, 4, 10, 14, 34, 51, 136, 168, 189, 190, 198, 214, 216, 233, 235, 261, 263, 275, 280
Masaryk, Thomas, 118
Mazzini, Guiseppe, 177, 189, 281
Meier, Golda, 282
Midgley, E.B.F., 136
Mill, John Stuart, 12, 98, 174, 183, 261
Milosevic, Slobodan, 131
Mobutu, President, 208
Modelski, George, 39, 40
Montesquieu, Charles de, 12
Morgenthau, Hans J., 5, 20, 23, 25, 123, 125, 126, 142, 150, 190, 218, 275, 278
Muhammed, Prophet, 55, 58
Mussolini, Benito, 19, 22, 105, 145, 175, 201, 247, 281
Myers, Norman, 268

Napoleon, I., 98, 102, 126, 148
Nasser, Gamal Abdul, 85, 112, 208
Nelson, Keith, 10
Nicolson, Harold, 154, 160
Niebuhr, Reinhold, 136
Nietzsche, Friedrich, 181, 182
Nixon, Richard M., 116, 250
Nkrumah, Kwame, 170
Noel-Baker, Philip, 19, 123, 197
Northedge, F.S., 25, 65, 117, 176, 178, 282
Nye, Joseph, 220

Olin, Spencer, 10
Organski, A.F.K., 151
Orwell, George, 265
Owen, Wilfred, 180

Palacky, Frantisek, 97
Palmerston, H.J.T., 143
Penn, William, 184, 198
Peron, Isabelita, 282
Peter the Great, 214
Philip of Macedonia, 52
Pillsbury, W.S., 98
Plato, 41, 177, 189, 280
Platt, John, 290
Pol Pot, 176
Prebisch, Raoul, 255, 256

Purnell, Robert, 54

Reagan, Ronald, 27, 128, 130, 146, 177, 253
Renan, Ernest, 98
Rhee, President Syngman, 186
Rhodes, Cecil, 168
Robespierre, Maximilien de, 14
Roosevelt, Franklin D., 147, 241
Rosenau, James, 26, 27, 106, 149, 220, 278
Rousseau, Jean-Jacques, 14, 70, 78, 101, 102, 190
Russell, Bertrand, 184, 282

Sadat, Anwar, 128, 162
St. Pierre, Abbe de, 198
Sargent, William, 60
Schoenberg, Arnold, 262
Schwarzenberger, Georg, 11, 20, 123, 125, 241
Scott, Sir Walter, 92
Shakespeare, William, 94, 95
Shaw, George Bernard, 189
Shevardnadze, Eduard, 288
Shute, Neville, 265
Singer, David, 151
Smith, Adam, 216, 231–3
Smith, Ian, 79
Spengler, Osvald, 262
Spinoza, Baruch, 218
Stalin, Josef V., 21, 98, 117, 146, 147, 148, 168, 170, 243, 245, 264
Stevenson, Robert Louis, 182
Suarez, Francesco de, 136
Sully, Maximilien, Duc de, 198
Sun Tsu, 8

Taylor, A.J.P., 63
Thatcher, Margaret, 71, 107, 110, 233, 280, 282
Thucydides, 8, 10, 51, 123, 139, 190, 275
Tippett, Michael, 184
Tito, Josip Broz, 117, 280
Tojo, General, 19
Tolstoy, Leo, 184
Trotsky, Leon, 109
Truman, Harry S., 247

Vattel, Emerich de, 218
Victoria, Queen, 92

Wagner, Richard, 168
Wallerstein, Immanuel, 172, 256
Waltz, Kenneth, 39, 151, 178, 188, 190, 275, 287
Webb, Sidney and Beatrice, 168, 177, 189, 280
Webern, Anton, 262
Wells, H.G., 264
Wight, Martin, 9, 10, 21, 50, 123, 125, 173–6, 190, 191, 192

William III, 69
Wilson, Woodrow, 18, 31, 118, 123, 149, 162, 177, 189, 197, 198, 199, 219, 275, 280
Wittgenstein, Ludwig, 6
Wolfers, Arnold, 136
Wootten, Henry, 159

Xerxes, 148, 222

Young, Oran, 144

Zimmern, Alfred, 19, 20, 123, 197

SUBJECT INDEX

Abhazians, 90

Afghanistan, 23, 77, 79, 80, 132, 134, 140, 141, 146, 147, 185, 220, 222, 253, 274, 277, 280

Africa, 3, 40, 53, 56, 61, 72, 101, 104, 123, 142, 146, 151, 171, 175, 206, 256, 268, 286
    colonisation/partition of, 168, 170, 171, 174, 217
    see also individual countries

Albania, 19, 32, 38, 77, 86, 128, 129, 145, 170, 174, 200, 202

Algeria, 114, 141, 179, 190, 234

Alignment, 143, 144, 148

Allies (alliance systems), 143, 144, 147, 156, 192, 220
    see also NATO, Warsaw Treaty Organisation (Warsaw Pact)

Analysis, levels of, 7

Anarchism, 264

Anarchy, 150

ANC (African National Congress), 27, 175

Anglo–German Naval Treaty (1935), 283

Angola, 27, 88, 132, 175, 191, 274

Anti-colonialism (anti-imperialism), 101, 102, 104

Anti-racism, 101, 104

Anti-slavery movements, 216

Apartheid, 131
    see also South Africa

Arab-Israeli conflict (*see* war)

Argentina, 155, 176, 238

Armenia, 56, 98, 112
    see Nagorno-Karabakh

Arms (weapons)
    conventional, 88, 285, 287
    nuclear, 21, 22, 24, 27, 151, 184, 187, 266, 284, 287

Arms control, 146, 161, 284–5

Arms race, 148, 151
    as cause of war, 285

Arms sales, 280

Ashanti, 170, 174, 217

Asia, 3, 38, 40, 56, 101, 104, 108, 123, 142, 151, 171, 256, 274

colonisation of, 168, 170, 171, 217
    see also individual countries

Association of South East Asian Nations (ASEAN), 210, 292

Atomic bomb, 22, 41, 180

Australia, 83, 106, 190, 238, 265

Austria, 19, 41, 62, 64, 72, 73, 98, 102, 145, 147, 240, 276

Austro-Hungarian Empire, 60
    see also Habsburg Empire

Azerbaijan, 112
    see Nagorno-Karabakh

Baganda, 171, 217

Balance of payments, 107, 251

Balance of power, 3, 24, 52, 64, 68–9, Ch. 10 *passim*, 249, 277, 286

Balance of terror, 151

Balance of trade, 107, 232

Balkans, 85, 109

Baltic Republics, 66, 174–5
    see also individual states

Bangladesh, 97, 104, 185

Basques, 90, 98, 99, 220

Behaviouralism, 22–4, 31, 32

Belgium, 71, 72, 147, 174, 208, 234, 235, 276

Berlin Wall, 135

Bipolarity (bipolar system), 142, 150–1

Boer War (*see* war)

Booker's, 224

Bosnia (Bosnians), 5, 28, 41, 79, 80, 103, 104, 106, 136, 140, 148, 151, 160, 175, 180, 185, 191, 220, 274, 275, 285

'Boston tea party', 70, 215

Bretton Woods system, 241, 243–6

Brezhnev Doctrine, 170

Britain (*see* Great Britain)

Buddhism, 49, 212, 282

Bulgaria, 55, 72, 131, 147, 200

Bureaucratic politics, 116

Burma, 103

Byzantium (Byzantine), 55, 56, 58, 62, 156–7

California, 77, 83, 169, 219

Cambodia (Kampuchea), 77, 83, 90, 112, 144, 165, 176, 220, 280
Campaign for Nuclear Disarmament (CND), 184, 265, 271
Canada, 83, 127, 165
Capitalism (capitalist), 14, 22, 33, 34, 35, 36, 38, 64, 93, 103, 172, 177–8, 182, 189, 190, 232–41, 257, 263, 280–1
CARICOM (Caribbean Common Market), 255
Central America, 185, 274
    see also individual countries
'Centre' – 'periphery' relationships, 36–7, 254–6
Chechen/Ingush peoples, 86
Chile, 223, 224
China, communist, 32, 38, 45, 71, 80, 86, 88, 117, 128, 129, 130, 132, 141, 142, 144, 149, 161, 162, 165, 171, 173, 221, 256, 270, 271, 280
    see also Taiwan (Formosa)
China, imperial, 7, 38, 48, 49, 58, 62, 79, 109, 133, 145, 168, 169, 215, 229, 235
China, post-imperial, 19, 201, 217
Christendom, 12, 55, 61–3, 77, 84, 197, 213
Christianity, 13, 14, 53, 55, 57, 61, 62, 65, 71, 126, 156, 168, 181, 182, 184, 190, 197, 221, 282
Civil wars (internal conflicts), 101, 123, 141, 144, 146, 147, 180, 181, 184–5, 208, 239, 278
Coexistence, peaceful, 222
Cognitive dissonance, 117
Cold war, 3, 21, 22, 45, 86, 118, 123, 128, 135, 140, 141, 142, 150, 158, 160, 169, 191, 219, 220, 279, 291
    economic relations and, 246, 249, 277
    evolution of, 82
    United Nations and, 205, 209, 210
Collective security, principle of, 200, 285
Collectivism, 7
Common Agricultural Policy (CAP), 135
Commonwealth (British), 128, 249
Communism, 3, 22, 32, 38, 48, 85, 86, 100, 104, 108, 113, 118, 129, 141, 146, 150, 160, 190, 191, 192, 198, 264, 281, 292
    containment of, 108
Communist countries, 32, 38, 141, 145, 146, 160, 161, 163, 219, 220, 221, 248–9, 252, 256, 269, 280
    see also individual countries
Communist International (Comintern), 129, 214
Community, definition of, 7, 11
Comparative advantage, doctrine of, 232, 239
Concert of Europe, 72, 89, 143, 199
Congress of Aix-la-chapelle, 159
Congress of Berlin, 235
Congress of Vienna, 159, 199
Conscription (levee en masse), 102, 187
Corn laws, 231, 234
'Correlation of forces', 141
Council for Mutual Economic Assistance (COMECON), 249
Crimean war (see war)
Critical theory, 294
Croatia (Croats), 5, 28, 62, 80, 83, 97, 103, 104, 167, 170, 185
    see also Yugoslavia
Crusades, 15, 61, 62, 63, 182
Cuba, 38, 82, 90, 114, 128, 130, 146, 253, 256, 265
Cuban missile crisis, 116, 165, 208
Cyprus, 82, 83, 209
Czechoslovakia, 19, 32, 41, 84, 115, 131, 132, 145, 161, 173, 174, 178, 202, 280

Debt problems, 207, 252–5
Decision-making, 116–7
Decolonisation, 87
Democracy, 189, 191
Denmark, 36, 133, 159, 179
Dependency, of developing countries, 36–7, 170–2, 178
Dependentistas (dependency theorists), 36–9, 170, 171
Deterrence, 121, 192
Developing countries, lesser developed countries (LDCs), 35–8, 87–8, 171–3, 206, 243, 252–6, 267–70, 277, 292
    see also Third World

Diplomacy, 50, 52, 58, 63, 64, 67–8,
     125–6, 139, 143, Ch. 11 *passim*, 192
Disarmament, 19, 20, 146, 148, 161, 283–4
Division of labour, 232
'Dollar gap', 107, 246

Eastern Europe, 3, 21, 22, 40, 86, 88, 101,
     102, 103, 131, 146, 150, 161, 170, 191,
     192, 243, 246, 248, 249, 256, 292, 293
     see also individual countries
East India Company, British, 215
East India Company, Dutch, 215
Ecological perspective, ecological crisis
     (*see* 'Green' analysis)
Economic development, 87, 89
     OPEC nations and, 251
     military spending and, 113,
          191–2, 238, 241
     population problem and, 269, 293
     war and level of, 192, 204, 206–7,
          239–40, 243
     UN and, 204, 206–7
Economists, 177–8, 216, 231, 232, 236,
     238, 252, 254, 255, 256, 269, 290
Egypt, 47, 48, 56, 72, 83, 94, 128, 130,
     141, 162, 174, 188, 208, 224, 229
Empire(s)
     death of, 55, 56, 60, 77, 79
     rise of European, 13, 62, 168–9,
          170, 231–2
     rise of non-European, 47, 48, 49,
          53, 55–8
     rise of Roman, 53–5
     see also colonialism; imperialism
England, 9, 12, 65, 77, 95, 99, 234
     see also Great Britain
Enlightenment, Age of, 68, 101, 214
Environment (environmental
     degradation), 3, 24, Ch. 18 *passim*,
     291, 293, 294
Equality, 81–3, 102
Eritrea (Eritreans), 28
     see also Ethiopia
Estonia (Estonians), 19, 28, 175
Ethiopia (Abyssinia), 19, 94, 131, 175,
     201, 235, 284
'Ethnic cleansing', 3, 27, 100, 106, 175,
     294

Ethnicity, 96, 97–8, 168
Europe, 3, 9, 12, 13, 14, 22, 32, 40, 51, 56,
     58, 60–9, 70, 72, 73, 77, 94, 102, 108,
     115, 118, 123, 142, 145, 168, 172, 186,
     198, 203, 213, 220, 230, 231, 234, 238,
     240, 246, 247, 248, 284, 290
     see also Eastern Europe; Western
          Europe
European Coal and Steel Community
     (ECSC), 26, 248
European Commission, 7
European Commission for the Danube,
     199
European Council of Ministers, 82
European Court of Human Rights, 82
European Court of Justice, 133
European Economic Community (EEC
     or EC), 26, 127, 133, 134, 142, 218,
     229, 249, 250
     see also European Union (EU)
European Free Trade Area (EFTA), 249
European Payments Union (EP), 248
European Union (EU), 80, 82, 83, 90,
     107, 163, 198, 210, 286, 290, 291, 292
Exchange Rate Mechanism (ERM), 90,
     135, 210, 254
Exponential growth, 269, 273
EXXON, 7, 218, 223

Falklands (Malvinas) war (*see* war)
Fascism, 19, 22, 104, 105, 107, 151, 160,
     187, 190, 192, 240
     see also Nazism
Federalism, 286
Finland, 19, 130, 202
Food and Agriculture Organisation
     (FAO), 205, 206, 218
Food crisis, world, 251
Ford, 223
Foreign policy analysis, 108, 115–7
Foreign policy decision-making, Ch. 8
     passim, 277, 288
France, 32, 56, 64, 65, 70, 72, 77, 84, 89,
     98, 99, 101–2, 109, 112, 113, 114, 131,
     133, 140, 141, 142, 146, 148, 159, 167,
     179, 202, 207, 215, 223, 234, 235, 238,
     243, 277, 286
Franco–Prussian war (*see* war)

Free trade, 231–3, 234, 243
Fuggers, 215
Functionalism, 32, 286

General Agreement on Tariffs and
  Trade (GATT), 88, 135, 210, 224, 293
General Motors, 223
Geneva Convention (on poison gas),
  186, 284
Geopolitics (geopolitical theories), 40–1
Germany, 22, 27, 32, 49, 62, 65, 69, 72,
  73, 84, 85, 88, 89, 95, 97, 102, 103, 106,
  113, 148, 168, 174, 200, 235, 238, 240,
  245, 290
Germany, East (GDR), 85, 129, 135, 191,
  280
Germany, Federal Republic of (West),
  135, 163
Germany, Nazi, 19, 20, 22, 40, 41, 71, 98,
  103, 108, 112, 115, 146, 170, 175, 201,
  202, 275, 286
Germany, unification of, 3, 210
Ghana (see Ashanti)
Global warming, 207, 272
Grading/ranking of the Powers, 89, 287
Graduated Reciprocation in Tension
  Reduction (GRIT), 288
Great Britain, 32, 72, 82, 84, 92, 97, 99,
  102, 106, 113, 129, 143, 159, 173, 231,
  234, 235, 240, 249, 271, 290
  and Albania, 129
  and Czechoslovakia, 161
  and the balance of power, 52, 142
  colonies of/British Empire, 40, 69,
    101, 108, 168, 170, 174, 179,
    217, 234, 235, 236, 239, 243
  and diplomacy, 163, 164
  and the EEC, 133
  and Egypt, 85, 130, 141, 207
  and the first world war, 180
  and France, 71, 84, 109, 146, 179,
    207
  and Germany, 84, 115, 202, 286
  as Great Power, 89
  and Iran, 146
  and Iraq, 147
  and the League of Nations, 202
  and New Zealand, 127

  and the second world war, 41,
    118, 275, 279
  and the Soviet Union, 41, 141,
    146, 170
  and the UN, 89
  and the United States, 130, 207,
    243
  and Yugoslavia, 161
Great Depression, 19, 107, 240, 244
'Great Power' status, 89
Greece, city states, 49, 50–3, 58, 124, 155,
  181, 229
Greek civil war, 146, 147
'Green' analysis, 266–70
'Greenhouse effect', 268, 271, 273
Grenada, 27, 196, 277
Group of, 77, 87
Guatemala, 145, 223
Guyana, 224

Habsburgs, Habsburg Empire, 239
Hague conferences (1899 and 1907), 199
Haiti, 129
Hanseatic League, 212
Hausas, 217
'Heartland' theory, 40–1
Hegemonial power, 39, 40, 52, 124, 143,
  148, 170
Hinduism, 49, 57, 146, 181, 184, 212, 221
Holism, 7, 34
Holland (Netherlands), 40, 65, 67, 72,
  89, 174, 179, 234
Holy Roman Empire, 55, 212, 213, 215
Honduras, 101
Hudson's Bay Company, 215
Human rights, 10, 205, 219, 291, 293
Hungary, 62, 85, 97, 103, 134, 280

IBM (International Business Machines),
  7, 218, 223
Iceland, 85
'Ideology', definition of, 70–1
Imperialism, 6, 8, 18, 22, 35, 103, 112, 137,
  Ch. 12 passim, 233–9, 269, 281, 290
  see also colonialism and neo-
    colonialism
India, 48, 49–50, 52, 56, 104, 146, 167,
  168, 173, 174, 181, 185, 221, 271

Individualism, 7, 10, 12, 34
Indonesia, 38, 88, 174, 175, 256
Industrialisation, 36, 234, 239, 252, 255, 256, 269–70, 292
Integration theory, 32
Interdependence, 27, 33, 37, 87, 106, 113, 149, 151, 268, 286
Interest groups (lobbies), 112
International anarchy, 7, 9, 11, 39, 190
International Bank for Reconstruction and Development (*see* World Bank)
International community, 7, 79, 291, 294
International Court of Justice (ICJ), 129, 133, 205
International economic order (international political economy; world economy), 216, Ch. 16 *passim*, Ch. 17 *passim*, 291, 293, 294–5
International Labour Organisation (ILO), 205
International law, 11, 13, 18, 19, 66–7, 68, 69, 77, 81, 108, 125, 127, 132–4, 135, 143, 149, 151, 205, 218–20, 276, 295
International Monetary Fund (IMF), 87, 88, 134, 229, 246, 250, 252, 254
International morality, 11, 13, 135–7
International order (world order), 12, 14, 66, 70, 71, 86, 114, 126, 127, 128, 132–7, 143, 151, 158, 162, 192, 222, 287
International organisation(s), 18, 81, 83, 131, 134, 153, 163, Ch. 14 *passim*
   governmental (IGOs), 210
   non-governmental (INGOs), 210
International Red Cross, 199, 275
International regimes, 135
International Relations (International Politics; World Politics), vii, 3, 4, 7, 8, 9, 10, 16, Ch. 2 *passim*, Ch. 3 *passim*, 52, 67, 73, 96, 106, 113, 123, 125, 132, 136, 139, 149, 163, 167, 179, 229, 288, 294, 295
International societies, 135
   pre-modern Ch. 4 *passim*
   modern, Ch. 5 *passim*

International society (international system), Ch. 1 *passim*, 17, 18, 21, 26, 27, 31, 41, 45–7, 58, 65, 66, 70, 79, 85, 90, 103, 108, 109, 111, 114–5, 126, 127, 132, 137, 143, 148, 151–2, 165, 190, 191, 197, Ch. 18 *passim*, Ch. 19 *passim*, 290, 293, 295
International trade, 27, 62, 131, 199, 221, 230, 233–5, 238–40, 250
IRA (Irish Republican Army), 27
Iran, 90, 97, 104, 133, 141, 144, 146, 147, 171, 176, 223, 252
   see also Persia
'Irangate', 107, 161
Iraq, 53, 56, 57, 90, 97, 103, 115, 129, 130, 131, 133, 147, 167, 173, 174, 176, 183, 185, 279, 293
'Iraqgate', 107, 147, 161
Ireland, 65, 97, 104, 274, 276
Islam (Islamic world), 55–8, 61, 62, 86, 106, 146, 168, 172, 176, 182, 213, 221, 251, 282
Islamic fundamentalism, 108, 148, 253
Isolationism, American, 290
Israel, 79, 104, 105, 128, 129, 162, 167, 175, 188, 191, 208, 221, 269
Italy, 10, 53, 58, 61, 67, 69, 103
   modern, 19, 22, 62, 102, 105, 131, 170, 174, 175, 202, 235, 243, 284
   Papal, 155–6
   Renaissance, 63–5, 157–8
IT&T (International Telephone and Telegraph), 218, 223

Japan, 7, 19, 22, 38, 48, 84, 88, 89, 109, 110, 133, 142, 145, 148, 170, 174, 178, 201, 202, 219, 235, 238, 243, 249, 250, 251, 269, 286, 292
Judaism (Jews), 45, 56, 57, 94, 95, 97, 98, 99, 103, 181, 197, 221, 269, 282
Justice, 4, 33, 142, 150, 288

Kashmir (Kashmiris), 28, 77, 83, 90, 185, 220
Kellogg–Briand Pact (1928), 19
Kenya (*see* Kikuyus)
Kikuyus, 217
Korea, 83, 147, 205

Korean airline disaster (1983), 187–8
Korea, North, 79, 86, 115, 129, 186, 206
Korean war (see war)
Korea, South, 38, 88, 115, 145, 256
Kurds/Kurdistan, 28, 77, 86, 90, 185, 220, 293
Kuwait, 109, 115, 129, 130, 176, 183

Laissez-faire, 216, 231–3, 235
Laos, 90, 165, 276, 277
Latin America, 27, 35, 36, 37, 94, 100, 101, 108, 144, 150, 170, 171, 185, 256
    see also individual countries
Latvia (Latvians), 19, 28, 175
League of Nations, 89, 96, 131, 143, 170, 197, 198, 199–204, 218, 241, 283, 291
League of Nations Covenant, 199
Lesser Developed Countries (LDCs)
    see developing countries
Liberal (Liberalism), 10, 29, 36, 71, 78, 98, 103, 148, 183, 184
Liberia, 220, 235
Libya, 90, 129, 131, 167, 174
Liechtenstein, 80, 81
Linguistic Analysis, 6, 11, 18, 46
Linkage politics, 27
Lithuania (Lithuanians), 19, 28, 103, 175, 200
Lobbies (pressure groups), 112
London School of Economics (LSE), vii, 6, 18, 32, 40, 163, 168
Luxembourg, 72, 147, 276

Malaysia, 38, 88, 176, 256
Manchurian crisis, 19, 170, 201
Marshall Plan/Aid, 192, 247–9
Marxism, 14, 21, 34–5, 36, 37–8, 93, 111, 172, 178, 183, 198, 240, 280
Marxism–Leninism (Communism), 35, 38, 108, 148, 281, 282
Mercantilism, 215, 230–33, 236, 291
Merchant Adventurers, 212
Mexico, 94, 253, 254, 269
Middle East, 38, 47, 48, 88, 112, 142, 151, 274
    see also individual countries
Migration, 269, 293, 294
Military aid, 51–2, 245, 247

Military–industrial complex, 184
Monroe Doctrine, 108, 142, 170
Montevideo Convention (1933), 79
Morocco, 56, 128
Mozambique, 88, 175
Multinational corporations (MNCs), 26, 153, 215, 220–1, 223–4, 250, 293
Multipolar system (multipolarity), 151
My Lai massacre, 189, 190

Nagorno-Karabakh, 112
Namibia (South West Africa), 131, 168
National interest, 110–11, 117, 221
Nationalism, 5, 69–72, 78, Ch. 7 passim, 176, 178, 190, 192, 221, 233, 237, 281
    see also individual countries/ peoples
National liberation movements (Liberation movements), 185, 219
    see also ANC, IRA, PLO etc
Nation, definition, 93–9
Nation state, definition, 96
NATO (North Atlantic Treaty Organisation), 134, 144, 218, 277, 291
Natural law, 66, 67, 136, 275
Nauru, 80, 83, 220
Navigation Acts, 231
Nazism, 85, 101, 104, 105
Neo-colonialism, definition of, 171
Neorealism (Neorealist), 39
Nepal, 147
Neutrality, doctrine of, 147, 276
New International Economic Order (NIEO), 37, 87, 207, 255, 277, 292
Newly industrialising countries (NICs), 38, 88
New Zealand, 84, 85, 127
Nicaragua, 71, 146, 277
Nigeria, 104
    see also Hausas
Non-alignment (Non-aligned Movement), 87, 130, 277
Non-intervention, doctrine of, 66, 90, 142, 183
Non-state actors, Ch. 14 passim, Ch. 15 passim
North American Free Trade Area (NAFTA), 134, 210, 292

North–South conflict, 87, 88
Nuclear capability (weapons), 287
Nuclear proliferation, 183, 207, 287, 292
Nuclear war, 27, 114, 187–8, 265, 266
Nuremberg war trials, 219, 294

Oil prices, 251–2
OPEC (Organisation of Petroleum Exporting Countries), 251
'Open diplomacy', 18, 162, 164
Organisational process model, 116
Organisation for European Economic Co-operation (OEEC) 247–9
Organisation of African Unity (OAU), 128
Orthodox Church(es), 55, 62, 213
Ottoman empire, 57, 72, 73, 102, 200, 239

Pacifism, 103, 183–4, 190
Pakistan, 56, 97, 104, 128, 185
Palestine Liberation Organisation (PLO), 128, 162, 191
Palestinians, 28, 90, 104, 220
Papacy, 55, 61, 62, 64, 66, 77, 78, 157, 159, 212, 213
Paradigms (see realism, rationalism and revolutionism), 9–10
Paris peace conference, 70
Peace, definition of, 288
Peloponnesian war (see war)
Persia (Persian), 47, 48, 49, 51, 52, 56
see also Iran
Personification, 5–6, 178
Peru, 253
'Petrodollars', 87, 252
Philippines, 167, 236
Pluralist theories, 26–8, 33, 107, 134, 149, 221, 232, 294
see also interdependence
Poland, 19, 22, 41, 65, 69, 85, 95, 97, 103, 106, 112, 130, 145, 174, 200, 202, 253
Population growth, 222, 268–9, 292, 293
Portugal, 40, 65, 85, 159, 170, 174, 179, 234, 235, 238
Post-behavioural revolution, 32–3
Post-modernism, 263, 284
Power, definition of, 5, 6, 282–3

see balance of power
'Power politics', 10, 11, 21, 123–4, 125, 179, 283
Preventive diplomacy, 208
Propaganda, 129, 164, 187, 275–6
Protectionism, 19, 106, 210, 234–5, 255, 290
Protectorates, 69–70
Protestantism, 65, 168, 213
Proxy war, 186
Prussia, 69, 71, 72, 85, 175
Puerto Rico, 236
Punjabi Sikhs, 90, 220

Quebeçois/Quebec, 28, 77, 219, 220

Rational actor model, 116
Rationalist theories, 9, 10, 12–4, 134, 275
Realist theories, 8, 9, 10–11, 20–1, 22, 23, 24–5, 28, 29, 31, 33–4, 39, 132, 134, 136, 142, 178, 221, 275, 278, 283, 294
Reformation, 65, 212
Republic of Northern Cyprus, 79, 129
Revolutionist theories, 9, 10, 14–5, 198, 275, 283
Revolutions, 6, 15, 192
American, 70, 71, 101, 214, 215, 231
French, 12, 45, 68, 70, 71, 100, 102, 150, 159, 187, 214, 276
Russian, 22, 45, 71, 109, 191
Rhodesia, 79, 129, 131, 206
Roman Catholic church, 55, 58, 62, 65, 159, 168, 213, 230
Roman empire (Rome), 53–5, 56, 58, 60, 61, 77, 95, 105, 147, 154, 155, 181, 197, 287
Romania, 19, 32, 55, 62, 72, 103, 128, 145
Royal Dutch Shell Group (Shell Oil), 223
Russia, 21, 22, 45, 55, 62, 69, 72, 73, 84, 85, 86, 88, 89, 98, 102, 131, 144, 145, 159, 210, 234, 238, 240
see also the Soviet Union
Rwanda, 132, 220, 293

Sanctions, 62, 131, 134, 136, 204, 229, 248, 285, 294

San Marino, 81
'Satisficing', 117
Scandinavia, 65, 85, 181
    see also individual countries
Scientific approach, to the study of IR,
    5, 24–5, 29, 294
    see also behaviouralism
Scientism, 168, 263, 264
Scotland, 53, 65, 92, 99, 219, 220, 223
Secessionism (Secessionist
    movements), 25, 192
Security dilemma, 39, 178
Serbia, 5, 55, 62, 72, 80, 103, 136, 137,
    167, 279
    see also Yugoslavia
Singapore, 38, 40, 88, 113, 256
Slovenes, 28, 97, 103
Socialism, 32, 34, 35, 37, 87, 88, 102–4,
    141, 184, 187, 191, 240, 257
Socialist Internationals, 214
'Society', definition of, 7, 11
Somalia, 79, 80, 98, 132, 185, 205, 209,
    220, 221, 222, 239, 274, 293
South Africa, 3, 106, 128, 131, 167, 175,
    206, 217, 235, 236
Sovereignty, 6, 66, 67, 69, 70–3, Ch. 6
    passim, 96, 100, 104, 113, 124, 127,
    134, 143, 150, 151, 169, 171, 183, 190,
    206, 210, 217–24, 286, 293
Soviet Union, 3, 5, 21, 22, 32, 38, 82, 86,
    90, 108, 113, 129, 131, 132, 141, 146,
    149, 168, 169, 186, 188, 192, 243, 245,
    247, 249, 284
    and Afghanistan, 140, 147, 253
    and Albania, 128
    and the balance of power, 142,
        146
    and China, 117, 130, 221, 280
    and the cold war, 82, 128, 141,
        158, 277
    and Czechoslovakia, 32, 132
    demise of, 141, 145, 173, 240
    and diplomacy, 163
    and Eastern Europe, 86, 243
    and Finland, 19, 130, 174, 202
    and foreign policy, 109–10
    and Germany, 22, 112, 191, 202,
        286

and Great Britain, 41, 141, 146,
    170
and the Greek civil war, 147
and Hungary, 134
and imperialism, 178
and Korea, 205–6
and Poland, 19, 130, 146
and the UN, 82, 205–6, 208, 243,
    283
and the United States, 22, 114,
    117, 128, 130, 141, 146, 158,
    163, 165, 206, 208, 251, 284
and the Warsaw Pact, 32, 144, 170
and Yugoslavia, 117
    see also Russia
Spain, 53, 56, 57, 61, 64, 65, 77, 94, 95,
    99, 100, 101, 128, 142, 159, 170, 173,
    174, 182, 215, 234, 235
Spheres of influence, 146–7, 170, 235
Sri Lanka, 185
'Stagflation', 252
Stalinism, 21–2
    see also Marxism–Leninism
State system (see international society)
Strategic Arms Limitation Treaty
    (SALT), 146
Structural Adjustment Package, 254
Structuralism, 31, 33–41, 172, 177, 294
Subnational movements (see
    secessionism)
Suez Canal, 23, 130, 207, 224
Suez Canal Company, 85
Supranational organisations, 7
Swaziland, 170
Sweden, 36, 174, 178, 179, 238, 279
Switzerland, 36, 72, 88, 102, 113, 133,
    147, 174, 238, 275, 276, 279
Syria, 56, 57, 97, 167, 188
Systems theory/analysis, definition of,
    24

Taiwan (Formosa), 38, 88, 235, 256
Territorial expansionism (see
    Imperialism)
Terrorism, 185, 207, 294
Third World, 3, 32, 85, 88, 150, 163, 223,
    251, 269
    see also LDCs

Thirty years' war, 65
Tibet, 48, 79, 185
'Totalitarianism' ('totalitarian'
   ideologies), 265
Transnational actors, Ch. 15 *passim*
Treaties of Westphalia, 65–9, 71, 125, 212
Treaty of Rome, 192, 249
Treaty of Utrecht, 68
Treaty of Versailles, 72–3, 162
Truman Doctrine, 247
Turkey, 72, 82, 86, 112, 144, 179

Uganda (*see* Baganda)
Ukraine (Ukrainians), 22, 28, 62, 103
UN Charter, 204, 206, 219
UN Educational, Scientific and Cultural
   Organisation (UNESCO), 205
UN Emergency Force (UNEF), 208
UN Food and Agriculture Organisation
   (FAO), 205, 206, 218
UN Force in Cyprus (UNFICYP), 209
UN General Assembly, 129, 163, 204,
   206
UNITA, 27
United Nations, 3, 7, 27, 81, 82, 83, 89,
   96, 109, 128, 129, 131, 133, 134, 170,
   183, 200, 204–10, 218, 241, 243, 291,
   293
United Nations Commission on Trade
   and Development (UNCTAD), 87,
   255
United States, 22, 25, 27, 40, 82, 83, 84,
   86, 101, 108, 110, 144, 146, 192, 203,
   235, 236, 238, 240, 244–51, 253, 269,
   276, 284, 290, 292
      and the balance of power, 142
      and Canada, 127
      and China, 128, 132, 162
      and the cold war, 82, 128, 141,
         158, 169, 277
      and Cuba, 82, 90, 114, 128, 130
      and diplomacy, 163, 165
      and the first world war, 162
      and foreign policy, 116
      and Germany, 163
      and Great Britain, 130, 207, 243
      and imperialism, 167, 169, 170
      and Iraq, 129

and Japan, 84, 110, 243, 286
and Latin America, 144
and Lithuania, 144
and the Middle East, 112
and MNCs, 223, 250
and the Soviet Union, 22, 114,
   117, 128, 130, 141, 146, 158,
   163, 165, 206, 208, 251, 284
and the UN, 82, 129, 183, 206, 210,
   243
and Vietnam (*see also* Vietnam
   war), 23, 71, 90, 113, 114, 140,
   165, 186, 189
Universal Postal Union, 199
UN Operation in the Congo (ONUC),
   208
UN Security Council, 81, 82, 89, 143,
   145, 204, 205, 209
UN World Health Organisation
   (WHO), 205, 218
'Utopianism', 18–9, 20, 22, 31, 123

Vanuatu, 77, 83, 220
Vatican, 62, 77, 276
Vietnam, 23, 38, 71, 90, 108, 112, 113,
   114, 140, 141, 144, 145, 165, 167, 176,
   256, 265, 280
Vietnam war (*see* war)

Wall Street crash, 19
War (Wars), 8, 11, 14, 18, 19, 22, 28, 35,
   50, 57, 65, 68, 73, 130, 133, 139, 140,
   143, 144, 147, 148, 151, 159, 160, 173,
   Ch. 13 *passim*, 239, 269, Ch. 19 *passim*
      Afghan civil, 140
      American civil, 101, 181, 217
      Arab–Israeli, 104, 188, 208, 251
      Boer, 236, 239, 262
      Crimean, 72, 181
      English civil, 9, 12
      Ethiopian civil, 141, 180
      Falklands/Malvinas, 27, 115, 176,
         188, 253
      First world, 18, 22, 28, 31, 51, 72,
         73, 98, 131, 149, 150, 151, 162,
         180, 187, 188, 189, 191, 192,
         197, 199, 235, 236, 239, 245,
         262, 264, 276

'Football', 101
Franco–Prussian, 235, 276
Gran Chaco, 203, 239
Grenada civil, 141
Gulf (Iraq–Iran), 133, 252, 284
Gulf, (Iraq–Kuwait/UN), 109, 115,
    129, 130, 176, 183, 188, 196, 208
'Just', doctrine of, 14, 63
India–Pakistan, 185
Indo–China (second) 'Vietnam',
    23, 31, 114, 140, 180, 185, 186,
    189, 294
Indo–China (third)
    Vietnam–Cambodia, 141, 221,
    280
Korean, 115, 180, 186, 191, 205,
    239
Napoleonic, 102, 287
Peloponnesian, 50–2, 86, 139
of the Roses, 99
Russian civil, 22, 144
Second world, 19, 21, 50, 114, 118,
    123, 131, 140, 145, 147, 150,
    151, 162, 184, 186, 187, 191,
    192, 202, 204, 219, 240, 243,
    244, 245, 274, 275, 276, 279
Seven years, 179
Sino–Vietnamese, 141, 221, 280
Spanish civil, 185, 202, 264
of Spanish succession, 68
Thirty years, 65, 67, 186, 275
Yemen civil, 141, 221
Warsaw Pact, 32, 132, 144, 170, 218
Western Europe, 32, 90, 99, 102, 113,
    133, 142, 163, 178, 214, 233, 248, 249,
    291
    see also individual countries
World Bank (IBRD), 87, 205, 246, 252

Yugoslavia, 3, 32, 93, 117, 129, 130, 131,
    147, 160, 161, 173, 200, 222, 291, 293
    see also Serbia

'Zero-sum' relationship, 139, 149, 150,
    221, 231, 279
Zionism (Zionist movement), 108, 112
Zulus, 217